REAL ESTATE
AND ECONOMICS

REAL ESTATE AND ECONOMICS

Thomas W. Shafer

Professor of Business, Economics and Real Estate
San Diego City College

RESTON PUBLISHING COMPANY, INC., Reston, Virginia
A Prentice-Hall Company

Library of Congress Cataloging in Publication Data

Shafer, Thomas W 1941–
  Real estate and economics.

  Includes bibliographical references.
  1. Real estate business. I. Title.
HD1375.S357   333.3'3   75-14465
ISBN 0-87909-715-9

© 1975 by
Reston Publishing Company, Inc.
A Prentice-Hall Company
Reston, Virginia 22090

10 9 8 7 6 5 4 3 2 1

Printed in the United States of America.

to
CHET
knowing teacher and friend

and to
M.E.
without whom this book would not have become fact

CONTENTS

PREFACE

This text is written with the intention of aiding the student and practitioner of real estate in the understanding of the economic forces behind day-to-day observations. Understanding, in the sense used here, implies more than mere facts and numbers. This text has the intention of helping the reader make an analysis of real estate in the market place. Throughout several years in a classroom situation, the author has found a great diversity within the student body with respect to background and analytical experiences. As a result, the goal of the author is to present a readable and beneficial text that will aid the student in the analysis and interpretation of the economic events of the time and their impact upon the real estate sector.

The text begins with a section on basic economic theory. Past experience suggests this as a necessary starting point for the student with little current economic background so that he will understand the concepts and conclusions of the later sections dealing with more specific real estate situations. Fundamental concepts of the school of economic theory are, however, repeated and applied throughout the text. Generally, the text begins with oversimplified situations which explain economic principles and progressively moves into more complex areas which tend to reflect real world situations more closely.

The major area of concern of the author is the application of such techniques of analysis found in economics to the actual situation on the local level in which the educator and his students find themselves. For this reason, the author has chosen not to include elaborate examples and case problems that are far removed from the actual situation of any particular reader. Both the student variation, which was previously mentioned, and the need for relevance to one's immediate situation guided the author in his preparation of this text. For those reasons the text is divided into distinct sections to allow flexibility in its use in the classroom or personal situation. The format is one which the author has found to be most comfortable and productive in his several years of teaching this specific course. Other educators will most surely find modifications and changes in subject order more productive for their approaches.

Above all, the author does not intend to substitute national statistics or regional biases for the more valid information found on the local level. One of the major inputs required in such a subject as real estate economics is the statistical data of the local region or community. Such agencies as the Federal Reserve Bank, local or regional banks, Chambers of Commerce, market and real estate research firms, and area colleges and universities all provide valuable information on the economic profile of the region, state and locality in which the reader and student live. Such inputs should be included at the appropriate times in the study of the economics of real estate and in the use of this text.

At the beginning of one of the author's courses, a real estate practitioner made the statement: "The amount of land is fixed and the population is ever growing, therefore the price of land can only go up!" It is the intention of the author that by studying the text such statements will not be made in earnest by those obligated to be more knowledgeable.

Thomas W. Shafer

I

ECONOMIC THEORY
AND APPLICATION

We begin our study of the possible relationship between real estate and economics by asking the general question: How significant is real estate as an economic good? Aside from our personal interest in real estate, does the size of the real estate sector justify intense study and examination with respect to the economic relationships that exist? The first chapter devotes its attention to that question, and examines the magnitude of the real estate sector on the national level from a variety of perspectives.

The second chapter introduces the principles of economic theory and discusses the concepts of supply and demand analysis, elasticity, and the concepts and assumptions implicit in the theoretical market. The focus of attention in the second chapter is generally upon the process by which goods and services are exchanged in the market place, and the relationships that determine how such goods and services are allocated among all the potential buyers and sellers of such items.

In the third chapter, the concepts and definitions that constitute economic thought are applied to the real estate sector in general. The concepts of supply and demand analysis are focused upon the characteristics of the supply and demand of real estate services. The development of economic characteristics of the general real estate sector is the primary emphasis of the third chapter. The chapter devotes considerable effort to developing the definition of the abstract services through use as the essence of the real estate commodity being exchanged. The differences between a physical definition of real estate, and one in the more abstract sense are developed. Finally, the chapter concludes with a discussion of the ways in which the real estate market in general differs from the basic assumptions underlying the theoretical economic model.

The final chapter in part one concerns the whole area of statistics. Numbers in various forms and combinations are the essence of the world of real estate and the focus of the real estate professional and practitioner, as well as a growing body of knowledgeable consumers. More than that, the very essence of the school of economic thought is in the world of data and statistics of various types. In the fourth chapter statistics are developed in terms of the time perspective and the reference to either supply or demand that data may reflect. External influences on data, and primary versus secondary sources of statistics are discussed. The chapter concludes with a presentation of input-output analysis, and a presentation of economic base analysis. Such analyses are becoming increasingly common in the real estate sector, and some understanding of such techniques is necessary for the student of real estate and economics.

In the subsequent chapters, more specifically defined aspects of the real estate sector are examined, but all have as their base the understanding of the principles of economics and the unique factors characterizing the real estate sector as the essentials.

INTRODUCTION

DEFINITION OF REAL ESTATE

What do we mean when we talk of real estate? Are we referring to so much land at a given location? Do we include other things attached to the land such as buildings? What about smaller items attached to the land? Is our interest focused upon the land below the surface? Are we interested in the space above the land as the source of value? In the study of real estate and the relationship between real estate and the fundamental principles of economics, the definition of real estate used can have a significant impact upon the results of the study. We could choose a narrow definition, such as only the physical "dirt," but then our study would have very little direct relationship to the real world of pragmatic economic functions. On the other hand, we could also choose a broad definition including many factors of marginal validity, in which our study would be hampered by vagueness and incompleteness associated with topics too big to be adequately covered in the allotted assignment.

Furthermore, the definition of real estate to be employed must also be similar in nature to the focus of the study. If the study is to be detailed and physical in perspective, then the definition of real estate should also be in those terms. However, if the study is to be abstract and somewhat apart from the physical aspects of the topic, then the definition of the subject must be in terms that can be treated in the abstract sense. As a result of the nature of the study, which is the study and application of the principles of economics to the real estate environment, an abstract definition of real estate was chosen.

Real estate is defined in terms of the services gained through the use or uses to which it is put. Since the yardstick of measurement in the area of economics (and the real world to a great extent) tends to be limited to dollars or money, the concept of real estate must be related to that form of measuring tool. Services through use as a definition of real estate also have one other major advantage, and that is that it focuses one's attention on the benefits received and sold and the measurement of those benefits in terms of dollars or money. This focus draws the student away from the physical peculiarities of the given real estate package in question. The study of an item of interest should, if the study is to be most productive, be divorced from the emotion and subjective feelings attached to the subject.

The fundamental subject of study from the economic viewpoint is the process by which goods and services are exchanged in the market place. The allocation of goods in the capitalistic countries tends to be a function of the prices being bid for those items offered for sale. Buyers willing to bid the higher price will tend to be allocated those resources. The estimation and interpretation of the value of the services in question is very much a personal task of the person bidding on the items. Therefore, in the study of such a market structure and function it is not mandatory for the student to duplicate the efforts of the parties involved. The higher bids are taken as indicative of more valuable services being accrued to the person bidding. The final point at which the seller and buyer agree to the exchange can be an accumulation of value estimates on the entire list of benefits to be derived through ownership of the given item in question.

In the study of the relationship between real estate and economics, we are focusing our attention upon the processes by which that arbitration and exchanging take place and the structure of the environment under which the arbitration between buyer and seller takes place. In such a study, the market characteristics, the market structure and the efficiency of the market and its measurement are the primary points under examination. As such, the use to which real property can be put and the benefits to be gained through such usage are the major elements of study.

THE ROLE OF REAL ESTATE

Every nation in the world is defined in the first sense in terms of its political boundaries, that is, in terms of its control and claims over geography. The peoples of the world occupy and use real estate resources in every spectrum of human endeavor. Although the law of gravity has a great deal of credit for this importance of real estate in the basic sense, there are many other questions that gravity will answer. The distribution of peoples is not uniform throughout the world, or throughout any one nation. There are certain benefits and advantages associated with particular locations, which, therefore, attract more people than other areas within the same country. Thus, real estate resources located in some spots are more useful than those resources in other areas. Consequently, the value of real estate resources in advantageous locations tends to be greater than the value of real estate elsewhere.

Furthermore, real estate services, their cost and their usefulness, are intimately related to nearly every aspect of human existence. We need real estate services suitable for living and raising our families in. We also need other real estate resources to work in or upon, and with which we can operate our business and vocational endeavors with success. We also need real estate resources suitable for recreation and cultural activities that are a vital part of human existence. Governmental and religious bodies, as well as other social needs, also demand the use of real estate resources to their individual ends. And by far the largest consumer of real estate services in terms of the area demanded is for the agricultural needs of a growing nation and world. Not one area in the human experience comes to mind where real estate services are not one of the major requirements. Every phase of life requires the consumption of real estate services in one form or another.

In addition to the physical need for real estate resources, and the resultant importance of real estate in the physical sense, there is the even more important position of real estate in the total economic health of a nation, and that nation relative to the entire world. For the majority of persons in the country, the financial commitment and the amount of investment involved in home ownership constitute the single largest form of investment that most families will make in their entire lifetimes. In addition, the monthly support and maintenance of such an investment also represents one of the largest single items of expenditures in the average monthly income of family units.

With reference to the commercial and industrial segment of economies of most developed nations in the world, real estate services in the form of land holdings and improvements placed upon the land for production and manufacturing purposes are the single largest investment in all industrial and commercial sectors. Real property in the form of real property services is at the very foundation of the economies of most of the nations of the world and the individuals within those nations. As such, then, real estate is closely entwined with the state of economic affairs of the nations of the world and the respective nations or nation under examination.

DEFINITION AND SCOPE
OF ECONOMICS

Economics is primarily a study of the manner in which goods and services of monetary or economic worth are distributed among the peoples of an area, region, state, nation or the world. The ultimate goal of such study is to be able to explain with a reasonable degree of accuracy why goods are distributed in the manner they are in the present scene. The implication is that to the extent we are able to explain the current distribution system of goods and services, then our ability to predict the future allocation patterns if certain changes are made is enhanced.

The perspective of the economist is fragile in that he/she is attempting to examine a social-economic system from the viewpoint of an impartial and unbiased observer. The role is similar to that played by the microbiologist studying life systems under a microscope. The major flaw in the role played by the economist is that he/she is part of the system being examined. Therefore, objectivity is extremely difficult to maintain, or even to reach, for most persons assuming the role or perspective of the economist.

With reference to the subject of the economists' studies, the allocation of goods and services includes all goods and services exchanged in the market place or provided through governmental programs. It also includes all people and all operating entities, and all the factors that have any economic impact upon the lives of those persons. Such problem areas as: inflation, deflation, unemployment, social programs, governmental budgets, taxes, subsidies, productivity, imports and exports, capital investment, savings, interest rates, banking, government debt, equity ownership and a multitude of other areas are all within the rein of the economic student. Virtually every area of human existence with reference to economic well-being is part of the study of economics. Likewise, the body of economic thought accumulated up to the present covers nearly every area of human endeavor in relation to the economic structure and function that surrounds such experience. One large body of economic thought, Micro-Economics, concerns the operation of individual firms and industries. Another segment, Macro-Economics, concentrates upon the operations of the federal and state governments and the national economy as a whole. Another body of economists concentrates only on the international economics scene; Economics of International Trade is what that sector is called. Other areas of more select concern include: labor economics, welfare economics, agricultural economics and a long list of specified areas of study within the overall scope of economic theory and analysis. Wherever there is an exchange of products and/or money or other goods or services, the principles of economic theory can be applied to that situation. Also, even those areas outside of the market processes are subject to study by the economist if they have impact upon the economic allocation of goods and resources at some further point in the economy. And, of course, every area of governmental expenditure and taxation is part of the operating area of the economist.

ASSOCIATION OF REAL ESTATE
AND ECONOMICS

From the point of definitions, it is clear that there is a very great association between real estate and economic theory. The importance of the real estate sector in the economic sense transcends nearly every activity of the human experience. The field of economics and economic thought also encompasses nearly every area of interaction between human beings as groups and as individuals in the economic arena. In point of fact, it is nearly impossible to consider many of the major areas of economic study, particularly on the governmental level, without perceiving some impact upon the real estate sector either directly or secondarily from those anticipated actions on the part of the government sectors. Policies relating to employment and wage levels, income taxes, investment tax changes, supply and growth of money and credit, specific government programs of subsidies and supports for certain economics groups, and a myriad of other possible areas are directly related to the real estate sector. Such policies would tend to have a very dramatic and direct impact upon the activity and productivity of the real estate sector in whole or in part. That there is a viable and substantial relationship between economic theory and real estate is clearly evident in understanding the substance of both fields of interest. Therefore, it is also clear that understanding and analysis of economic theory and principles can be and are of immediate benefit to those participating directly in the real estate markets.

Furthermore, the subject of real estate itself often is considered in isolation as though it were separate from the economy and the dynamics of the regions, states, and countries of the world. Such treatment in conflict with the concepts of real estate and the market processes can only hamper sound analysis and judgment in the decision-making process relating to the real estate sector. The entire real estate sector is concerned with the production and exchanging of real estate services in a multitude of forms. Such services are most often measured in terms of the monetary yardstick, which does not recognize the subjective or emotional aspects of the real estate product. The demand for services is competitive to a high degree, and the available supply is most often competitive for the highest sale price. As such, the health or lack of it of the entire economic spectrum of the area, region, state, nation and world has a tremendous influence upon the economic profile within the real estate sector.

The real estate sector cannot be divorced from the economic realities of the economic system that it functions within. The interaction of businesses and individuals, as well as the government, has a direct impact upon the real estate sector. And, therefore, it cannot be ignored in the analysis of the real estate market in general or the real estate submarkets in particular. The extent to which the principles of economic theory are valid in the commercial sector, those same economic principles will tend to be appropriate in the analysis of real estate.

Purpose of the Association

The relationship between economics and real estate is rather clear and direct. The relationship between real estate and the immense variety of operating economic influences within the economy of the regions, states and the country and the world is also well established. However, the degree and the complexities of such influences between segments of the operating economy and the real estate sector are not nearly so clear or precise. A more thorough understanding of the principal relationships outlined in economic theory and analysis, and the application of the tools and techniques from the economist's tool kit to the analysis of the dynamics of real estate within the operating economy of which real estate is but a part, will result in more efficient production, planning, use and distribution of real estate resources. That such understanding and usage of economics will directly benefit the participants in the real estate sector is a nearly predetermined consequence.

Approach Employed   Before one is able to employ the tools of the economist in a skilled analysis of a segment of the complex real estate industry, some basic understanding of the elements of economic theory must be possessed. In the first section to follow, the basic theory of supply and demand analysis is presented. The assumptions under the purely competitive market situation are discussed, as are the elements of elasticity and the supply and demand schedules and the adversary motivations between buyers and sellers. The application of such basic theory is then discussed employing a general and oversimplified concept of the real estate market. The real estate product is defined in the economic sense, and the economic yardstick is discussed and explained. A chapter on statistics follows the two chapters employing economic theory and the application of that theory to the basic real estate product. Since data are the primary tool of the researcher and particularly the economic researcher, some knowledge is required of the pitfalls of data and what correlation means are required.

The following section focuses attention upon the concept of land use. Use of real estate resources and the benefits to be derived through such usage were earlier established as being the major element in the exchange process within the market. The history of land use and land use patterns and the parameters of the time are discussed in relation to the current shape of our oldest cities. The regulation and control over land use is then discussed and the role of the constitution and the governing bodies in the determination of land use is then discussed. The elimination of the old parameters affecting land use patterns and the controls that seem to be dictated in the present scene are explored.

Up to this point, real estate has been discussed and analyzed in the simplistic overgeneralized concept of one national real estate industry. The third section introduces the concepts of the various submarkets in the national real estate perspective. The submarkets are studied in terms of their being distinct and separate markets in many respects. The role of the real estate professional in each market is explored. The market structure and motivations of those within the markets are discussed. The real estate services being exchanged in each market are distinctly different, and the impact of that difference upon the structure and operation of the submarket is developed.

As the goal in analysis—from the standpoint of the operating real estate professional, and the majority of the buyers and sellers in the real estate market and submarkets—is the determination of economic worth or the value of a given prospective purchase or sale, then the concept of value is at the very heart of the subject of economics and real estate. The fourth section focuses attention upon the basic nature of value and what it really means. The measurement of value is discussed and the different types of value are explored. The concepts of value and appraisal are developed, as well as the basic approaches to estimating value found in the appraisal sector. The elements of each appraisal approach are outlined and discussed. The shortcomings and advantages of each approach are discussed in terms of the impact upon the economic aspects of the market.

As the measurement of value is most often, if not always, ultimately reduced to money terms, and as the role of finance is so complex, section five turns to finance and real estate. The basic nature of the real estate commodity that requires financing is developed along with the economic structure that tends to make financing so important. The financial framework of real estate is developed from the economic analysis point of view. The history of finance in real estate is then discussed as a partial determinant of the current profile of financing in real estate. The economic structure and flaws of historical finance are discussed, then the current development of financing patterns as a result of the impact of those flaws is analyzed.

The final section focuses attention upon areas of special interest that have impact upon the allocation of real estate resources and the economics of the distribution process. The first chapter concentrates upon the investment analysis of real estate. The more elaborate techniques of Present-Value Analysis and the Internal-Rate-of-Return are increasingly being employed in the evaluation of investment alternatives. As the investment types of real estate are really a submarket, and in most instances the returns required through an investment are predefined in terms of the media, these techniques are increasingly appropriate for real estate investment analysis. The size of real estate investment projects, the financial commitment, and the number of persons involved in the evaluation dictate that a more refined knowledge is required on the part of the real estate professionals attempting to function in this market. Additionally, the principals in such projects should have some grasp of the techniques employed to reach the value estimate in the proposals. The fact that outside research firms are growing in number to provide the labor of such research means that the individuals in the project must have a sound grasp of the techniques to be able to use the services of such firms.

The second chapter in the final section is a closer look at the actual production process in the real estate sector. The industry and its economic structure greatly explain some of the major problem areas in the industry. The differences from the purely competitive model are discussed as is the impact of such differences on the product, costs and cyclical ills that plague the construction industry in the private sector. The major elements within the market that are responsible for such market structure are also discussed as well as the economic importance of the construction sector to the national economy. The role of local, state and federal governments in perpetuating the ills of the industry is also examined.

The final chapter examines the development of government participation in the real estate sector of the nation. The primary emphasis is upon the role of the federal government from the beginning of the nation to the present. The changing role of federal government participation from one of total neglect, to national economic survival, to the present era of specific problem solving, is developed. The various acts and agencies that were born along the path are also discussed. The chapter concludes with some of the author's modest predictions about future federal government involvement in the real estate sector, and a brief explanation of the justification behind such predictions.

REFERENCES

1—U.S., Department of Housing and Urban Development, A Decent Home. Report of the President's Commission on Housing, Washington, D.C.: U.S. Printing Office, 1968.

2—U.S., Department of Commerce, Bureau of Census, *Statistical Abstract of the U.S., 1973.* Washington, D.C.: U.S. Printing Office, 1973.

WHAT IS ECONOMICS?

BACKGROUND

Whenever something is bought or sold, whenever a buyer and seller come together in the market place, something takes place that is governed by a set of principles that is called economics. The amount to be sold and the amount to be bought are dependent upon those principles. Without such common ground the buyers and sellers could never come to terms, and indeed would find it all but impossible to communicate at all.

One of the elements of this common ground would be the money or value terms both the buyer and seller used in the market place. If the seller used the concept of money as his measurement of value, and the buyer used rocks as his measurement, they would not be able to come to agreement on the value of the particular item discussed. If they had a common translation for each other's currency, then they would be able to talk in the same terms. Economics, and more particular, certain concepts and principles of economics, provide those common means of communication in the world of commerce.

MONEY

One of the cornerstones of economic thought is the concept of money. As measured in a currency, it implies a yardstick of value. Nearly every place in the world has a currency. Most currencies of the world are exchanged for others, so that an exchange rate has been and is maintained for nearly all currencies. Such exchange rates provide a commonality between all currencies, such that they are all a measurement of value. International exchange of goods and services is enhanced by the ability to translate from one currency to another, and thus provide a virtual worldwide system of value.

Without a currency many communities are precluded from joining the wealth brought about by exchange between countries. Consider, for example, the problem of communication in the market place when the buyer and seller are trying to come to terms in two completely different languages. Imagine for a moment the situation in which the seller is attempting to sell his wares at $5.00, and the buyer is attempting to purchase the seller's items at price expressed in terms of prayers, say two prayers. Without some method to establish a ratio of one value system to another, dollars to prayers, the buyer and seller in the above example could not consummate a transaction.

Societies without a money system usually conduct transactions in terms of the exchange of physical goods. An example would be two pigs equal to one milk cow. This type of limited commerce is described as a barter economy. The yardstick of value in such societies is limited to physical goods already in wide use in the society, and physical goods of such size and weight that they can be brought to the market place. Under such circumstances, goods must be equal in value for any transaction to take place. There is no method for making change in situations in which either buyer or seller has goods worth slightly more or less than the other. Another major handicap of the barter economy is there is no method for deferred payments. Every transaction must be complete and final in the time frame in which it occurs. Since there are no monies or near monies in the form of notes or checks, every transaction must be completed in the day it occurs.

The ultimate impact of the two conditions cited in the previous paragraph is that fewer transactions can take place in the market, thus there tend to be fewer buyers and sellers, and thus the economy tends to be slower and smaller due to these conditions.

POST-INDUSTRIAL REVOLUTION

One major characteristic of the developed nations of the contemporary world, in the economic sense of developed, is they all tend to have a well-defined money system that is readily converted into the currencies of other nations of similar degrees of development. Money, as a common denominator for economic growth and development, appears to be rather well established. Money, as a necessary element for international commerce and exchange, is clearly a mandatory item. It has been established as the only common yardstick of value through which people can come to terms with the value of an object or service.

Money as the Value Concept

The central relationship being discussed in relationship to money and other value yardsticks, is that the measurement in terms of the yardstick implies the value present in the item. That is, if an item sells for $5,000.00 to a willing buyer and by a willing seller, then the implication is that that item in total has a value of $5,000.00. The task of assigning a certain dollar value on each and every part of the item is not necessary in terms of the value system we have been using. When an object is exactly two feet long, it is not necessary to measure further in terms of inches, centimeters or millimeters the various parts of that item to determine its value in terms of length. Likewise, the value of a new car is the total price paid for the car, and the value estimate is not compounded by the task of adding up all the individual characteristics of the car and attaching a dollar value to each of those characteristics.

The complexities of the value systems of individual persons is such that a common language and yardstick is necessary before more than one person can convey his assessment of value to another. This is the task of a money system in the economic world, to act as the common language and yardstick for measurement of value in the areas of exchange between persons in the market place.

ECONOMICS AS A SUBJECT

Economics is a body of thought assembled in an attempt to explain why goods and services are distributed in the world as they are. It is only concerned with goods of economic value, those suitable for use and not in infinite supply. The economist focuses his attention on the prices of certain commodities or services, and the supply of those same services and commodities. The economist attempts through his studies to answer two primary questions: (1) Why did that price prevail in the market place for that commodity or service?; (2) Why did that amount of the good or service reach the prevailing level it did in that market situation at that time? The level of supply of goods in the market place and the price at which those goods or services are exchanged, are the major areas of study to the economist. These two areas have been collectively called supply and demand analysis. We will now examine these two elements of economics individually.

Definition of Supply

Supply of a commodity in the economic sense is a schedule of the various amounts of a commodity that will be made available for sale at varying prices. It should be noted that it is a schedule and not one fixed point or quantity. The use of a single supplier may illustrate the point: Mr. Jones sells potatoes in the market place. Let us assume that his cost of production is 50¢ each, at his current output. He has normally produced 1,000 potatoes and been able to sell them all at $1.00 each. His current output would look much like Table 2–1. Upon interviewing Mr. Jones and looking at his past history of

TABLE 2–1

Quantity	Price	Profit
1,000	$1.00	$500.00

TABLE 2–2

Quantity	Price	Profit
500	$ .75	$125.00
1,000	1.00	500.00

production, we find that if the market price were only 75¢ each he would not grow as as many potatoes, but would choose to grow some other crop that is more profitable. He would still produce potatoes, but not as many. Table 2–2 shows this comparison.

Further conversation with Mr. Jones and looking at past history reveal that he would double his production if the price of potatoes rose to $1.25 each. He reasons that it would not cost much to expand current production to that level, and the profit margin would exceed the profit in the products currently being grown on that land. A table of the three estimates of production at the three various prices is depicted in Table 2–3. This table is a simple illustration of a supply schedule. It is a listing of the various amounts sellers are willing to sell at various prices in the market. In economics it is commonly implied that such relationships can best be seen when the table is presented in graphical form. Such a graph is illustrated in Figure 2–1.

The three points represent the intersection of the price on the vertical axis with the quantity supplied on the horizontal axis. Through such a graphical presentation, many subtle relationships are brought to light. The amount of probable supply between the points of the measurement is illustrated. In addition, the relative amount of change in the supply with a shift in the price is also depicted. This relationship between price changes and the corresponding change in supply is an important concept in economics. It is called elasticity versus inelasticity. The tendency of supply to adjust to changes in price is the amount of price elasticity in the supply segment of the market. The example above shows that if price decreases by 25 percent from $1.00 to $.75, the amount supplied will decrease by 50 percent from 1,000 to 500. The supply schedule in the above example would be described as being elastic relative to price because the quantity supplied varies more than price when price changes. An inelastic supply curve would be much like that one depicted in Figure 2–2.

In the supply curve illustrated by Figure 2–2, the same changes in price as de-

TABLE 2–3

Quantity	Price	Profit
500	$ .75	$ 125.00
1,000	1.00	500.00
2,000	1.25	1,250.00

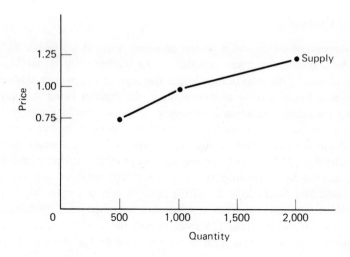

Figure 2–1

picted in the previous supply schedule are maintained in the present schedule, and the amounts being brought to the market by Mr. Jones are much different than the previous schedule. In the present case, a shift in price of 25 percent from $1.00 to $1.25 results in an increase in supply from 550 to 600, or less than ten percent. When price changes occur, there is a less than corresponding change in supply. Such a relationship is described as being a relatively inelastic supply in relation to price of the commodity.

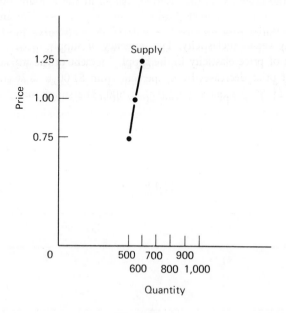

Figure 2–2

Definition of Demand

The demand of a commodity, in the economic sense, is a schedule of the various prices paid for a commodity made available in the market place at varying quantities. Another way of stating the relationship is that the amount that will be demanded in the market place is a function or is dependent upon the amount being supplied. Another way of stating the demand function is to determine the amount or quantity that will be demanded by consumers, that amount they would be willing to buy at various prices in the market. As in the illustration of supply, perhaps the use of a single consumer may clarify the relationship. Mrs. Smith consumes potatoes in the market place. The normal price is 50¢, and she feels she can afford to purchase 100 potatoes each period (say one year in this case). Mrs. Smith feels that if the price of potatoes were only 25¢ she could afford to purchase more and use them as substitutes for other starchy foods she normally uses. Let us say she would purchase 125 potatoes each period if the price were 25¢. Likewise, Mrs. Smith feels that if the price of potatoes rose to 75¢ she would not purchase as many, but rather substitute other starchy foods that are less expensive. At 75¢, Mrs. Smith feels she would reduce her normal consumption to 75 potatoes each period. If we constructed a table to represent these quantities and prices, it would resemble Table 2–4.

As in the discussion regarding the supply portion of the market, the raw data appearing in the table form do not bring out the relationships nearly as clearly as the graphical analysis. The graph of the above table would likely appear similar to Figure 2–3.

As in the graphical presentation of the supply function, the graphical analysis of demand is very revealing in terms of the trend of the demand function, and the likelihood of quantities that would be demanded or sold at prices other than the prices that were presented in the table. Also, the relative change in the amount demanded by the consumer as the price varies is also indicated by the graph above. The major differences between the supply curve presented earlier and the demand curve presented above are the slopes in opposite direction. The supplier will tend to supply more at a higher price while the consumer will tend to purchase less at a higher price and more at a lower price. Also, the elasticity of demand is in the opposite direction from supply. However, both the demand and the supply functions are relatively elastic as presented in the two examples so far. It will be recalled that if the amount demanded and supplied varies rather equally with a change in price, then the cure is described as being relatively price elastic. An inelastic demand curve would be more vertical as depicted in Figure 2–4.

TABLE 2–4

Price	Quantity
$1.25	75
1.00	100
.75	125

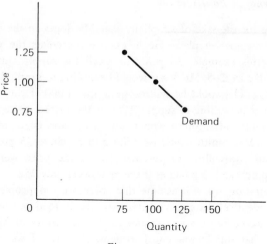

Figure 2–3

It would, however, continue to be negatively sloped, reflecting the interests of the consumer and his choice of having more rather than less for nearly the same expenditure. In the less elastic curve the same changes in price are illustrated as the previous example. The amount of change in the amount demanded in response to the higher or lower prices is less than in the prior example.

As in the definition of supply, the demand curve presents a schedule of quantities demanded at varying prices. It is a schedule of many prices and quantities, and is not limited to only one price or one commodity quantity. Any point along the curve represents the same demand curve or the same supply curve. It is only when the amount supplied or demanded changes for a pre-existing price that the supply has changed or shifted.

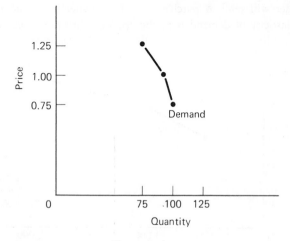

Figure 2–4

Definition of a Market at Equilibrium

Let us assume for the sake of simplicity that Mr. Jones in the supply example is the sole supplier in the market place. He in essence represents the whole industry of potato producers in this example. As you will recall his supply curve was presented as depicted below in Figure 2–5. Mr. Jones would be willing to supply 500 potatoes if the market price were 75¢. He would be willing to supply 1,000 if the market price were $1.00. Mr. Jones would be willing to supply 2,000 if the market price were $1.25.

As you will recall, Mrs. Smith would have a demand curve much like that depicted in Figure 2–6. Mrs. Smith would be willing to purchase 75 potatoes if the price were $1.25; she would be willing to purchase 100 if the price were $1.00; and she would be willing to purchase 125 potatoes if the price were only 75¢.

For this illustration we will assume that there are ten people like Mrs. Smith, each with the same identical demand curve for the staple food potatoes. If we do this, then the ten people would be able to consume all of the market of Mr. Jones supply if the price were such that supply was equal to demand. Now, if we present the supply curve of Mr. Jones and the ten demand curves of the Mrs. Smith's, the graph would look like Figure 2–7.

If the price charged and predicted by Mr. Jones were $1.00, then the ten consumers would purchase or demand 100 potatoes each, or 1,000 potatoes in total. Mr. Jones would produce only 1,000 at the price of $1.00 as illustrated by his supply curve. At that point, the supply curve and the demand curve intersect, and equal each other. This point of equality between supply and demand is termed market equilibrium. The reason it is called the equilibrium is that neither buyer nor seller has a tendency to depart from this point of perfect equality.

Market Adjustment and Correction   To explain why the point of equilibrium illustrated previously tends to persist, consider Figure 2–8, which shows a quantity below the equilibrium quantity of the previous example.

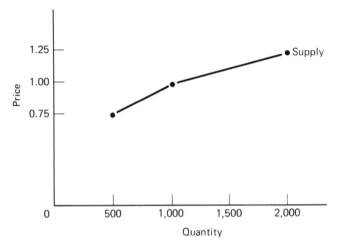

Figure 2–5

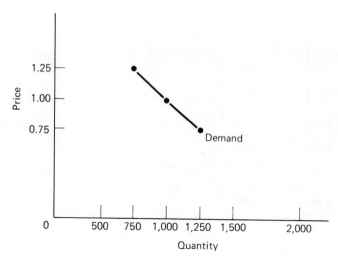

Figure 2–6

Let us assume that point (1) indicates the level of both the current supply and the consequent demand. The amount demanded at the price illustrated is well below the quantity that the suppliers would be willing to supply at that high price. The amount currently being supplied is an amount that would be supplied at a much lower price than that being paid. The higher-than-normal return the suppliers would be receiving at this artificial low level of output would attract other producers into the market who would be willing to sell at a lower price and still maintain a reasonable profit. Thus, the suppliers would tend to increase in number or in output and push the artificial limit represented by (1) toward the true equilibrium point, which is the intersection of supply and demand. For the new suppliers to sell their product they must be willing to sell at a lower price than is currently being charged, or the consumers of the potatoes would not

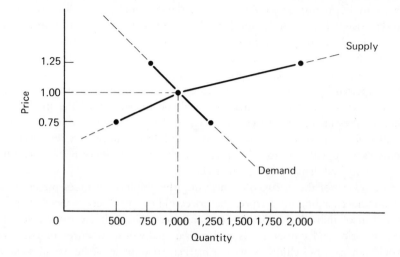

Figure 2–7

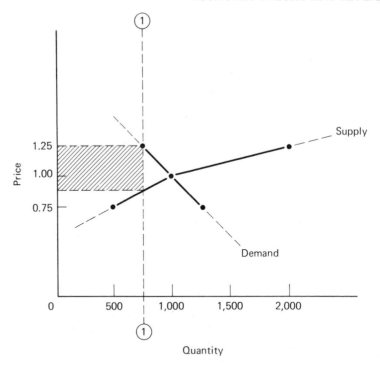

Figure 2–8

increase consumption. It is important to understand that the market does not operate in a vacuum, but it can attract increased production through the rates of return or earnings it is capable of producing.

Figure 2–9 illustrates another false output level, this one to the right of the equilibrium. The point represented by (2) is the new and artificial output assumed for this new example. At this new level of output the consumers are willing to pay only a much lower price than at equilibrium. It is also true that for suppliers to produce at this expanded output level, they must be expecting a much higher price than that price that prevailed at the equilibrium. The shaded area represents the difference between the prices. In the current example, the prices paid by the consumers are much lower than the prices expected by the growers of potatoes. The result of this situation is that the growers using expensive and marginal land will be forced out of the market because of the losses represented by the shaded area. The cutback in supply because of this loss of return will tend to move toward the previous equilibrium illustrated. Furthermore, the reduction in supply will tend to drive prices up toward the higher price at equilibrium where the supply and demand curves intersect.

As a review of the discussion concerning the graphical analyses presented so far, it might aid understanding to interpret the prices and output levels as those of the industry rather than of individual producers or consumers. The industry market actually determines the price and output levels and not an individual producer or consumer. A seller would not gain by selling below the market price for long; he would soon sell all his product and the market would tend to return to the higher price. His net gain would

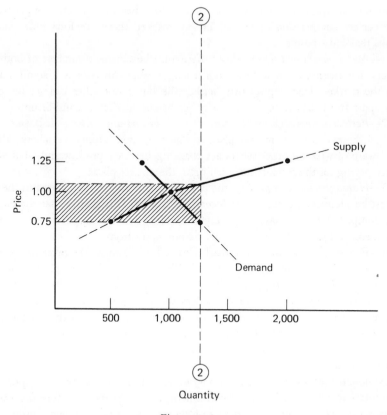

Figure 2–9

be less than selling at the market that would also be able to absorb all his product at equilibrium. He would not gain anything at all by attempting to sell above the market, because all the buyers would be buying from the other producers at a lower price.

The role of the buyer would be relatively the same as the individual seller in the market. A buyer would not pay more than the market price for an item, for he could get all that he required for a lower price represented by the going market price at equilibrium. Likewise, the buyer would find it impossible to acquire his desired amount of the commodity at a price below what the market was. None of the sellers would sell him his desired amount at a price below what they could receive from the other buyers in the market place. Thus, it can be seen what is meant by saying that the price and quantity at the market equilibrium are determined by the entire market of buyers and sellers and not by any one individual buyer or seller.

ASSUMPTIONS IN THE PURELY COMPETITIVE MARKET

There are examples in our daily lives that attest to the fact that many products do not behave exactly as the illustrated example of potatoes in the previous discussion.

The previous examples are set in market that is described as a purely competitive market. For perfect competition to prevail in any market, there are four fundamental assumptions that must be met.

1—*Many buyers and many sellers*: there must be sufficient numbers of both buyers and sellers that neither a single buyer nor a single seller can possess a significant influence on the market. This implies that neither the buyer nor seller can set his price or quantity apart from that price and quantity set by the market at equilibrium.

2—*Perfect knowledge on the part of both buyers and sellers*: all buyers must be aware of all the prices in the market place so that they have alternative sellers. All sellers must be aware of what all other sellers are charging for their product and what all other buyers are paying for the product he is selling in the market place.

3—*Homogeneous commodity*: the product being sold and purchased in the market place must be identical among all producers and buyers. This assures that the buyer will not feel compelled to purchase from any individual seller because the buyer receives identical merchandise no matter what seller he purchases from.

4—*Free price mechanism*: the market must be able to set the price of the equilibrium point that most freely expresses the equilibrium in the market place. Price in the terms of a currency has been presented at length as the most common, if not the only, yardstick of value measurement. For the sellers and buyers to come to agreement on the quantity and price at equilibrium, they must both be free to bid on the available supply in the terms of that yardstick of money or currency. Without that yardstick the entire market would not be able to reach agreement on the value of the product or service under consideration.

Although the foregoing assumptions severely limit the ability of the purely competitive model to fit the real world environment, it is important to note the impact of the assumptions. They allow the student to interpret the market by comparison with the purely competitive model. Where the market is acting very differently from what the outcome may be expected to be under pure competition, those differences most generally can be attributed to the four assumptions being invalid under the real world conditions. The degree to which some or all of the assumptions under pure competition are true adds greatly to the ability of the student to predict market behavior.

The relationships described under the purely competitive model are valid economic relationships that do exist in the economic world of reality. How supply and demand are determined and interact is the subject of economics, and the purely competitive model most clearly illustrates those relationships. As the subject of this text proceeds further, the analysis will become more complex. The underlying analysis will, however, be the same as in the purely competitive model discussed in this chapter.

SUMMARY

In discussing the subject of economics, we found that money was a basic yardstick of value in the world of the economist. The refinement in the money system is amplified by the post-industrial revolution and international economic development. Economics was defined as a body of thought assembled to explain the distribution of resources. The concepts of supply and demand were illustrated and defined in the context of the purely competitive market. The adjustments of supply and demand to each other were also illustrated. The concepts of elasticity of supply and demand were also explained. The purely competitive model was presented in which the concept of market equilibrium was explained. The adjustment process of supply and demand in the pure competition model was also illustrated. Finally, the four fundamental and key assumptions that underlie the model of pure competition were discussed and explained. Finally, the importance of understanding the impact of the four assumptions was highlighted and established for the remainder of the analysis portion of the text.

REFERENCES

1—Bach, George L. *Economics: An Introduction to Analysis and Policy.* 7th ed. Englewood Cliffs, N.J.: Prentice-Hall, Inc., 1971.

2—Heilbroner, Robert L. and Thurow, Lester C. *The Economic Problem.* 4th ed. Englewood Cliffs, N.J.: Prentice-Hall, Inc., 1975.

3—Joseph, Myron L. *Economic Analysis and Policy.* 3rd ed. Englewood Cliffs, N.J.: Prentice-Hall, Inc., 1971.

4—McConnell, Campbell R. *Economics.* 5th ed. New York: McGraw-Hill, Inc., 1972.

5—Robinson, Marshall A., et. al. *An Introduction to Economic Reasoning.* 4th ed. Washington, D.C.: Brookings Institution, 1967.

REAL ESTATE ECONOMICS

SIGNIFICANCE OF REAL ESTATE
AS AN ECONOMIC GOOD

Real estate as a commodity in the world of economics ranks as the largest single product in our economy. There are many ways to measure the value of real estate in comparison to other goods. The merits of various methods will be covered at length in later chapters; however, it may prove appropriate to look at one method or measure at this point.

Amount of money borrowed or owing on various assets is one common measurement in the economic scene. The federal government owes money in the form of the national debt. Consumers owe money on charge accounts and installment loans. Businesses owe money in the form of commercial paper such as debentures and promissory notes. One product that is separated from the others by type of asset borrowed against is real estate. Table 3–1 illustrates these four classes.

The significance of real estate as an asset in the national economy is well documented by the above table. Real estate is as large as the federal government in terms of economic impact of its debt (see Figure 3–1). The fact that real estate is from the private sector of our economy and that it represents only one form of assets, adds importance to the figures cited in the previous table. The private sectors of the national economy clearly outweigh the national government in terms of total debt financing (see Figure 3–2). The real estate commodity clearly represents the single largest item securing that debt in the private sector.

TABLE 3–1
Debt in $ Billions

Class of Debt	1940	1950	1960	1970	1971 (est.)
Federal debt	45	218	244	339	366
Real estate	26	55	151	321	352
Commercial paper	10	16	31	76	83
Consumer credit	8	22	56	127	137

Source: U.S., Department of Commerce, Bureau of the Census, *Statistical Abstract of the U.S., 1972*, pp. 441, 451.

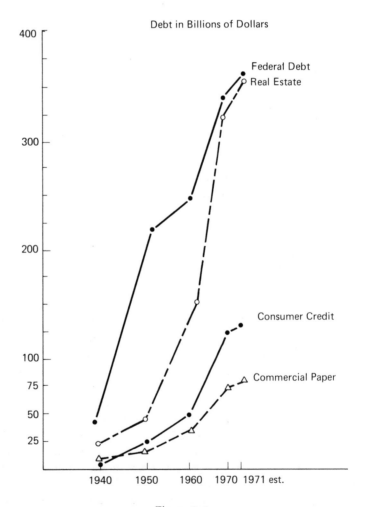

Figure 3–1

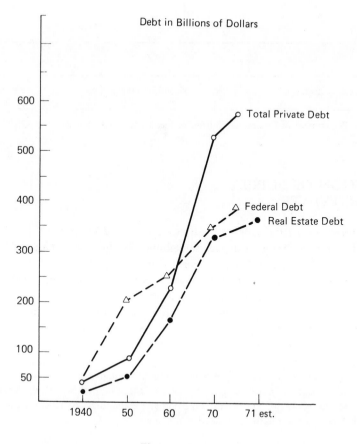

Figure 3–2

Another point to be aware of, indicated in the previous table, is the rate of growth in real estate debt. Between the years 1950 and 1970, the federal debt grew by approximately 68 percent. Real estate debt during the same period grew by more than 585 percent. The trend indicates that real estate is becoming a much larger or more significant debt asset than any other single form of asset, and that if the current trend continues, real estate will secure more debt than the entire federal government of the wealthiest nation in the history of the world.

Table 3–2 shows the amount of taxes collected on real estate for the nation as a whole. The importance of tax revenue is twofold: first, it is collected nearly entirely by local governments and not national; and second, it represents value in the terms of cash rather than security for a loan. The importance of cash is that the real estate sector of the economy must generate cash through service and use to pay taxes that are due on the basis of the value of the property. It means that not only is real estate worth a great deal of money, but that it also generates a lot of money in the economy through its use. The impact of $34 billion on the local economies within the national sense is surely ample evidence of the importance of real estate as an economic good.

TABLE 3–2

	1950	1970
Property taxes collected	$7,359,000,000	$34,054,000,000

Source: U.S., Department of Commerce, Bureau of the Census, *Statistical Abstract of the U.S., 1972*, p. 318.

DEFINITION OF SUPPLY OF REAL ESTATE

To most persons the supply of real estate is defined in terms of the physical supply of land. The typical argument goes something like this: since the supply of land is fixed, and the number of people in the world is growing, the prices of land can only go up. The problem with such a simplistic analysis is that it fails to adequately define the concept of real estate. The supply of real estate is much more than the physical supply of land or "dirt." By defining real estate supply in terms of "dirt" we have a fixed supply, but that supply is so large as to be of little economic constraint. As stated by the President's Committee on Urban Housing:

> The United States is rich in land. All two hundred million Americans could be housed in single-family homes in an area roughly the size of the state of Iowa. If all Americans were to move to the states of Texas and Oklahoma, the population densities of those states would then be comparable to the United Kingdom or West Germany.[1]

If all the United States population could inhabit two states comfortably, or one state of single family homes, then surely the amount of dirt in the entire 50 states is not the primary consideration when we speak of the supply of real estate.

The element of supply in the real estate sector is the services that one can derive from the use of the real estate for a specific purpose. It is the value of the use of real estate, and not the land itself, that is of value in the economic sense. Although the supply of land in the physical sense is relatively fixed, i.e., it is difficult in the extreme to manufacture land, the supply of land suitable for a specific use is more a function of the market forces. Marginal land can be cultivated and fertilized for crops if the price of the specific crop is high enough to warrant it. Hilly terrain can be made suitable for housing if the price of housing is high enough to cover the higher construction costs. In this way, the supply of real estate services is relatively more elastic than the supply of physical "dirt." The supply of real estate services is more dependent upon the amount of capital expenditures required to convert the land suitable for that use, than supply is dependent upon the amount of physical "dirt" upon which such uses can be made. Figure 3–3 illustrates the differences between the concept of supply as the physical amount of "dirt" and

---

[1]The President's Committee on Urban Housing, *A Decent Home* (Washington, D.C.: U.S. Government Printing Office, 1969), p. 135.

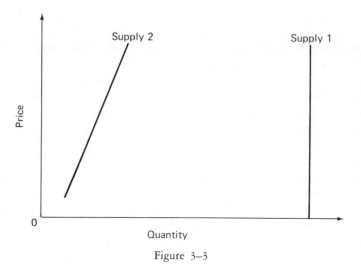

Figure 3–3

the supply of real estate defined in terms of the total property services available through the use of real estate. S_1 represents the physical definition. It is a vertical line because of the fixed amount of land mass in the world. At any price, the amount of available land in the physical sense is the same. Even at a zero price, the amount of land is the same as it would be if the price were at the highest possible. The amount of land does not respond to changes in the prices at which that land is exchanged in the market place. S_2 represents the supply of real estate in definition of use and the value of the services resulting from the use to which the real estate may be put. S_2 is sloped upward and to the right because it tends to increase in quantity as the price of its services increases. At a very low price, there would tend to be real estate that was so productive that it would be able to generate revenue at even a very low price. Other land would not be as nearly productive and could only be worth cultivating if the price of the product were high enough to justify the added expense of making or converting the land to the newer use. Therefore, as the price increases, the supply of land services tends to increase, reflecting the conversion of less productive land to the new and more profitable use.

In real estate, single family homes would be an example. As the price of homes went up, and the returns earned by developers likewise went up, it would then pay to build homes on land previously thought to be too hard to landscape or make into useable lots for homesites. The increase in the supply of real estate services again would respond to higher prices paid by purchasers for land of a specific use (single family homes), and not merely for the land or "dirt" having a higher value.

Real estate as an economic good in the market place is extremely varied and differs a great deal from the assumptions made in the previous chapter on the supply in the perfectly competitive market. Aside from the concept of real estate services and use, rather than the physical supply of "dirt," real estate is quite different from other economic goods exchanged in the market place. There are four concepts that tend to make real estate unique as an economic entity: (1) fixed location, (2) a very long life, (3) large economic units, and (4) decisions relating to real estate as long-term decisions.

The fact that real estate services are fixed to a particular location has dramatic effects on the market function. Sellers are incapable of moving their product to suit the market. A commercial building that was suddenly found to have lost its appeal because of a rerouting of a freeway would put the owner of that building in an extremely poor position. The owner rents or leases real estate services associated with that location and its surrounding environment. Suddenly he finds that people are not willing to pay for the services his building offers because of its location. Unfortunately, he cannot move his product to a better market as the potato grower would be able to do. There are many other areas of concern that are affected by the fixed location of real estate; many will be covered in later chapters on more specific topics.

Whenever the physical properties of land are modified to yield specific and marketable real estate services, the life of those services is a valid and extremely important consideration by both the producer and consumer. One of the more obvious points is that the product must be thought to be of economic value for a long period of time. The possibility of the market making necessary adjustments in the short run to take advantage of temporary and short-lived demand is reduced by the long life of real estate assets. The prospects of a developer having to live with a mistake for 40 years compels those owning and developing property services to be very sure of their market prior to committing themselves to improving the physical property and selling the property services. It also tends to make buyers more cautious in their bargaining in the market place, because they too will have to live with their decision for many years.

The single most obvious aspect of real estate to the ordinary citizen is that it costs a lot of money. The magnitude of real estate is a very real factor to all buyers and sellers in the real estate market. One of the first conclusions is that fewer buyers are eligible or in the market because of the large economic units involved. Another major fact of life in the United States is that for most buyers the price of the real estate necessitates that some of the money for the purchase come from other people besides the buyer. The fact that most buyers must borrow money from other people to make the purchase means that other people besides the buyer and seller are involved in the negotiations and determination of the value of the commodity being exchanged. Furthermore, the mere magnitude of real estate services tends to make the entire market more conservative and less volatile. Part of the reason for less of an immediate adjustment process is the complexity of the decision as to the value of the proposed or offered real estate services. As with all four of the factors under discussion, the magnitude of the price of real estate reflects the fact that the services gained are not realized in total at the time of the transaction. The benefits of use are spread over a period of time that is in the realm of the future. Prediction of the future is at best a tenuous guide of value. The magnitude of price in real estate multiplies the importance of this estimation of the future.

As with the real property services themselves, decisions made in the market place relating to those property services are long-range decisions. That is, not only the physical life of the asset, but decisions about the asset are long-run. If you or I purchased a candy bar at the local store, and it turned out not to be the kind we liked, we would merely buy another one of the kind we did care for. If the first candy bar was spoiled or damaged, we would simply buy any additional bars at a different store. Our decisions about the candy bar and the store are short-term decisions, lasting only as long as it takes us to buy another candy bar. A decision about real estate, however, is not nearly so trivial.

If we invest all of our savings in a house that turns out to be not to our liking, or that is totally unsuitable to our needs, it will tend to be a long-term decision. The reason is that we will have to wait until we again have savings adequate to cover selling costs and the buying and moving costs that would be involved in another move to more suitable quarters.

Another implication of the long-term decisions relating to real estate is the impact of improvements on real estate. If I decide to build a single-family house on a piece of vacant property, and the town suddenly turns down in the economic sense, there may not be any buyers in the market for my house. That house is not suitable for growing agricultural products, which may be the only remaining economic enterprise in that town. The decision to build the house is a very long-term decision, and may not lend itself to correction.

DEMAND FOR REAL ESTATE

As with the supply of real estate, the demand for real estate is more than merely the demand for the physical "dirt" involved. The demand for real estate is a demand for the benefits that may be derived from the use of the physical land for a specific purpose. Demand for real estate tends to be much like the demand for other commodities in certain respects. Demand tends to be a negatively sloped line in the graphical analysis. Such an aggregate demand curve is depicted in Figure 3–4. In the illustration, the amount demanded by consumers of real estate services tends to increase as the cost or price of real estate decreases. This tendency reflects the basic assumption in economics that people as consumers will generally prefer to have more rather than less for the same amount

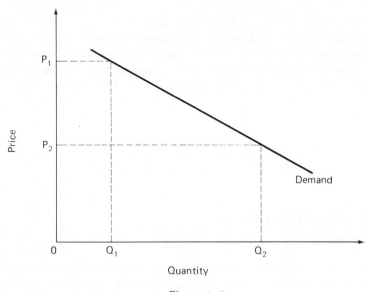

Figure 3–4

of expenditure. If the price of the item is P_1, the consumers in this market will then demand the amount at Q_1. That is, suppliers will be able to sell their wares until they reach the level of total sales represented by Q_1. If the price of the commodity is reduced to P_2, then consumers will be willing to purchase the total amount represented by Q_2. The reason for this increased consumption is twofold. First, at the lower price more people may be able to afford the commodity. Second, at the lower price some consumers will find it to their advantage to buy more of the commodity instead of other commodities that were purchased before.

In the field of real estate, the fact that lower prices of real estate services tend to increase the demand for the service is rather well established. The second concept of substitution is not so clearly known by most persons. The substitution effect is evident in the second home market and in the vacation condominium market where the consumer of the real estate is not the occupant on a year-round basis. The costs as well as the returns in such substitutions tend to limit the impact of such a concept to the higher income groups. However, the concept of substitution that was described in the previous section on supply of potatoes is just as valid when one is discussing the demand side of the equation in the real estate sector.

The fact that the demand function or curve for a commodity tends to a negatively sloped curve—that is, it slopes down and to the right—is the exact opposite of the positively sloped supply curve characteristic of supply. The opposite slopes of the curves in the graphical presentation reflect the conflicting objectives of the consumers versus the suppliers. The sellers of a commodity prefer to receive the most money for the least amount of product. The consumers on the other hand prefer to receive the most commodity for the least amount of expenditure. In a free enterprise economic system, the point at which the two parties come to agreement in the market place is called the market equilibrium.

The elasticity of the demand schedule or curve is an important factor, as it was in the supply analysis preceding this discussion. Figure 3–5 illustrates the elasticity of the demand curve for real estate services. The demand for real estate services tends to be relatively responsive to changes in price. If the price of real estate drops from P_1 to P_2 the amount demanded by consumers in the market place will increase from Q_1 to Q_2. The amount of change in the amount demanded as a result of the price change is slightly more than the same relative change in the price. The change from P_2 to P_3 results in an even greater change in the amount demanded from Q_2 to Q_3. Real estate generally tends to have a variable elasticity as depicted above. Only when price changes are significant in terms of suddenly allowing previous groups that could not afford real estate to enter the market are there major impacts from the elasticity of the demand curve.

SUPPLY AND DEMAND IN THE MARKET

Now that the individual concepts of supply and demand have been studied, it is appropriate to analyze them as they react in the market place. Such a presentation is described as a model of the market. Recently, such models have been widely used in real

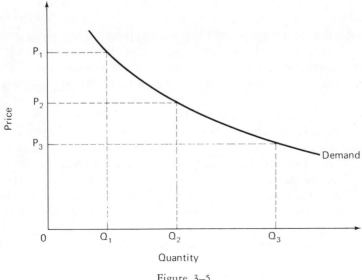

Figure 3–5

estate research and development. The advent of the computer has enabled many re-searchers to represent the market in the form of mathematical equations assembled in what is called simulation models. Figure 3–6 illustrates the supply and demand curves of a hypothetical market in real estate services. The demand curve is negatively sloped for the reasons given in the previous discussion on the demand for real estate. The sup-ply curve is highly positively sloped, representing the opposite values of the seller of

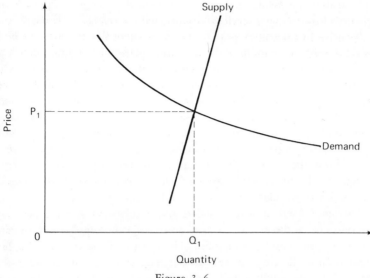

Figure 3–6

real estate as opposed to the buyer of real estate. The point at which the amount demanded and the amount supplied are equal is called equilibrium. At the equilibrium
point, all the sellers in the market will sell all their products, and all the buyers in the
market will be supplied all they demand. Since we are concerned with only one commodity, there is only one price and one quantity at the equilibrium point. Such a market
as is illustrated above is called a perfectly competitive market, and equilibrium under
perfect competition.

Perfect competition is an ideal situation that tends not to occur in the real world.
However, for the sake of analysis it is mandatory to deal in the simplistic assumptions
under perfect competition. There are basically four key assumptions in the perfect
competitive model: (1) many buyers and sellers, (2) one homogeneous commodity, (3)
perfect knowledge on the part of both buyers and sellers, and (4) freely competitive price
mechanism. Because of these four basic assumptions, buyers would not pay more for the
commodity because they could get all they needed at the lower price at equilibrium.
They would not pay a lower price because the suppliers could sell all their product at
the higher price The suppliers would not charge a higher price because they would not
be able to sell any of their commodity because the buyers could get all they demanded
at a lower price The suppliers would not charge a lower price because they can sell all
they have at the higher price. The entire market, both buyers and sellers, tends toward
the equilibrium point at all times. The four assumptions cited earlier are largely responsible for the tendency toward equilibrium in the manner described.

Process of Market Adjustment

Because we do not live in a static or unchanging world, the ability of a system
or society to adjust to changing conditions is a real test of its viability and strength.
Surely one of the major attributes of the private enterprise system is its ability to adjust
to changes with a relatively high degree of success. Figure 3–7 depicts a market at
equilibrium that suddenly finds itself confronted with a change in demand to a higher
level. The demand at equilibrium was D_1, which suddenly shifted to a new higher level
represented by D_2. Such a sudden shift in demand cannot be accommodated by an increase in the supply to the same extent. As was previously discussed in the supply side
of the real estate market, it often takes more than one year for the supply of real estate
services to be increased to any major extent. Because the increase in supply is more likely
a consumption of the marginal services, it is less than that necessary to fill the new
demand, and generally results in higher costs. With the amount of pressure on the market because of the new higher prices and excess of demand over supply, more suppliers
will be attracted into the market. The temporary equilibrium point is the intersection of
P_2 and Q_2, which will prevail until supply can adjust to the new demand pressures.

The temporary equilibrium set after the first shift in the demand for real estate
will tend to maintain itself until the builders and developers can bring new supplies of
real estate services on to the market. Such an increase in the supply of real estate usually
requires more than one year to accomplish. The impact of the increased supply on the
previous equilibrium following the shift in the demand is seen in Figure 3–8. The increased supply shifts the supply curve to the right (S_2), which implies that even at the

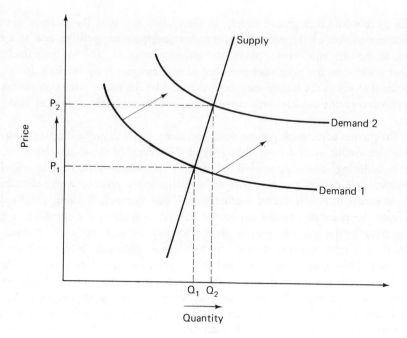

Figure 3–7

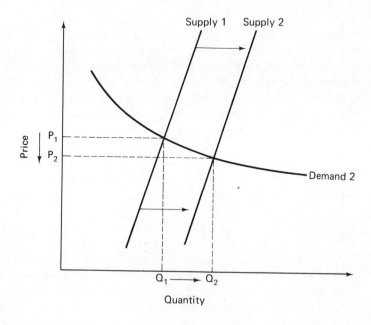

Figure 3–8

old price there would be a greater supply. In the market situation, the increase in supply will cause the market on the part of sellers to become more competitive, and as a result the price at the new equilibrium point (the intersection of D_2 and S_2) will tend to be somewhat lower than the price that prevailed in the short-term equilibrium. In fact, the mere point that prices are higher than normal would be the major attraction on the part of sellers to enter the market with newer projects and a greater supply of real estate services.

The market adjustment process described above tends to prevail in most situations in which the market is in an expanding trend. However, in those cases in which the market is declining, where demand is falling, the adjustment process is drastically altered. Figure 3–9 depicts the first part of the adjustment process, where demand has fallen while supply has remained unchanged. When demand declines, graphically it moves from the point of equilibrium to the left, or away from the equilibrium point. When moving to the left, the amount demanded declines, and the price at which that quantity is exchanged is lower than at the previous equilibrium. When demand drops from D_1 to D_2, the price drops to P_2, and the quantity demanded drops to Q_2. The impact of this decline is a lower return on investment for the seller of real estate services and a lower level of sales. In such situations, some of the supply will be directed to substitute uses so that the supply will tend to drop to some minor degree at least. Such a substitution could be in the form of apartment houses being converted to rooming houses or to invalid care facilities.

When the market has sufficient time to adjust supply, as in the over-one-year period of the expansion of supply, one finds that supply seems unable to contract even

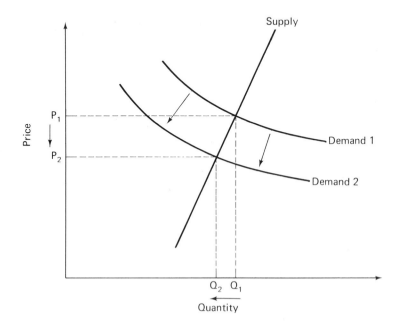

Figure 3–9

in the longer periods. What this means is that the first phase of a market decline, as depicted above, is also the long-run phase of the adjustment process in a declining market. The reasons for this one-way action on the part of the supply of real estate services are many and very complex. However, much of the cause for such behavior lies in the basic elements that make real estate services unique as an economic good. The fact that real estate is confined to fixed location, has a very long life physically, and comes in very large economic units, and that decisions relating to real estate are long-term decisions, all have much to do in contributing to the nearly one-way market adjustment process. One cannot move real estate to a more viable market. One cannot change the use of large real estate developments or projects without major expense and losses being incurred. One tends to ride out temporary poor climates when the amount involved is large in terms of the original economic commitment. One tends to stick to a decision when that decision was made with 40 or 50 years in mind, and the project comes under severe economic strain which it is believed will not continue for the life of the decision project.

In this chapter, we have been discussing real estate and economics with the broad brush of the generalist. The basic principles of economics were applied to the general area of real estate. The elements of real estate that constitute the subject matter of this text were analyzed and discussed. With this general background into the relationships between economic principles and the economic good of real estate, we will now turn our attention to the more detailed analysis of the elements in the real estate market and the economic impact and evaluation of those characteristics.

REFERENCES

1—Barlowe, Raleigh. *Land Resource Economics*. 2nd ed. Englewood Cliffs, N.J.: Prentice-Hall, Inc., 1972.

2—Ely, Richard T. and Wehrwen, George S. *Land Economics*. Madison, Wis.: University of Wisconsin Press, 1964.

3—Richardson, Harry W. *Urban Economics*. Middlesex, Eng.: Penguin Books Ltd.: 1971.

4—Smith, Herbert C., et. al. *Real Estate and Urban Development*. Homewood, Ill.: Richard D. Irwin Co., 1973.

5—Unger, Maurice A. *Real Estate*. Burlingame, Ca.: Southwestern Publishing Co., 1964.

6—Weimer, Arthur M., et al. *Real Estate*. 6th ed. New York: The Ronald Press, 1972.

STATISTICS

USE OF STATISTICS

Whenever one is in the position of trying to gauge or measure any element in the world of business or economics, the first obstacle encountered is the choice of what types of information are the most relevant to the question. If we wished to know the "average age" of the persons in a certain job or business, we would decide on whether we wanted the mean age, the single age most common, the middle age of the population or perhaps some age grouping or class. In all instances, the data we would be collecting would be the same, the ages of the individuals in that job or business. In the area of economic questions, the choice of data becomes much more involved—how to group the data, and what measurement to observe. Also, the data itself becomes open to much broader judgmental decisions. If we wished to know the "average" income of all four-unit apartments or less in a given area, the data we set out to collect are not at all as clear as the example dealing with ages of the population. Would we attempt to collect gross incomes, net incomes, cashflow, reported incomes or any of a multitude of other possible figures that may be indicative of income, or allow the researcher to arrive at the net income impartially? What costs, expenses and depreciation schedules would be considered, if any?

It is clear that the matter of deciding what data are needed and collecting that data are extremely important considerations in the mind of the researcher. Clearly, many areas are open to opinion and compromise before actual data collection begins. Every statistical study or survey has some area of judgment entering into it prior to the actual collection of data. In the areas of business, economics and real estate, statistical studies and surveys are abundant in every sector of our world. The major caution that should enter the mind of every person using or relying upon such statistics is the possible compromises that were made prior to the collection of the data, and how those compromises may reflect on the validity of the conclusions drawn by anyone using those statistics. Stated another way, are the statistics employed most suitable for the purposes of the researcher? The uses to which the person collecting the data had in mind may or may not be the same or compatible with the uses to which we may wish to put the data.

SUPPLY AND DEMAND STATISTICS

In collecting and using statistics, the distinction between supply and demand should be made. As discussed in Chapter 2, there is a direct difference between the supply and demand sectors of the market. If one is to use statistics to aid in reaching a conclusion or judgment, it is extremely important that the figures used actually measure elements of what the investigator wishes to study.

Supply is the easier of the two sectors to measure, but even then questions must be answered prior to collecting data, and also prior to using data collected by other sources. The sector chosen must be the supply segment data are collected from. The demand for housing is most often separated into single-family units, apartments and condominiums or planned unit developments. Likewise, if one is to measure the supply of residential real estate services, a similar classification must be used. Another consideration that must be entertained is whether only completed units are to be included in the data analyzed, or should the researcher also include units currently under construction? In the event units under construction are included, when should they be completed? In other words, at what stage in construction should the line be drawn between units included in the supply figures and those excluded from such figures. Additional consideration should be given to the number of mobile homes in the market area under study. The number of mobile home parks currently open and those under construction may also be a significant factor in the supply of residential housing. Indeed, considering the rising costs in the residential as well as other real estate areas, mobile homes may soon become a very significant factor in the available supply of real estate services for the middle- and lower-income families.

Demand statistics in the field of real estate are much more involved than are the supply statistics. The measurement of demand is totally based on the bias of history. Whatever statistics are employed, they all either measure what the demand was in some past sequence of time, or they are based on some type of inference that itself is based on past performance of demand in the market. In either case, one can never measure with complete confidence what the demand for a product or service will be.

The impact of this difference was illustrated more dramatically in the discussion of elasticity of supply and demand, and the importance of the time frame of supply and demand earlier in Chapter 2. The factors making real estate a unique commodity in the market place are the same factors that tend to make supply much easier to measure than the demand for real estate could ever be.

The most common indicators of demand in the real estate sector are the sales figures for the various types of real estate services changing hands. Sales are obviously measurements of what has already taken place in the market place, but nevertheless they constitute one of the most common statistics in analysis of the demand for housing. Transfers of real estate often provide a more complete set of data than do sales because of the inclusion of all real estate transfers. Sudden increases or decreases in population are also indicators of demand or the lack of it in a given area. Vacancy rates of apartment and commercial real estate are often used as indicators of the demand for those particular real estate markets. Again, it should be noted that in demand also, the real estate market of interest should be well defined. Single-family, multifamily, commercial, industrial, manufacturing and special-purpose real estate must be discerned in the data for the statistics to be useful at all.

External Elements

Although factors outside the immediate real estate sector affect both supply and demand of real estate, in the collection and study of data most externalities affect the demand for real estate more than they will the supply factors. Again, the major reason for this is the historical bias of demand analysis. Therefore, the discussion of external forces that follows will be devoted primarily to those factors affecting the demand for real estate and the statistics devoted to that demand.

The first major classification of external factors affecting demand is the market itself. Within the given market area under examination the employment climate, the regional or local economy, the availability and terms of financing, the business cycle of the region (if it has a definite cycle as many regions do), the influence and programs of the various governmental agencies active in the area under study—all have or may have a great deal of influence over the demand for real estate services in the area. The use of data collected for analysis and consideration is highly dependent upon many of these factors for any validity or accuracy in the study and its conclusions. It is important for the user of reports as well as for the person producing them to understand the factors affecting the data upon which the study is based. Furthermore, when a sudden change occurs in one or more of the factors cited above, the practicing real estate student should make the necessary adjustments in his reasoning and conclusions that the new information would indicate should be made. It is not uncommon to find oneself making a judgmental error based on outdated information or data sometime in one's career. Attention to many of the external influences mentioned may save the disappointment that comes with conclusions based on outdated, inappropriate or inaccurate data inputs into the decision.

A second major area of external influences is in the area of monopolistic characteristics that may prevail in the social and economic environment of the market area. There appears to be a rather strong tendency for most people to congregate and live near other people that have a similar income and ethnic, religious, racial and social values. In some instances this tendency may enhance the community and thus the regional economy of an area. However, in many instances the result is that inhabitants of a given area will endure many adverse elements merely because they feel intimidated by the prospects of living in another area in which the people do not have the same religious, ethnic, economic or social values. It is not an uncommon occurrence to find physically inferior buildings renting for higher than the average for like units when the renters are not English-speaking, or are nonwhite, or of an ethnic or cultural minority. Oftentimes some of the contributing factors include the monopolistic position occupied by the land owners in areas in which such congregating peoples inhabit larger or more metropolitan cities.

Many theories and publications center upon the phenomena of business cycles. Whether such cycles actually do exist in fact is an issue open to debate on many fronts. The major consideration is the most likely impact on the immediate area under examination. The individual area or region may or may not be subject to such cycles. In any event it is almost certain that each area or region will register changes that are not in direct proportion to whatever evidence there is for national business cycles. However, certain relationships show up in cycle analysis and theory that do tend to occur in the real estate sector. When there is a sudden increase in the demand for real estate services, that in turn is the same as saying there is a sudden decline in supply relative to the amount demanded. Whenever the amount of available supply is significantly less than the amount demanded, there prevails what is described as a seller's market. In the seller's market, the seller is able to generate a higher than normal rate of return on his product. Likewise, the buyer is in the position of taking what he can get, and often does not have the option of substituting for better accommodations at perhaps a lower price.

On the other hand, the situation also occurs in which the available supply is more than enough to meet the available demand. Where the supply is greater than the demand for an item, there is what is called a buyer's market. In a buyer's market, the buyer has the advantage, and will tend to get a lower price than normal for his money. Likewise, the seller is at the disadvantage and must take what he can get for his product. What happens in a buyer's market is essentially a situation in which there is an oversupply of the commodity under examination.

Other, more limited external elements such as architecture, soils, transportation, education, cultural attractions, history and a multitude of other factors may play a major part in shaping the demand function for real estate services. The important point to be stressed here is that whatever the external elements may be that are important in shaping the market for real estate services in the individual areas, it is vitally important for those in real estate to be cognizant of what those factors may be and to what extent and in what direction they influence the supply and demand for real estate services in that particular area.

TIME PERSPECTIVE OF THE DATA

In every study or research project, one of the most important limits or parameters that must be set is the time frame of the study and of the data upon which the study and its conclusions are based. In economic studies the time frame is divided into two major segments. The first is the short-run analysis, which is a period of time that does not provide for an increase in the facilities of production or technologic advances. It is usually a period of one year or less, but may be longer for specific industries. In real estate, the

short-run period generally does not allow for an increase in the number of units produced, while at the same time the demand for real estate may shift either up or down
rather dramatically.

The second perspective, the long-run perspective, allows sufficient time to increase
the supply of real estate services. Even in the longer run there is usually not sufficient
time to include major technology changes unless they are near production scale during
the time covered. The very-long-run perspective is used on occasion to study the trends
and relationships over a period of many years or decades. Historical studies of industries
or trends in certain measurements are the most common types of very-long-run projects.

The time perspective of the data you inspect may have a dramatic impact upon
the results and credibility of your study. Suppose you were attempting to predict what the
market for single-family homes in your area might be six months from now. From
the information about the market structure you have so far, you know that the primary
segment that will influence the market in such a short period of time is the demand for
the services you are studying. Therefore, you would not devote much time or energy to
gathering data relating to the supply of real estate services within the next six months.
The only changes in supply will be the units currently under construction that will be
ready for sale within six months. The factors relating to the demand for the services
under study will be the major emphasis of your efforts. In gathering data relating to the
demand for housing in your area within the next six months, you must use considerable
discretion in deciding which factors are relevant in that short time span. In most instances, data such as national economic trends, fiscal and monetary policies of the federal
government, federal and state programs relating to housing, business cycles, tax considerations would be too long range to have a significant impact on the housing market of
a local area within the next six months. What is the most important consideration is the
fact that only data that reflect changes in the immediate future are those data that should
be included in your study. Current trends in terms of financing, units size and price
ranges, sales figures by area, size, price and types of units, opening of a new road, shopping center, school, park or other such amenity should be included in your analysis.

The major concept to adhere to is that if your study or analysis is a short-run
project, then the data you include in your analysis should be data that are relevant
in the short-run. Any data that are primarily long-run data should be included only if
they indeed have an immediate impact in the short-run.

When anyone attempts to undertake a very large project in terms of the size of
the project and in terms of the time span involved in the completion of the project,
they must account for some of the long-run economic indicators relevant to the project. It is not uncommon for any significant commercial project to become trapped
in a time frame of three to seven years from the time of initial planning to opening the doors of the completed project. In such projects there is the inherent danger
of the market changing rather drastically between the initial planning stage and the
completion date. For that reason, it is vitally important for the management of the project
to account for the economic indicators relevant to the next three to seven years. Indeed,
for such a project to get off the ground and gender the financial backing it must have,
it must be thoroughly projected and documented into the future. Such future projections
must also include indicators relating the market to the entire life of the project. There

must be some assurances that the financiers and the purchasers will benefit from the project over the life of the project, otherwise it will not be financed or sold. Such a time frame as would be entailed in a large commercial project, which would be 40 or 50 years in most instances, would include most all indicators of both supply and demand over the time frame studied.

As a result of the scale of the projects in the long-run market, it has precluded individual developers from conducting adequate economic studies suitable for such projects. A few very large national firms may have adequate research staffs to conduct such thorough studies, but most firms are not large enough to have such resources at their disposal. As a consequence, a growing number of firms on the national and regional level specialize in such research. Although they may sometimes appear expensive (most studies cost from $25,000 to over $1 million), the quality and depth of the research is usuallly much greater than most research staffs are equipped to conduct. There are also many research staffs for most of the large banks and newspaper firms of the nation. In addition, many special interest publications carry extremely useful data relating to various economic elements in our world.

The major overriding concern of this text is that no matter how good or detailed the available data may be, the people making the real estate decision must be able to understand and interpret the data that apply to their areas of concern.

SOURCES OF INFORMATION

Whenever information in the form of data is used in a study to reach conclusions relating to the topic, the source of the information is a very important consideration. Just as people in our daily lives vary in the degree to which we value their judgment, the sources for information vary according to the researcher collecting the data and the researcher using the data.

The most ideal situation is one in which the person using the data is the same person collecting it. All the judgments that must be made in gathering the data are made by the one using the information. In such a case, all the judgments are made with the purposes of the study in mind. Such a source of data, the person using the data is the person who collects it, is called "primary." Data are usually most complete and most accurate when they are obtained from primary sources. The major overriding drawback of such data is that they are usually very time consuming and very expensive to collect. As a result, most market studies done on the local level by private parties are seldom based upon primary information sources.

Because of the time and cost factors that handicap primary data gathering, most persons employ "secondary" information sources. A secondary source of information is that in which the researcher using the data is not the one who collected the data. The researcher is compelled to accept data that were obtained by someone else, and that may or may not be most appropriate for what the researcher has in mind for his study. The major advantage in using secondary data sources is the tremendously reduced cost in gathering the data inputs into the study.

However, the cost advantage of secondary data can be quickly lost in those cases in which the data from secondary sources are not completely appropriate to the study being conducted by the second person. In most if not all cases, the purposes of the second study are not identical with the purposes of the first study. Therefore, even the most minor adjustments or compromises made during the original collection of data may have drastic implications in the second or future studies employing the same data. For this reason, it is vitally important for the user of secondary information sources to understand the assumptions and compromises made by the persons collecting the original data. One famous example is that in which a survey was taken among the business community to determine the outcome of a presidential race. The conservative candidate was favored by a large percentage of those questioned. The surveyor concluded the conservative candidate would win hands down in the coming election. What actually was the case, however, was that the conservative candidate was soundly beaten in the election. The assumption made by the magazine that business represented the nation's populace was a totally invalid assumption; indeed most members of the business community are rather conservative in their political views. The general populace of the nation was leaning toward the more liberal candidate. The point to keep in mind is that the assumption that the business community fairly represented the national political feeling was not a valid assumption. The study fairly represented what that portion of the nation was feeling politically, but the assumption that that was the same as the national opinion was misguided.

Another example would be a dual meet between country A and country B. Country A reported that it had placed second in a world meet, and B had placed next to last. The manner in which data are presented as well as the number of observations in the study can have a very distortive influence on the study and the reliability of the study. Studies published by supporters of specific programs or points of view are usually poor studies upon which to base further research. The most reliable forms of secondary information are those published by research and governmental bodies. The Bureau of Labor Statistics, the Bureau of the Census, and the Department of Commerce publish volumes of reliable material on a monthly basis. Most major colleges and universities have bureaus of economic and business research that offer very reliable sources of information to the local communities. Also many of the major financial institutions, including the Federal Reserve Banks, have ample resource material available to the public free or at a nominal charge.

Statistics is primarily a study of associations. It is the attempt to gain some insight into the future through study of the details of the past. The study of the past can reveal certain associations between events; when one event occurred, it was usually preceded or followed by a certain other event. When such an association happened on a rather consistent basis in the past, then both parts of the association are observed in the current scene to see if such turning of events may occur in the near future. The important thing to keep in mind is that the entire study is one of association—the likelihood that one event is associated with another event. There is, however, nothing in the entire study of statistics that denotes or even attempts to establish a cause-and-effect relationship between the two events.

The difference between association and cause-and-effect relationships is perhaps best illustrated by the following example. There is almost a perfect association between the water temperature off southern California beaches and the number of persons who drown each year. As the water rises in temperature, the number of persons drowning increases proportionately. As the temperature falls, the number of persons who drown falls in a nearly identical proportion. Nothing in the data or in the analysis concludes that the temperature of the water causes people to drown.

When statistical information is available on the more complex world of economics and real estate, the distinction between association and cause and effect is not so easily made. The more aware is the researcher or the consumer of research of the external factors affecting data in the subject area, the greater the likelihood of him being able to spot false implications and conclusions relating to studies in his area. The earlier section on external factors can be readily appreciated in light of the potential problems that may arise in trying to establish cause-and-effect relationships on the basis of simple associations.

The single most important principle upon which any study or research should be based is the unbiased collection and analysis of the raw data at the time of collection. Whenever a researcher begins with an opinion or conclusion as to a cause or relationship, and then proceeds to collect data from a sample in attempts to prove his preconclusion, the study and the data are seldom if ever valid in terms of analysis or reliability of data for subsequent research projects. The purpose of research is to answer the question of what relationship exists between two or more events. Research does not have value when it starts out to prove a presupposed relationship.

Input-Output Analysis

In addition to economic research with a real estate market and finance orientation, there are two relatively common statistical studies that are well established in the national, regional and state levels. These two are input-output analysis and economic base analysis. Input-output analysis attempts to identify those areas that are producers and those areas that are consumers in the economic area under study. The end goal of this type of study is to guide governments in the areas that will most benefit the entire area if the government encourages production or consumption in certain patterns. Table 4–1 contains a division of the economy between producers and consumers. In the example, two producers, A and B, are also the only two consumers. Such a situation is referred to as being a closed economic system. Most barter and primitive cultures are of this type.

TABLE 4–1

Consumers	Producers		Total
	A	B	
A	1	1	2
B	1	1	2
	2	2	4

TABLE 4–2

| | Producers | | |
Consumers	A	B	Total
A	1	1	2
B	1	1	2
C export	1	1	2
	3	3	

From the table it can be seen that each sector produces two units of output, and each consumes two units of output. Given such a situation there is absolutely no possibility of export or cash imports that would enable this community to expand beyond its current point. Such exclusion of all outside trading possibilities is the reason it is called a closed system.

Table 4–2 illustrates the first possible area of changing to an "open" economic system. Although there are still only two producers as before, there is one added consumer category—exports. Sectors A and B now produce one third more than before, and what would be a rotting surplus in the previous closed system now becomes a viable export product. Capital would begin to accumulate in the country because it is not importing anything, only exporting. If the government of the country wished to expand these exports even further to accumulate more capital stock for future industrialization or whatever, it would not be able to distinguish between A and B as to which sector would be the best to expand. As far as the table indicates both are exactly the same in their impact on the foreign trade issue.

Table 4–3 illustrates another matrix of distribution that is a bit different. A and B are the only producing sectors of the country, and A, B and Export are the three consuming sectors. However, the major fact in the new matrix is that the distribution for export, as well as within the country, is much different than in the previous examples. Both A and B produce three units as before; however, B does not export any

TABLE 4–3

| | Producers | | |
Consumers	A	B	Total
A	1	1	2
B	0	2	2
C export	2	0	2
	3	3	

while A exports two. If this country wished to expand its exports and international trade position it would now have some basis upon which to make a firm decision. It would no doubt choose to expand the production and employment associated with industry A and choose not to do much if anything with the capacity of industry B.

The major point of the illustration is to understand the basic idea behind input-output analysis. It is used primarily by governmental bodies to measure the impact of certain sectors of the local, regional or state economy in terms of imports versus exports. The logic of the approach can be used on a local scale to briefly review the economic structure of a particular area of interest. Also, input-output analysis provides some statistical study of the relationship between certain industries or sectors and other sectors in the same area.

Problems in Input-Output Analysis   Input-output analysis is subject to some very serious problems that are not easily solved. The first major problem is the data inputs upon which the model matrix is based. Sales are not a very accurate measure of output or of input. Dollar figures reflect more than what one particular industry segment produces. Raw material and input factors are reflected in the final price of industrial products. Double counting such as this may seriously distort the comparisons between industry segments. Sales are, however, the most common measure because of the ready access to such figures and the relatively low cost of using such data input measurements.

The net value added at each stage of the production process is a much more accurate input statistic. However, obtaining such figures is extremely costly and virtually impossible for most industry sectors in any sizable area under examination. Individual firms are very reluctant to identify the exact amount of gross profit attributable to their special skills. Furthermore, the methods of accounting vary so greatly between various industries and firms within each industry that it is a virtually impossible task to ascertain the value added at each stage of the production process.

The number of employees is another alternative form of measurement of the importance economically of various industry segments. The single largest drawback in relying upon employment statistics is that they ignore completely the productivity of those employees in various industries. Through introduction of new machinery the output per employee may be drastically increased. Relying upon employee inputs, the study would totally ignore the increase in output of that particular industry.

Economic Base Analysis

In nearly every area there are industries that export products or services outside the area, and thus generate income into the area from outside sources. Such industries are usually regarded as the key industries that determine the extent of growth of the community or region. In the recent oil exploration activity in Alaska, when the oil is drilled for and found, brought to production and then transported for refining, there are many persons and companies involved in the process. As a result of the expansion of the personnel involved, facilities such as roads, air services, schools, restaurants, hotels, food producers and importers and a variety of other service-connected industries grow as a result of the one basic industry in petroleum being generated. This illustrates the difference between those types of industries that are basic (oil exploration and development), and those industry sectors that are considered nonbasic (hotels, restaurants, stores, etc.).

The previous example about oil also points out another important consideration in basic industries. Basic industries generally tend to have a multiplier effect on the nonbasic sector. That is, one unit of basic industry will generally support more than one unit of nonbasic industry. The employee working in the basic industry sector has a family and needs that he demands be met by many sectors other than just the firm where he works. It is this basic relationship between base industry and nonbase industries that it supports that is the reason for economic base analysis.

The economic potential of a given area or region is the primary reason for economic base analysis. It is most commonly conducted through the governmental bodies in cooperation with private research firms in some of the more involved or complicated studies. The first point is the taking of an inventory of the current industries and their importance in terms of dollar magnitude and number of employees. Each industry is listed in order of magnitude and whether it is considered basic or nonbasic. In cases in which limited funds are expended on the study, very often it begins with the assumption that all manufacturing and agriculture are totally for export, and are therefore basic industries. All other industries are then regarded as nonbasic. This indirect method is by far the most inaccurate, but it is also the cheapest and entails the shortest time span.

Another technique is to compute percentages for the list of industries in the inventory as a percentage of the total. Then the national profile of percentage for each industry segment is compared with the local percentages in the inventory. Those making the study, usually governmental bodies of some level, then make decisions about stimulating or dampening certain area trends of industrial growth. Such an approach is generally called the *location quotient technique.*

Local governing bodies sometimes use the minimum requirement technique, in which they compare their local area under study with other localities in the nation. Beginning with one of the base industries in the area under study, one hundred or so communities are ranked in order of the percentage of their economies that are due to that industry. Then the local area people who are in the decision area will choose where they feel their community should place among the one hundred other towns or communities. For example, if community A has 40 percent in agriculture, and community C has 30 percent in agriculture, then perhaps community B will feel they are about the same size and general climate and therefore will decide to be at or near 35 percent in agriculture. If community B is currently only at 20 percent agriculture in its economic makeup, it may then decide to institute some program to encourage the growth of the agriculture sector.

The problems in the economic analysis are many, in addition to the outline of the approach explained previously. The first major problem is attempting to define "basic" and "nonbasic" industrial sectors. The case of national firms of the conglomerate type presents the most obvious type of difficulty. Vertical firms also present some of the same problems in trying to separate their basic manufacturing features from their marketing or distribution features.

Defining the economic area presents some serious compromises in the study.

Exactly where the local economic areas end and the export areas begin can have a drastic impact on the figures and relationships generated from the study. In some cases it may be impossible to study an economic region much smaller than most of one or more states. In other cases it may be relatively easy to study one single town. In either case the consideration of economic units in close proximity must be made.

What measurements or yardsticks are to be employed will have a major impact on the reliability of the study and the conclusions upon which it is based. Dollar measurement has serious drawbacks when based upon sales or exports as an indication of the economic worth of a given industry. The dollar amounts may reflect costs of partially finished components by other sectors used by the exporting company. The cost of obtaining value added figures is usually totally prohibitive for any study of much detail. Employment figures when used are totally irrespective of the productivity of the labor in that industry. The fact that one sector may be more labor intensive than another is totally ignored in the type of study that counts only the number of employees. The garment industry is quite labor intensive, as compared with the petroleum industry which is quite capital intensive. The relative importance of the two would be greatly distorted if only an employee measurement were used in the data included in the economic base study.

Because of the data problems and the mere scope of such an economic analysis or study such as we have been discussing, one of the major problems is the mere cost in terms of time and money that such a study must entail to have any meaning. Knowing that to maintain total integrity data should be from primary sources, and that the economic measurements should entail more than one yardstick, the data problems that naturally arise whenever any compromise is made are indeed rather major in terms of the ultimate impact on the study.

REFERENCES

1—Reichmann, W. J. *Use and Abuse of Statistics.* Middlesex, Eng.: Penguin Books Ltd., 1971.

2—Rigby, Paul H. *Conceptual Foundations of Business Research.* New York: John Wiley and Sons, Inc., 1965.

3—U.S., Department of Housing and Urban Development, *A Decent Home.* Report of the President's Commission on Housing, Washington, D.C.: U.S. Printing Office, 1968.

4—U.S., Department of Commerce, Bureau of the Census, *Statistical Abstract of The United States, 1973.* Washington, D.C.: U.S. Printing Office, 1973.

PART

LAND USE

After studying the theoretical principles of economics and the application of those principles to a simplified version of the real estate sector, we now turn our attention to the product itself in the real estate exchange process. We have carefully defined real estate in the more abstract terms of the services gained through use of the real estate product for some specific purpose. That use and real estate services are a more complex definition of real estate than the physical definition based upon so much land area or "dirt," goes without saying. The point of the current section is to examine the implications of that definition and to study some of the past and current trends within the market process and from without that have a dramatic bearing upon the economic distribution of this most important resource in the human experience.

CHAPTER

FOUNDATIONS AND PATTERNS OF LAND USE

WHAT IS LAND USE?

Land use is the ultimate product of the market place. Between the interaction of supply and demand forces in the market place, and the initial constraints that are or may be imposed by governing bodies, is a subject property being used for some specific purpose. It is this last purpose that results from the market forces that is the subject of the real estate professional. Land use may encompass a broad definition, but for the purposes of study all economic uses must be included. All uses would include certain nonuses in the normal sense such as: speculative land holding in margin areas; open space of social benefit, greenbelts also of social benefit, public historical or recreational lands, also of public good, and in some cases buffer zones of nonuse to protect given areas of residential or city and town development. In all cases the use of land as measured in terms of return or price is the actual commodity being bargained for in the market place.

A given parcel of land may be suitable for more than one type of use. Thus, the measurement of the returns that parcel may generate for various uses is the basic determinant of the ultimate use to which that piece of land may be put. These various returns enable all the potential buyers to bid for that parcel of land. The bidder that is able to get the highest returns from the use to which he wishes to put that land will be able to outbid all other potential buyers who may have other uses in mind. It is through this process that land use is dependent upon the market forces, and, therefore, is the end result of the market situation.

Inasmuch as the use of land is dependent upon the market processes, the multitude of factors that influence the functioning of the market structure are serious elements relating to land use. Through the police power of the government sectors, government regulation of the market and the elements of land use within their jurisdiction have become a very strong limiting influence on the ease of the market functioning within the more traditional patterns of pure competition as described in earlier chapters. Most of the laws relating to real estate are of state and local origin, but in reference to certain programs of national origin, the federal government also plays a large role in regulating the real estate sector. The multitude of regulations relating to transfer, financing, zoning, building codes, various subsidy programs, taxes on real property, price and rent controls and many other more specific regulations create a more difficult environment for the process of bargaining and exchanging of goods in the real property sector to operate efficiently and with minimum time delays.

HISTORY OF LAND USE

Historical patterns of land use and the development of our major metropolitan areas were dependent upon distinct advantages those sites had in relation to trade routes, ports, raw material resources and some man-made trade advantages such as breakpoints in the rate structure of railroads. The pattern of growth within these areas largely followed the wishes of the persons owning the land. Major cities such as New York, Chicago, Denver, Seattle, San Francisco and New Orleans, were all based on certain advantages they had in relation to trade routes, natural resources, deep water ports or railroad lines that tended to make them flourish, whereas other lands did not possess the same advantages. Furthermore, these communities tended to grow with a perspective of the short term and within the desires of the private land owners. As a result, nearly all of these major cities have vastly overcrowded central areas with a wide diversity of building types and architecture, and a very noticeable lack of open areas or overall planning. To a large extent the reasons for the historical patterns of land use were centered around the technologic constraints that prevailed at the time many of the larger cities began to emerge. Transportation and most communication facilities prior to the 1900s made living more than a few blocks from the main metropolitan area extremely difficult. In fact, a distance of one or two miles from the center of the city would put one nearly in the rural area.

Without refined fiscal and monetary systems, even on the national level, large-scale planning by city and state authorities was impossible. Therefore, the entire impetus in the growth process was in the hands of the private sector of the economy. As such, the decisions of the many private individuals in relation to construction and building in the growing cities, when combined with the fractionalization of land ownership, led to the intense use of real estate services in the major marketing areas of the cities and minor emphasis placed upon the long-range aspects of city growth.

PRIVATE PROPERTY AND LAND USE

The institution of private property as compared to the feudal system of land ownership had a distinct impact on the pattern of land use in a city, or the lack of a formal pattern. Without the one overall decision-maker as in the feudal system, there generally was a lack of any planning on a municipal scale. The power to decide what use was to prevail on a given piece of land was in the hands of the owner of that land. When ownership of most of the metropolitan land is divided into many individuals owning many pieces of land, the decision-making process becomes extremely blurred on any regional or municipal basis. In the feudal system, the lord or king owned all the land and could therefore dictate the land-use plan for the entire region by virtue of his owning it. It is in this way that private land ownership had a great deal to do with the pattern of land use that developed in the older cities in the US. The role of private property has and has had as much effect on the transaction phase of the market as on the land use patterns.

By its very nature, the institution of private property requires a governmental body to protect and enforce the property rights of those owning land. As such, private property becomes more a product of law and the courts of the land than of the real world of physical facts. Indeed, as a nation grows from the small agriculture-based country of the 1700s and early 1800s to a metropolitan and industrial nation that we see today, the types of property rights develop with the same degree of complexity and refinement. In many areas of the country today there are lawyers who practice only in areas involving real estate, because that area has become so complex and developed that one man could not keep up with the developments in that area and also be able to practice confidently in the many other areas of legal controversy.

Estate Interests

The ownership of real property is historically termed "estate" ownership. Through time several classes of estates have developed to fit the various ownership rights common to real property. Freehold estates are interests in real property that do not last for a fixed period of time. Less-than-freehold estates are generally fixed in duration. Freehold estates include estates in fee, both absolute and qualified by condition or limitation, and life estates. Less-than-freehold estates include: estates for years, from period to period, at will and estates at sufferance. Table 5–1 further displays the types of estates and the more general classification of estates by fee or freehold and nonfreehold.

Estates in Fee

Sometimes called fee simple estates, estates in fee may be absolute if the owner may dispose of his estate at anytime during his life, or after his death. Such fee simple ownership is most common. If you own a home, you may sell it, rent it, lease it, remodel it or dispose of it in any form of inheritance upon your death. If you bought a piece of real property under the condition that it be used as a church or other specific purpose your interest would be a qualified fee estate. Qualified fee estates may be qualified by a condition or a limitation, but in either case the estate remains an estate in fee.

Life estates are the other types of estates in fee. While the one enjoying the life estate is living, he has all the rights normally associated with those having fee simple ownership. The major difference is the life estate is limited to the life of the one contained in the contract; after that life is complete, or after the death of the one enjoying

TABLE 5–1
Estates of Real Property

Freehold Estates	Less-than-Freehold Estates
Estates in fee	Estate for years
(A) Absolute	From period to period
(B) Qualified	Estates at will
Life estates	Estates at sufferance

the life estate, the estate reverts to the grantor of the life estate. This means that a life estate cannot be willed or inherited after its completion like a normal estate in fee can be willed or inherited.

Leasehold Estates

Estate for years is one type of less-than-freehold estate, in which the lease is for a fixed number of weeks, days or months as determined by the mutual agreement between the lessor and lessee. Periodic tenancy is another name for the estate for years classification of leasehold estate.

Estate from period to period is much like the estate for years in that the lease may be for any period of year to year, month to month or week to week.

Estate at will is terminable at the will of the lessee or by will or unilateral decision of the lessor. There is no designated time period for the lease as in the previous two examples. Some states, including California, have a requirement of advance notice of termination to prevent the abrupt termination of such a lease.

Estate at sufferance is an estate in which the lessee retains the possession of the land if he has rightfully come into possession of the land originally in the lease. This estate prevails at the completion of a previous lease agreement, while the lessee still occupies the land.

Economic Implications

Unlike most other economic goods exchanged in the market place, estates in real property are abstract and highly complex. The package of real estate services represented by the various types of estates is actually a variety of different commodity services. Each type of estate is a different commodity being exchanged in the market place. The quality of the estate is much like the varying quality of various raw materials, and the lower the quality the lower the price such a commodity will get in the market relative to what fee simple ownership of the same property would get. The type of estate relates more to the quality of the real property interest than to the ownership or legal ramifications of the contract of the estate interest. The complexity of the estate classifications is one of many reasons that real estate is a highly specialized and complex product in the economic world. This complexity also contributes to the ease or lack of ease in real estate transactions occurring in the market place.

Title to Real Property

Estates are really just more detailed descriptions of the nature of what is owned in owning real estate services. Title, however, refers to how the asset is owned. All property has an owner, from some governmental body down to some individual. In private ownership, there are many ways property may be owned. Two broad classes of private ownership are separate and concurrent. Where one has complete ownership, also called severality, he or she may do as they wish with all the rights of real property.

In many cases sole ownership is not the case. In these instances, concurrent ownership in one form or another prevails. The particulars of each class may vary among the 50 states, but essentially the types or classes of concurrent ownership are generally recognized. Concurrent ownership includes: tenancy in common, joint tenancy, community property and tenancy in partnership.

In tenancy in common, each individual has title to his separate interest. They may be uneven interests, and there may be any number of persons in the estate. Each person may convey his interest any way or time he wishes, including through will or probate.

In joint tenancy, there may be any number of persons, but the interests must be equal to each other. There is only one title to the entire property, and at death the demised partner's interest passes to the remaining partners. There is no right of inheritance or will.

Community property applies only to a husband and wife. In most states the interests under community property are exactly equal between husband and wife. Each is prohibited from conveying his or her interest without the other doing the same. At the death of either partner, the remaining spouse receives one half the interest of the deceased spouse, and his heirs receive the other half as designated by his will or the probate law.

In addition to the manner of legal registration of the ownership of real property, there are also a group of legally defined interests that may preclude the ownership interests in real property. Such legally defined interests are called encumbrances.

Encumbrances

Encumbrances are of two general categories, those that affect title to real property and those that affect the use of real property. Those that affect title are generally called liens, and include: mortgages, trust deeds, mechanics liens, tax liens, special assessments, attachments and judgments. Liens generally denote a financial interest in the property, and do not affect the use to which the property is put. The second class of encumbrances pertains to the use of the property. Easements, zoning regulations, building regulations and encroachments are examples of encumbrances that relate directly to the use of property.

Encumbrances as well as estate designation have a very real and serious impact economically. Fee simple ownership without encumbrances of any sort represents the purest form of real estate service. In those instances in which the estate is less than fee simple, and the property is subjected to encumbrances of various sorts, the economic worth as reflected in the market place is less than the property would generate if it were of a higher form of ownership. Leasehold estates do, however, offer added flexibility in the real estate market. In those instances when one is able to purchase only those real estate services he is intending to consume in the immediate future, the financial outlay is much less than in the case of purchasing an infinite amount of real estate services through fee simple ownership.

ECONOMIC IMPLICATIONS

Until the past 50 years of American history, land use was basically a function of the private decisions of individual land owners enjoying fee simple ownership. The major parameters that dictated land use were the natural forces such as terrain and pro- ductivity of the land for specific purposes. It was rare to find instances where entire land use concepts for an entire town or region were instituted under the conditions of private land ownership. The motivation on the part of land owners was the returns they were able to gender through their land as a function of the immediate trade advantages associ- ated with that site. Such concepts as open space, congestion, public areas and future growth patterns were essentially ignored through the role that private land use decisions maintained in the market.

As a result of the growth of the towns and cities in certain areas, concerns such as public services and the overall benefit of the entire citizenry became significant enough to garner adequate support for such public services as police and fire protection, schools, hospitals, libraries and many of the other public services that have a more drastic impact on land use. As a result of these services, and the need to generate funds from all the land owners in the area or municipality, more overall planning and land use be- came a viable element in the use of land and private fee simple ownership was displaced as the major guide in land use decisions. Instead, private land use decisions were inte- grated with public land use planning for the overall land use planning in the commu- nities of most larger areas of the United States.

The historical trends resulting from the nature of the fractionalization of land ownership, and the ultimate confrontation between the profit motive and the social or overall good of the citizenry, naturally led to a more well-defined spectrum of land use planning and control.

The profit motive working through private land ownership and private land use decision-making on the fractionalized ownership maps were the major determinants of land use in our historical development. The growing complexity of land use services defined in the legal estate and the registration of ownership and title merely added to the great complexities involved in land use decisions. By the turn of the century, the rate of growth for the metropolitan cities of the nation had reached a point where the conflicts between private or profit good and the social good of the communities at large were not necessarily the same, and indeed had shown some dramatic differences. For the benefit of the population as a whole and to insure most of the public services necessary for growth and development, overall land use planning began to be a truly recognized part of most urban area governance.

The trends in modern land use planning began to emerge nearly 50 years ago. The following chapter is devoted to the current land use planning techniques and changing parameters of growth.

REFERENCES

1—Brown, Robert K. *Real Estate Economics: An Introduction to Urban Land Use.* Boston: Houghton-Mifflin Co., 1965.

2—Laurenti, Luigi. *Property Values and Race.* Berkeley, Ca.: University of California Press, 1961.

3—McClellan, Grant S. *Land Use in the United States.* New York: H. W. Wilson Co., 1971.

LAND USE PLANNING
AND CONTROL

HIGHEST AND BEST USE

The concept of highest and best use may have a variety of meanings depending upon who is employing the term. In the spectrum of economics, highest and best use has a very specific definition. The yardstick of measurement most commonly used in economics is money. Although there are many areas of question when employing money as a yardstick, as discussed more thoroughly in Chapter 2, it remains the most useful of tools. The highest and best use to which a subject property may be put, then, is the use that returns to the owner the maximum money return in comparison to alternative uses.

It is in this context that the land use patterns of historical nature were left to the devices and interpretation of the individual and private property owners. With the fractionalization of land ownership as one of the major characteristics of America, it is rather easy to see how the highest and best use to which property may be put was not uniform in the individual minds of the many owners.

The great complexity of land ownership, and thus the ownership and sale of real estate services, lead to many problem areas that are not so simply solved in analysis. Through some instances of uncommon cooperation between land owners, patterns of land use developed on a larger scale than individual lots. Deed restrictions were a common way for land owners to control the use of property they owned and leased or sold to others. It was a result of the knowledge gained through the higher returns they could expect if they controlled the uses to which parcels they sold could be put. This trend was most common or prevalent in subdivisions and housing tracts involving many smaller parcels being sold by one large land owner. Through assurances to potential buyers that their neighbors could not build or use adjacent sites for unsightly or obnoxious uses contrary to what the major portion of the sites was being used for, the owner selling the sites began to realize a better price for his sales and thus a higher return than could likely be generated without the restrictions. In some areas, deed restrictions pertaining to racial composition of the community limited land purchases to white buyers. In such cases, those potential buyers to whom that was an important part of their choice of housing, such deed restrictions did indeed raise the attractiveness and thus the profit to the seller of the land having such deed restrictions. Through such experience with deed restrictions, many land owners have discovered that they may indeed raise the value of their real estate services through some forms of deed restrictions. It should also be pointed out that most deed restrictions not attached to the use of the land have been declared unconstitutional, and most surely such deed restrictions as those pertaining to racial discrimination have been soundly declared unconstitutional.

The concept of the highest and best use of real property in terms of the highest return to the seller and user, and the legal details of land and deed restrictions comprised the major elements in the land-use planning spectrum existing prior to municipal zoning regulations. It is also important to understand that the economic factors in the market were and are the major determinants of land use. Without the economic returns being present deed restrictions and other forms of land use control would have little or no impact whatsoever. Economic returns are the motive for using land for any purpose, and without economic advantages attached to certain uses, there would be no economic reasons to put such land to any specific use. Such land would not have any worth in the market place, and thus would not have any value as an economic good.

ERA PRIOR TO ZONING

Highest and best use of land was confined to the individual property owner and his measurement of that use that would generate the highest return. As such, the planning function prior to municipal zoning ordinances was actually quite short-sighted. The land owner was in most instances concerned with the immediate returns to him in land use, and not the long-run impact of his decisions.

In addition to operating in a relatively free market place, where the laissez-faire capitalistic attitudes prevailed for the most part at this time period in our history in the U.S., the technology and state of the research and planning arts were nearly unknown. As a result, even the few powerful persons in a position to implement long-range planning ideas, and who may have had some social interests for the highest and best use of all land in an area, were also without the tools necessary to define the goals or the problem areas that may arise, and indeed did arise as a result of many private land owners doing with the land as their own best interests and personal fortunes dictated.

As a result of the characteristics of the market place that prevailed during this era in our history, the major elements in land use planning were the individual measures applied to individual land exchanges and development. Such instruments as deed restrictions and various qualities of estates were the major tools. Some specific building restrictions did occur in regard to public health and specific land use within cities.

In summary, the control over land use and planning was vested in the private owner of land, and the use was primarily the result of his opinion of the use that would garner him the highest return. As a result of the decentralized nature of planning and control, land use was very short-sighted in terms of social benefits accruing to the society of which it was a part.

PUBLIC CONTROL OF LAND USE

Public control over land use within municipal jurisdictions began to appear shortly after the turn of the century. The first national definition and recognition of zoning regulations occurred as the result of a Supreme Court decision set down in 1926. In the City of Euclid v. Ambler Realty Co., the court held that zoning regulations fell within the police power of the government under the constitution and declared that such regulations: will make it easier for fire protection, increase the safety and security of home life, tend to prevent street accidents by reducing traffic and congestion in residential sections, decrease noise and other conditions that condone nervous disorders, and preserve a more favorable environment for children (U.S. Supreme Court, 272 U.S. 365 [1926]).

Although there may be some room for argument over the court's reasoning in some instances, the important point is that such local zoning ordinances were upheld as being constitutional. Furthermore, it is worth noting that such zoning ordinances were not based on the older law of some pre-1900 decision or legislation. Zoning as we know it in its present form in most U.S. cities is a relatively new phenomenon on the scene of land use planning and control through the power of local municipal jurisdictions.

One important facet of zoning must not be overlooked. Zoning is applicable only to future land use within the area under jurisdiction. Zoning cannot be made retroactive to cover land used for specific types of improvements prior to the zoning law being implemented. What this means is that the legacy of a patchwork quilt of land usage within many areas cannot be overturned with the passage or implementation of local zoning ordinances. Such ordinances will apply only to new construction within the area under its jurisdiction.

Zoning applies only to future changes in land use; it has virtually no impact upon the land use currently being enjoyed in the area under examination. Furthermore, zoning has impact only where the economics of the market place equate with the zoning level of use or exceed the use intensity allowed by the zoning regulations. To illustrate, if the land and location dictate multifamily density, and the zoning regulations permit multi-unit construction, the area will most likely become multifamily. However, if the economics of the area under consideration dictate agricultural use, zoning that area as commercial will not in any stretch of the imagination result in that area suddenly changing to office buildings and other structures of the intense use of commercial.

The point to remember is that zoning does not determine the use to which land will be put. If we suddenly zoned the South Pole as R-4 multi-unit residential, there would most likely not be a sudden interest on the part of developers to build multi-unit residential structures in that region simply because of the new zoning regulations. Zoning is rather like the steering wheel of an automobile, and the economics of the region are like the motor. Once the motor is running forward, then zoning as the steering mechanism can guide the direction of economic improvements that take place. The steering wheel is totally ineffective until the motor is running. Zoning is totally ineffective until there is growth in land use and improvements in the economy of the region.

Table 6–2 illustrates a typical page of zoning types and descriptions. The sym-

TABLE 6–1
Zoning Types and Description

Section	Zone	Description	Density
101.0403	FW	Floodway control	
	FPF	Floodplain fringe	
	A-1	Agriculture	
	R-1	One family residential	Low
	R-2	One, two, and multifamily residential	14/acre
	R-2A	Multifamily, walkup, low-rise residential	29/acre
	R-2B	Multifamily, walkup, low-rise residential	36/acre
	R-3	Multifamily, apartment	43/acre
	R-3A	Multifamily, apartment	73/acre
	R-4	High density residential	
	RV	Small hotel/motel, visitor accommodation	
	R-4C	Highest density residential, high rise	
	CP	Commercial parking	
	CR	Commercial recreation	
	CO	Commercial office	
	CN	Neighborhood commercial	
	CA-S	Area shopping center, restricted signs	
	CA	Area shopping center	
	C-1S	Older commercial center & strips, sign restrictions	
	C-1	Older commercial center & strips	
	CS	General commercial, sign restrictions prevail	
	C	General commercial	
	CBD	Central business district, centre city	
	SR	Scientific research	
	M-1D	Distributive industries	
	M-1P	Industrial parks	
	M-1B	Light industry, certain "heavy" commercial	
	M-1A	Manufacturing with open area requirements	
	M-1	Manufacturing	
	M-2A	Manufacturing and storage, with open areas	
	M-2	Any use not specifically in conflict with the law	
	LC	Land conservation, environment protection	

TABLE 6–1

Continued

Special Zones

Airport approach zones
Airport approach and turning zones
Airport approach zones, height limitations
Airport turning zones, height limitations
Airport instrument approach zones
Airplane flight training zones
Height limitation zones
        Point Loma, 30 feet
        Point Loma, 60 feet
        Coastal, 30 feet
        La Jolla, 50 feet
        West Peninsula, 50 feet
        Mission Hills, 30 feet
        West Clairemont, 30 feet
        Mission Beach, 35 feet
        Pacific Beach, 50 feet
        South San Diego, 30 feet
        South Peninsula, 30 feet
        Midway-Mission Bay Park, 30 feet
        University Community, 30 feet
        San Diego Ave., 30 feet

Source: City Planning Department, *Municipal Code of the City of San Diego*, Planning and Zoning Regulations for the Use of Property, January 1, 1973.

bols in the left column denote each zone classification. The figures reflecting the allowable density are stated in terms of the number of units by each type per acre of land. The number of zoning classifications as well as the number of zones have increased over what existed prior to the 1970s. In the more recent years the attention and concern paid to social goods and environment have led to a more complete zoning ordinance consistent with the regional general plans of land use and growth. Nine different zones for residential land use, and twelve different zones for commercial properties, are indicative of more detailed land use planning. Height limitation zones and the land conservation zone are aimed more directly at controlling growth and open space.

    The General Plan and the zoning code prevail over all lands in the region under jurisdiction. Uses beyond those authorized by the local zoning codes and master plans are granted only through variances issued by the planning commission, or through special use permits granted by the city council and mayor. It is worth noting that in the area under study, the planning commission has not granted a variance of much substance for more than three years. Additionally, the last special use permit was granted more than two years ago. If this community is indicative of the national populace, one would have to conclude that land use regulations are becoming more detailed and more firm. The federal government has tended to enhance the effectiveness of land use controls by requiring a master plan for land use in every region prior to that region being eligible for federal funds in the development and renovation areas. Under such trends land use and control by regional and local authorities are becoming more stringent within the regions and certainly more well defined in terms of individual land uses within each area. The impact on development has been even more acute. In addition to the land use controls, there have emerged a group of environmental study requirements that extend the planning stage of private development several months. Environment impact studies and the agreement of the Environmental Protection Agency, as well as agreement by the majority of the citizens, are all growing elements in the decision-making process of land use and changes in the use of real property.

ZONING AND THE MARKET PROCESS

Zoning and land use controls affect all future land use decisions after the date of the regulations' adoption. The fact that zoning and controls focus on the future has specific impact on the market. In general, the uses to which land is put prior to zoning or zoning changes are unaffected by the new zoning regulations. The only uses that are affected are future uses and land held in speculation of future use, which the new zoning either now permits or forbids. To the extent the value of a current use includes the anticipation of a future change in use that is affected by the zoning change, then that property will also be affected by the zoning regulation.

If a single-family dwelling is in an area that is rezoned to a multifamily use, any increase in value will relate to the land and not to the house. In addition, the increase in value for the land will reflect only the future value if the land is put to use in a multifamily residence. In the instance of a downzoning from multifamily to single-family use, vacant property held for future use as multifamily will show a sudden decrease in value because of the decreased return with single family use than with the more intense use of multifamily. The impact of the zoning and land use control legislation remains on the future uses to which land in question may be put. To the extent that current values reflect future anticipated changes in the use of the subject property, then to that extent the current value will be affected by the new zoning regulations.

CITY AND MUNICIPAL PLANNING

Nearly all zoning regulations such as the one cited earlier in this chapter are local in their impact. By that we mean that the authority upon which such ordinances are based is local authority and does not extend beyond the boundaries of the municipality that enacted the zoning restrictions. Because of the local nature of such plans they do not have the effect of overall land use planning that they are aimed at. To the extent that the locality is small relative to its environment of developed area, then such elements as congestion, pollution, density and proximity to heavy industry could persist just beyond the boundaries of such a locality and be immune to the zoning and land use planning of the local municipality. If a street was one of the boundaries, the situation could exist in which the side of the street within the locality would be zoned residential single family, and the other side of the street outside of the jurisdiction of the town may have a heavy-metal smelting plant. No matter what the best-planned community may have in the order of ethics and intentions, it has power to restrict land use only within the confines of its municipal boundaries.

Another problem with local zoning and land use control is the limited economic strength of many municipalities. One example would be in a previous case in which the smelting plant was the only major industry in the area and employed practically all of the town directly or indirectly. In such a case, it is virtually impossible for the town to institute a land use ordinance that would be contrary to the motives of the firm or seriously impair even its short-term profits. Another example of the impact of limited economic strength of smaller towns is a situation in which a small community is surrounded by many larger neighboring communities. Small municipalities such as this may exist in the greater Los Angeles area as an example. Any innovative or highly restrictive land use plan that such a small community may enact will have virtually no impact on the overall patterns of land use in the area. Additionally, if such a code were highly restrictive or had serious economic implications the net effect could be to make that community segregated from the economic well being of the overall area. Growth and development would tend to skip over the area and the areas surrounding the community may develop fully while the more restrictive area would be left to stagnate because of the higher restriction and costs of economic development associated with it. As a result of local enactment of land use plans that were not coordinated with entire economic areas, and the resultant array of land use planning, the federal government, through the Department of Housing and Urban Development, directed funds for regional planning agencies and master plans for land use within each designated economic region. It was the recognition that land use is a regional concern and cannot be adequately dealt with on the local level that led to this commitment on the part of the federal government.

There are many more potential and actual areas in which local jurisdictions have a distinct disadvantage over the regional approach. Among them are: adequate research staffs containing well-trained professional land use planners and researchers; and adequate financial resources to pay the costs of relevant and adequate research and study, in addition to paying salaries and publication and distribution costs of the projects under consideration.

Probably the single largest handicap of planning in nearly all levels of governmental structure is the paradox of planning staffs having only the power to investigate and recommend solutions, and at the same time not having any power to insure that the proper solutions are considered in earnest and the results and conclusions based upon research and study are implemented into the action phase of actual land use decisions. Nearly all land use plans and the planning staffs behind those plans have the authority to advise only, and the action bodies most often have no obligation to adhere to that advice at all. The political bodies that implement land use and zoning decisions listen to the economic impact on property valuation and tax base as well as employment and development that generally accrue to the areas near where a new $100 million residential or commercial development is requesting to build. The recent movement into the areas of environmental impact studies, and comprehensive planning commissions and regional planning authorities financed through state and federal monies, tends to give confidence to the future role of land use planning and decision-making that will tend to have a broader base of support and power to implement the often-long-term socially desirable growth patterns that short-term profits in isolated areas have previously tended to ignore and pass over.

FUNCTIONS OF PLANNING

Although planning bodies are to promote objectives of the citizenry that they represent, two factors must be pointed out. First, those objectives must be firm and concrete in definition. General objectives that are too vaguely defined lead only to hap- hazard planning and land use control. Second, the citizenry must include the economic region of impact and not merely the area within a particular municipal district. The recent trend toward regional economic area planning agencies illustrates this objective.

Aiding and guiding sound economic growth and development within the subject area are surely other functions of planning. In fact, this may well fall within the govern- mental duties outlined in the Constitution referring to the health and welfare of the people. Such would be the overall function of planning, with reference to all the people within the economic area under study.

Finally, planning agencies should aid in the communication and coordination of the efforts of the various governmental activities within the areas under their study. The myriad of governmental agencies requires such coordination if well-organized and well- planned land use patterns are to develop within an area. Such diverse agencies as Forest Service, military, U.S. Postmaster, General Services Administration, various agencies and projects under the Health, Education and Welfare Department, transportation and pub- lic utilities commissions, port authorities and many other governmental bodies both federal and state or local need coordination and cooperation if they are to work for the common good and welfare of all citizens within the area.

PURPOSES AND OBJECTIVES OF ZONING

Through the dividing of land within the jurisdiction into land use districts, zon- ing has as an objective the successful implementation of the city plan or community master plan. Zoning has been and continues to be the primary tool in the arsenal of the city planning and legislative bodies to direct the land use patterns within their areas to comply with the plans approved by the community involved.

Certain uses to which land may be put are by their very nature self or mutually exclusive or nonharmonious. Such things as a slaughterhouse and a housing development and schools would be an example of nonharmonious land uses. One of the objectives of zoning is to provide a method through which such confrontations can be avoided before the land is actually improved with such uses in mind. The overall plan approved by the community should, and most often does, recognize such nonharmonious uses.

Certain health and safety standards dictate the segregation of land use within population districts and areas that have direct impact on such population centers. Such items as protected watersheds, reservoirs and traffic patterns within the capacity of major or critical thoroughfares would tend to illustrate the types of considerations that generally fall within the health and safety of the populace. Zoning has the objective of insuring that such standards of health and safety are adhered to in land use patterns within the community.

The recognition that zoning generally tends to insure the value of properties within the zoning area has come to be an accepted objective or justification for zoning regulations. There is little doubt that zoning does help to insure property values in areas zoned for specific uses. The owner of a house may find it easier to sell at a reasonable price if the potential buyers were assured that through the zoning regulations someone could not build a junkyard next door to his home. Such assurances that zoning regulations may provide to maintain and promote property values, then it could be said that zoning has the purpose of maintaining property values.

LIMITATIONS OF ZONING

There are some very serious limitations as far as zoning and its impact on the land use patterns of an area are concerned. The first major limitation of zoning has already been discussed earlier, and that is the relatively slight impact on current land usage. Zoning is most effective as it regards new developments and improvements and any conversions of preexisting improvements.

Structures and improvements existing at the time the zoning laws are implemented, including those that do not conform to the new laws, are not corrected by the new zoning laws. It has been held all the way to the Supreme Court that zoning laws cannot be made retroactive, with the intent to force nonconforming uses to conform to the new zoning laws.

Furthermore, zoning does not have control over the architecture or esthetic characteristics of improvements within the zoning area. As long as the structures conform to the zones established at the time they were built, then no matter what the architectural style or esthetic qualities of the buildings, they are within the law and cannot be forced to change. It is not possible for a community zoning commission to enforce a particular architectural style in its land use plans. Zoning applies to the use to which a subject property may be put. Through regulation and requirements attached to certain uses under the zoning codes, there are many controls over density that specific elements of the zoning code apply. Among them are: residential zones restricting the number of units per acre of land, commercial and manufacturing zones restricting the number of employees for each firm operating within the zone, various parking requirements for multi-unit zones, certain bulk, height and setback requirements in certain zone areas, and the always present special use permits and controls along with variances to uses contrary to what specific properties are zoned.

REFERENCES

1—Babcock, Richard F. *The Zoning Game.* Madison, Wis.: University of Wisconsin Press, 1972.

2—Fellmeth, Robert C. *The Politics of Land.* Ralph Nader's Study Group Report on Land Use in California. New York: Grossman Publishers, 1973.

3—Haar, Charles M. *Land-Use Planning: A Case Book on the Use and Misuse and Re-Use of Urban Land.* 2nd ed. Boston: Little, Brown, and Co., 1971.

4—_____. *Law and Land.* Anglo-American Planning Practice. Cambridge, Mass.: Harvard University Press, 1964.

5—Ottoson, Howard W. *Land Use Policy and Problems in the U.S.* Lincoln, Neb.: University of Nebraska Press, 1964.

6—Paulson, Morton C. *The Great Land Hustle.* Chicago: Henry Regnery Co., 1972.

PART

III

THE REAL ESTATE MARKET

After studying economic theory and the application of economic theory to the real estate situation, and then studying the subject of land use and its determination and the role of land use planning, we are now ready to begin the study of the real estate market in particular. The economics and land use concepts form the foundation upon which the real estate market as a whole, and the real estate specialized markets in particular, are based.

The chapters in this section will begin with analyzing the structure and function of the real estate market. Following the overall structure, market analysis will study the particulars of the various submarkets that actually prevail in the general real estate situation.

CHAPTER

MARKET STRUCTURE AND FUNCTION

DEFINITION OF A MARKET

A market is a situation in which there is a free contact between all willing buyers and all willing sellers such that the same commodity or service will tend everywhere to gender the same price. The major elements in that situation are: (1) an unrestricted adjustment of the price of the commodity or service to the movement or fluctuation of either supply or demand or both; and (2) as close to a purely competitive market as possible. A purely competitive market is one in which there exists: (1) a sufficient number of both buyers and sellers that no one buyer or no one seller can influence the market on his own behalf; (2) the product or service being exchanged in the market place must be a homogeneous good that it is essentially the same no matter which buyer or seller is involved in the individual transaction; (3) all buyers and all sellers are knowledgeable about both the product or service and the actions of all other sellers and buyers in the market place; and (4) a highly organized market with free entry and exit.

The market equilibrium price represents that point at which all the sellers will sell their product and the output will be bought by all the buyers entering the market (see Chapter 2). The only way such a smoothly operating situation in the market could be maintained is through the four principal assumptions in the purely competitive model as depicted above. It is through no one buyer or seller having control over the market that they individually can react to their competitors' price changes and reach a market equilibrium as described. Indeed, the definition of market value used by most states and courts as well as appraisers is:

The price at which a willing seller would sell and a willing buyer would buy, neither being under abnormal pressure; . . . as defined by the courts, it is the highest price estimated in terms of money which a property will bring if exposed for sale in the *open market allowing a reasonable time* to find a *purchaser with knowledge* of property's use and capabilities for use.[1] [italics mine]

Such terms as willing buyer and willing seller, open market and reasonable length of time refer nearly verbatim to the conditions of a purely competitive market.

To the extent to which one or more of the assumptions is not valid in the market situation, the market will not conform to the theoretical analysis developed to explain how the market functions. Even in the instances in which the market is deviating from the pure competition model, through an understanding of the market theory, one is better able to make an accurate assessment of the impact on price or number of units likely to be available for sale under such deviations. In the real estate sector, factors such as location, amenities and financial terms of sale have the effect of individualizing each transaction. The more such factors raise the price of an item, the fewer potential buyers in the market place and the longer it will take to sell such a product. The extent to which these terms lower the price of the item relative to other similar items, the faster it will sell because of the increase in the number of potential buyers.

CHARACTERISTICS OF THE REAL ESTATE MARKET

Few Buyers and Sellers

One of the most noticeable characteristics in real estate is the small number of sellers in any one particular area, and the small number of buyers actively in the market for a property in that small area. Furthermore, the real estate market in general tends to be a local market. By local we mean that people living in New York are not in the market for homes in Kansas City. The market tends to be limited to the general geographic location. It should be acknowledged that the market for real property may be more well defined if one uses distance in time from the business or major employment center as the defining criterion for geographic market. The real market, according to that definition, may encompass several states if the transportation system is adequate (such as around New York City), or it may limit itself to very small compact areas as most towns in the far northern reaches of the nation.

Another reason for the limited number of buyers and sellers for any particular area is the fact that the number of individuals interested in any single class of real property is also limited. The largest class is single family residential, and the smallest may be special-use properties such as churches, oil refineries, grain elevators and similar unique structures. For any given class of real property there is a limited number of po-

---

[1]California Department of Real Estate, *Real Estate Reference Book Vol I* (Sacramento: State Printing Office, 1971), p. 661.

tential buyers and limited number of potential sellers for such structures. The reason is the limited nature of the real estate services that can be derived from such specific use buildings.

Nonhomogeneous Product

Real estate by its very nature is not a homogenous item. In the market example, to freely substitute among the various sellers, buyers must be able to buy the same product from all the sellers in the market place. If buyers cannot freely substitute one seller's product for another seller's, then the price mechanism will reflect the premium of one over the other. Also, this same factor will tend to limit the size of the market. To the extent that a certain product is unique and not easily substituted or replaced by that of another seller, a separate market will develop for that individual product. The seller or sellers become fewer, and the potential buyers also become less in number. Under such situations, the market operates much more crudely and the advantages of the buyer or seller become powerful as the market fluctuates between a buyer's market, with many sellers and few buyers, and the seller's market with many buyers and few sellers.

Insufficient Knowledge

A third major characteristic of the real estate market is the lack of sufficient knowledge on the part of both the sellers and the buyers. Knowledge is used in terms of knowing what the market forces are and what the product is in relation to the substitutability of one for the product of another seller. The major importance of such knowledge is that for the sellers to meet competitors' prices and for buyers to pay a fair price and not one in excess of what another seller would charge for similar products, knowledge of the market and the actions within it is one of the major assumptions of the purely competitive model. The lack of perfect knowledge in the market place means that prices will fluctuate and range more for similar units, and that comparables may not be reliable as measures of true market value in the economic sense.

The reasons behind the lack of knowledge include the fact that most sellers and buyers are infrequent entrants in the market for real estate services. In a recent study in the state of California it was found that the average homeowner in the southern part of the state retained his/her home for five to eight years. Although that is undoubtedly low for the nation as a whole and for many areas in particular, it translates into the fact that most persons enter the market for real estate only six or seven times at most in their entire lifetimes. The real estate market is a dynamic market subject to many outside and inside factors that would change the complexion of the market rather dramatically in a five- to eight-year period. Consequently, the number of changes and their magnitude in terms of impact on the real estate values that take place during the interval that most people are out of the market make those same persons quite unknowledgeable in the immediate real estate market no matter what their intellectual abilities or interests may be.

Another factor attributing to the inadequate knowledge on the part of most buyers and sellers in the real estate market is the limited number of offers to sell or buy that occur in any one class of real estate within which the properties are comparable.

Without many transactions taking place, and those transactions being well publicized, both buyers and sellers have a poor base upon which to establish the most accurate selling price at which the subject properties will transfer. There is, in other words, a definitive lack of knowledge available even to those professionals within the market.

Probably the single largest factor contributing to the lack of knowledge on the part of both the sellers and the buyers is the extremely complex nature of the real estate good itself. Because of the factors we discussed earlier that tend to make real estate unique as an economic good (fixed location, long life, large economic units and long-term decisions), every real estate parcel being traded in the market place is by itself to a very great extent. The legal description of the rights actually being traded and the physical attributes of the property, as well as the amenities and subjective assets attached to a single property, make the job of knowing all possible substitute properties a task so large that rarely does anyone become capable of claiming "sufficient knowledge of the market."

Buyers and Sellers

The fourth major characteristic of the real estate market is the idea of willing buyers and sellers in large quantities. There are a limited number of potential sellers of properties of any one single class. At the same time there is usually a limited number of potential buyers for properties within any single class. As a result, there is most often compulsion on either the buyer's or the seller's part that forces him/her into the market. To the extent of the compulsion, the market behavior of either party to the transaction will be modified from that normally expected to prevail in a free market of normal competition. The resulting price at which the exchange takes place may be high, accounting for the compulsion on the part of the buyer, or the price may be low, accounting for the compulsion on the part of the seller. In either case the resulting price in the market is not what a normally competitive market would yield.

So it is that certain characteristics of the real estate market are a bit different from those characteristics held to be true in the purely competitive model. However, by accounting for these differences, and making the necessary adjustments in the analysis, one is still able to apply the principles of theory to the real estate situation.

THE FUNCTION OF THE REAL ESTATE MARKET

The ultimate function of any market in the economic sense is to facilitate adjustments in price and quantity in response to changes in either supply or demand for the product or service in that market place. The market does this by bringing the buyers and sellers together in the physical sense, and by providing them with a common measurement upon which to negotiate. Among barter economies uniform measurement is lacking. In more economically refined economies money of one type or another is used as the accepted medium of exchange and measurement of value.

Assume that at a given instant all the buyers and all the sellers in a specific market are completely satisfied, and that the market is at an equilibrium point; suddenly a significant rise occurs in the demand for this product or service. The ability of the market to translate this new demand into the form of increased prices being bid for the product, and communicating this fact to the sellers in the industry, will determine the capacity of the market to adjust supply to meet the new demand. To the extent that market is able to adjust to such a change it would be said to function well. If the market adjusts very poorly to such changes that market would be said to function poorly.

For a market to function well and to be very efficient, it must be able to facilitate adjustments in both directions. That is, the market should be able to perform equally as well with a falling demand or supply as with a rising demand or supply. Assuming an equilibrium point, if there is increase in the number of sellers in the market place without any rise in the number of buyers, the market must translate this new imbalance in terms of lowered prices bid for the commodity, and it must attract a greater number of buyers to the lower price. It is the function of the market to facilitate this adjustment process, and the extent to which the real estate market in general differs from the assumptions of the purely competitive market determines in part the extent to which the functioning of the market is impaired from what it may otherwise be under purely competitive conditions.

The diagrams below depict the two situations we have described in the preceding paragraphs. Figure 7–1a depicts the rise in demand from the preexisting equilibrium point, from D_1 to D_2. If the market is functioning as it should, the price should rise to P_2 and the amount exchanged in the market should rise from Q_1 to Q_2.

Figure 7–1b illustrates the situation in which an increasing number of sellers is coming to the market. This increase is represented by a shift of the supply schedule from S_1 to S_2. With no subsequent change in the demand schedule, the price will fall to P_2 and the amount exchanged in the market place will rise from Q_1 to Q_2.

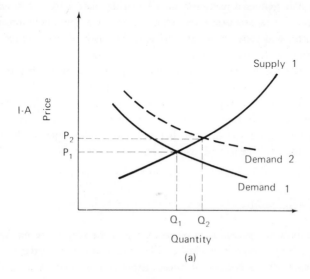

Figure 7–1a

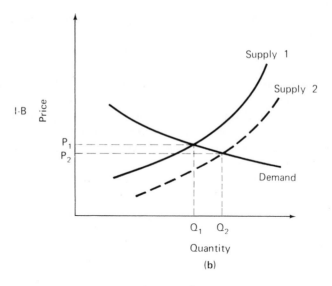

Figure 7–1b

Continuous Site Competition

One obvious factor in the real estate market is that every parcel of real estate is unique, and therefore the market cannot function nearly as smoothly because substitution is not a perfect relief between competing sellers and competing buyers. However, one general principle has a vast impact on the real estate market. This principle is the principle of continuous site competition. What that term means is that every site is in competition with every other site suitable for the same use for potential buyers. Although certain locations may gender a premium in the market place based on their location, the sellers of such properties are prevented from extorting a monopoly profit by the fact that competing sites will prove more attractive as the price of preferred sites rises above the economies attached to that location.

It is through the principle of continuous site competition that the market generally determines land use patterns within a given geographic area. Although zoning may restrict land usage to certain types, the market provides the sole motivation for using land for any purpose, and in that way determines the ultimate worth of all subject properties. The pattern of those uses of land then becomes the product of the functioning of the market and the effectiveness of continuous site competition is a vital part of that market function.

The Function of the Broker

We have discussed some of the areas in which the real estate market differs from the model of the purely competitive market. The overall function of the real estate broker is to overcome as much as is possible those imperfections that exist in the real estate sector. One of those areas is the limited number of buyers and sellers in any one geographic area. Through advertising and promotion the broker is able to increase the number of buyers and sellers that are effectively in one market. The more people in the market, the more activity there is likely to be, and consequently the most likely there will tend to prevail a fair market price for those properties exchanged.

The lack of knowledge and the inexperience on the part of both buyers and sellers in general is an acknowledged defect in the real estate market. The abuses and misfortunes that have occurred in the market because of this lack of knowledge have made it obvious to the public as well as those in the industry that some education must be instilled. The average consumer of real estate services in the form of owner-occupant enters the market only five to ten times in his/her entire lifetime. Consequently, it has fallen upon the real estate professional to gain knowledge and convey it as required to the consumers of real estate. Knowledge as a factor in the efficient functioning and the consumer sector benefiting from the market imperfections that are overcome by such knowledge has been increasingly recognized by the various licensing agencies of many states. Consequently, most licensing boards now require a growing academic as well as vocational knowledge on the part of the real estate profession and all the segments that operate around and within that classification. It is the ultimate end of such trends in education in the real estate field that the market will function more efficiently and that the consumer of real estate services will be better served.

STRUCTURE OF THE REAL ESTATE MARKET

The real estate market in general may be structured according to a variety of formats. However, a structure based upon the marriage of the concepts of type of use with the motivation of the owner of such properties offers several advantages. Such a structure as is shown in Figure 7–2 illustrates the type described in the previous statement. The various categories of use have been grouped into those of residential and those of nonresidential nature. The more specific categories further designate the specific type of use and the relative intensity of such usage, as well as the motivations of each class of consumer of the various real estate services associated with the type of use. In the residential section, the categories of owner-occupant, renter-occupant and investment multifamily are more closely connected to the motivational aspects than perhaps some of the other classes. In any such organizational description of the structure of the

REAL ESTATE

Residential	Non-Residential
— Owner-Occupant	— Commercial
— Renter-Occupant	— Industrial
— Investment	— Manufacturing
	— Agricultural

Figure 7–2

real estate market in general there will be ample real world situations that overlap these distinctions in the previous illustration. Nevertheless, the structure as described in the figure provides an adequate base upon which to analyze the submarkets within the real estate sector. The following chapter will discuss the details of the submarkets in real estate in the manner presented in the foregoing table, as well as the implications as to function that each submarket characteristic implies.

REFERENCES

1—Bach, George L. *Economics: An Introduction to Analysis and Policy.* 7th ed. Englewood Cliffs, N.J.: Prentice-Hall, Inc., 1971.

2—Joseph, Myron L. *Economic Analysis and Policy.* 3rd ed. Englewood Cliffs, N.J.: Prentice-Hall, Inc., 1971.

3—McConnell, Campbell R. *Economics.* 5th ed. New York: McGraw-Hill, Inc., 1972.

4—Heilbroner, Robert L. and Thurow, Lester C. *The Economic Problem.* 4th ed. Englewood Cliffs, N.J.: Prentice-Hall, Inc., 1975.

5—Robinson, Marshall A., et al. *An Introduction to Economic Reasoning.* 4th ed. Washington, D.C.: The Brookings Institute, 1967.

CHAPTER

MARKET ANALYSIS

The real estate market differs greatly from the general picture we have discussed up to this point. The preceding chapters have set the foundation of the operation within the real estate sector. The economic principles govern the relationships that exist in the real estate sector. The differentiation between physical and service definitions of real estate is essential to all of real estate. The concept of land use is also fundamental to the discussion of how the market measures that land use in terms of the highest return.

This present chapter represents the departure from the general concept of the real estate sector. However, within the departure it must be clear that the principles underlying the relationships and various submarkets are the same throughout.

The distinction of submarkets has been made in a manner that is comfortable to the author, and adequately presents the differences of the sectors discussed. Other market definitions may exist; however, the substance of the definitions will remain the same. The elements of each submarket are unique to those sectors, but may be defined or reclassified in many ways. The dynamic nature of the real estate field is ever changing and many overlaps exist in any arbitrary classifying that may be employed by various authors. The fundamental idea is that characteristics do alter the behavior within the market, but still are inputs into the fundamental relationships that prevail in the economic sphere.

THE OWNER-OCCUPANT MARKET

The residential market in real estate comprises three major sectors, as presented in the illustration in the previous chapter. The largest submarket in the residential sector is the owner-occupant market, which includes mostly single family dwelling units. The residential sector as a whole amounted to nearly $763 billion dollars in asset value in 1973. Given the magnitude of this sector of the industry, the characteristics of this sub-market are well worth the effort of examination.

From Chapter 2 and 3, it will be recalled that the market description of supply and demand interaction and the ultimate price and output at equilibrium point were based upon a rather uniform market that was based on four major assumptions. Those four assumptions were: (1) many buyers and sellers, (2) perfect knowledge by both buyers and sellers, (3) a homogeneous product, and (4) a free price mechanism. It should be kept in mind that whenever one or more of these assumptions is not valid in the market the resulting price and output at point of exchange will not truly reflect a free market, but rather a distortion.

In the owner-occupant market, four major characteristics stand out in the analysis. The first is the common factor of both buyers and sellers having very little experience in the market. Most buyers and sellers in the single-family and owner-occupant market buy and sell a home no more than seven or eight times in their entire lifetimes. The implications as far as comparable prices, locations, quality of the product and details of the area, legal and financial scenes are not at the disposal of the owner-occupant seller or buyer. Second, the market of buyers and sellers is a widely scattered one. There are generally few buyers and sellers in one very small neighborhood. As a result, the market is quite unorganized and there is no central market place for buyers and sellers to meet and bargain over the relative merits of bid and asked prices. Third, by far the majority of both buyers and sellers in the owner-occupant market enter the market with their major motivation being something other than the profit motive. Surely, most sellers expect not to realize a loss, but selling once every five to eight years essentially ensures that. The major point is that there is generally some compulsion on the part of either buyers or sellers or both. They sell because they have a new job, or the physical plant no longer fills their needs. The buyers tend to buy for the same basic reasons. Family and personal considerations tend to play the major role in motivating both buyers and sellers in the market. This fact is further demonstrated by the major determinants of the demand for single family housing cited earlier in Chapter 3. It will be recalled that family income and the terms of financing are the two largest determinants of the demand for housing. The price of the product is not nearly as high on the list of demand factors. As a result of these three factors characterizing the owner-occupant market, the fourth factor is a real result. The fourth characteristic of the owner-occupant market is the need for and the role played by the real estate professional. The professional is needed to a very great extent in this market because of the expertise he can provide the parties, that they tend not to have access to on their own. It should be recognized that the fear of selling below the fair market value and buying above the fair market value are the major justifications for paying for the expertise of the real estate professionals. Additional factors include his/her ability to increase the market for properties, and bring more buyers and sellers to the market place; also to insure that the products are suitably explained to buyers and sellers in terms of the complex nature of the bundle of legal rights that actually are being purchased; and finally that both parties to any transaction are negotiating for a product that is what they actually mean to sell or buy.

The recent development of consumer exchange services at reduced cost, as well as negotiated commission schedules, are recent innovations into the market. However, they reflect a more knowledgeable consumer as much as a more economical market device. The role of the real estate broker remains the greatest in the owner-occupant market both in terms of the need for his services and the latitude of his negotiating capacity.

THE RENTER-OCCUPANT MARKET

The second major sub-market in the residential sector is that of the renter occupant. The differences between the renter and the owner as an occupant are obvious in the practical sense. However, in the market analysis they actually indicate two entirely different markets in structure as well as in performance. The first major difference is the knowledge possessed by both renters and owners of rental housing. This comes about through the frequent exposure in the market by the renting population. They change dwellings rather more frequently than do the owner-occupant population. As a result, they tend to know the current market to a much greater extent. Second, they tend to generate more contacts within the market because of their frequent entry. Rents are rather well advertised, so the market price and value of rental housing are well known by the consumers in this market segment. Last, because of the rather well-organized and -publicized market and the well-informed buyers there tends to be little need for the real estate broker from the renter-occupant market. In select instances, and where time to shop is at a premium as well as the product definition rather exacting, which usually accompanies a rather high-priced product, a few real estate professionals can provide a service to the renter-occupant market.

Demand Characteristics
in Residential

Residential housing in the owner-occupant and the renter-occupant submarkets tends to be a consumer good. Therefore, demand for these submarkets tends to focus on the amount of outlay in terms of cashflow, and the capacity to accommodate that outlay in terms of income. Overall in any region, the population and its demographic profile dictate the general demand for housing. Such factors as immigration, age, marital status and family size establish the parameters of demand for the housing in that region. The second major factor affecting demand in the residential market is the income and income prospects of the population. Not only does this affect the capacity of the family units, but also it affects the decision to rent versus buy, which is the major option of most of the residential consumers. The trends of the income and the incomes of new immigrants versus the current population give a great insight into the possible impact upon the demand for housing within the region studied. Third, is the amount and terms of credit within the local financing community. Such items as down payment required, monthly payment amount and length of the loan have a great impact upon the demand for residential housing. Again, these relate to the monthly income of the family units and the proportion of that income that must be dedicated to housing. The fourth factor affecting the demand for residential housing within an area would be the monthly costs of upkeep and maintenance for housing in that region. Such items as taxes, repair, fuel oil, utilities and routine yard and house maintenance often can amount to as much as the loan costs over the life of the building. A fifth group of factors that have varying impact upon the demand for housing would include such items as social pressure among family and peers, customs within the community and tastes of certain community groups or populations. It should be recognized that such impacts upon the demand for residential housing sector affect the two major elements, which are the upgrading consumer seeking to improve or change his type and quality of residence, and the consumer weighing the rent-versus-buy decision. As the costs involved in ownership far outweigh the costs of renting suitable housing, the present owner-occupant will tend to remain where he is and the new family units will tend to rent rather than buy. Where the two sectors begin to approach each other in terms of costs, renters will tend to buy and owners will tend to upgrade their present housing.

Contrary to our previous discussion of supply and demand analysis in Chapters 2 and 3, there has been a noticeable neglect of the price of housing in the owner-occupant market. The major reason for this is the income and financing considerations. If the consumer can afford the monthly payments and costs, and the financing terms are liberal enough to allow little down and a very long-term loan, then there is little buyer resistance as long as the housing under question adequately meets the needs and desires of the buyer making the decision. Such facts are testified to by the guideline of monthly payments being within 20 percent to 25 percent of the family take-home income, which is frequently used to approve real estate loans for single family dwellings. In more recent times increased fuel costs and higher maintenance costs have tended to lower this percentage. The neglect of price as the major criterion in purchase as well as sale is a result of the nature of the owner-occupant market. Terms of financing can make a great difference in the impact of price on the monthly cashflow of the purchaser. As a result, financing terms have become more directly affective in the market place than the mere price of various real estate products in the single family owner-occupant sector.

The supply of housing in the residential market tends to be rather easily defined. Supply includes newly constructed units, conversions of one use to another and demolitions. Affective supply would usually include all new units currently under construction that are expected to be completed during the current year. Conversions occur in both directions, increasing the residential units and decreasing them. Both need to be accounted for in the supply figures for any economic region. Demolitions are in one direction during the current period, that is they reduce the supply of residential units. Demolitions occur most often because of two trends. First, there is a change in the highest and best use to which that property can be put. Such change would be the case of the central business district spreading into previously residential areas, or commercial strip development spreading into adjacent residential areas, the reverse case of agricultural land being used for residential suburbia would be some cases. The second trend that may lead to some demolition would be that in which the returns associated with an improved use were so poor that owners abandon such buildings. Raw land may be useful for agricultural products without a near population, but the land would have to be cleared prior to such use. Abandoned properties may be converted to such unimproved uses as agriculture, but the structures would have to be removed first. Supply of real estate services in the residential sector includes not only the currently existing structures, but also those under construction, those under conversion and those that may be marked for demolition.

MULTIFAMILY INVESTMENT

The remaining sector of the residential submarket is that of the ownership of multifamily residential investment properties. This part of the residential submarket is quite apart from the consumer-oriented parts discussed so far. In fact, the producers of new housing units, including single family housing units, could be included in this same submarket. The characteristics of this market are quite different from those of the other two submarkets in the residential sector. First, the buyers and sellers in this market are well informed and have considerable experience. They tend to know quite well what the market conditions and trends are, and what the investment world uses in terms of techniques and measurements of investment quality.

The second major market characteristic is that the product itself tends to be highly complex, and requires highly specialized knowledge. The techniques of investment strategy are highly technical, particularly in regard to the financial structure and the tax consequences. As a result of the second characteristic, the third market characteristic is the necessity for many specialists in the market. Such specialists as real estate lawyers, accountants, economic and market research people and others are common in transactions involving multifamily investment properties. The fourth major characteristic of this market is the motivation of the buyers and sellers. The primary motive in this market is profit, and more specifically, after-tax profit. As a result, there tends to be heavy emphasis upon the forecasting of future costs and revenues. Such a specific and well-defined objective as the profit motive makes the market operate within much tighter constraints. The real estate professionals that concentrate in this market are those that have a great deal of expertise in the detail aspects of taxes, financing, legal aspects and quantitative and qualitative procedures. As a result, fewer real estate professionals are in this submarket and those that are in it are highly specialized. Additionally, there tends to be much less latitude in terms of the bargaining and possible negotiating that the real estate broker may perform. As a result, the commission schedules in this submarket vary much more than the more common rates that exist in the single-family residences market.

In addition to the market characteristics already mentioned, the magnitude of the investments involved in the investment submarket is also a large factor accounting for some of the differences in this market. Because of the amounts of money involved in most of the projects in this area, there are people involved other than the buyer and seller. In addition to multiple banks or financing institutions conducting their own analysis, there is the fact that in many instances the financial commitment is such that the project is not obvious in its ability to protect the capital invested. It is for this reason that the financial structure, management, marketing and tax and planning consequences become so important. The number of diverse specialties called into the project is such that they must nearly all reach the identical solution and profit potential for the project to become fact. The role of the real estate professional in this realm is to facilitate the communication and exposure of the interested parties. His role in actually selling the project is quite minimal; the project will have to sell itself more than be a function of the marketing expertise of the real estate broker.

As a result of this market structure there are fewer and much larger and more specialized real estate firms that become involved in marketing the majority of these types of residential investment projects. The skills required are usually far greater than those normally required in the single-family residential market.

Factors Affecting Demand

Whenever we speak of investment, it seems that this is somehow different from when we speak of consuming real estate services. In the residential sector there are two submarkets essentially—the owner or renter occupant, and the investor. The occupant is consuming real estate services associated with the location he has chosen. His primary motivation is not return or profit, but rather the use or services he receives from the expenditures he/she makes in the real property in question. The investor, on the other hand, is not necessarily planning to occupy the real estate under question, but rather to sell or lease the services associated with that location for a suitable return on the capital he has invested.

As an investment, real estate is in the position of having to compete with all other forms of investment in terms of return on each dollar invested and the risk associated with that return. The common yardstick of measurement is even more well defined in terms of net dollars after taxes, often expressed as a percentage rate of return on the amount invested. In this respect, some factors affect investment demand a bit more intensely than they do other forms of real estate demand. (1) The first general principle is that as the magnitude of the investment increases so does the project's sensitivity to the conditions of the market. As the amount of money invested increases, so too does the number of people involved in the analysis and final approval of a project. In addition to the dollar size of the project, the larger and more complex the investment becomes in the physical terms, it too involves more persons and agencies. The number of local, county, state, and federal agencies involved in large development proposals and the impact upon the environment and natural resources by such projects is but one example of the increase in complexity with the increase in physical dimensions. Such more intense use of land resources, with its increased complexities and risks, calls upon more than a "horseback" conclusion about the total payout time and amounts.

(2) Second, the terms of credit are extremely important in the investment area. Soft dollars are strongly preferred in most projects, as opposed to hard dollars. Soft dollars are monies that can be deducted from income for tax purposes. Such items as prepaid interest, management fees and return of principle in cashflow are examples of soft dollars to a firm. However, payments on principle, down payments and interest received are examples of hard dollars that must be reported to the IRS and taxed as regular income. The essential point in preferring soft dollars is that they allow the investor to accumulate his capital, or to recoup his initial investment earlier than he otherwise

might. This means that his initial investment is subject to risk for a shorter time, and also that he will have sufficient cash to invest in other projects sooner than he might otherwise have.

(3) The third major element affecting demand is the amount of relief from income taxes that the investment provides. The difference between soft and hard dollars discussed in the preceding chapter was mostly referring to the tax advantages of soft dollars as they relate to the federal income tax. The net effect of tax deductible items is to lower the net costs of the investment, thus increasing the investor's return of principle. Again, the quicker he/she may recoup the initial investment, the sooner they can reinvest in another project and the less time their original investment is subject to the risks that go with any and all investments.

NONRESIDENTIAL MARKET

The nonresidential real estate submarket comprises primarily commercial and industrial properties. Agricultural properties are really a whole separate category of real use, and will be discussed in a separate section. The market characteristics of the nonresidential sector are quite apart from those of the residential sector. It should be pointed out that the business and commercial sectors are much more concerned with such factors as economic trends and conditions for the near and future as well as the advantages of certain real estate parcels as they relate to their business. The primary focus of the business and industrial sectors of our economy is one of which those parties within the real estate market are a part. As a result, the first general market characteristic is that the supply and demand segments in the nonresidential real estate market tend to be much more sensitive to the general business conditions and conditions within their own industry. This concern overrides nearly if not all other concerns of those within the market. Buyers and renters of commercial and industrial properties must feel that the future for their particular industry must look positive, or they withdraw from the market and wait until economic conditions improved. Likewise, the sellers of freehold and leasehold interests in commercial and industrial property must forecast the market for such uses to make their investment an economically feasible one.

The second major factor in the characteristics of the nonresidential submarket is the location and supply of necessary labor needed in the particular industrial or commercial clients in the market for such nonresidential real estate uses. Additionally, the location and supply of adequate material inputs is similar to labor as a partial determinant of the demand and supply for nonresidential real estate services. Again, the implications are that such factors as labor and material are vitally important to the profitable operation of businesses in nearly all types of industries that potential buyers and sellers as well as lessees of nonresidential real estate are a part.

The location of the markets that consumers of commercial and industrial products serve and depend upon for their business is the third major characteristic of the nonresidential real estate submarket. What this and the previous characteristic referring to the supply of labor imply, is that the entire community within which the subject properties and market lie must fully complement the business and commercial firms that make up the individuals in the market for nonresidential real estate services. The physical aspects of the area, in terms of population and supplies, and the future prospects for the area are of vital importance to business firms thinking of expanding or entering the area. Just as schools, utilities, parks, transportation and other factors are important to potential homeowners in the residential sector, so are the supply of labor and material and access to the market important factors in the nonresidential market.

The fourth major market characteristic in the nonresidential market is the attitude of the community in terms of its acceptance of certain industries, or all industry, and the acceptance of the particular firms involved in the subject under consideration. There appears to be a rather well-defined trend on the part of major cities to discourage the extractive type of industries and the heavy industries (otherwise called the "dirty" industries), and at the same time to attract the "clean" industries of finance, research, medicine and home offices. Such trends, to the extent that they may exist in the community under study, may have far reaching impact on the type, extent, and pattern of land use devoted to nonresidential purposes.

It should be restated at this point that the size of the financial commitment involved in nonresidential development is such that the market considerations tend to be much broader and much more researched than in most residential sectors. In the very large residential sectors involved in the new town developments, the size of the commitment far exceeds most nonresidential investments. But much of the uniqueness of nonresidential market is at least partially due to the magnitude of the projects themselves. In those instances in which the project rapidly grows beyond the capacity of only a few investors, then the number of people involved in decision-making expands. As a result the number of studies and the extent of the analyses broadens far beyond what would be the case with smaller projects involving only a few people. It is for that reason that very large projects of nearly any use will follow the same pattern of research and specialization beyond what is to be found at the common single-family broker and salesman level.

Responsiveness to the Market

The nonresidential market is slower in its reaction to the fluctuations in the market than is true in the residential sector. The reasons for this are relatively clear upon examination. First, the lead times involved in the building and/or renovating for such use, or the site location time and studies for the suitable location are so long that there is little flexibility after the initial commitment decision has been made.

The second major reason for a lack of adjustment to temporary or relatively short-run business turnarounds is the size of the financial commitment involved. When a group of financial corporations finally makes a commitment for a $25 million building they are very reluctant to sacrifice perhaps up to $2 or $3 million dollars of preparation simply because of a market turndown that is not expected to last more than three to five years. Not only is the amount of investment commitment large, but also the preparatory time lag is approaching five to eight years before the larger business and industrial buildings are actually ready for occupation. In many if not most instances, temporary economic downturns seldom last more than three to five years. When a project is found feasible over its expected economic life of forty or more years, it would seem foolish to give up such a project after initial investment of up to $1 million or more predevelopment dollars because of some temporary economic downturn that is expected to last only a few years. The fundamentally important factor is that the research and economic analysis be correct in not showing a basic change that will represent a permanent alteration in the economic structure or health of the market under examination.

Role of the Broker

In the nonresidential real estate submarket, the role of the broker is considerably different from the position of the broker in the more traditional residential market. The levels of expertise on the part of the buyers and sellers in the nonresidential market create less demand for the same skills and knowledge on the part of the broker. Generally, the buyers and sellers have researched the positions in the market and the feasibility of the projects under consideration to such an extent that there is little margin for negotiations left to the broker in the transaction.

As a result of the market conditions, those firms that concentrate in nonresidential brokerage are usually large, well-integrated real estate companies with many specialties included in their staffs. As such, they are equipped to perform some of the detailed analysis that is required in this market. Of the smaller firms that do engage in nonresidential brokerage business, the specialty they most often provide is access to board rooms and top management of firms that their clients would have a difficult time exposing to the potential property offered for sale.

The real estate specialties that dominate the nonresidential market include: leasing specialists, property management, industrial realtors, shopping center specialists, commercial and industry specialists and various appraisers of special nature, as well as site location analysts, economic and feasibility researchers, economic impact and environmental impact researchers, and the many facets of the legal profession as it relates to the special nature of segments of the real estate industry.

As a result of the many specialists servicing the nonresidential submarket of real estate, the role of the normal real estate broker is greatly diminished. This is not to say that the broker is not needed or useful in this submarket, only that there is a need for fewer of them, and the ones that do service this market must provide rather refined and sophisticated services that require specialized knowledge and skills. Further evidence of the lower profile taken by the broker in the nonresidential submarket is the occurrence of negotiated sales commissions below the normal ten percent range in unimproved land and six percent on improved properties. The incidence of such negotiated rates appears higher in the highly refined nonresidential market than in other submarkets in the real estate sector.

INDICATORS OF BUSINESS ACTIVITY

In attempts to analyze and to interpret the trends of the various segments of the real estate sector of our economy, certain activities are more important than others. Some areas have a greater or quicker impact on the real estate markets than do other areas. The following tabulation is by no means a complete listing of all indicators of business activity that may or may not have an impact on the real estate sector. However, the items listed are quite well publicized and relatively easy to gain access to on a current and consistent basis.

The first group of business and economic indicators are those that are quite sensitive. These tend to fluctuate quite frequently, and in response to sometimes rather brief changes in the business or economic climate. As such, they should not be taken on their own merits to indicate significant trends in the prospects for such long-life assets as real estate, but rather temporary conditions that may affect the market in the short term, or, when combined with one or more of the stable indicators, that may indicate the beginning of a trend. Short-term or very sensitive business indicators would include:

1—The number of business failures

2—The rise or fall of stock prices

3—Orders for durable goods

4—Residential building permits

5—Commercial and industrial construction

6—Manufacturing work week

7—New business formations

8—Basic commodity prices

As a group, the short-run indicators generally reflect the attitudes of the consuming public. Public confidence or lack of it is a major factor influencing the demand for residential services as well as the prospects for all consumer-related industries. Any steady trend of falling in the above list would seriously affect the long-term prospects for those in real estate industry.

The second class of indicators would be those that are less volatile than the first class. These more sluggish indicators reflect current market conditions more than future attitudes. These indicators fairly accurately describe where the economy is at in this current time:

1—Nonfarm employment

2—General unemployment

3—Corporate profits

4—Bank debits

5—Freight car loadings

6—Industrial output

7—Wholesale prices (excluding food and farm prices)

This second class of indicators generally reflects the conditions from the business-man's point of view. The first class was focused primarily upon the consumer. The business sector generally responds to the consumer needs and the prevailing attitudes in the market. As such, this second class of indicators is more sluggish than the first group. It is important to recognize that what trends develop in this class generally will determine the supply of products and services in the forthcoming months. As a result, the implications as to price movement in the following periods can be indicated to some extent in this sector.

The third class of business indicators that are readily available to most everyone is the class dealing with the more stable economic indicators that reflect the national scene. These indicators move very slowly and more gradually than do the other two classes we have discussed. Sudden changes in the indicators of this type generally indicate a rather drastic change in the economy. By sudden, we are referring to from one quarter to another, as these indicators are usually published quarterly, and move rather sluggishly from one quarter to another. During any one-year period significant change can be noticed, but between any two consecutive quarters the change should not normally be too drastic. Such stable indicators of a national nature would include:

1—Personal income

2—Retail sales

3—Installment debt

4—Bank business loan rate

5—Factory inventories

There are significant seasonal cycles in some of these indicators that must be compared to the previous quarter at the same point in the cycle to have any meaning to most observers. A growth in magnitude roughly the same as the amount of inflation for the previous and current quarter should be expected, and not interpreted as a significant change in the national economic profile. Such indicators as retail sales climb drastically in the normal Christmas season. Likewise, inventories on the retail level climb prior to the Christmas season. Such trends would be grossly misinterpreted if not compared with the similar build-up in the appropriate quarter of the preceding year.

REFERENCES

1—Barlowe, Raleigh. *Land Resource Economics.* 2nd ed. Englewood Cliffs, N.J.: Prentice-Hall, Inc., 1972.

2—Lippold, Richard W. *Urban Housing Market Analysis.* Washington, D.C.: U.S. Department of Housing and Urban Development, 1969.

3—Ratcliff, Richard U. *Real Estate Analysis.* New York: McGraw-Hill, Inc., 1969.

4—Weimer, Arthur M., et. al. *Real Estate.* 6th ed. New York: The Ronald Press, 1972.

PART

IV

THE CONCEPT OF VALUE

After studying the economic theory and application of such theory to the real estate industry, we developed the concept of the market in which such economic principles tend to operate. The subject under study was real estate. We have now defined it more specifically in terms of real estate services associated with a given use. Land use was defined and the patterns of land use were discussed. We have also considered some of the controls that are exerted over the use of land resources. In the preceding section we analyzed the market of real estate services. The development of three general submarkets was presented and the differences discussed.

Up to this point we have discussed two aspects of the real estate subject. The first was the economic aspect of the general subject and the definition of the object under examination. The second major emphasis was on the product and product demand characteristics and how to judge and interpret them.

In the present section we will develop the concepts of value and discuss what actually constitutes something of value. What must prevail in the market situation for anything to have value as an economic entity. The present section will also entertain the task of ascertaining how to measure value and what various attempts and approaches are made. The task of appraisal and its relation to value will be explored. The three basic approaches to appraisal will be analyzed in terms of the traditional value theory and contemporary valuation analysis. The concept of value and the social integration of human beings will be discussed and explored as an interrelated part of the ongoing social processes.

CHAPTER

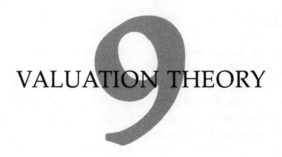

VALUATION THEORY

In the study of real estate in the economic sense, we are involved in the analysis of the product definition under examination. In the earlier chapters we concluded that the real subject of real estate in the market and economic sense was the use and benefits to be gained from the use to which various properties may be put. We are also concerned with the market structures and substructures that exist within which the economics of the situation operate. We studied rather intensely the relationships that exist between the buyers and sellers in the market place, and the resulting supply and demand analysis that results in a point of equilibrium. The equilibrium point, it will be recalled, is the point at which the available supply is exchanged according to the available demand, or the point at which the supply and demand are equal in the market place.

In actuality we were discussing the economic concept of value when we observed the equilibrium point of exchange in the market analysis. Value in those terms is defined as that point at which an exchange will take place between the buyer and seller. Value is defined in terms of the market price at which an item will be exchanged. The assumptions are that at that point on the scale the product or service is equal to the amount of money offered in exchange. The other assumption is that the yardstick of dollars or money is the sole objective measuring stick for value. There are ample arguments for holding that money is not as appropriate as other criteria as a measurement bench mark. However, in the realm of economics we have generally accepted the monetary units as a yardstick while at the same time acknowledging the imperfections of such a tool. The realistic world of alternatives to money as a measure of world economic choices is quite lacking in any consistent measure being offered. Value as the major goal of analysis, therefore, is generally confined to dollar definitions. Furthermore, value is generally defined in the economic environment of the free market.

TYPES OF VALUE

The preceding definition of value is not the only value concept that occurs in the world of humanity. One of the most common trends is to generate a concept of value for the express purpose for which the analysis is conducted. Such concepts as cost, intrinsic, replacement, appraised, antique, insurance, salvage and many other qualifications of the word value are common. It is therefore vitally important to explicitly define the concept of value one is using in any discussion.

Intrinsic value is a particular definition that needs some elaboration and discussion in the current context. Intrinsic value refers to that value, if any, that an item has by simply being that item. In some circles certain items have a predefined value by definition. Gold was such an item when the U.S. dollar was defined in terms of $35 equaling one ounce of gold. Under such special conditions, gold could be said to have an intrinsic value. It becomes a very moot point, however, when the market price at which people are willing to sell and buy that same gold is more than $35, approaching $200 at times.

It is not uncommon to find members of the general public accepting the logic of some few unethical and unknowledgeable land promoters who sell real estate on the same intrinsic value concept. "There's only so much land and a growing population, so the price can only go up!" is the type of logic not too infrequently heard. Somehow land is believed to have value simply because it is land. Such a concept of intrinsic value is highly vulnerable to misunderstanding and misinterpretation. The single largest handicap of such a concept of value is the lack of sound and reliable data upon which to base such conclusions. Just because the seller or the agent of the seller says that something is worth so much in terms of dollars does not necessarily mean that the item under negotiation is actually worth that much.

ELEMENTS MAKING UP VALUE

Value is a function of four primary conditions. The term value in the context here is that value measured in terms of money that a particular item will be exchanged for in the market place. We are concerned with economics in the text, and therefore will confine our use of the word value to those economic conditions of which it is a part. The four major determinants of value for all goods and services in the physical world are: use or utility, a demand for that use or utility, a limited supply of the item or service, and the capacity to transfer or exchange that use or service from one party to another.

Use

An item or service must perform some function to have any value. That function may be productive, as in a knife with which one may cut and form materials. That function may also be abstract as in a gold knife or a display of adornment, which provides its owner with abstract benefits such as pride, status or honor. But the item must fulfill some function to have value. After all, if there are no benefits to be derived from the ownership of some item or service, why would anyone anywhere be willing to bid any price for it?

Demand

Not only must an item or service perform some function, there must also be some demand for that same use or service. Demand is a result of a willingness on the part of potential buyers to exchange dollars for the product or service in question. Without such a willingness there would be no demand for the item, and as a result there would be no price at which it would change owners. If its worth cannot be measured in terms of yardstick chosen (dollars), then it has no value according to the value so defined by that criteria. Essentially, value is determined by the intersection of supply and demand at the equilibrium point. Therefore, it is obvious that demand is an important element in the determination of value defined in the economic sphere.

Limited Supply

If the supply of a product or service is such that there is so much of it that the amount demanded is available for free because the supply is so much more, then it is clear that the item in question has no value in the economic sense. An example of an item that fills the previous two characteristics and fails in the current one is air. We all need air to live, so it provides a very vital function. There is also a great demand for air, in that the nearly $3\frac{1}{2}$ billion persons on earth all need it constantly to survive. However, because all that is needed is available for free it has no value in the economic sense. In unusual situations such as 90 feet under water, air has almost an infinite value. But in the economic world of normalcy, the infinite supply of air for breathing eliminates the possibility of an economic value for air. Oil on the other hand has a very limited supply in the world, and as a result of that limited supply (as well as the other three elements of value), the reserves of oil in the world have a very real economic value.

Transferability

For any product or service to have an economic value, it must be able to be exchanged from seller to buyer in the market situation. The essence of value is defined through the market process of exchange. Therefore, for something to have an economic value it must be able to be bought and sold between buyers and sellers. In some instances, such as real estate, the legal rights to access or use are transferable rather than the object itself. Nevertheless, the value object, which is the right to use or to access, is transferable from one party to another. Examples of items that have use, demand and limited supply, and at the same time have no economic value because of the lack of transferability, would be such things as a rare singing voice, or artistic talent. There is virtually no way for an individual to purchase the voice of Bing Crosby or the artistic talent of a Picasso. The inability to transfer such an asset in the market place prohibits that object from having an economic value defined through the market place. The material results from such talents may indeed be marketable as records or paintings, but the talent itself has no economic value.

In the real estate sector of our economy, the transferability of the rights to use property are governed through a complex system of laws and regulations that tend to have dramatic impact upon the market determined value of such real property. Because of the importance of the element of transferability in the value determination, the legal and legislative areas of our economy have a tremendous impact upon the value of real property. Real property in the United States is essentially a legally defined set of rights to use specific portions of land in or within prescribed boundaries. Real property is essentially a bundle of *rights* to certain *uses* and the returns from those uses, that a subject property may be put. Rights and uses are abstractions from the physical world, and as such are defined through the legal and governmental structures within the nation of which it is a part. As a result of such abstraction from the physical world, real property has become highly subject to the influence of the legal and legislative sectors of our economy. The element of transferability that constitutes the fourth element of value is probably the largest area concerning real property that is influenced by the legal sector.

REAL ESTATE AND THE ELEMENTS OF VALUE

To stand the risk of repetition, it is of benefit to relate the four elements of the value to the subject of real property. Earlier in the second chapter and in the third chapter we defined real estate in terms of use. It was important at that time to understand the distinction between the physical definition of real estate and the definition in terms of real estate services or use. In the value concept it can be seen again why the distinction is made. The benefits of use are the actual product being exchanged in the market place. The concept of use or benefits is fundamental to any concept of value. Real estate, therefore, has been defined according to the uses to which it may be put. In the market analysis chapters, the market structure again was defined principally along the lines of the uses to which real property may be put.

In the second element of limited supply we see again why real estate must be regarded from the standpoint of the uses to which it may be put. The physical supply of "dirt" in the world is nearly unlimited in terms of the majority of the uses to which it may be put in the market. However, the supply of land suitable for specific uses is indeed limited in many categories. The use again is the major qualification. The suitability of a given site for a specific use, and—considering the intensity of the use or uses—the supply of suitable sites for such uses are indeed limited from the market standpoint. Increasingly, the number of sites suitable for specific uses and the laws, regulations and policies authorizing such use are quite limited. The limitations as to use are increasingly more limiting than the mere physical supply of land or "dirt" within the areas of study or concern. The ways in which real estate services are limited in supply are far more complex and involve a great range of factors that normal supply situations and supply decisions in the more traditional product sectors do not.

The demand for real estate services is fundamental to the human experience throughout the world. That demand is not for the "dirt" at the particular site under examination, but rather for the benefits through use that may be derived from that particular location. The occupants of a particular building site are not concerned with the dirt involved in that location, but rather the advantages and benefits to be enjoyed through the use of that particular structure located as it is. A brief look at a multistory building will convey the distinction between the concept of "dirt" versus the concept of real estate services through the benefits from use. The demand ingredient of value as it relates to value in real estate is the demand for specific real estate services and uses.

The element of transferability as it relates to the value of real estate services is a highly complex one. The complexity derives primarily from the nature of real estate itself. Real estate is essentially a bundle of various rights to the benefits of use for prescribed parcels of real estate. Those rights are a product of legal sanctions and definitions. As with nearly everything deriving its definition through the legislative and regulatory sectors, the result is a highly complex and often vague pattern of rights associated with given locations within given jurisdictions. As a result of the complexity of the definition of the bundle of rights associated with any given parcel of real property, the transfer of those same rights is also highly complex. However, even though the physical property itself cannot in most instances be moved from one seller to one buyer, the rights to the benefits through use can be so transferred. The entire world of title transfer and the line of liability involved in a clear versus a "clouded" title have given rise to entire industries such as the title insurance field. There are various methods of transfer of title to various classes of interests and type of real estate services involved that have evolved in various parts of not only the United States, but throughout the world. The fundamental fact of such transfer methods is that the principle of private property ownership must exist.

PRIVATE PROPERTY AND THE REAL ESTATE PRODUCT

Through the principle of eminent domain and police power, the definition of private property in the United States is very much a governmentally defined and enforced concept. The principle of *escheat* is the vested and continuing interest of the governmental body in the real estate product. As such, the roots of the definition and control of private property reach back to the very beginnings of this country as an independent nation. As a result, the value of the real estate product is very much a function of the governmental participation in the entire spectrum of the real estate field. Not only are the various levels of the governmental sectors involved in the real estate product through the definition of and protection and enforcement of private property rights, but the role and the extent of that role of participation in real estate are continually changing and developing at varying degrees throughout all the segments of the real estate sector. From the federal programs such as FHA and VA; and departments such as HUD and FRS; through such state programs as state support programs, title regulations and property description, to the local level in municipal zoning, environmental impact studies, building codes and permits and local market organization, changes in the role of participation occur at every session of the legislatures and policy committee meeting. The definition of the property rights within such jurisdictions is an integral product of the system that prevails.

The quality of the interest in the private property is also a fundamental factor in the real estate product. Table 9–1 illustrates the types of estates generally found in real property. The purest form of ownership in real property is fee simple absolute, in which the owner can alter, use or dispose of his property in any manner of his personal choosing. In real life there are few, if any, instances in which one may enjoy absolute fee simple ownership. Because real property is very much a function of the region and geography of which it is a part, and such interests are essentially a product of government and laws, rarely does the situation exist in which absolute fee simple ownership can exist without being qualified and limited to some extent by the very bodies that created it. As a result, the purest form of ownership found in most developed areas is that of the qualified fee simple nature. The owner has nearly all the advantages of fee simple absolute, but must be sure he/she does not violate the rules and regulations established for the benefit of all in the community of land owners in the land.

The important point in this discussion of estates is to realize that as the estate becomes more diluted in ownership, the less authority one has in usage, and as a result the market value or economic value of such an interest is less than that of a more complete nature.

OWNERSHIP AND VALUE OF REAL ESTATE

In addition to the qualities of estates in real property, how the ownership is declared of such real property estates may have a very real and dramatic impact upon the

TABLE 9–1
Types of Estates in Real Property

Types of Estates	Quality of Estates
Freehold estates	
Fee simple	Highest
Absolute	
Qualified	
Life estate	
Nonfreehold estates	
Leasehold	
For years	
Period to period	
At will	
At sufferance	Lowest

Source: California, Department of Real Estate, *Reference Book Vol. 1*, 1973 ed., Sacramento, Calif., p. 73.

marketability of such interests. Generally, ownership is confined to the following categories:

1—Separate

2—Concurrent: Tenancy in common, joint tenancy, community property, tenancy in partnership.

Separate ownership refers to one person or party having ownership and all the rights and responsibilities of such ownership. Concurrent ownership refers to simultaneous ownership by two or more persons each having or sharing the rights and responsibilities of such ownership.

The implications in the market place are as varied and as complex as the multiple of classes of estates times the options of ownership that each may take. The implications of the classes of concurrent ownership are severe in the market place. The degree of autonomy on the part of the sellers of real property is not obvious. The ramifications that such lack of total authority may have in the exchange in the market place have led to many specific interpretations of the authority of one party or another to sell any estate in which ownership is in a concurrent state with other parties. The whole field of title insurance has also grown in partial response to such conflicts that develop.

It should also be observed so far as estates and ownership are concerned in many instances the more limiting the estate and the more group ownership patterns may in fact make the marketability of specific real estate services more attractive. For example, if a manufacturing firm desires to locate closer to a new market, and the firm has very specific requirements in terms of the physical characteristics of the plant site, it may be far more economical and suitable for the firm to purchase a leasehold interest, perhaps in a group financing situation. Under such terms the firm would find what meets the physical requirements, and yet would not have to purchase the entire real estate product, which may be excessive in terms of cost or of needed space. If the only property services available were huge fee simple parcels with very high price tags, this potential buyer would not be able to enter the market. So, through segmenting ownership rights and classes of estates the real estate product becomes more adaptable to the needs of the market it serves, and also makes the market for real estate services a highly complex one.

THE VALUE ESTIMATE

The economic concept of value developed in this discussion so far has been defined in terms of the amount of money or goods in exchange that will be offered and accepted for a product or service in the market place. It is important to recognize the importance of the market place in that perhaps new definition of value. In economics, the yardstick of measurement has traditionally been the monetary one, that is, dollars as the major measure of value. Although there are many drawbacks and shortcomings associated with money as the yardstick of value, there has been a noticeable lack of any adequate objective measure to substitute for it. As such, value has been defined as primarily market defined. That is, there is no acceptable intrinsic value for real estate services of any other marketable item. By market defined, we mean that value is defined by

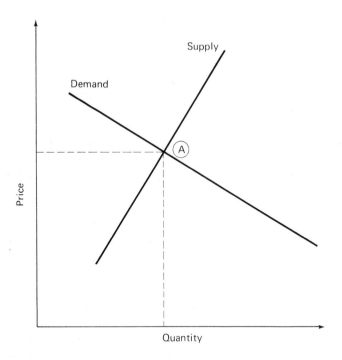

Figure 9–1

the point at which the supplier or seller will exchange his product or services with the buyer for the buyer's money or item of barter or trade. In other words, value is defined by the intersection of supply and demand in the more traditional graphical presentation of economic theory.

In Figure 9–1, point (A) represents the equilibrium point between supply and demand of the product or service under examination. At point (A) the seller will be willing to sell and the buyer will be willing to buy at the quantity and price indicated on the axis. The value of the particular item in the economic sense would be defined as the point on the left axis coinciding with point (A) on the graphs. The price at which exchange will take place is the value of that particular item or service in the true market place. No other point will persist. At a lower price more will be demanded than is available for sale. The result would be to bid prices up. At a point above the equilibrium, the supply would exceed the demand and the sellers would lower price to attract buyers. The important point to recall throughout this discussion of value is that the concept of value is a dynamic concept and a function of the real world and economy. Just because buggy whips once sold for $5 does not mean that they are worth at least $5 now. Likewise, just because a piece of property sold for X amount of dollars last year does not necessarily mean that it will sell for X plus in the current year. The economic value of any good or service is determined by the economic conditions defined at the time the value estimate is made, and are at the point of exchange between the good in question and other goods or monies.

REFERENCES

1—Bach, George L. *Economics: An Introduction to Analysis and Policy*. 7th ed. Englewood Cliffs, N.J.: Prentice-Hall, Inc., 1971.

2—Heilbroner, Robert L. and Thurow, Lester C. *The Economic Problem*. 4th ed. Englewood Cliffs, N.J.: Prentice-Hall, Inc., 1975.

3—Joseph, Myron L. *Economic Analysis and Policy*. 3rd ed. Englewood Cliffs, N.J.: Prentice-Hall, Inc., 1971.

4—McConnell, Campbell R. *Economics*. 5th ed. New York: McGraw-Hill, Inc., 1972.

5—Robinson, Marshall A., et. al. *An Introduction to Economic Reasoning*. Washington, D.C.: The Brookings Institute, 1967.

CHAPTER

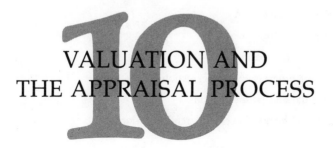

VALUATION AND THE APPRAISAL PROCESS

WHAT IS APPRAISAL?

Appraisal is fundamentally an opinion or judgment as to value of the object being appraised. The object of appraisal is the value estimate. It is, therefore, fundamental to the appraisal process to understand and keep in mind the points relating to the formation of value itself as discussed in the preceding chapter. An appraisal is an attempt to answer the question: "What is it worth?" Essentially, the appraisal estimate is expressed in terms of what the subject item would likely garner in terms of money if placed on the market. Again, the market definition of value is the goal of the investigation. The definition of economic value given in the preceding chapter is the value goal of the appraisal process.

Being defined through the market place and the interaction of supply and demand, valuation through the appraisal process is subject to many factors of varying influence. Among those factors are the following:

Supply and demand principles

Principle of change

Principles of substitution

Principles of highest and best use

Principles of balance

Principles of increasing and decreasing returns

Principles of economies of scale

Principles of contribution

Principles of competition

Principles of conformity

Principles of anticipation

Principles of progression and regression

Governmental and political trends

Economic and market forces and trends location

Operating expenses

Capitalization rates

Utility and scarcity

Depreciation and obsolescence

In recognizing the interaction of market forces as the thermometer of all general business conditions and attitudes, the price mechanism that reflects all the judgments of all the parties in the market provides a most useful tool. By starting with the price at equilibrium all the decisions leading to that equilibrium are accounted for, without having to analyze each factor of the decision process independently.

However, in the task of appraisal the end product is the prediction of what future prices will be for specified properties. As such, the appraiser must account for the factors that lead to the price at the point of exchange in the market place. Therefore, the appraiser should have a thorough understanding of the factors and relationships that go into the final value estimate in the market.

APPROACHES TO THE
APPRAISAL PROBLEM

The real estate product is essentially a product of three dimensions. First, it is a physical asset in terms of land and improvements. Second, the real estate product is value judgment on the part of the market and submarket of which it is a part. Last, the real estate subject represents income to the owner of the asset, whether in the form of dollars or in the form of services associated with use by the owner. The three classical approaches to appraisal reflect these three different definitions: the cost approach, the market comparision approach and the income approach. All three approaches have as their goal the prediction of the economic value of the asset in question. However, all three approach that value from a different assumption or set of assumptions. From the complexities of the real estate commodity itself and the fact that the entire economic world deals with human beings making a multitude of independent decisions and judgments, it is clear that no one approach has the capacity to provide all the answers. As a result, most professional appraisers will employ all three approaches to reach the final value judgment in the subject appraisal they are performing. It is a vitally important point to understand the assumptions underlying each separate approach so that the applicability of one approach over another can be determined as far as possible. Furthermore, the shortcomings of each approach involve more than the underlying assumptions, and should be explored for the benefit of all those parties employing the results of appraisal estimates in the decision-making process in the market place.

The Cost Approach

Essentially, the cost approach attempts to estimate the cost of building the improvement at today's prices and subtracting from that amount the total services or use that have been consumed up to the current date, and then adding the value associated with the land. The steps would be listed as:

- *step 1:* Estimate cost of improvement new.
- *step 2:* Estimate the amount of depreciation.
- *step 3:* Estimate the land value based on comparable sites.
- *step 4:* Estimate total value by adding land value to the depreciated cost.

The situation in which the cost approach would be most applicable would be in those cases of a new building on a property that is at its current highest and best use. The cost approach is also applicable when the appraisal is for fire insurance purposes. It is also employed to a great extent in situations involving special use types of property such as breweries, grain elevators and the like. In the cases involving new buildings, the costs reflect current costs that would be involved in replacement, and the property being employed at its highest and best use. Although a considerable time lag can occur between construction and the final occupancy in many if not most instances, the assumption of current figures is generally true. Also, for fire insurance purposes, the insurance is to replace the structure if it burns and would, therefore, reflect the true cost of such coverage. In the case of special-use properties, the choice of the cost of replacement method is most often dictated by the inappropriateness of any other method of approaching the value estimate. The market value of such structures is minimal except in instances in which the market reflects all buyers and sellers who are in the market for the same type of special-use structure. As most special-use buildings and structures are built for consumption by the owner and builder, the income approach is next to useless because in most instances there is no income in the measurable form to use as a bench mark.

More general problems in the cost approach are: what is the definition of replacement, whose costs are to be used, what do costs ignore, and what approach is there to depreciation? In the definition problem, what is meant is the difference between replacement as duplication and replacement as similarity. In many older structures, the costs involved in duplication are extreme, and in some instances it may be totally impossible to duplicate because of certain types of material no longer being available. The costs involved in replacing with a similar structure may be drastically different from the costs of replacement in duplicate. However, the newer structure may be drastically different also.

In the question of costs, the economies of scale, such as they are, that exist in the construction industry make some builders more efficient than others. As a result, the cost of replacement by one firm may be greatly different from the costs of replacement by another firm. Also, such items as quality of workmanship and the time to construct may extensively alter the end product and the costs of the product.

A big problem of cost estimates to appraisal is the tendency to ignore such facts as misplaced structures and over-improvement and under-improvement of real property. In the cost approach, these factors would be totally ignored. As a result the value estimate would materially differ from the economic value of the given property. The problem of nonconforming uses with existing zoning regulations would also fail to be accurately appraised in terms of economic value by the cost approach. As was discussed earlier, if such a structure were destroyed, any new or rebuilt structure would have to conform to the new zoning regulations no matter what use the previous structure may have been built for.

In arriving at an estimate of the amount of life or services that have been consumed up to the date of the appraisal, the market comparison technique is the only one available. Normal depreciation schedules would not provide one with accurate value figures. Such book values would necessarily relate to the economic value involved in the current appraisal estimate.

More fundamental than all the foregoing discussions of details in the flaws of cost approaches to appraisal estimates of value, is the more basic question of the relationship of costs to value. Exactly what is the relation between cost and value, if any? To begin with, it is quite apparent that costs do not determine value in the economics sense. The Hope diamond is obviously worth more than the costs incurred by man to find and cut the stone. We have already established the fact that economic value is market-determined concept. The free exchange between potential buyers and potential sellers establishes the value in the economic sense. The fundamental concept behind value is the benefits that will accrue to the owners of an item or service in use or possession. If value were a cost-determined concept, objects such as diamonds or other precious stones and metals, art objects, antiques and many other items would certainly be worth much less than they currently demand in the market place. Likewise, oil, wood and paper products and many other items would trade at much more stable levels and perhaps at lower levels than are currently seen in the petroleum field. Value is simply not a cost-determined concept. The cost of an item or service must be below the market price or economic value of that item or service, or it would not be produced and offered for sale in the market. Costs affect the supply of available goods and services in the market place, as they reveal the profit potentials and margins, but costs most certainly do not determine the economic value of anything.

Market Comparison
Approach to Value

The market comparison technique of appraisal is descriptively the most simple approach. One must perform essentially three basic steps to arrive at a value estimate. First, sales data are gathered of like pieces of property. Second, differences are adjusted between the subject property under consideration and the sales figures of other parcels. Finally, the value of the subject property is estimated on the basis of the adjusted sales figures of comparable properties.

The major strong points of the market comparison approach to value are: that it is the most widely used method of appraisal, and that by observing sales figures one is actually accounting for what people are in reality willing to pay and to receive for such property. However, there are many pitfalls in the market comparison technique that one should be aware of so as not to be led "down the primrose path."

First, there are no two properties anywhere that are exactly alike. As a result of the uniqueness of real estate as opposed to more homogeneous products, the accuracy of any two comparisons is by definition bound to be open to some degree of question. Not only are the sites different and to some extent each unique but also that uniqueness is even compounded when any improvement is added to the real estate site. As a result, the accuracy of any comparisons conducted are open to considerable debate and variance.

One of the most frequent problems encountered, especially in the older and more stable areas, is the unavailability of comparable sales. An area may be so stable or small or unique that sales in the area are few and infrequent. In such instances, the accuracy of the market comparison may be seriously open to question. In some instances, the lack of relevant data makes the approach impossible to apply at all. Sales figures more than a year or two apart tend to preclude the applicability of the market comparison technique. Of course, in some small stable communities there may still be some relevancy in using data more than one or two years old. On the other hand, in some of the more active real estate areas data on sales more than a couple of months old are already outdated and virtually useless for the market comparison technique of appraisal.

One of the fundamental problems in the real estate industry, and more particularly the residential owner-occupant submarket, is the lack of information on the terms of the sale in addition to the gross amount of the sale. As was discussed in the market analysis chapter, the terms and availability of financing generally constitute the second most important factor determining the demand for housing. The price fluctuates considerably between a situation of cash-in-hand sale versus a sale with 95 percent financing. The extremes are especially true in situations involving seller being cashed out to the existing loan or seller taking back a large long-term note or trust deed. Terms of sale are very important in the residential market, and price itself is not quite enough to determine the market value of real estate that has sold or been offered for sale.

The final problem area in the market comparison approach to determination of value is the adjustments made to comparable sales figures. Such adjustments are really value judgments on the part of the appraiser and are difficult if not impossible to quantify in terms of objective data. With the knowledge that no properties are exactly alike, and that the terms of sales are not included in the sales figures, and that the time and location of sales used in the market comparison are varied and not exactly current or exact, then some adjusting must be made to the data to reflect more closely the true aspects of the comparisons. The appraiser must call on experience and expertise to provide some benchmarks for adjusting the figures. However, no matter what the talents of the appraiser may be, the resulting adjustments are highly subjective and constitute more personal opinion than measurable fact. After a thorough analysis of trends and the real estate profile of the community, and a truly objective analysis of the supply and demand considerations making up the market, the professional real estate appraiser may be more able to adjust such comparable data to truly reflect objective fact.

Acknowledging the pitfalls in the market comparison approach to the appraisal of value, one final comment should be made. The market comparison approach to value estimates is the closest to the real value estimate. The data inputs, comparable sales figures, when adjusted for terms of the transactions actually measure what people are willing to pay and receive in the exchange of the goods and services of the real estate sector. As such, they consider the real objective evidence of economic value, which is the price persons are willing to pay and receive in the exchange in the market place. Economic value has been defined as a market-determined concept, and in that regard the market comparison technique of appraisal comes closest to measuring that aspect of the appraisal task.

Capitalization of Income Approach

The income-capitalization method of appraisal is a much more complex and involved analysis than the more traditional methods of cost and market comparison. However, conceptually the income capitalization method is not that strange. Essentially, the real estate under examination represents a bundle of income checks—the promise of one check each year of the life of the asset, and at the end of the economic life another check for the salvage or resale value. The underlying logic is that money is always worth more now than later. Thus, the check for the current year is worth more than the check for the following year. That is, each year's income over the future life of the project is worth progressively less starting with the current year. Furthermore, the promise of a certain sum of dollars 20 or 30 years in the future is worth less than that same amount of dollars if paid in the current year.

Essentially, the steps in the income capitalization approach are as follows:

- *step 1:*   Amount of net income on an annual basis.
- *step 2:*   Capitalizing the net income at the appropriate capitalization rate.
- *step 3:*   Estimate of salvage or resale value at completion.
- *step 4:*   Capitalize salvage by same rate.
- *step 5:*   Add value of income stream and salvage value to reach total.

These steps are abbreviated and somewhat generalized. The format, however, is generally correct in the appraisal technique employing the capitalization method. In many instances, the net income is simply capitalized at some rate of return plus recapture. And even in some cases, the gross rent schedule is capitalized by some percentage rate. Such concepts as gross rent multipliers are reflective of the professionalism on the part of some of the less knowledgeable real estate practitioners.

The first area of problems and hazards in the income capitalization approach to appraisal is the income projections themselves. How accurate are the net income estimates, and are they more reflective of the good or poor management of the property than of the market level to be expected? Also, what is the duration of the income stream depicted in the net income estimates? More will be discussed about the time element later in this chapter. The problems in estimating the future income stream as well as substantiating the current net income figures can present formidable tasks for the appraiser.

The second major problem area is that having to do with the portion of the building or project that is owner-occupied. In most cases, the area being owner-occupied has always been so and there is little if no information available as to the market value in terms of a leasehold interest in that portion occupied by the owner. Comparables are not generally accurate enough to substantiate accurate income figures for such dwellings or portions of dwellings. As in most cases in the residential sector, the owner-occupant pays more for his ownership interest than the renter-occupant would pay. The fact of his ownership and pride of the asset often are major inducements for the higher premium. So, in those instances involving a major portion of the asset being owner-occupied the net income projections are quite difficult to substantiate.

Another problem area in the income capitalization method is the impact of amenities on an asset. The attempts to quantify the impact that amenities may have on the income prospects of a project are extremely difficult. It is assumed that if one building has more amenities than another and also has a greater income stream than the other, the amenities are to some degree responsible for the difference in income. The point that is a problem is that the life of amenities is usually much shorter than the life of the entire project, and also that amenities reflect the efficiency of management as well as the physical aspects of the amenities. If the amenities cost $1,000, how much additional income annually can be attributed to those amenities as separate from the location, size, management or other factors associated with the more profitable project?

Capitalization-of-Income Examples   If we deposited $1,000 each in two separate banks, one paying 8 percent interest and the other paying 12 percent interest, for a period of 20 years the amount of our total investment at the end of that period of time would be:

Bank A (8 percent)	$4,660.90
Bank B (12 percent)	$9,646.20

As a result of such a comparison, we know that the rate of return or interest being earned by our investment is an important aspect of the worth of our investment during the time period. However, the other element in the analysis (time) is also a vitally important determinant of the total amount of worth for the investment at the end of the time period. Let us deposit the $1,000 in the same eight percent bank, but let one remain for ten years and the other remain for 30 years. At the end of those two time periods the two amounts would be:

Account A (ten years)	$ 2,158.90
Account B (thirty years)	$10,062.60

It can be seen that time can be as important factor as the rate of return being earned by a principle investment in terms of the total worth of such an investment at the end of its life.

Traditionally, in the real estate sector, net income has been capitalized at a pre-determined rate of return to reach a capitalized value for that income producing asset. Such technique may be illustrated as in the following example: An income property has the net income stream of $50,000 annually, and the capitalization rate is at .ten per-cent. The simplistic formula of A/r is employed, where A is the amount of annual income and r is the capitalization rate. In our example, then, the $50,000 income would be divided by the ten percent capitalization rate to arrive at a value of $500,000 for the project.

$$\frac{50,000}{.10} = \frac{500,000}{1.0} = 500,000 = 500,000.00 \text{ value estimate}$$

The major flaw in the approach illustrated above is the total neglect of the time element in the return analysis. We would surely look upon the above investment with a different view if the income were only for five or ten years, than we would if the income would continue on into infinity. When we account for the time element in such an analysis, the ultimate value estimate is quite different from the estimate above in cases of limited time, and quite similar in cases approaching infinity. As an illustration, assume that the above example was an income stream relatively secure for 50 years, with $50,000 yearly and a capitalization rate of ten percent. We would then find the value as follows:

$$50,000 \times 9.915 = 495,750.00 = \$495,750.00 \text{ value estimate}$$

The major reason that the two estimates are so close in value is the major time period involved. Fifty years is so long as to be approaching infinity in terms of normal life of investments in use. If we now shorten the time period to 15 years, which is more rational (the average life of one ownership in many real estate sectors is less than ten years), the results are quite different:

$$\frac{50,000}{.10} = \$500,000.00 \text{ estimated value of income property}$$

$$50,000 \times 7.6061 = \$380,305 \text{ estimated value of income project}$$

A difference of $119,695.00 is a significant difference of opinion as far as the estimate of value of the particular income project under examination. The reason for the differ-ence in the two value estimates is the assumption in the first equation. Whenever the element of time is ignored in the calculations of investment return and worth, the result-ing value estimate must also be short of complete, and may be terribly misleading to anyone relying upon such appraisal of value for decision-making.

To illustrate a more complex example that may reflect a somewhat simplistic example in the real estate sector, let us examine the following example:

A building with $10,000 net annual income has a firm dollar option of $300,000 sale price at the end of the tenth year.

$$\$10,000 \times 10 \text{ years} = \$100,000$$

Net sale in 10th year $\underline{300,000}$

$\$400,000$ Total dollars to be received

Now, the question to be answered is what is this investment worth today to the prospective investor? If we use the A/r formula we would show:

$$\frac{\$10,000}{.10} = \$100,000 \text{ plus sale proceeds of } \$300,000 = \$400,000$$

The major flaw in the approach is the time element that is assumed to be infinite in the A/r equation is not supported by the project itself. It is a sad fact of life that many unknowledgeable investors and less-than-knowledgeable real estate professionals continue to use such approaches to arrive at initial value estimates.

Referring to the tables at the back of the text, it can be seen that a more efficient and accurate value estimate may be made to account for the unique elements of the project. The first step is the evaluation of the annual income estimate through the proper technique accounting for the proper capitalization rate and the time frame of the investment project. The net income stream from the investment represents an annuity payment over the life of the investment. The value of each year's income is progressively less as the time into the future extends. Just as $1 next year is worth less than $1 immediately, so the $1 two years from now is worth a little less than $1 next year. Each extension of time diminishes the value of the proceeds from that time period. Using the table at the back of the text for the present value of $1 per period at ten percent capitalization rate for ten periods we have the following:

$10,000 × 6.1446 = $ 61,446.00 present value of the income stream

300,000 × 0.38554 = 115,662.00 present value of proceeds from the sale ten years from now

$177,108.00 present value of the investment in the subject project

Likewise, the sum of money to be received in the tenth year upon the sale of the project is subject to evaluation in the same terms as the annual income sums of the first ten years. The factor employed to evaluate the sum upon sale was the table at the back of the book referring to the present value of a sum of dollars due in the future capitalized at the same ten percent rate.

What this type of analysis does is to allow the investor to evaluate the income promised by an investment separate from the physical attributes of the investment itself. In the foregoing analysis, the source of the income is really immaterial to the analysis of the investment as an investment. The criterion of investment is return on the dollars invested when accounting for the risk factor. The dollars invested versus the dollars returned is the fundamental relationship under analysis in the investment decision. Other factors such as liquidity, size of investment, terms, leverage and length determine to some extent the general field to be analyzed as well as the appropriate capitalization rate to employ.

What the analyst is really attempting to do in the capitalization approach to appraisal is to determine the present value as of this moment of the total dollars promised by the project under consideration. In the previous example, the project was extremely limited and simplistic. The income stream during the ten-year life was secured through a secure lease contract. Therefore, the income stream was relatively secure under such a lease arrangement as a triple net lease where the lessee pays all taxes, upkeep and monthly expenses entailed in the project. Also, the salvage or residual value at the end of the lease period was assured through the hard dollar option at a fixed price. Under such circumstances, the contract is binding on both parties and the price at time of sale is assured. The one major item totally ignored in the example used was the possibility of leverage, which is so crucial in many real estate projects. Since we were attempting to evaluate the project rather than the investment for a given purchaser, the element of leverage had no place in the analysis.

When applying the same general outline to a specific project for a specific individual investor, many other factors may be included in the analysis. First, the quality of the income stream, that is, the probability of the net income continuing to remain at the same level as currently observed, is measured in terms of risk. The major element in the overall evaluation of risk is the capitalization rate chosen for the particular investment. A guaranteed lease will provide less risk in terms of the net income of the future than will a month-to-month lease to a small retailer in a highly competitive industry. In such instances one would be more inclined to capitalize the lease project at a lower capitalization rate than the month-to-month project. The higher the risk of an investment the higher the capitalization rate employed in the analysis. A low risk investment such as U.S. government bonds carries a lower interest rate than a small corporate bond issue. The higher rate charged or demanded by the market on the corporate issue reflects the increased risk in the corporate issue when compared to the little risk of the federal government issue.

The choice of appropriate capitalization rate can also be influenced by the tax aspects of the project. In a project involving first-user 200 percent depreciation, the tax shelter aspects can be considerable. In such an instance the project may be best evaluated in terms of the after-tax rate of return. The tax profile of the probable investor is included in the income and tax consequences of the project. The rate of return or the capitalization rate chosen to be used in such case would be a lower rate to reflect the fact that the income would be after tax or tax free. It is not uncommon to see the rate charged on municipal issues, which are tax-free, generally three or more percentage points below an issue that is similar in terms of risk but that is not tax-free. That three-point differential would likely be reflected in any capitalization rate that was employed in the comparison of a tax-free or after-tax investment to a more conventional investment not enjoying the tax advantages of the first.

Capitalization Rate and the Market   It is important to recognize that real estate does not operate in a vacuum subject only to its own rules and norms of behavior. The real estate sector is an integral part of a dynamic economic system and is subject to great influence upon that system and influence from that system upon real estate. Likewise, the capitalization rate, which reflects what most investors expect in terms of returns on their investment considering the risk involved, is also a function of the economy and the investment community. Generally speaking, the capitalization rate is synonymous to the interest rates prevailing in the market both locally and nationally. Interest rates may be thought of as the price of money in the free market.

Figure 10–1 represents a simplistic and hypothetical money market in its totality. All the potential borrowers in the market bid on the available funds and, as the figure illustrates, at the level of bidding the suppliers of funds will lend all the available funds to all those bidding at the market price. Where all the suppliers committed equal all the buyers buying, the market has reached equilibrium. At the equilibrium point the market price of money (interest rate) is r_1 and the amount of funds exchanged at that price is equal to Q_1. The fact that the supply of funds may be a partial, or in some instances a complete, monopoly may seriously distort this process of arbitration, but the market will ultimately determine the equilibrium point. If one could get all the money he needed at a point below that represented by r_1, then so could anyone else in the market. The lenders of funds would have to meet that lower price, or not lend any money. Since their business is to sell money on loan, then they would be inclined to meet their competition in the market through lower prices (interest rates). Likewise, any borrower who was being charged more than r_1 for his loans would tend to go into the market and borrow at the lower market rate. His lender would meet the competitive price just as before.

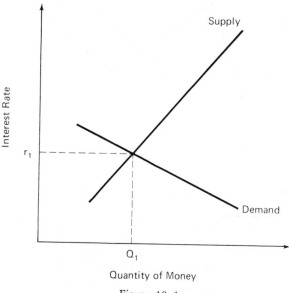

Figure 10–1

Figure 10–2 is a depiction of two elements in the money market on the national as well as local scale. It illustrates the difference between the risk factors in two different classes of loans and lenders. Supply (1) represents high-risk capital in the money market. This type of capital tends to be the domain of the private lenders rather than the institutional lenders because of the risk factors and the corresponding premiums such borrowers must pay. Such ventures as venture capital in new small businesses, secondary financing and marginal personal loans are some examples of high-risk loans that are not normally initiated by the bigger commercial banks. As a result, these funds carry a higher, and in some cases a much higher, interest rate than more conventional loans. Supply (2) represents the more conventional loans of the commercial banks. There are more of these funds available because of the lower risk factor, and there are more demanded because of the lower interest rate. Now, it would be terribly naive to believe that risk was the only factor influencing the difference in rates and amounts demanded or supplied. The major overriding factor, however, is the overall risk of the investment or loan. That risk in the overall sense represents more than the risk of capital in terms of whether it will be returned by the borrower. It may reflect any number of factors including:

- *interest rate risk*   that interest rates will go up after the loan
- *inflation risk*   that cost of money will go up

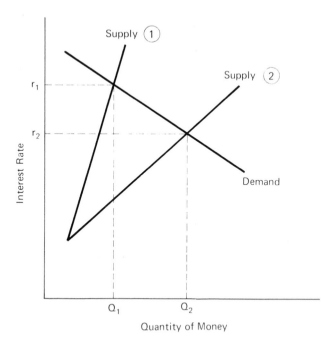

Quantity of Money

Supply$_1$ — High Risk: Private Lenders

Supply$_2$ — Low Risk: Public Lenders

Figure 10–2

- *liquidity*   loss of flexibility in investment strategy
- *political risk*   government may penalize fixed assets
- *tax risk*   taxes may go up causing income to go down
- *income risk*   income stream may not subsist into the future
- *time risk*   long-term investments mean a long time for changes

These risks represent the market for funds more than any single aspect of real estate itself. That is, they reflect the market conditions of which investment real estate is a part. The major portions of the risks listed previously are comparative. That is, how does real estate compare with alternative investment forms? As such, the investment decision as it relates to real estate is not unlike the investment decision as applied to stocks, bonds, commodities, futures or objets d'arts. The analysis is a comparison of what is expected in this investment as compared to what is expected in that one. The only single facet of the two investments that may exist in common is the dollar analysis at the completion of the investment term. As such, those dollars represent the below-the-line return to the investor no matter what the investment is in. The income stream is the aspect being evaluated in the capitalization approach, and it makes little difference what the physical characteristics of that investment may be; if they do not show any impact upon the income stream of the investment during its life or at the completion at time of sale, then they are not considered in the income-capitalization approach to the real estate appraisal problem.

Recapture and Present Value Analysis

The idea that buildings that wear out over the life of the investment should be treated separately from the normal concept of capitalization is widely held in appraisal circles. The validity of the concept that an asset that is consumed during its income-producing life should be accounted for in the cost of the investment is not particularly debatable. The method of accounting for such consumption is. In the preceding analysis we established the concept that the return on investment is a market-determined item considering risks entailed in the investment type. The flaw in the recapture concept is that it is considered part of the return on capital invested, rather than a cost of the investment. The major problem is that such a capitalization rate that includes a rate for recapture will in nearly all instances exceed what suitable rates for suitable risks would exist in the market for rates of return.

Therefore, in the present approach to present value estimation of the investment value the amount of the original investment consumed in the production of income for that investment should be reflected in the amount received at the termination of that investment. Through such treatment, capitalization rates for competing investments may be more comparable and the investor may be availed of a more competent conclusion. In addition, such recapture rates are contested in extremes in documentation. Such trends as tax-approved methods of depreciation as well as the varying rates of physical consumption of real estate assets leads to a rather vague definition of recapture rates defined through consensus rather than one defined through analysis and documentation. A most simplified example of the use of recapture rate in the capitalization of income method would be the following:

Return attributable to land and site   8%
Recapture of building with a 25-yr. life   4% annual recapture
                Combined capitalization rate   12%

Annual net income: $10,000

$$\text{Value:} \quad \frac{\text{Net income}}{\text{Cap. rate}} = \frac{\$10,000}{.12} = \$83,333.33 \text{ value of income stream}$$

The areas of definition are the crucial problem areas for the recapture concept, as well as the problems of documenting the analysis with the real world examples of investors' desires and expectations in regard to the returns expected and accepted in various investment media. The overall criticism by this author is the assumption that the capitalization in whole or in part can be made separate from the influences of the market. The concept that a structure has a predetermined capitalization rate irrespective of the market forces is totally contrary to the fundamental nature of investments and the allocation of scarce resources.

MARKET IMPERFECTIONS

Real estate investment property is a much broader and more national and international market than some of the other submarkets in the real estate sector. As a result, market imperfections peculiar to many local or regional economies are not as common in the investment field. Also, the expertise on the part of the buyers and sellers in the large-scale investments diminishes the impact and the life of certain more subjective imperfections. Nevertheless, where certain monopolistic or monopsonistic tendencies distort the returns on investment property in that area, those same factors must be acknowledged in the market inputs used in the various approaches to the appraisal of value.

Through the foregoing discussions we have presented some methods by which one can analyze a given income-generating investment in terms of the abstract realities of that investment. The methods discussed make it feasible for one to evaluate separately the annual income prospects and the income to be derived at time of sale of an individual investment. The present technique allows one to employ some form of yardstick by which one may compare unlike physical properties on the basis of their investment quality. Real estate is merely one of many alternative investment forms that a prospective individual may choose to concentrate his funds.

The physical characteristics of alternative investments do not lend themselves to a realistic comparison for the decision-making task. If common stocks are currently earning a 15 percent return for investors, and real estate is earning a 10 percent return, investors will leave the real estate sector and go into the common stock medium. As long as the rates of return on both are based upon the same dollar returns, the validity of the analysis is established. Until real estate improves its return, or common stocks fall in the return they are earning, the movement from one investment to the other will continue. The market factors of each are not isolated from the impact of competing investment returns. The internal logic of subjects such as recapture will not alter the comparative advantage or disadvantage of one medium over another. The expected rate of return to be earned by investors is a market-defined concept and is virtually totally immaterial to the physical characteristics of the investment type.

Because the rate of return expected and demanded by potential investors is a market-defined concept, the markets involved must be realistically evaluated in terms of their prospective returns. In those instances in which certain markets show abnormally high or low returns compared to those normally found in the market place, the details behind such returns must be investigated carefully and completely. Such market imperfections as social, ethnic, cultural, economic and educational monopolistic and monopsonistic tendencies may have dramatic influence upon the returns associated with those localities containing such market-distorting influences.

Furthermore, if a certain concept is generally accepted as the basis of arriving at the market value of an investment, it may make little difference that the logic of the concept is or may be erroneous. As an example, if the gross rent multiplier is the generally accepted method of evaluation in a given locality, then the conclusions based upon that concept in fact become the market definition of value. It is in this manner that such simplistic approaches to value as the gross rent multiplier may in fact become valid in the market place, in spite of the lack of logical and analytical consistency, and the enormous variation such reasoning can have in the rates of return earned by such investors. Through the increasingly expanding scale of investments in real estate, both in money magnitude and in the number of persons involved in the value conclusion, the level of analysis and the consistency of logic are becoming more developed in the world of the real estate professional. In such light, the role of analytical study in the realm of rates of return and present value analysis will play an increasing role in the ability of the real estate professional to serve his industry, and indeed to survive in some markets.

REFERENCES

1—American Institute of Real Estate Appraisers. *The Appraisal of Real Estate.* 6th ed. Chicago: American Institute of Real Estate Appraisers, 1972.

2—Kahn, Robert. *Real Estate Appraisal and Investment.* New York: The Ronald Press, 1963.

3—Ring, Alfred A. *Valuation of Real Estate.* 2nd ed. Englewood Cliffs, N.J.: Prentice-Hall, Inc., 1970.

4—_____. *Real Estate Principles and Practices.* 7th ed. Englewood Cliffs, N.J.: Prentice-Hall, Inc., 1972.

5—Unger, M. A. *Real Estate Principles and Practices.* 4th ed. Burlingame, Ca.: Southwestern Publishing Co., 1969.

PART

REAL ESTATE
AND FINANCE

Having defined real estate in the precise terms of real estate services accrued through use, and the application of traditional economic theory to that product definition, we next considered the land use patterns and control of land use in the physical sense. The role of planning was established as a fundamental consideration of the real estate function. We then turned our attention to the market and submarkets that such uses are exchanged in, and the influence of the varying elements that constitute the real estate market and submarket. The function of the market in facilitating the buyers and sellers in arbitrating their opinions as to value was also examined. Finally, we examined the concept of value itself and the four elements that constitute value in the economic sense. The appraisal approaches to value determination were examined and criticized. The idea of a broad band of varying value estimates constituting the equilibrium price of varying real estate services was alluded to at varying points in the discussions to this point.

We now turn our attention to the role of the financial market and the financial structure within the real estate markets themselves. The role of financing is a dominant one in the real estate sector. As such, it has a dramatic impact upon the interaction of supply and demand within the market place, and indeed upon the level of activity that prevails in all of real estate at any given time. First, we will examine the role and function of money systems and the activity of banking in general as they relate to general economic activity of a region or nation. Second, we will examine the history of finance in the real estate sector prior to the depression of the late 1920s and early 1930s, and the great impact of the federal government after that time. Last, we will examine the development of modern real estate finance from the post-depression era up to the current date.

FINANCIAL FRAMEWORK OF REAL ESTATE

BARTER ECONOMIES

In simpler societies where money is not used, the only system of exchange between parties is the barter system. In such cases, persons come to the market place with items they offer for trade and purchases they wish to make in exchange for the items they have to trade. One goat may be brought to market by a man who may need a bushel of corn and one knife. As long as there is one seller in the market place who has both corn and knives, they have the potential for making a trade. If the one having the corn and knives is also in want of or need of a goat, or can easily trade the goat for something he does want, then there will be an active market with goods and services being exchanged.

However, the moment the goat is worth more than what any one trader has to offer, the whole system begins to break down. The owner of the goat must find one seller of other items who wants the goat and has enough other items to trade in exchange for the goat. Unless he does find such a person in the market, the goat is not a tradeable item in the market place. Every single transaction must be complete and final in the time frame and in the terms negotiated at time of exchange. Each party comes to the market place with certain goods, and each party takes home either those same goods or other goods that are considered to be of exactly the same value as those brought to the market place. There is no system to equate disparities in value between items bartered in the market place. Also there is no system by which future payments may be made, or by which installments may be made upon the purchase value of a particular item.

Under such a system, it is virtually impossible for exchange of goods to take place between two or more separate societies. The economic system of such societies becomes essentially a closed system. There is little room for arbitration between societies because of the requirement for complete agreement on value of two partially unlike items being bartered. As a result, the barter system is most typical of very small closed economic units. Such systems include only easily portable items in its trading spectrum, for it requires the physical exchange of unlike goods upon the consensus of value. Consequently, dwellings, land, services and highly prized items are usually absent from such markets.

There are no methods for "making change" when one item was worth more than another, but the trade was still desired by both parties. Every transaction was complete within the time frame that it occurred. Time payments are completely unknown. The essential element for such societies is that they are virtually completely closed economic systems. Figure 11–1 illustrates such a system:

When each and every transaction that occurs within the economic system is complete and equal, as illustrated for persons A and B, then the whole economy is illustrated by A and B. The flaw in such a system is that at no time does a surplus enter the picture, and at no time does a shortage enter the scene. The possibility of a third party entering the economic scene is completely ruled out in such a simplistic barter system. Every person produces exactly enough to fill his needs plus what he must buy from his neighbor, and his neighbor does exactly the same. As a result, most such systems are both small and nonindustrialized. The system does not have the capacity to produce more than is produced now so that the population in the industrialized sector could survive. Additionally, there would be no way for wealth to accumulate to the point that capital goods used in production could be purchased. As a result, the entire society is on the backs of people producing so they can survive to produce again. The accumulation of wealth, savings, investment and other major elements of more economically affluent systems are absent from the barter economy in total.

INTRODUCTION OF MONEY

With the introduction of money into the barter economy, the profiles of individual transactions became significantly different. First, there was the immediate capacity to make change in transactions in which the goods were not exactly equal in value. As a result, one party or another now had the capacity to accumulate wealth. In addition, there was a system by which larger needs could be accommodated through the gradual

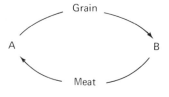

Figure 11–1

building up of funds to the point where one party could combine his money and his goods to purchase a larger item than would be possible under the barter system. As a result, the level of activity in the market place was significantly enhanced through the introduction of a money system. To a great extent the introduction of money overcame the cumbersome process of barter.

Second, the introduction of money allowed some items too large or too immobile under the barter system to be bought and sold in a market setting. Items such as real estate and homes could be exchanged without meeting the requirement of physical exchange in the market place that the barter economy required. Although at the time of the introduction of money into the economic systems of the world most land and property was owned by the power group under monarchy and kingdoms, or was considered part of that belonging to all people and not subject to being owned (as in some Indian cultures), the presence of money within the market system allowed transactions to occur involving such commodities as land, water, forests and so forth.

Finally, the introduction of money allowed a system of deferred payments to develop. With money on the scene there was a method by which one could "buy now and pay later." Even in earlier times, before charge cards, there were situations in which one party wished to purchase an item, but did not yet have the full purchase price in goods or in money. With the introduction of money there was a standard unit of measure for value, and thus a standard established for all payments in the present and in the future. Money allowed all items in the market place to be defined in terms of so much money for each. As a result, such goods could be paid for in the future based upon that definition.

FUNCTIONS OF MONEY

All monies perform certain functions that are required of them to be considered money. The first universal function of money is that it be an acceptable means of exchange. That is, it must be accepted for goods and goods accepted for money. The ratio is defined by the market place and the market value of the goods or services involved, but money must be acceptable as payment for the amount specified. To be an acceptable medium of exchange, the people of the country must be willing to accept that money as payment received for goods and services sold in the market place.

Second, and part of the first function, money must be a standard of value in the country of which it is a part. Money must be able to be used as the yardstick of value within the nation of which it is defined. If the money of a country is the acceptable medium of exchange, it would be the only single item that is defined in terms of all other items traded in the market place. If all items and services traded in the market place are defined in terms of so much money, then that money system will be the standard of value within that market place. If such a money system is in fact used as the accepted medium of exchange, then that money system must also be the standard of value of that same community.

A third function of money is to be a store of value or purchasing power. If a money system has not a store of value, then all monies accepted in exchange for goods would have to be converted into goods for fear of its being worthless in the immediate future. If I am going to accept money for goods I am selling today, I must have confidence that the same money is going to be worth something tomorrow or the next day or I would not accept money for the goods I sold. I would instead demand equal barter.

Perhaps a fourth function, although closely related to the previous three functions, is that the money system must be acceptable as a standard for deferred payments. The money system must be accepted as a standard of value in the present tense as well as in the future. Future payments to be a reality must be in terms of something in the present. For money to be the established money system in an economy, that money system must be that standard of value for deferred payments as well as present value.

Money systems became established because of the tremendous burden that all barter systems entail as a result of the cumbersome process of physical exchange of all commodities within the confines of the market place. Primarily because of the monetary systems' having alleviated such cumbersome processes, money was readily adapted to the market place. However, the four functions cited above are the details of the advantages of such money systems over any barter economy that may previously exist. Such money systems must perform all four functions to be accepted in the market place at all. As such, the four functions of money discussed are the four legs upon which the definition of money must rest.

DEVELOPMENT OF BANKING

The first consequence of the introduction of money into the barter type economic system was the increase in economic activity within the area. This was a natural consequence of the new capacity to make change to equate the multitude of transactions that were negotiated in the market place. Also, the capacity for future payment was a stimulant to current transactions. In this sense, money was like a fine lubricating oil. Its introduction initially made the system run more efficiently and more productively.

As a result of the economic refinements brought on by the introduction of a monetary system, the first natural consequence was the beginnings of the accumulation of wealth by others than the monarchy or ruling class. With the new capacity of deferred payments, it is a natural consequence that those selling for payments into the future are accumulating wealth in the form of debts and money accumulation. This in time led to the capacity for innovation and the introduction of capital equipment and investment.

The third major consequence of the introduction of money was the new possibility of international and interregional trade through import and export. Where the monetary system of the two countries or regions was the same, they could trade with each other for items of mutual interest. The specialties of the country could be sold to others through the import-export relationship as long as they both had the same money standard. Eventually, there developed the refinement in monetary systems and international trade of the exchange ratio being established between unlike currencies of trading nations in the same or similar international trading circles. With such exchange ratios, there evolved essentially a uniform money system such that any transaction could be translated into the currency of another nation to arrive at the same value estimate for all.

The whole world of international banking was a direct outgrowth of such trading practices. The banking system was the focal point of establishing such exchange rates between the money systems of various countries engaged in international trade.

Fundamentals of Banking

Throughout modern history banking has been closely and directly related to economic activity throughout the world of commerce and industry. Banking is fundamentally concerned with safekeeping and loading funds to business and individuals for economic stability and sound economic growth. Economic activity is vitally dependent upon the availability of funds for operation and expansion. The banking system is largely the focal point for such money transactions.

When a deposit is made in the account of a firm at the bank, that deposit becomes both a liability to the bank and an asset from which loans can be made. If all banks were required to have all deposits backed in total by cash within their vaults, then such banks would be nonfunctional as banks, and would merely be safe deposits for cash. As an example of what such an account would be is illustrated in Figure 11–2. In such a situation the bank does not have the capacity to lend money in any form to any party wishing to borrow. The deposits on the right side of the ledger must be covered in full by available cash on hand listed on the left side of the ledger. Under such circumstances, all claims to deposits could be fulfilled upon demand at any time. The bank in question would also go broke for a lack of any way in which to make any profit from the operation of the bank accounts.

The functioning bank, functioning as a bank, would more accurately be described in the manner presented in Figure 11–3. On the right side of the ledger account is the entry recording the deposit made by the individual, shown. On the left side, however, there is a great difference. With the assumption of a federal or state requirement of 20 percent reserves on hand for all deposits in accounts, the remaining 80 percent of the

BANK OF NOTOWN

Reserves Req.	$100.00	Deposits	$100.00
Total Assets	$100.00	Total Liabilities	$100.00

Figure 11–2

BANK OF SOMETOWN

Reserves Req.	$20.00	Deposit	$100.00
Loans O/S	80.00		
Total Assets	$100.00	Total Liabilities	$100.00

Figure 11–3

deposits are loaned by the bank to customers who are willing and able to pay interest in excess of that paid to the depositors.

These persons who borrowed from the bank, let us assume, deposited their funds in other banks and will draw against their deposits. Additionally, the other banks will also have to meet the 20 percent reserve requirement matching deposit claims with 20 percent cash reserved. The second bank can also lend out the other 80 percent of its deposits, that portion not covered by the reserve requirement. In this manner, the banks are able to earn a return on the function they perform. Through lending funds into the economy, banks have the ability to fuel economic expansion and development. Without the banks performing such a function, the economies of most nations would be hard pressed to accommodate the needs of economic developing systems for credit and financing. Through the flow of funds from one bank to another within an economic system, the impact of banking and financing function is felt throughout the economies of individual countries and, indeed, throughout the world.

The Multiplier Effect

From the previous example illustrated in the last section, let us examine the flow of funds from one bank to another through an economic system. Bank A receives an initial deposit of $100.00. That deposit must be matched by a 20 percent reserve requirement, or $20.00. The $80.00 remaining can be loaned out to customers and businesses within the community. The ledger of Bank A now looks like this:

The $80.00 in loans made by Bank A become deposits in some other person's account. For illustration, assume that the borrower has an account with another bank, Bank B. As a deposit in another bank, that $80.00 must be backed by the same 20 percent reserve requirement as the original $100.00 deposited in Bank A. Bank B now can loan out the remaining 80 percent of deposits not required as reserves. Bank B therefore loans out $64.00. Again assuming the borrower has an account at a bank other than A or

BANK A

Reserves Req.	$20.00	Deposit	$100.00
Loans O/S	$80.00		
Total Assets	$100.00	Total Liabilities	$100.00

BANK B

Reserves Req.	$16.00	Deposit	80.00
Loans O/S	64.00		
Total Assets	$80.00	Total Liabilities	$80.00

BANK C

Reserves Req.	$12.80	Deposit	$64.00
	51.20		
Total Assets	$64.00	Total Liabilities	$64.00

Figure 11–4

B, the $64.00 in loans become deposits in another bank, Bank C. Bank C also keeps 20 percent in the form of cash reserves to cover deposits, and then loans out the other 80 percent of the deposit, which amounts to $51.20.

This process of turning over money accounts and keeping only the amount needed by law to cover reserves results in that original deposit of $100.00 amounting to nearly $500.00 by the time it percolates through the economic system. With a reserve requirement of 20 percent, that $100.00 cash will become the reserve requirement for loans of which that $100.00 is only 20 percent. The multiplier in that case would be 100/.20 which reduces to 5. Actually, the multiplier is always the reciprocal of the reserve requirement. The 20 percent reserve requirement is the same as a 1/5 reserve requirement. The reciprocal of 1/5 is 5/1 or the whole number 5. The true multiplier will never reach the potential amount because of the infinite amount of time it would take for the transactions to get through such a system so completely. However, the impact of the multiplier can be felt in the relatively short period it takes to perform perhaps three or four transactions. Without the reserve requirement and the capacity to loan excess funds, the banks could not perform the function they do.

From the possible ramifications of the multiplier effect, it can be seen why the addition or subtraction from the money supply is a vitally important subject in the economic circles of a nation or region. For every unit added to the system through monetary expansion or increase of funds through growth of exports, assuming a 20 percent reserve requirement, there is a potential fivefold increase in economic activity and national or regional product.

THE GOLD STANDARD

The United States was officially on the gold standard until 1933. Under the gold standard, money was convertible into gold and gold coins. The supply of money was directly related to the total gold supplies within the country. At this period in the development of the United States, most of the world was also on the gold standard. The fundamental point in the gold standard is that the money supply is not under the exclusive management of the nation of which that currency belongs. The supply of gold in the physical sense has a tremendous impact upon the money supply of those nations whose money may be exchanged for gold. Without gold reserves such money would not be able to be exchanged, and thus would tend to lose its value relative to those currencies that were convertible into gold coin or bullion.

Under the international gold standard, adjustments in the balance of payments between two trading countries would be facilitated by the transfer of gold from one country to the other. The impact of such transfers would be that one country would lose deposits of gold and another country would gain. More than that, however, would be the resulting impact upon the money supply of both countries because of the multiplier effect. The gold exporting country would realize a magnified loss in its internal supply of money, and the economy of such a country would suffer from the sudden and/or severe shortage of credit. It is for these economic reasons that most countries on the gold standard attempted to maintain their exports above their imports.

During the deteriorating periods of the late 1920s and early 1930s attempts by individual countries to maintain their export profile above their imports led to currency devaluations as a last resort. When a nation's exports were falling the influx of gold into the nation would also decline. When gold transfers began to balance in the direction of exports of gold, those nations facing such deposit withdrawals were in a very poor profile. In attempts to make their goods cheaper relative to other countries they would devalue their currency relative to gold. The result would be an increase in exports for the devaluing country, and a resultant increase in gold transfers into the nation's economy. Through the banking system and the multiplier effect, the impact on the economy would constitute a big "shot in the arm."

The major problem with the gold standard as it existed prior to 1935 was the lack of control over the currency of a nation by the government of that nation. The movement of gold from one nation to another was more a function of relative returns and value of currency relative to gold than to the needs of the economy of the nation or nations. In an expanding economy on a global scale, the changes in relative advantage between common nations in the worldwide economy tend to be rather minor and quick changing. It was the long-lasting and severe situation of the depression of 1929 to 1932 that forced the recognition of the inflexibilities inherent in the gold standard as it was defined and used at that time. As one nation was experiencing a serious depression the shifting of gold from one nation to another resulted in the exportation of that depression to other nations. The result was a continuing scene of musical chairs, or "hot potato," in which each country attempted to right its economic condition through a matrix of import controls and devaluation of its currency relative to other countries.

The ultimate impact was the deterioration of public confidence in the financial and monetary management of the nation. Such doubts were first manifested in the stock and investment areas and led from those to the confidence in the banking system as a whole. Much of the ultimate outcome was attributable to the lack of internal management over the nation's money supply, and the lack of financial security measures to qualify and limit risks and speculation assumed by the elements in the banking community at large.

OTHER MONEY SYSTEMS

In addition to the gold standard, there were and are other monetary systems that exist. The United States had what is called a "Bi Metalism" in existence at the time of the international gold standard. We had gold coins and silver coins containing metal content of the same value as the face value of the coins. In addition, we also had the silver and gold certificates in paper money that were convertible into gold and silver depending upon which certificate was converted.

The only other monetary system that has existed in the United States, and exists in most other developed countries of the world, is the paper money system. The fiat paper money system is essentially a money system that has value in the form of purchasing power in exchange rather than value through conversion into some metallic form. The U.S. dollar is simply a dollar, and has value to the extent it is acceptable as means of payment in trade and commerce. The U.S. dollar is not convertible into anything else that can be considered money in the currency form, within the legal boundaries of the United States. The value of the paper money system is a function of the economy of the nation from which it originates, and not from the worth of the substance contained in the instrument or any substance it may be convertible into.

A fiat paper monetary system such as exists in the United States is a money system that provides elasticity to the money supply. The economic activity and health of a nation require that the supply of money be elastic. By elastic, we mean that the money supply can be expanded in times of economic growth and recovery, and that the supply of money may be contracted during times of rapid inflationary pressure and marginal speculation. Because there is a direct relation between the economic and business activity of a country and the supply of capital, it is highly desirable to have a monetary system that is capable of expanding and contracting as needed and indicated by the economic conditions of the time. The paper money system was introduced as a response to the elastic money supply under the international gold standard that led into the depression of the 1930s.

ABANDONMENT OF THE GOLD STANDARD

When the United States went off the international gold standard in 1935, most other nations also left the gold standard. Shortly thereafter the world economic community was embroiled in World War II. It was not until after the war that the International Monetary Fund was established as the central market for establishment of exchange rates for all the currencies of the trading world. Upon leaving the gold standard, most currencies were defined in terms of other currencies and the United States dollar. It was the United States that continued to define the dollar in terms of gold for international payments. The Bretton Woods agreement of the IMF in the middle 1940s added official sanction to the concept of all currencies being defined in terms of the dollar rather than gold or other precious metal. It was also at that same meeting that the dollar was defined in terms of $35 per ounce of gold. Thus, indirectly, all currencies were still defined according to a gold standard. The only difference was that for the purposes of the internal nature of the economy and its people, the United States was off the gold standard. The reason for this was that citizens of the United States were prohibited from keeping in their possession any gold, and that the currency was not convertible into gold for the purposes of the people within the country. The international scene was not the same. With currencies of most other nations defined in terms of the U.S. dollar, and the U.S. dollar defined in terms of gold pegged at $35 an ounce, the world monetary system was still on a modified gold standard.

As a result of this system, most other countries' currencies were adjusted over the years in terms of their relation to the U.S. dollar. The U.S. currency was not readjusted to reflect inflation or deflation from 1935 through 1970. The result of continued worldwide inflation for a period of more than 30 years led to a final confrontation with this dilemma in 1971. At that time the United States made its first adjustment of the dollar relative to gold since 1935. With the dollar pegged at $35 an ounce, and the world market price of gold above $100 an ounce, the United States had to address itself to the issue of a gold standard monetary system in the international realm. The fact that a monetary system cannot be both pegged to gold and at the same time be an elastic currency under management by the federal government was finally presented in terms of its bold realities.

INTEREST RATES AND THE MONEY SUPPLY

Interest represents the price of the use of money either for a short term or a long term. That price is a market-determined value based upon the same supply and demand relationships that prevail in the commodity or service markets. Figure 11–5 depicts a hypothetical market for money. If we assume there is only one market, and only one type of borrowed money in terms of time and increments, such a market would perhaps resemble the graphical market. Just as in all other markets the motivation of buyers is contrary to the motivation on the part of the sellers. In the case at hand, the buyers of loaned money wish to acquire the appropriate amount of money at the lowest cost to themselves. On the graph this is represented by a negatively sloped demand function down and to the right. As the cost is reduced, the demand for funds is greater. The objective of the seller of loanable funds is to maximize the amount he can get for the funds he has available to loan in the market. As a result, the supply function is positive to the

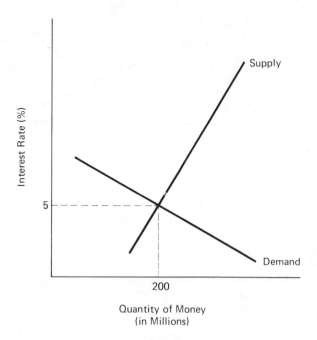

Figure 11–5

right. The supply schedule represents the tendency of higher prices to attract more funds into the market.

This second point is extremely important. The market for loanable or debt money operates in competition with other debt instruments and with the entire gamut of equity capital. The general tendency is that where debt money is earning a rate of return approaching equity capital, there will be a shift from the equity capital into the debt instruments. The reasons are many, but one major factor is clear. Equity capital is higher risk in the general sense than is debt capital. When people are no longer earning a premium for assuming such increased risk they will shift to the less-risky forms of investment that are earning the same or nearly the same rate of return. Probably no other market in the world is as purely competitive as the market for money, both equity and debt, and both long and short terms. As a result, there is constantly a shifting of prices in both the equity and debt markets that reflects the competitiveness of this particular market. The actions of the monetary and fiscal authorities in the federal government have great impact upon the market in a relatively short period of time because of the sensitivity of this particular market.

Figure 11–6 illustrates the concept of short-term and long-term money actually comprising two different markets. Generally, the long-term money markets demand higher prices in the form of interest rates than do the short-term markets. The increased risk associated with the longer terms is the primary reason for the higher rates. When-

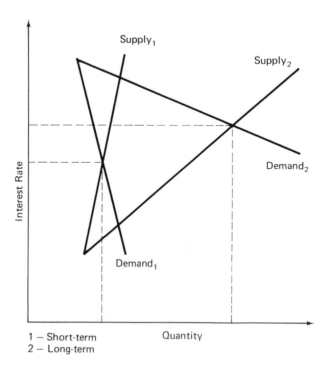

1 — Short-term
2 — Long-term

Figure 11–6

ever the price of short-term money approaches the price of longer-term money, there will be a rather dramatic shift from the long-term market to the short-term market.

The shift of money from the longer-term markets into the shorter-term markets is dramatic in the real estate sector at times. This is particularly true when the short-term money rates become higher than what are currently being earned on longer-term money, often running 20 or 30 times longer than the short-term money market. The competitiveness and the activity in the money markets is so acute that competition becomes very refined and the market very sensitive. As a consequence, minor changes in the comparative rates of return between short-term and long-term commitments in the money markets have dramatic impact upon the volume of funds shifting from one to the other.

Under the gold standard, the supply of money in the nation was relatively fixed. The adjustments that were made in the money supply were more the result of international trade than concerted effort on the part of the government. The money supply was not manageable in terms of its being able to expand or contract according to the needs of the country's economy. As a consequence, rather dramatic swings occurred in the interest rates and rather frequent and severe economic recessions prior to the period of the Great Depression. Under the current system of managed paper standard within the United States itself, the money supply can and is expanded and contracted as the nation's economy dictates. As a result of the managed paper currency system, the economic fluctuations in the United States national economy have been fewer and less severe than previously under the gold standard. Interest rates continue, however, to be market determined and rather sensitive to changing condition in terms and maturity rates of return in alternative investment forms. The underlying principle of interest rates being a market-determined price for the use of money remains the heart of the money market and the movements of private capital.

REFERENCES

1—Balassa, Bela, ed. *Changing Patterns in Foreign Trade and Payments.* New York: W. W. Norton Co., 1970.

2—Barger, Harold. *Money, Banking and Public Policy.* Chicago: Rand McNally, Inc., 1962.

3—Chandler, Lester. *The Economics of Money and Banking.* 6th ed. New York: Harper-Row, Inc., 1973.

HISTORY OF REAL ESTATE FINANCE (PRIOR TO 1930)

NEED FOR CREDIT

It will be recalled that in Chapter 2 we discussed the four major factors that make real estate unique as an economic good. One of those four factors was the large economic units required in real estate transactions. Because real estate generally is available only in large dollar units, there is a corresponding need for refined financial instruments to aid in the transactions involving real estate. In the majority of instances the potential buyers of real property do not possess the capacity to pay the total agreed upon price in cash at the time of sale. In the earlier development of the real estate industry, the need for financing was not wholly met by the financial institutions and policies existing in the period prior to the 1930s. As a result, the market for ownership and sale of real property was not fully developed in terms of the size of the ownership population.

BANKING AND SAVINGS

Commercial banking in the traditional sense was focused primarily upon fulfilling the needs of the world of commerce and industry. Real estate was not a fundamental part of the commercial banking industry, in much the same proportion that residential real estate is not the major element in the commercial banking industry of today. The savings banks that existed prior to the 1930s were even then a major element in real estate and land ownership segments of the economy. There were some major differences between savings banks of that time and those of today.

Although the Federal Reserve system came into existence in the early 1900s, it concentrated its functions upon the commercial banks and banking system at the exclusion of the savings industry. Even in the commercial banking segment the Federal Reserve system was not as clearly defined and did not regulate nearly as closely the commercial banking segment until after the depression of 1930. Nevertheless, the Federal Reserve system made the commercial banking system a national organization. As a wide network of national cooperation to some extent the commercial banks did enjoy some coordination on the national level with each other.

The savings industry was not so fortunate. The many savings banks in the nation were essentially independent and totally isolated as far as their banking functions were concerned. Savings banks were essentially local in nature, and very little interregional or interstate cooperation existed in the savings industry. There was no central bank set up in the savings industry comparable to the Federal Reserve system of the commercial banks. Savings banks drew their deposits from the local economy and in turn marketed their loans in the same local area. Facilities for transfer of funds into or out of a local savings area were largely absent until after 1930.

Mechanics of Savings and
the Multiplier Effect

The savings banks operating prior to 1930 were limited to the immediate economic area and/or political jurisdiction of which they were a part. This characteristic limited the impact of savings and investment on the economy of most of the nation. The one major characteristic was the elimination of the capacity for a multiplier effect as existed in the more organized commercial banking system discussed in the previous chapter. Table 12–1 illustrates the mechanics of savings and investment in the savings banks and the savings and loan associations prior to the 1930s.

As in the commercial banks, a deposit by a customer must be backed by a fixed ratio of a reserve requirement. In Table 12–1 the reserve requirement is 20 percent. The remaining 80 percent of the original deposit is still available for loans, or may be kept in the form of cash on hand in the bank. Since loans and investments earn a return for the bank the amount of money beyond the reserve requirement is normally invested in government securities or in loans to customers. In the case of real estate loans, prior

TABLE 12–1
Savings and Loan Bank A

Reserve Requirement	$ 20	$100 deposit
Mortgage Loan	80	
	$100	$100

to the early 1930s, although they earned a return for the bank, they were not subject to the expansion under the multiplier effect. The major point in the above example is that the $80 in the form of a mortgage or real estate loan is not subject to being deposited in another bank. The entire process of money flow is confined to the area being served by Bank A in the example. If the local area is rather slow in terms of real estate activity, then the $80 would go into forms of investment other than real estate. If the local real estate market is extremely active, it is limited to the proportionate amount of new deposits that are available for loans. There is no capacity for Bank A to sell the loans initiated and generate more capital for further loan commitment.

The reasons behind such limitations are several. First, there was no formal central banking system for the savings and loan industry. The physical capacity to cooperate was missing from the industry. Second, there was no uniform accounting system throughout the savings and loan industry that was well supervised and implemented. There were great differences between individual banks in loan policies, appraisal and value estimates, in terms, and throughout nearly all of the banking policies and procedures of the individual banks in the savings and loan industry. As a result, there was no functioning system by which money from capital-rich regions could be moved to capital-poor areas where demand for funds was in excess of the amount of money available for loans.

Prior to the early 1930s, the only organized system on the national level was the Federal Reserve system. It came into existence in the middle teens, only a few years prior to the depression era of the 1930s. The nation was on the formal international gold standard, as were most of the other major trading countries of the world. The savings banks and the savings and loan associations that were in existence were primarily under state jurisdiction and confined to fulfilling the local needs of their areas and drawing capital from the same local area.

REAL ESTATE PRIOR TO 1930

The characteristics of real estate as a commodity in the market place were the same prior to 1930 as they are now. The extent of private home ownership and the percentage of the population with enough capital resources at its command have certainly changed since that time. But one of the major factors that makes real estate unique as an economic commodity exchanged in the market place is the magnitude of the investment required in nearly all real estate situations. Because the price of even small and modest real estate products is rather high relative to other commodities, there is now and was then a basic necessity for credit and financing in the exchange of real estate services. As a consequence, the demand for financing in the real estate market increased with the passage of time and the growth in the nation and its economy.

Real Estate Financing
Prior to 1930

The details of financing in the real estate market were quite different in the period before 1930 than what we know as the real estate financial markets of the current day. The first fact was that only conventional loans existed at that time. Such factors as government-subsidized loans and various mortgage and loan insurance programs that we tend to take for granted in today's world were not in existence until after 1930. As a result of all loans being conventional, the advantages and lower costs associated with the more contemporary loan programs were missing and not available to the real estate market of the pre-1930 era.

Just as conventional loans have higher equity requirements than other loan programs, in the current market practices, so did the conventional loans of pre-1930. Because of the increased risk due to the lack of the loan insurance programs of today, the conventional loans of the 1930 era required higher equity positions by the purchaser. Loans were common that were for only 40 to 60 percent of the value of the subject property. Rarely were conventional loans initiated for more than 60 to 70 percent of the value.

Without federal government involvement in the real estate financing area with underwriting and mortgage insurance programs, the risk involved in such financial arrangements are generally greater. As with most other instances in which risks run higher, higher interest rates generally persist. So, as in the pre-1930 era, the risks were greater, and the capacity on the part of the savings banking system was less in its ability to assume such risks, ending with the result that interest rates were relatively high when compared to the whole history of real estate mortgages and loans.

In addition to the interest being rather high, reflecting the higher risks associated with an uninsured loan, the term of the average real estate loan or mortgage was considerably shorter than that to be found common now. The role of the federal government in the monetary policy and economy of the country, as well as the role of gold in the international trading scene, contributed to the rather frequent and severe fluctuations in the economic condition of the country and the world's trading complex. With such dramatic fluctuations being common, the risks of very long term loans were far beyond the normal business risks that the savings and commercial banks could assume. The shorter term of the real estate loans was also combined with a trend of nonamortized loans. Many loans were 10 to 15 years in length, with interest-only payments during the life of the loan and the principal of the loan due at the end of the term. Although the annual payments may in fact have been lower because of the interest only nature, very few persons were in the capacity to pay in full at the end of the loan period.

The major faith for payment of the loan as well as the major consideration for the initiation of such loans was the value of the real estate involved and not the personal financial characteristics of the persons buying the land under question. The major commitment was in the belief that the value of the property at the end of the term of the loan would be more than adequate to cover the loan principal. As a result, there was very little emphasis placed upon the ability of the purchaser to cover the loan and the payments. The assumption was that there was little or no chance of the value of real property ever falling. Generally, that assumption may not be too risky if on a national scale and over a very long period of time in a growing economy and nation. However, in specific instances and localities over the short life of most term loans in real estate, such assumptions were risky indeed. In addition, when the borrower was mostly ignored in the loan process the property was overemphasized in terms of its importance in the profitability of the loans. In the instances where property values fell the amount of the debt would tend to exceed the value of the real property. Such cases would virtually guarantee a loss to the banking system behind such loan portfolios.

The final lending characteristic of the pre-1930 era was the great number of junior or second loans on real properties exchanged. The low loan-to-value ratios of the first loans fell short of the total financing required by the purchasers in the real estate market. The second loans were even higher in interest rate than the first loans, which tended to be rather high, and they also tended to be more marginal in terms of the capacity of the purchaser. In terms of the foreclosure rates in the early 1930s, the second loans were the first to go into default, and were, therefore, the ones most likely involved in the foreclosure. Part of the foreclosure rate in the 1930s could be attributable to the marginal and rather common use of secondary financing in the real estate area prior to 1930.

Economic Implications of Pre-1930 Lending Practices

Conventional loans in the real estate sector limited the total market for real estate in that the high equity requirements prevented more than a few potential buyers from entering the market place for real estate. Furthermore, without the advantages of various loan insurance and subsidy programs we now expect in the real estate industry, the risks were often higher than would otherwise be the case. With those higher risks came the accompanied higher interest rates. These too tended to limit the market for real estate.

Term loans had some far reaching impacts on the economics of the real estate industry. First, the term loans were rather short term. With the life of the real estate loan or mortgage running 10 to 15 years at most, the monthly burden in terms of support was very high. Second, the terms of the loans were so short that amortization was virtually impossible for all but the very wealthy. As a result, most loans were interest only until the end of the loan. The interest payments varied widely from monthly fixed payments on interest to annual payments tied into the productivity of the land as in agricultural areas. At the completion of the loan period, the entire principal amount of the loan would often be due in full.

As a result of the terms of the loans, and the absence of amortizing the principal over the life of the loan, the principal payment in full at the term of the loans was not always possible. In most instances, the borrowers expected to be able to refinance the principal amount of the debt at the due date. Such built-in optimism was indeed admirable; however, it proved also to be quite foolish in the underlying assumption of continued growth and availability of financing. What happened to those term loans that fell due in the early 1930s? There were no sources of adequate capital, and the profitability of many segments of the economy had deteriorated to the point that even where money was available, the profits needed to pay the interest and principal were not apparent. As a consequence, those properties that had debt falling due were simply abandoned and the banks suddenly found themselves without money but with a lot of rather depressed collateral.

Because of the interest-only features of the majority of real estate loans during the pre-1930 era, the principal amount of debt was never or rarely reduced by those owners of such real estate assets. As a result, the majority of property owners were never out of debt. In essence, the typical property owner buying property over time actually never obtained a clear title to the property because of the never reduced debt. The result was not much different from a typical leasehold interest in real property. In the event of an unprofitable operation of a real property interest such as agricultural land, the owner would simply abandon his property interest, which had not increased in equity through the reduction of the debt. Also, in the event of a failure to refinance the debt at the end of the term loan, many owners simply let the banks take the property.

Economic Implications of the Structural Differences

Real estate by its very nature tends to be unique as an economic good, as was discussed in Chapter 2. The four factors of long life, large economic units, fixed location and long-term decisions account for the major uniqueness of the real estate product in the market place. The size of the commitment, the long life of the product and commitment, and the lack of mobility all had serious implications in the economy and lending practices prior to 1930, and the dominance of the international gold standard also conflicted with the nature of real estate itself.

The monetary structure under the gold standard was subject to rather frequent fluctuations and there was a major lack of management on the part of the individual governments under the gold standard. Gold going out of or into a country at that time would shortly have an impact upon the basic money supply of the nation. As the supply of funds fluctuates, so does the price level of the nation's exports and general economy. Such swings in the economy could and often did have rather dramatic impact upon the productivity and economics of real estate. These temporary short-term, and occasionally long-term, fluctuations were common in the economy prior to 1930. In addition, the banking system in the United States was quite provincial in character. The savings industry segment of banking was even more provincial and limited in scope. Each savings bank operated relatively separately from the rest of the banking industry. Each bank was essentially confined to its own local area both in terms of deposits and in terms of its loan customers. As such, the banking system was oriented in the same short-term perspective as the national monetary system and the economics of the times.

Real estate by its very nature is committed to the long-term perspective. The real estate asset has a very long life, which rules out its capacity to adjust to short-term changes. The decisions relating to the use of real estate are long-term decisions also. These decisions on the part of the consumer of real estate services include those decisions relating to the financial aspects of the real estate product also. In addition, the relatively large scale of real estate in terms of the dollar magnitude places heavy emphasis upon the ability or lack of it to finance purchases and exchanges through debt.

Real estate is intimately connected to the economy of which it is a vital part. Real estate is also closely married to the financial profile of the nation of which it is a part. As a result, insofar as the world and national monetary system and economy were magnified in the short term, and real estate by its nature is magnified in the long term, it is not difficult to see what contributed to the spread and depth of the depression in the 1930 to 1933 era.

CONCLUSIONS OF THE 1930 ERA

One of the first facts that became evident as a result of the depression of 1929–1931 was the vulnerability of the real estate sector to such shifts in the economic profile of a nation. Granted, there were some natural turns in fortune, such as the dust bowl of the midwest, that contributed to the plight of real estate activity. However, some of the basic elements of the real estate sector were major contributions to the extent of the depression. Such elements as the never-reducing debt, high interest rates, nonamortized loans, and the short terms of real estate loans in general were all major contributors to the fall of real estate during the depression era. The vulnerability of the real estate sector to such elements in the national and local economy were certainly underscored by the depression.

The second and most major conclusion of the depression experience was the importance of real estate as a mainstay of our entire economy. It was made quite clear that real estate ownership and productivity were one of the foundations of our national health, both financially and physically. As a result of such a lesson, it was also recognized that if the national economy was to recover from such adverse economic events as the depression, the viability of the real estate sector would have to be one of the major elements in such recovery. As a result, it became clear that the federal government had a vital stake in the health of the real estate sector of our economy. Furthermore, that recovery would necessitate some immediate action in the real estate area.

Third, the role of federal government could no longer be confined to subtle transactions relating to federal acquisition and disbursement of lands, but rather, would have to be explicit and direct in the activity and augmentation of the real estate sector of our economy. The financial areas relating to real estate were too important to the health of such a vital part of the nation's economy to allow the financial sector to impede the growth and operation of the real estate sector. It was recognized that the real estate sector required a stable and secure financial base. The monetary and fiscal policies of the federal government were very much at the center of such a financial system. Consequently, many of the modifications in the financial and banking markets were attempts to stabilize those sectors and such stabilization would aid in the recovery of the real estate sector. Such situations of overheated expansion and speculation on margin and the leverage factor employed to such an extent as it was, simply were recognized as detriments to a sound and stable banking industry. A stable banking industry was fundamental to the health of the nation, and to the real estate segment of the national economy, which constituted one of the pillars of the democratic world.

REFERENCES

1—Bogen, Jules I. et. al., eds. *Financial Handbook.* 4th ed. New York: The Ronald Press, 1968.

2—Bryant, Willis R. *Mortgage Lending: Trends and Practices.* New York: McGraw-Hill, Inc., 1962.

3—Hoagland, H. E. and Stone, Leo D. *Real Estate Finance.* 4th ed. Homewood, Ill.: Richard D. Irwin Co., 1969.

4—Wiedemer, John P. *Real Estate Finance.* Reston, Va.: Reston Publishing Co., 1974.

MODERN REAL ESTATE FINANCE (POST–1930)

THE ROLE OF THE FEDERAL GOVERNMENT

In the early 1930s, under President Hoover, the federal government was faced with the major task of stimulating the economy out of the depression. Until this period in our history the role of the federal government in the real estate sector had been rather subtle and quiet. Though it acquired lands in the movement west, and opened those lands to development through the various homestead land rushes, the federal government had not explicitly declared what its objectives were in relation to the real estate of the country. Under President Hoover, however, the federal government was specifically addressing itself to the task of getting the national economy back into shape. At that time the credit and financing institutions in the real estate related sectors were near total collapse, and the general unemployment picture was indeed grim. Nearly one out of four persons was unemployed at the depth of the depression, and many others were able to find only part-time and marginally productive employment.

As a result of the situation that faced the nation at that time, the federal government stated that one of its major objectives in participating in the real estate sector was to get the national economy back on its feet. One of the notable features of such a statement was the recognition that real estate was indeed one of the basic elements in the overall health of the national economy. When the real estate sector of an economy is in poor condition, the tendency is that the economy itself will soon follow. In addition, the real estate sector is the first area of any recovery for most economic downturns. Improving the real estate sector was recognized as one area where the impact upon the rest of the economy and supportive industries could and would play a major part in any recovery effort on the part of the federal government.

Since the savings and loan industry was the primary financial support of the real estate sector, it was the first area to receive the attention in terms of definitive and concrete programs. The importance of finance to real estate, as has been discussed in the preceding chapter, was so basic to the industry that nothing else was thought to work if the confidence in the financial institutions was not restored first. As a result of this thinking, the Home Loan Bank System was established.

THE FEDERAL HOME LOAN BANK SYSTEM

One of the fundamental shortcomings of the banking industry prior to 1930 was the localization of the savings and loan industry. There was the rather general tendency of savings banks to be local in their capacity to borrow as well as lend. Unlike the commercial banks, which had the Federal Reserve system, there was no central bank for the savings and loans. In 1932, the Home Loan Bank System was created to help solve the abuses and problems leading to the general failure of the banking system in the 1929–1931 period. The system consisted of 12 federal home loan banks that supervised and regulated the savings and loan member banks. The major element of the system was a systematic ability to transfer funds from one savings and loan bank to another, and the ability to provide advances to member banks in the event of temporary liquidity crises. The impact of these two measures was significant. First, the advances prevented panic withdrawals of funds beyond the cash reserves on hand at the local banks. Through advances from the federal home loan bank, the local savings bank could meet such sudden cash demands without failing, as had happened to many banks before the program.

The second major element was the ability to loan funds from a capital-rich bank to a capital-poor bank, thereby enhancing the ability of the entire system to meet the national financing needs, particularly in the real estate financing area. The addition of the Home Owners Loan Corporation in 1933 allowed an arm of the FHLB to buy mortgages threatened with foreclosure and thus shore up the position of the savings and loans that might otherwise be threatened with losses due to foreclosure.

In 1934 the Federal Savings and Loan Insurance Corporation was first established, with the purpose of insuring the funds of depositors in case of a bank failure. It was essentially the same as the FDIC, which insures the deposits of commercial banks. The importance of the savings and loan industry to the viability of the real estate sector was the major factor in these decisions. It was recognized that just increasing employment was not sufficient to rehabilitate the real estate sector. The entire financial support structure that lubricates the exchange of real property was seen as a fundamental aspect of economic recovery in real estate.

NATIONAL HOUSING ACT OF 1934

The importance of finance in the real estate sector was seen also in terms of the instruments used in the financial arrangements involving exchange and sale of real property. The National Housing Act of 1934 was probably one of the most visible programs involving financing in real property. It was through this act that the Federal Housing Administration (FHA) was established. It will be recalled that the terms of real estate loans prior to 1930 were much different from what is common in today's real estate industry. The FHA was mostly responsible for those changes.

The first element in the FHA program was the insurance of the mortgage by an arm of the federal government to reduce the risks associated with real estate loans. As a result of the reduced risk the terms of real estate loans changed in length, interest rate and structure. Loans were extended beyond five to ten years, and loans of 20 and 25 years became more common. Also, with the lower risk the demands were reduced for higher returns through interest rates. The lower interest rates were fundamental to the success of the program. Last, the loans were no longer structured as term loans with interest-only payments until term. The newer loans were more fully amortized over the life of the loan so that the buyer was actually building up his equity and reducing his debt over the life of the loan. As a result, the lump sum payments in full principal at the end of the loan were no longer common. There was also the tendency to increase the loan-to-value ratio to a more realistic figure, primarily because of the insurance factor and the reduced risk. The total impact was the near elimination of second and third loans at high interest rates, and the need for total refinancing at the end of a rather short term. The characteristics of the real estate financing support were more nearly like the basic long-term characteristics of the real estate product itself.

Other Elements of
the FHA Program

Some additional elements of the FHA program had rather significant impact upon the real estate industry and the financial support that it generated in the period after 1930. Although many of these elements were not in the area of financing directly, they were significant in terms of their impact upon the financial health of the industry. The most significant of all elements of the FHA program was the insured mortgage concept. The lower risk associated with real estate loans was fundamental to recovery.

Another element of the FHA program was the emphasis placed upon the person borrowing the money. Prior to 1930, the emphasis was solely upon the property securing the loan. The value of the property and the future potential of such property value was the sole basis of the loan. As a result, the capacity of the buyer to pay the loan was ignored, as was his character. Additionally, the widespread use of second and third loans upon real estate further complicated the financing of most real estate transactions. We know today that the credibility of the buyer is a vitally important element in the estimation of the total risk in any given loan situation. Such factors associated with risk were nearly totally ignored in the lending practices prior to 1930. The FHA program set certain standards in regard to the profile of the potential buyer and borrower. Such factors as employment record and character, annual income, monthly take-home income and total other debts incurred on the part of the borrower became part of the normal loan procedure and qualifications for certain loan and risk limits.

The estimate of value prior to 1930 was highly subjective and local in application and technique. There were no general standards for the appraisal industry to follow that were consistent and uniform throughout the country. As a result, only those familiar with the local areas and values in real estate at the local level would be in the position to loan funds in such a market. Through the stimulus of the FHA programs, and the requirements that such qualifications had to be met before such loans would be covered under the mortgage insurance programs of the FHA, the financial community in real estate began to accept the criteria put out initially through the FHA. Such items as number of bedrooms and bathrooms, number of square feet, type of plumbing and wiring, conforming to zoning and land use regulations, the type of material used in construction and many other elements in the basic structure itself and the land associated with that structure were becoming part of the basic value analysis. Additionally, the format of the value estimate, the appraisal report, was also basically outlined in the FHA requirements for information. As a result of such impetus on the part of the FHA and the federal government, some uniformity began to emerge in the appraisal industry and the national approach to valuation of the real estate sector.

Such standards for the value estimate were basic to the ultimate success of the real estate sector to recover from the depths of the depression that hit real estate so hard. It was recognized that real estate was a national concern and that the recovery of the nation partially depended upon the ability of the real estate sector to recover. As a national concern, it also became apparent that the solution to part of the real estate situation would come from the national perspective. If the financing of real estate was to have the necessary national access that it required, it was fundamental to that issue that the appraisal approaches to value for such financing were necessary. The FHA program, for being the first attempt of the federal government to directly enter the real estate industry, was almost surprisingly successful. That success was not the result of only the direct programs such as mortgage insurance, but equally of the other stimulus in the financing and appraisal areas that were and are at the heart of the real estate sector.

THE FEDERAL NATIONAL MORTGAGE ASSOCIATION

FNMA was also part of the federal government's intent in the 1934 Housing Act. Although incorporated in 1938, FNMA was part of the same scene that produced the FHA. The role of the FNMA was and is to provide a market through which the mortgages insured through the FHA could be both bought and sold. FNMA provides those market facilities required for such exchange to take place. Its major role is to keep funds in the market for residential real estate activity. The FNMA is primarily a wholesale or behind-the-scenes type of entity. The public consumer or borrower does not come in contact with the FNMA. FNMA deals mostly as a federal government central bank in many ways. Although a private corporation, it sells bonds to raise capital with which it buys the mortgages from the savings and loans that wish to sell their loan portfolio to raise more capital to lend at the retail level.

THE OBJECTIVES OF THE THREE MAJOR ELEMENTS BORN IN 1930

Perhaps one of the easiest ways to illustrate the interrelationships of the programs born out of the 1930s would be simply to look at their basic objectives. First, the FHA had three basic objectives: (1) to attract mortgage money into the market, (2) to help establish a secondary mortgage market, and (3) to help meet other socially desirable goals and objectives. The FNMA had two basic objectives: (1) to provide a secondary mortgage market and (2) to attract funds into the mortgage market from non-real estate entities. The FHLB had three major objectives: (1) to make advances to member savings and loans as needed, (2) to examine and supervise the management and accounting practices of members, and (3) to help provide for a secondary mortgage market.

Although all three placed particular emphasis upon certain elements in the national real estate financing market, and each was delegated such responsibility in their creation, it is interesting to note that all three had some goal in one common element of the real estate financing area. All three elements had one eye on the secondary mortgage market, and the other eye on the particular segment they were active in. The importance of the secondary mortgage market cannot be more emphasized than through such concentration of effort on the part of the federal government.

ROLE OF CREDIT AND THE
SECONDARY MORTGAGE MARKET

Because of the very nature of real estate being such that it nearly always requires some extension of credit to accomplish the exchange in the market place, the availability of credit is at the very heart of real estate in the nation. As was seen in the analysis of the conditions that existed in the real estate financial markets prior to 1930, the inflexibility of the credit mechanism and the localization of financial resources are too severe of restraints to a healthy and active real estate industry. The role of real estate in terms of the national economy and the economic health of the nation is such that action to eliminate imperfections is almost mandatory for the national good.

Because of the national importance and scope of real estate, it is a most obvious fact that financing of such an element of our economy must also be national in scope and nature. For financing to become national, the measurement of risk and value, the methodology of appraisal and the flow of funds should be relatively uniform throughout the nation. It was with the flow of funds in mind that the secondary mortgage market takes on such monumental importance. Since real estate markets, just as other markets, do not move uniformly throughout the nation, it is important to have a system whereby adjustments can occur in the markets throughout the nation without depressing the national market as a result. Those areas where the market demand for housing and real estate services is active must have some way of satisfying their financing needs. The ability of the local bank to sell its loan portfolio in the market place and realize more cash funds with which to continue to meet the demands of the local area it is in, is a basic ability required for the health of the real estate sector. The ability to transfer funds from one area with excess cash and low loan demand to other areas of low cash and high loan demand is fundamental to the nature of the national real estate industry.

In effect, the secondary mortgage market makes the market for real estate loans financing a national market. As the entire country and its people benefit from the real estate industry, the entire nation through the secondary mortgage market mechanism is involved in the flow of funds from one region or area to another on the basis of demand and ability. The role of the appraisal standards and the regulation of the financial agents involved cannot be ignored. Nor can the impact of insured mortgages and the reduction of risk associated with them. But such programs would be nearly entirely non-effectual if a national secondary mortgage market could not be established and maintained. As a result of this recognition, all three of the major agencies growing out of the depression accepted the development of a secondary mortgage market as part of their function and responsibility.

THE ERA OF THE 1940s AND FINANCING

In 1944 the federal government entered a new phase of involvement in the real estate sector by instituting programs aimed at specific problems in the real estate sector. The passage of the GI Bill of Rights included the veterans' loan guarantee program. Under the administration of the Veterans' Administration, a veteran of military service could borrow up to 100 percent of the cost of a new home and have the loan guaranteed by the insurance provisions under the GI Bill of Rights. The need to provide housing for the thousands of returning veterans and their families was what the program was addressing. As a result of the programs instituted through the Veterans' Administration, the production of housing in the post-World War II era reached an all-time high in the late 1940s.

In 1949 another housing act was passed expressing the interest and intent of the federal government in the real estate sector. Although there had been several programs dealing with the need for public housing and low-income housing for the poor, there had not been a national move in this direction until the early 1950s. In the Housing Act of 1949 the federal government stated its second major goal in the real estate area. It will be recalled that the first declaration was to get the economy back on its feet in the 1930s. In the Housing Act of 1949, the federal government declared its intent to assure a "decent home for every American family." It must be recognized that this is far more ambiguous and political than the more specific economic declaration of the 1930s.

From the early 1950s until the present time the government has been addressing itself to various elements of the decent home goal. The poor, the discriminated, the aged and the young have been the objects of various programs since the passage of the 1949 bill. The underlying issue behind such programs has been the fact that certain elements of our national population lack the economic resources necessary to own and maintain a home adequate for their needs. To such an extent that these conditions are the result of a conscious or unconscious discrimination on the part of the financial community toward or away from certain geographic areas, then such specific abuses can be addressed by the federal and state government programs in the real estate sector. However, where such inability on the part of the population to secure adequate housing is a function of their lack of economic resources, then it is at least questionable whether specific real estate programs can rectify the problem.

In the economic sense, when an individual does not have the money with which to enter the market place and purchase enough to fulfill his needs, it would seem that the focus should be upon enabling that individual to reach an adequate income level so that he or she may fill their needs. Such a focus upon the educational and employment elements of the nation would not be nearly so identifiable as the real estate sector.

THE HOUSING ACT OF 1954

Although the Housing Act of 1954 essentially endorsed the programs of the previous two major acts, it did make one major innovation. In addition to endorsing the FNMA and the efforts in the slum clearance and urban renewal programs, the 1954 Act required that all local agencies have a workable master plan in terms of land use for their respective regions before they could be eligible to receive funds from the various federal programs. This was the first time that a master planning concept in terms of urban growth was mandated by a federal agency. In the act were various items referring to uniform building codes, adherence to zoning regulations and fire standards. Relocation and financing were also discussed in the content of the 1954 Act. However, the master plan requirement was the single most far-reaching element of the act. In most instances, the building codes, fire regulations and the municipal zoning restrictions were each implemented and administered by a separate entity without much coordination and communication between each of the separate segments. As a result, land use patterns and the growth of the urban areas were relatively unregulated in terms of an overall planning. The fact that most areas now have master plans in terms of land use, and that such master plans are periodically updated and revised, is the result of the Housing Act of 1954.

SUPPLY OF MORTGAGE MONEY

The basic prerequisite to any loanable funds is the accumulation of wealth. There must exist those individuals and organizations that have accumulated wealth in the form of money or near-money assets before there are assets for anyone in need of capital to borrow. In the developed societies such assets are in terms of money, and are usually on deposit in various financial institutions. The underlying concept is that there must first be savings or the accumulation of wealth by individuals and businesses before there can be any borrowing. Savings on the part of individuals and businesses is the sole basic source of loanable funds in any economic system.

With savings as the sole source of loanable funds, it is apparent that such savings must be beyond the needs of the normal business fluctuations and cycles before there are funds that could be committed for the long terms normally involved in the real estate sector of the economy. The size of the demand for funds in the real estate sector in addition to the length of the loan periods place unusual demands upon the financial markets of a country. Referring to Chapter 2, it will be recalled that real estate debt in the United States was nearly equal to the total national debt of the federal government. Such magnitudes are indeed great in their impact upon the financial capacity of a nation. The savings by businesses and individuals must be rather well managed and a national banking system must be rather well established for such funds of that large a magnitude to be accumulated and invested in debt form throughout the entire real estate sector of the economy.

SOURCES OF CREDIT IN CURRENT REAL ESTATE

Conceptually, any agent or institution through which money is or can be accumulated constitutes a possible source of funds for investment in the real estate sector. The banking industry has traditionally been looked upon as the primary source of mortgage capital. Commercial banks concentrate their efforts in the commercial and industrial sectors of our economy and in the real estate financing associated with those sectors. The savings and loan industry has been highly concentrated in the residential real estate sector since the early 1930s. In addition to the banking industry, however, a growing list of sources for real estate capital would include:

Insurance companies

Pension and trust funds

Credit unions

Investment groups and clubs

REITs

Partnerships

Limited partnerships

Syndications

Governmental programs

Insurance companies accumulate large fund accounts with which to insure the payouts that may occur in the future. Generally, they are active in the construction financing phase of real estate in the larger projects. Pension and trust funds also do some construction financing, but they are also quite big in the investment property area of real estate. Credit unions provide limited small loans for members to buy home improvements and modest real estate purchases.

Real estate investment trusts were not a major factor in the real estate field until the Internal Revenue Service changed their tax situation in 1968. At that time it was upheld that the "conduit" theory of taxation should apply to funds in REIT, which pass through the trust into the hands of the investors. If 90 percent or more of the funds received by the REIT are passed directly to the investors in the trust, then the funds are not taxed while in the trust. As a result of the change in tax situation, the REITs have grown tremendously since that time. From a few million dollars invested in such funds, the total is more than a billion dollars within five years from the change in tax status. REITs concentrate their efforts in the medium-size investment properties and some agricultural lands.

Small partnerships provide the scale of investment to the partners that could not be accomplished as individuals. Partnerships exist in many areas of real estate, but are rather small in terms of the size of the projects. Syndicated partnerships generally are larger than simple partnerships and include upwards of 100 limited partners and one general partner. They, too, focus on the medium-size investment properties and speculative land acquisitions.

Finally, there are specific governmental programs to gain desired social benefits that finance private enterprise projects. Such programs as Model Cities, Small Business Administration and specific programs for the benefit of economic disadvantaged make funds available to those who may not otherwise be able to compete in the more restrictive financial markets.

Types of Real Estate Credit

The various forms that real estate credit may take are quite common and not difficult to understand or to describe. Such documents as mortgages, trust deeds, land and land sales contracts, real estate trust certificates, sale and leasebacks, long-term leases and a variety of smaller, more individualized credit forms are common types of real estate credit forms that are used.

What is more fundamental to the understanding of the forms various real estate or edict arrangements take in the market place is that the market forces within the financial and real estate markets will always adjust in the details of the instruments to meet the demands of the consumers and sellers of money in the financial markets. As the real estate market has become more refined and more complex in the period since the late 1930s, so the forms of financing in the real estate field have become more refined. As the needs of the various investors in real estate and the types of real estate properties that are exchanged in the market place have changed, so too has the list of forms and types of real estate financing also changed to meet the more complex requirements.

THE FUTURE OF REAL ESTATE FINANCE

As the values associated with real estate in the more developed areas of the world have escalated in the past 30 years, the quality of estate interests has come to include a wide range of interests. The quality of interest in real property can be looked upon as an element of the financial profile of real estate. The growing importance of leasehold properties, condominium residential and commercial projects, planned developments and the sale and leaseback arrangements all lower the burden of cost on the purchaser and consumer of real estate services. The bundle of rights associated with real estate has begun to be broken into smaller bundles of rights that can be more readily exchanged in the market place. Such trends in property interests will continue as long as the total costs that are associated with real estate continue to reach the upper limits of what the majority of potential consumers of real estate services can afford to commit themselves to.

Additionally, the role of government and private enterprise in meeting social goals in a cooperative effort will continue and increase in the future as such needs become more identifiable. The role of the federal government in designing specific programs to meet some of the specific and individual problems in the whole area of real estate finance will continue into the future. The importance of real estate as a national element in our economy dictates that the role of real estate will also be a significant national interest in the years to come. Although the whole real estate financial mechanism does not operate entirely perfectly at present, the efforts on the part of federal and state governments and the principles within the real estate financial market itself will continue to focus upon improving the efficiency of the financial market.

REFERENCES

1—Pugh, J. W. and Hippaka, W. A. *California Real Estate Finance.* 2nd ed. Englewood Cliffs, N.J.: Prentice-Hall, Inc., 1973.

2—Wiedemer, John P. *Real Estate Finance.* Reston, Va.: Reston Publishing Co., 1974.

PART

SPECIAL AREAS
OF CONCERN

Although many areas relating to real estate have not been treated in the text, some areas of special study should be discussed that do not fall within the format of the preceding chapters. The first area of such study is the role of real estate as an investment medium. Under such objectives the evaluation of real estate and the motivation of the participants is significantly different from that found in the areas covered so far. The role of investment analysis and the tools and techniques employed by the investment analyst are significantly different from those to be found in the more traditional approaches to real estate. The more contemporary approaches of Present Value Analysis and Internal Rate of Return Analysis are relatively specialized techniques of investment evaluation that are not common to the general nature of the real estate market. The role of competing investment alternatives and evaluation of alternative investment strategies in the investment sector of the real estate market dictate that such methods should be discussed.

The role of the production process in real estate and the role that such process plays in the overall economy is of increasing concern on the part of various public and private sectors of our economy. The complexities of the production process and the structural problems that contribute to its problems are of specific concern. The increased attention paid to the national and regional needs to provide better and lower-cost housing facilities is another reason for the following discussion. The current trends in terms of costs associated with the production process also point to the increased concern to be paid to this area of the real estate sector.

The final chapter reviews the role of the federal government and its participation in the real estate sector directly. The role of participation on the part of the public sector, and more particularly the federal government, seems to be expanding considerably during the past two decades. The current trends toward participation seems to be continuing that increasing role played by the federal government. Some review of the historical development of federal government participation seems in order for the student to gain adequate perspective of the current trends. The role played by the federal government since the era of the depression of 1929–1935 has been expanding, especially since the 1940s after World War II. The current trends and needs within the industry seem to point to further inroads on the part of the federal government in an attempt to overcome some of the disadvantages associated with higher costs and a rather uneven allocation of real estate resources among the citizens of the nation.

CHAPTER

ECONOMIC ASPECTS
OF REAL ESTATE
INVESTMENT THEORY

INVESTOR TYPES

There are nearly as many types of investors as there are persons in any one market. However, broadly speaking, there are three major investor types. First, there is the investor who looks upon his expenditure in the market place more in terms of consumption than in terms of pure investment. The single-family homeowner to a large degree typifies the consumer orientation. The average homeowner looks upon his real estate interest in terms of providing the services that he/she desires in a home residence. The homeowner as described is consumption oriented in the approach to the real estate investment being made. Other examples may be the retail firm looking for the right location to complement its primary business. Again the motivation is the consumption of real estate services at a given site so that the primary function (domicile, marketing hot dogs, gasoline, etc.) is complemented by the real property chosen.

A second major investor type would be one who is attempting to secure a reasonable return on his or her invested capital without undue risk or sophistication. Many single-family residences are exchanged for this degree of investment return and trade-off in terms of all the possible desired benefits through consumption. Additionally, many smaller multifamily and commercial real estate projects are exchanged for this purpose. Some smaller scale undeveloped lands may also exemplify this type of investor. The amount of risk and the degree of sophistication are minimal in this type of investor, who would not sacrifice security for higher returns.

The third major investor type would be one who would embrace higher-risk projects in the prospect of higher returns. The amount of speculation as well as the amount of and degree of investment knowledge brought to the market by this third type of investor is much greater than the previous two types of investors. This third type of investor is more knowledgeable in terms of investment criteria and investment analysis. The knowledge of the market and the understanding of the financial implications of various investment projects is much more within the normal operating realm of this third type of investor. Finally, larger projects involving intricate financial and legal planning are the types of investment projects most typical of the third type of investor in real estate services. Capital gains speculation and leveraged equity buildup are generally much more common objectives in the third type of investor than in the first two types of investors.

INVESTOR MOTIVATION

Just as there are different types of investors, there are also various forms of motivation in the real estate investment market. Some of the more common motivations on the part of real estate investors are:

Safety of principal

Safety of income

Higher rates of return

Greater cashflow

Higher leverage, yielding higher returns on equity

Speculation on appreciation in the future

Investment and use mixture

Cashflow and appreciation married in one investment

The noticeable lack of liquidity in real estate highlights the general nature of real estate in general. In most instances, investors in real estate are willing to give up liquidity, access and, in some instances, safety for the higher overall returns in terms of cashflow and appreciation of principal that characterize investment properties. Liquidity also relates to the unique nature of real estate, in that real estate is long lived and involves long-term decisions, and also requires large economic commitment relative to other forms of investment.

A second major element in the nature of the motivation on the part of investors in real estate projects is their overall tendency to seek an equity position and the higher risks associated with equity, rather than the more conservative debt positions associated with the more liquid and more flexible savings accounts through traditional banking and fiduciary agencies. The motivation for higher returns through equity in real estate is accepted in full view and recognition of the greater safety and flexibility and liquidity given up by not committing those funds at a lower return in the debt instrument areas. As a result of the analysis and decisions that must be made for the knowledgeable investors in real estate investment property, the level of sophistication in general is greater than in the more consumption-oriented real estate interests.

LEVEL OF KNOWLEDGE IN THE INVESTMENT MARKET

Because the investor in real estate is not concerned primarily that the real estate services in a given location are to be consumed by him or her, the attention must be focused upon a much greater and more complex issue of services to be offered in a market of real estate services. The trends of consumption by an entire market population are the area of concern, and measurement by a yardstick of dollars rather than the more subjective yardstick of likes and dislikes that constitute the measuring device of the consumer purchaser. Because the scope of the analysis is extended to include an entire market, the possible investment locations must also include the majority of the market for such real estate services.

As a result of the extension into a more comprehensive market as described above, the level of knowledge on the part of investors in the investment real estate market is greater than the knowledge on the part of the more common single-family owner-occupant consumers. This knowledge includes a more thorough awareness of what is and is not a suitable return on invested capital in the light of various attributes of given investment alternatives. What that means is that investors in investment property are aware of the rates of return earned in the market on properties with similar risk and return ratios. In addition, the more knowledgeable investors are aware of what alternative investment media are earning compared to the returns associated with real estate projects. They tend to be more aware of alternative yields, the trends of the yields of various investment alternatives and the relative management burden associated with various yields of real estate and other investment projects. Additional insight into the quality of income streams, the capacity and advantages of the possible use of leverage and the expense-to-income ratio as an indication of operational efficiency are rather common knowledge in the market place of refined real estate investment projects.

ACCELERATION AND MULTIPLICATION THROUGH LEVERAGE

When a person owns a given investment free and clear of debt, there is no leverage in that investment. Examples of such media would be the normal savings accounts at the commercial or savings institutions. The format of such an investment is outlined below:

$$\$10,000 \text{ certificate of deposit at } 8\% = \$800$$
$$\text{in earnings annually}$$

$$\frac{\$800}{\$10,000} = 8\% \text{ return}$$

When an investor borrows some of the capital with which to make an investment, that investment then becomes leveraged. Using the same case example as before, let us assume the investor borrowed $9,000 from a good friend for one percent interest. He also contributed $1,000 of his own funds.

$$\$9,000 \text{ borrowed } + \$1,000 \text{ equity } = \$10,000$$

$$\$10,000 \text{ invested in a certificate of deposit}$$
$$\text{at } 8\% = \$800 \text{ earned annually}$$

$$\frac{\$800}{\$10,000} = \text{return on overall investment}$$

However, if we consider the return on only the amount invested by the one party of his own money we get an entirely different rate of return. From the gross earnings of the investment we must deduct the cost of the borrowed funds to arrive at the net income figure. That net income is then expressed as a percentage of the amount of equity dollars the person has invested in the project of his own.

Gross income of investment	$800.00
Less: cost of borrowed money (1% of $9,000)	(90.00)
Net Income	$710.00

$$\frac{\text{Net Income}}{\text{Equity}} \qquad \frac{\$710}{\$1,000} = \text{Percentage rate of return} = 71\%$$

Although the project itself earned a flat eight percent annual return, through the use of leverage the rate of return for an individual investor could be made significantly more attractive. Higher yields in certain investments allowed the principals to accumulate their invested capital quicker. The ultimate objective of wealth accumulation is accelerated through the use of leverage.

Referring again to the previous two examples, it can be seen that with a given amount available for investment ($10,000), leverage will allow that individual to invest in more than one project with his given amount. Without leverage, he or she is limited to one investment of $10,000 in our example. However, with 90 percent leverage (the ability to borrow 90 percent of necessary invested amounted amount) that same person can spread his or her $10,000 into ten different projects each with 90 percent leverage and a total overall investment of $100,000 dollars. Such multiplication of investment capital is available only through the principle of leverage. As a result of the impact of leverage upon investments and investment capital, investors who are knowledgeable about leverage can accumulate wealth through equity buildup at a quicker rate than would be true otherwise. Also, through the use of leverage in an appropriate manner the cashflow or dollar return from investments can be increased above what would normally accrue to the investor in a total equity situation.

It should be recognized that leverage is a very efficient principle in magnifying both returns in sound investments and losses in poor investments. In a depressed market situation, where a given investor is leveraged to the 90 percent extent in the previous examples, a 10 percent drop in value of the asset represents a 100 percent loss in equity because of the leverage factor. To illustrate this principle:

$$\frac{Equity}{Value} \quad \frac{\$1,000}{\$10,000} = 10\% \text{ equity} = 90\% \text{ leverage}$$

$$\frac{Returns}{Equity} = \text{Rate of return} \quad \text{(1) Value increases by } 10\%$$

$$10\% \text{ of } \$10,000 = \$1,000$$

$$\frac{\text{Return} \quad \$1,000}{\text{Equity} \quad \$1,000} =$$
$$100\% \text{ return}$$

(2) Value falls by 10%

$$-10\% \text{ of } \$10,000 = (1,000)$$

$$\frac{\text{Return} \quad (\$1,000)}{\text{Equity} \quad \$1,000} =$$
$$(-100\%) \text{ return}$$

As you can see from the example, leverage magnifies both profits and losses. Therefore, in most situations the investor utilizing leverage must be in a position to assess the possible risks of loss that the leverage position will magnify if employed.

Real estate has traditionally been one of the areas where investment has tended to be rather highly leveraged. Since the early 1930s loans in the real estate sector have ranged between 60 and 95 percent. In other words, the equity requirements have ranged between 5 and 40 percent. Such leverage possibilities account to some degree for the wide interest and acceptance of real estate as a viable investment medium. An example of the leverage situation would be the following:

Total investment requirement	$50,000
Annual net income	5,000

$$\text{Rate of return:} \quad \frac{\text{Income}}{\text{Value}} = 10\%$$

Use of leverage:

(A) 90% loan at 5% = annual cost	$ 2,250
(B) Net income after debt	$ 2,750
(C) Total equity invested	$ 5,000

Leverage rate of return:

$$\frac{\text{Net Income}}{\text{Equity}} = \frac{\$2,750}{5,000} = 55\%$$

Through the use of 90 percent leverage in available real estate money markets, the investor in the above example was able to generate five and one-half times the return normally available in the same investment without the benefit of leverage. The assumption in the above example is that the interest costs were the only payments on the borrowed funds. When payments must be made to principle as well as interest on the borrowed capital, the net income is lower and the equity higher, resulting in a lower rate of return overall.

To illustrate the efficiency in magnifying both losses and gains, consider the following: The annual income from the previous project drops to five percent on the total investment project. Instead of $5,000 annual net income, the same project now yields $2,500 in net income. Setting the project up in the same manner as before, we then see:

(A) Annual net income $2,500

(B) Interest costs of 90% loan at 5%   2,250

(C) Net income after debt service $ 250

(D) Total equity invested   5,000

(E) Leveraged rate of return:

$$\frac{\text{Net Income}}{\text{Equity}} = \frac{250}{5,000} = 5\% \text{ rate of return}$$

As a result of the leveraged position, the net return dropped 96 percent as a result of a 5 percent drop in the overall return earned by the project. The project earned 5 percent on asset value as opposed to the previous 10 percent, but the leveraged investor earned only 5 percent on his equity as opposed to the previous 55 percent return.

As a result of these examples for illustration, it can be seen that the principle of leverage operates very efficiently in both an up market and a down market. It is important, therefore, that the investor employing leverage in a given investment project be somewhat more knowledgeable in terms of the details of the project and the inherent risks associated with the project that leverage only magnifies. One of the first considerations in the investment decision process is often whether there is the possibility of leverage. Without leverage capabilities, many investment alternatives are eliminated at the outset.

FINANCIAL ANALYSIS AND INCOME ESTIMATION

The starting point in the investment analysis is the estimation of the expected income to be derived from the proposed investment. In the economic perspective, we are focusing our attention upon the yardstick of dollars and the relation between alternative investments and the dollar benefits to be realized as a result of investing in them. After completion of the cashflow analysis, and the formalizing of the income estimate from the proposed investment project, then evaluation and comparisons can be made with alternative investment opportunities. However, the initial estimation of the income to be derived from the single project under analysis is the most important step in the process. The following example illustrates the steps and process of income estimation:

Scheduled income	$29,000	
Less:		
allowance for vacancies	$\dfrac{(1,450)}{27,550}$	
Less:		
operating expenses	$\dfrac{(9,200)}{18,350}$	Net Income
Less:		
debt service	$\dfrac{(13,300)}{5,050}$	Net Cashflow
Add:		
net tax savings	$\dfrac{2,700}{7,750}$	Total & Return

The analysis of the income estimate and the final formation of the net income to be expected from the investment requires detailed knowledge and research if it is to be wholly accurate or realistic. Referring to the illustration above, the expected vacancy level will be a function of the scheduled income and that income compared to the rents being charged by competitive units of similar quality. Through a knowledge of the market for such units the researcher can make the judgments necessary to establish a realistic income schedule and vacancy allowance. The vacancy allowanace is also a function of the overall supply and demand factors governing the rental market in this region. The trends and possible future levels of both supply and demand must be eliminated with reasonable accuracy for such a project to be successful.

The overall operating costs of the proposed project must be examined rather thoroughly and compared to what the operating norms are within the industry and region within which the project is located. Such items as architecture, material, weather, tenant turnover, demographics of the tenant mix and trends in terms of maintenance and repair costs are all factors that should be included in the estimation and evaluation of the operating expenses predicted for a given structure. Such facts as abnormally low operating expenses for a given project offered for resale may indicate an attempt to inflate the net income stream by neglecting necessary repairs that would constitute large expenses for more major repairs to the new owner. Additionally, a thorough and complete audit of the operating accounting reports for the project is a mandatory task for a prospective investor to validate and confirm the operations of the project and the vacancy and operating expenses of the investment project.

Having reviewed the operating nature of the project and arrived at the net income to be expected from the investment, the prospective investor next needs to account for service on the total debt he or she expects to incur if the investment is chosen. The initial inquiry on the part of the investor was partially related to the total amount of cash required to enter the investment at the outset. As a result of the initial estimate of cash required, the investor should have a fairly accurate idea in terms of the total amount of financing he or she would have to incur to complete the project negotiations. The amount of debt is not nearly as important as the terms of the financing chosen. The complexities and variables associated with the entire field of real estate finance require extensive knowledge not always possessed by all investors. Nevertheless, the financing of the proposed project should be thoroughly analyzed to arrive at the most complementary format in terms of the project transfer and the returns to the individual investor.

Here, one important point should be noticed. When referring to returns to the investor, what investment analysis concerns itself with is the net dollars to be realized by the investor in his pocket as a result of the investment under examination. The net income of the operating accounts of an investment project are not the same as net income in the forms of cash realized by the principal investor. It is at this point that project feasibility and individual investment analysis differ. Since the investor in the project under examination must borrow part of the capital with which to make the investment, the costs associated with that borrowing are real costs to him or her and must be accounted for in the overall analysis of the investment project. Fundamental understanding of the monetary markets, and access to current trends within the financial community, are vitally important points the investor should know, or have a party on his side of the bargaining table who does know. Since the funds that will cover total debt service are from the net operating income of the project, the amount of cashflow committed to debt service is a vitally important element in the total amount to be returned to the investor over the life of the project. An accurate estimation of the amortization schedule at an obtainable interest rate is fundamentally crucial to the investment appraisal.

Last, when accelerated depreciation schedules are elected, which was 150 percent of straight line in the above example, the amount of dollar cashflow attributed to the project will be only the amount of taxes that the investor will not have to pay as a result of the "paper" loss recorded in the earlier years of the investment. In the above example, the operating loss in the first year was $5,570. This resulted primarily from the high depreciation charges in the early years. The investor in the example was in the 50 percent marginal income tax bracket. As a result, 50 percent of the operating loss was the amount the individual actually saved in dollars or cashflow he or she would normally have paid in income taxes. The increase in dollars retained as a result of the tax treatment of the operating loss resulting from the accelerated depreciation employed constitutes a real dollar gain by the investor as a result of the investment project. Therefore, those net dollars earned are attributable to the investment and are counted as part of the total return earned as a result of the investment. The important tax implications and provisions of the Federal Income Tax laws are highly complex and most investors need the assistance of competent tax counsel to accurately interpret and quantify the effect of various tax treatments of various methods of accounting for depreciation and other expenses.

EVALUATING THE DOLLAR RETURNS OF AN INVESTMENT

Once the net after-tax dollars are determined for a given investment project, the investor is confronted with the task of determining how well or how poorly that investment compares with alternative investment media in which his or her dollars could be invested. Real estate, from an investment point of view, is not unlike all other investment areas in that the worth of the investment is the relative position of the promised returns on invested capital compared to the returns possible through all competitive investment media. When one begins from the point of investment and returns on the invested capital, there is a rather uniform basis for making any judgment, and the analysis and decisions are generally more objective. Factors such as amenities, location, neighborhood, floor plan and room decor or design are not evaluated at all except in the terms of the impact of such factors on the income expected from the investment project. The analysis is confined to the income stream of one investment as measured relative to time and the initial investment amount in comparison to those income stream characteristics of all alternative investments.

AVERAGE RATE OF RETURN

One of the earlier ways in which investments were evaluated was in terms of the average rate of return earned by the investment. Initially, the net income of the investment was compared to the appraised value of the same investment to form a rate of return. The problem with such an evaluation was the rather high range that developed among similar investments and the separation from the ownership interest represented by equity. In the previous example of the apartment complex:

$$\frac{\text{Net Income}}{\text{App. Value}} \quad \frac{18,350}{172,135} = 11\% \text{ Average Rate of Return}$$

In such a complex investment as the project used in the example, the more common average rate of return approach is somewhat deceiving. In the more contemporary average return approach, the after-tax income to the investor is compared to the investor's equity in the project. In our example of the apartment complex:

$$\frac{\text{After Tax Cashflow}}{\text{Owner's Equity}} \quad \frac{7,750}{73,315} = 10\frac{1}{2}\% \text{ average return in year 1}$$

$$\frac{7,404}{75,802} = 9.8\% \text{ average return in year 2}$$

$$\frac{6,890}{78,476} = 8.8\% \text{ average return in year 3}$$

The major reason for the dropping average rate of return in the second example is depreciation. As the amount of dollar depreciation declines, the net after-tax income also declines because of the reduced tax shelter through a book expense item such as depreciation, and also the contributions to principal in the debt service schedule increase the owner's equity in the overall project. The net impact of each of these items on the above example is to reduce the rate of return by approximately one-half percent in the earlier years of the investment.

Although the average rate-of-return method is rather common, there are some major comments about the method that should be made. The strongest reasons for the popularity of the average rate of return approach are its basic simplicity, which most people can easily understand and follow without much of a background in investment analysis. Also, because the technique employs readily accessible information from the standard accounting reports, the information is easily and cheaply attained. The biggest major flaw in the entire approach is the complete neglect of the time value of money. The idea that $1,000 today is worth more than the promise of $1,000 two years from today is rather well accepted. However, in the average rate of return analysis all income is treated alike without modification for the fact that some income may be several years from the time the initial equity portion was contributed. Also, the average rate of return generally employs accounting income and equity rather than cashflow and the out-of-pocket equity contributions that constitute the essence of the investor's position. It should also be noticed that appreciation in asset value is totally ignored in the traditional average rate of return approach. In the field of real estate, appreciation is often one of the major, if not the major, contributor to the overall returns associated with the investment project. Because appreciation is not recognized until the time of sale, it rightfully does not belong in the rate of return in the operation of the project, but it certainly should be considered at the completion of the income stream at time of sale or revision. The time value concept certainly could not be ignored under such analysis, and, therefore, the average rate of return type of approach is grossly inaccurate when applied to the real estate investment situation.

PAYBACK PERIOD FOR BREAK-EVEN POINT

The break-even approach to investment analysis has been commonly used in industry and capital investment for many years. It has been used occasionally in the real estate investment community, but suffers some serious shortcomings in such long-term investments as real estate. Essentially, it is seeking to answer the question: "How soon would the investor recover his original investment?" What is done in the analysis is illustrated in the example that follows. The total amount invested is divided by the annual expected cashflow, to arrive at the number of years required to recover the original investment.

$$\frac{\text{Fixed Investment}}{\text{Annual Cashflow}} \quad \frac{73,315}{7,750} = 9.5 \text{ years}$$

The logic of the payback or break-even analysis can be seen more clearly perhaps in Figure 14–1. The initial investment remains unchanged in the example. With income from that given investment at a more or less constant amount annually over the life of the subject project, the total income from the investment project gradually and constantly builds over time until the total income received equals and then exceeds the initial investment amount. At the point of intersection of constant cost curve or line,

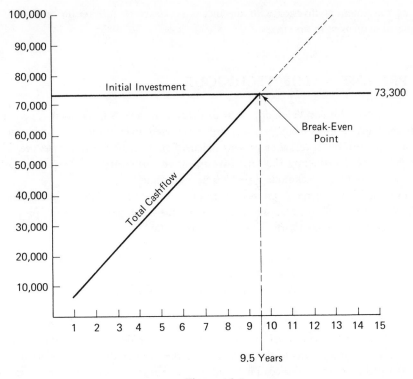

Figure 14–1

and the rising income line, the investment will have reached its break-even point. On the horizontal axis, this point of intersection is between the ninth and tenth year, or more nearly the nine and one-half year point from the date of the original investment.

Again, the major flaw in such a technique is that it totally ignores the time value of money. The income received 25 years from the point of initial investment is treated in the same manner as income received in the same year as the investment. Yet, we are all generally aware of the notion that income promised in the future is not worth the same per unit as income to be received in the current time period. Another major flaw of the payback or break-even approach is the complete disregard of potential profits above costs that investment by its very nature holds to be important. It is the returns above the invested amount or in addition to the amount that is invested that investment psychology concerns itself with. It is quite difficult to compare the payback or break-even point in years with an expected amount of return on invested capital expressed either in terms of dollars or in terms of percent of the original investment. The break-even analysis is traditionally applied to capital equipment when the user is looking to con-sumer for the working equipment and to reap labor and capital savings as a result of the equipment addition. Those savings would tell the manufacturer how long he had to use the machine to recoup the price of the machine in labor or capital and material savings.

The real estate sector of the investment community differs greatly from such a comparison and the payback or break-even evaluation approach falls terribly short in

providing the potential investor with the means necessary to fully evaluate one investment and its returns with another.

NET PRESENT VALUE TECHNIQUE

In the Net Present Value approach to investment analysis, the total expected returns from a given investment proposal are discounted in a manner to arrive at the
worth of those returns in terms of present dollars. The sum of the returns expressed in
current dollars after deducting the total investment requirement should equal or exceed
zero. Let us illustrate this technique through a new example:

Proposed Investment: A project on a net lease yielding $10,000 annually for ten
years. Lessee has a hard dollar option at the end of the tenth year to buy the project for
$300,000. Total price listed for the project is $250,000.00.

$10,000 times ten years	$100,000
Sale in the tenth year	300,000
Total returns of project	$400,000

The project is not worth $400,000 in the current time frame, but the vital question is
how much is it worth? The seller is asking $250,000, but that does not mean that the
project is worth that amount. In the evaluation of the project, there are essentially three
steps that should be accomplished. First, the present value (in terms of today's dollars)
of the $10,000 income for ten years should be determined. Referring to the tables on
page 000 we determine that any investment of this character must yield at least six percent to the investor. Using the six percent table refer to the column giving the present
worth of an annuity for ten years at six percent. In the tenth row is the factor 7.360087.
Multiply that factor times the amount of the annuity to arrive at the present worth of
the income stream during the ten-year lease period.

$10,000 times 7.360087 $73,600.87

The second step in the problem is to determine the present worth of the $300,000
promised in the tenth year at the completion of the lease. In this case we again refer
to the table on page 000 but more specifically to the present worth of one table and the
tenth row. We have a factor of 0.558395, which is multiplied times the amount of the
dollars to be received in that tenth year.

$300,000 times 0.558395 $167,518.50

The total present worth of the dollars to be returned from the proposed investment is:

$10,000 times 1.360087	$ 73,600.87
$300,000 times 0.558395	167,618.50
Present worth of returns	$241,119.37

The final step in the Net Present Value approach is to subtract the total invest-ment requirement from the present worth of the total returns and arrive at a net value. If the difference is zero, then the project equals the required rate of return (six percent in the current example) and should be accepted. If the difference is positive, meaning the proposed yields a higher return than required, then the project should also be accepted. In the case in which the difference is a negative number, meaning that the present dol-lars given up to secure the investment are not equal to the present worth of the total dollars received from the investment, the investment should not be accepted at the price level used in the analysis. In our example we have:

Total returns from the project in present worth	$241,119.37
Less: investment required in current dollars	(250,000.00)
Net present value of investment	(8,880.63)

Accordingly, the proposed investment project should be turned down in the negotia-tions. The alternative is to offer $8,880.63 less than the investment project is currently listed. Under such an offer, the project would meet the investment requirements in terms of rate of return that the parties have chosen.

Since there is a great similarity between the present value analysis and the in-ternal rate of return approach, we will critique them jointly after the discussion of internal rate of return analysis. Both are rather complex for the uninitiated and, there-fore, should, in the author's opinion, be discussed somewhat in parallel.

INTERNAL RATE OF RETURN ANALYSIS

The internal rate of return analysis is not terribly unlike the present value analy-sis discussed in the previous section. The object of the analysis is to determine the rate of return that the income stream represents when compared to the original investment. The income stream represents an annuity for the purposes of analysis. In the earlier example, the apartment project had a net income stream of $5,050 from a building com-plex of an expected life of 25 years. We look at that income stream over the life of the project and attempt to find what rate of return that represents on the original invest-ment. Table 14–1 on the following page shows this process.

The initial investment requirement for the project was a total of $73,315.00. The closest present value amount was the six percent capitalized amount, which totaled $70,-306.50. The investment amount was $3,008 more than the six percent capitalized amount, thus the effective internal rate of return for the project was between five and six per-cent. The sum of the difference was $3,008 more than the six percent capitalized amount, and there was $7,210 difference in total between the five and six percent capitalized amounts. The difference was 42 percent of the range less than six percent return. There-fore, the internal rate of return for the project for the 25 year life is 5.58 percent (6.00 percent less .42 percent = 5.58 percent).

TABLE 14–1

	Factor	Income	Present Value
4%	15.662	$5,050.00	$86,141.00
5%	14.094	$5,050.00	77,517.00
6%	12.783	$5,050.00	70,306.50
7%	11.654	$5,050.00	64,097.00

If the project yields an internal rate of return less than the norm for that firm or industry, the project is not accepted. If the internal rate of return equals or exceeds the normal return for the firm or industry, the project is accepted. In the above example, the internal rate of return would indicate that the project would not be acceptable. It is part of the shortcomings of the internal rate of return technique that it evaluates only the income stream from a given project and not the total bundle of benefits to be derived from the project. Among alternative investments, the internal rate of return technique allows one to list them all in order of their internal rates of return and then choose the single one that exceeds all the others in terms of the internal rate of return. To account for all the returns of an investment, the present value analysis would have to be employed for salvage and resale values in addition to the income stream projections. This approach would be particularly appropriate in the case of real estate investment projects in which appreciation in land value plays a major part in many investment decisions.

REAL ESTATE AND INVESTMENT ANALYSIS

When approaching real estate from a purely investment standpoint, many of the more common elements in the buy-versus-not-buy decision are missing. It is the investment requirements and opportunities for return on investment capital that play the major role in the decision-making process. Other factors that would be important for owner-occupant would not necessarily be appropriate for the investor not expecting to occupy the subject real estate project under consideration. With this rather dramatic change in priorities on the part of the potential buyer of investment properties, there is also a much greater refinement in the examination of those areas that do take precedence. In addition to the motivation on the part of the investor segment of society, there is also the general trend in the investment field for properties in the refined investment categories to be on a generally larger economic scale than those projects in the owner-occupant categories. As a result of the large economic commitments, there are also more detailed analysis and more conservative risk-taking as a result of the number of professional investors included in any one project.

Although real estate in general offers some highly attractive incentives for potential investors, some persistent problems are found that plague complete analysis in the investment sphere. Cashflow and salvage value at resale are two of the largest obstacles in the accurate estimation and evaluation of a real estate project from the investment return standpoint. Cashflow is most often a function of the efficient operational aspects of a given real estate project, rather than a result of the attributes of the given asset itself. No analyst of the human species has a perception of the future so flawless that exact net profits from a given operation of a given real estate project in a dynamic society can be predicted with complete accuracy. Furthermore, that same imperfect human is no more adept at ascertaining the value at time of sale of a given project even a few years from the time of purchase, let alone 10 to 30 years after initial purchase.

Because of the vague parameters set in the time frame of an investment, and the even more vague insight provided by economic and environmental trends in existence at the time of purchase, any refinement in the analysis of the data available should be greeted with a mixture of salvation and skepticism. The techniques should be used and studied with an attitude of improving the tool kit of the financial diagnostician, but at the same time not be looked upon as being something so precious as the Dead Sea Scrolls.

This is particularly true of the analysis techniques that treat the time value of money concept in their analysis. It is a relatively new concept to be employed at the pragmatic level of the practicing real estate professional in his task of ascertaining and conveying his ideas of value. There is, however, ample room for the present value theory and the internal rate of return theory to be employed beneficially in the everyday world of real estate transactions. As the economic commitment required by many of the more feasible real estate projects grows, the amount of analysis and study of costs versus returns will likewise grow in intensity and depth as well as technique. The practicing real estate professional, and the wise investor too, will find it increasingly more important to embrace the logical consistency and the time value of money concepts included as a part of the present value theory and the internal rate of return theory. The old habits of using gross income multipliers and general capitalization rates simply will not hold up under the close scrutiny increasingly required in the investment segment of the real estate industry. It is for that reason that real estate investment analysis has begun to encompass the present value and internal rates of return concepts in the analysis of real estate for investment purposes.

The payback and break-even approaches, along with the average return analysis are less accurate and precise in a field that is growing more analytical and complex nearly daily. In addition, because of some of the unique characteristics of real estate—its long life, large economic commitment, fixed location and long-term decicions and commitments—more accurate and complete analysis and evaluation techniques are very much in demand. The basic characteristics of real estate are unlikely to change dramatically. Thus, continued refinement in analysis and continued intellectual development of the practicing real estate professional and investor are needs that seem unlikely to be completely fulfilled in total within the foreseeable future.

REFERENCES

1—Archer, Stephen H. and D'Ambrosio, Charles A. *Theory of Business Finance: A Book of Readings.* New York. The Macmillan Co., 1967.

2—Casey, William J. *Tax Shelter in Real Estate.* New York: The Institute for Business Planning, 1957.

3—Cohen, Jerome B. and Zinbarg, Edward D. *Investment Analysis and Portfolio Management.* Homewood, Ill.: Richard D. Irwin Co., 1957.

4—Prime, John H. *Investment Analysis.* 4th ed. Englewood Cliffs, N.J.: Prentice-Hall, Inc., 1967.

5—Sauvain, Harry. *Investment Management.* 3rd ed. Englewood Cliffs, N.J.: Prentice-Hall, Inc., 1967.

6—VanHorne, James C. *Financial Management and Policy.* Englewood Cliffs, N.J.: Prentice-Hall, Inc., 1968.

7—West, David A. *Readings in Investment Analysis.* Scranton, Pa.: International Textbook Co., 1969.

8—Beaton, William R. *Real Estate Investment.* Englewood Cliffs, N.J.: Prentice-Hall, Inc., 1971.

15

PRODUCTION PROCESS
OF REAL ESTATE

ECONOMIC IMPORTANCE

When we speak of the production of real estate resources, we are focusing our attention primarily upon the construction industry in structures and real estate improvements. Although significant improvements are made in the agricultural sector of the economy, the major construction activity is almost solely confined to the more urban forms of improvements. Table 15–1 provides an indication of the size of the construction industry and the relative size of the residential construction segment. In 1965, total construction in the United States amounted to more than $73 billion. Residential construction amounted to nearly $28 billion. In 1972, total construction had grown to nearly $124 billion, and the residential portion to nearly $54 billion. Figure 15–1 shows the relationship between the level of overall construction activity and the level of national growth as expressed in the Gross National Product (GNP). Consistently the level of construction activity has been nearly equal to ten percent of the total economic wealth of the nation.

As such, the construction industry represents one of the major segments of the entire economy of the nation. Residential construction, which is the production of housing units, constitutes a major portion of that total economic activity. When one takes time to consider all the supportive industries related to the production of real estate services, including material, maintenance and the real estate marketing and supportive industries, the importance of the production of real estate services is immense in any measurement.

TABLE 15–1
Value of New Construction Annually
(in $ Millions)

Year	Total	Residential
1972	$123,836 million	$54,186 million
1971	$109,238 "	$43,268 "
1970	$ 94,167 "	$31,864 "
1969	$ 93,368 "	$33,200 "
1968	$ 86,626 "	$30,565 "
1967	$ 77,503 "	$25,568 "
1965	$ 73,412 "	$27,934 "
1960	$ 54,632 "	$22,975 "
1955	$ 46,519 "	$21,877 "

Source: U.S., Department of Commerce, Bureau of the Census, *Statistical Abstract of the U.S., 1973,* p. 673.

Another indication of the economic impact of the real estate production segments of the economy is the relative level of employment directly in the construction and production areas. In 1972 there were over three and one-half million persons directly employed in the construction industries. With a work force of nearly 70 million persons in the entire United States, real estate production accounts for nearly five percent of the total employment in the nation. Again, if one attempts to account for the vast number of employed persons in the related industries servicing construction, the total manpower commitment in production of real estate services is immense.

It can be seen why the federal government was so concerned with the construction industry during the depression years of the early 1930s when the nation was attempting to recover from the economic basement. It is partially a result of the influence and dedication on the part of the federal and state governments to maintain a healthy and active real estate production sector that the industry and its related industries have grown to the national magnitude they have.

INDUSTRY CHARACTERISTICS

The construction industry, and more particularly the residential construction segment, is a unique industry in its structure and in its behavior when compared to other major industrial segments of relatively the same size. The first characteristic that comes to mind is the small size of the firms operating in the industry. When one thinks of large and complex industry, such industries as steel, automobiles, drugs, aerospace and others come to mind. Such firms are large and highly integrated, with a great deal of centralization. For the largest, or one of the largest industrial segments in our country, construction is typified by rather small operational units with very little concentration.

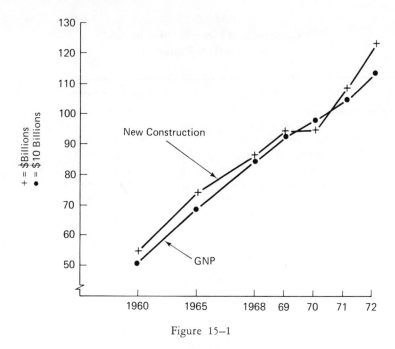

Figure 15–1

Table 15–2, showing construction firms by size of total sales, illustrates this point. Over half of all the firms in the construction industry are less than $25,000 in total annual production. Of the total in construction, 83 percent reported less than $100,000 in total output during the year of observation. Such figures have many implications in the real estate production in the nation. The production of real estate services is an extremely small-scale industry. With total sales or receipts of less than $100,000 annually, there is no capacity for large-scale technology and managerial techniques. With over half of the construction firms in the nation making less than $25,000 annually, there is also a high number of sole proprietors who lack the time or capacity to employ major innovative measures. Such operational scale precludes the possibility of major technological or managerial innovation originating from within the industry itself. Since the table includes all construction firms, most of those in the higher operational levels would have to include the large government contractors that build the major federal and state projects such as dams, highways and the largest commercial and industrial complexes. It is a well-known characteristic of the residential construction industry that most builders are generally from the communities in which they operate.

LOCALIZATION OF THE INDUSTRIAL UNITS

Because of the operational scale, or perhaps the reason behind it, the great proportion of residential construction firms in particular are local in their operations. By local is meant that the firms building residential structures within an economic region gen-

TABLE 15–2

Construction Firms by Size in 1967

(in Total $ Receipts)

Class Size	Number of Firms	
Less than $10,000	351,747	firms
$10,000 to $24,999	130,592	"
$25,000 to $49,999	97,602	"
$50,000 to $99,999	80,429	"
$100,000 to $249,999	70,746	"
$250,000 to $499,999	30,129	"
$500,000 to $999,999	17,456	"
$1 million or more	16,137	"
Total Firms	794,838	

Source: U.S., Department of Commerce, Bureau of the Census, *Statistical Abstract of the U.S., 1973*, p. 677.

erally tend to originate from the same economic region. There is a distinct and extreme shortage of firms of national scale that operate in the residential construction industry. In the few that have appeared in the 1970s several have suffered from such severe losses and lack of acceptance that many have since withdrawn from the residential construction scene on a major scale. The small scale of operations by the majority of construction firms dictates that they will be local in their operations. As a result, most firms that make up the construction industry are highly susceptible to the local fluctuations in demand for residential properties in their areas. Being local, any change in the local market characteristics affects those firms more than would be the case if they had activities in other areas to emphasize in such temporary down turns.

UNORGANIZED INDUSTRY NATIONALLY

Partially because of the localization and resultant smaller economies of scale being performed by the residential construction industry segment, there is also very little organization within the industry itself. Most operators conduct their business on a local perspective and very little coordination exists beyond the local level. As a result, supply and marketing data have a vitally important influence on the operation of the construction segment in any local area. The building standards, codes, zoning and the state of the arts in terms of management of construction companies are not as developed and refined as they are in the dynamic industries of steel, autos, transportation and many other big industrial segments of the economy. Additional advantages that would accrue through organization, such as adequate supply of necessary raw material on a scale necessary to sustain growth within an economic area, are missing.

The result is an industry that is the innocent victim of economic fluctuations,

rather than a dynamic force in the elevation of some of the ill effects of economic fluctuations and temporary maladjustments in the supply and demand accommodations
within the market place. With a product as universally held and economically significant
as real estate, such lack of organization within the market place will surely be a focal
point of concern on the part of academicians and leaders in the national scene of real
estate in the future.

The lack of organization and the small economies of scale practiced in the real
estate sector contribute substantially to the cyclical over- and under-building that occur
in the industry. Table 15–3 and, more particularly, Figure 15–2 illustrate this fluctuation
and cyclical pattern in the housing starts or production of housing in the United States.
When one begins to examine local building patterns these cyclical trends become magnified. In local areas there is sometimes extended periods of construction of new housing
as a result of sustained growth through immigration. Such trends have been noticeable
in the far western and the southeastern parts of the nation for the past several years. As
a footnote to the table cited, current indications are that the 1973 statistics will fall below the levels of 1972 and 1971.

On a local level the cyclical characteristics of the construction area are more
defined than on a national scale. Generally, when demand for housing increases and
monies are also available with which to finance the construction process, then local firms
enter the residential construction market. Since they are generally small and local these
firms do not have significant research departments and follow one another on the basis
of whether they possess the skills and manpower to do the job and can obtain the construction financing to go through with it. As a result, they complete their projects within

TABLE 15–3
New Housing Starts, 1960 to 1972

Year	Number of Units
1972	2,379,000
1971	2,085,000
1970	1,469,000
1969	1,500,000
1968	1,546,000
1967	1,322,000
1966	1,196,000
1965	1,510,000
1964	1,561,000
1963	1,642,000
1962	1,492,000
1961	1,365,000
1960	1,296,000

Source: U.S., Department of Commerce, Bureau of the Census, *Statistical Abstract of the U.S., 1973*,
p. 683.

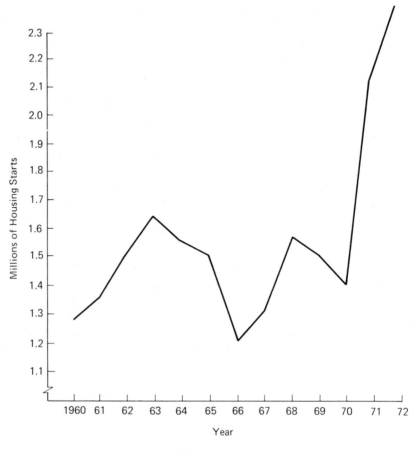

Figure 15–2

a short time of one another. The result is usually a temporary oversupply of units. Then there is a slowdown in construction until the empty units are sold and the market recovers. Figure 15–3 illustrates this tendency in a descriptive sense. With a fairly steadily rising demand for housing in an area, the supply characteristics generally move in a step-ladder fashion. The result is the alternate excess and shortage.

THE "RATCHET EFFECT"

The staircase trend of supply in relation to the demand for real estate services, particularly urban land use services, also reflects some of the fundamental factors associated with real estate. Because of the very uniqueness of the real estate good being exchanged, that market of such goods also behaves a bit unlike most other commodity or service markets. The long-term considerations involved in the production of real estate goods makes real estate highly inflexible in the market. This is particularly true in the circumstances of a sudden and prolonged market depression or decline.

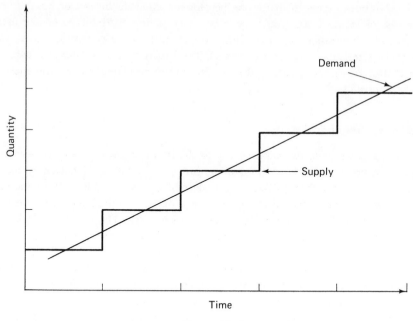

Figure 15–3

In the situation of a falling market, the supply of real estate services is not normally capable of reducing in the normal manner. The only force of reduction is the deterioration of the physical real estate resources. Because of the trends of real estate in construction, such a market decline would produce reduced supply of real estate services in sudden drops as a result of deterioration of the structures from long neglect after abandonment. The general trend of groups of structures to be built around the same period would correlate with similar groups of structures falling out of the market through deterioration at rather sudden points during such a long-term market decline. The inability of the real estate market to adjust downward on the supply side in response to sudden drops in the demand for structure gives rise to the description of the nature of the market adjustment processes as a ratchet.

ECONOMIC IMPACT OF INDUSTRY CHARACTERISTICS

At the beginning of this chapter we reviewed the economic significance of the residential and general real estate construction industry in terms of the national economy. Accounting for nearly ten percent of the national output annually in direct terms, and surely much more than that in terms of the auxiliary industries supporting the construction and maintenance efforts in real estate, the production process in real estate is at the very foundation of our economic well being. Therefore, even the slightest of imperfections or distortions in the industry has a dramatic impact upon the welfare of the entire nation.

It has been estimated that a one percent reduction in the cost of housing, either in purchase or maintenance, would result in a total saving of $1 billion on the national level (Kaiser Commission, p. 114). Therefore, to address the economic impact of the industry characteristics is indeed a large task. The following discussion will confine itself to the characteristics we have described so far, and some of the major consequences of such characteristics.

Small Economies of Scale

The size of the firms operating within the major segment of the real estate construction industry is unusually small for an industry so large. Nearly 75 percent of the firms in the industry are less than $100,000 in total annual receipts. As a result of such small size, most of the construction firms operate on a nearly marginal level with very little capital investment. They enter and leave the industry often. The result is a lack of stability within the market itself, and instability contributes to the lack of capital investment and economies of scale that may be possible. Additionally, the small size of most firms within the industry rules out the capacity for extensive innovation within the residential construction industry in particular, and the construction industry in general. On the scale on which most construction operates, the profit-saving advantages of most innovation techniques would not substantially change the below-the-line profits of the typical firm. As a result, the motivation for change and innovation, particularly if it entails substantial investment capital, is missing from the largest segment in the construction industry.

Local Nature of Construction Firms

The fact that the majority of firms engaged in the production of real estate improvements are local in origin has a dramatic impact upon the nature of the industry. The first element is the high susceptibility to market fluctuations. Although national real estate trends are rather steady in their trends over the five-year periods, the impact upon local areas in most cases is dramatically different in nature and in the extent of the movement within the common real estate cycles that persist. Housing starts may increase by ten percent nationally, but a given local area may incur substantial construction declines because of the many market factors that may affect one market more than another. Thus, a local firm is much more subject to these local variations than is a national firm. The national firm may have the capacity to shift resources and material from one local market temporarily slowed down to another local market experiencing a significant rise in construction activity.

A second element relating to the local nature of the construction industry is that being local, such firms are much more subject to the local political and financial forces and capacities of the area. Factors such as material supply, labor, financing for construction, planning and building permits and codes magnify the vulnerability of the firm that is local in nature and capacity. The ability to attract capital from outside sources greatly enhances the ability of the contractor to negotiate a fair rate of interest and

TABLE 15–4
Participants in Production Process

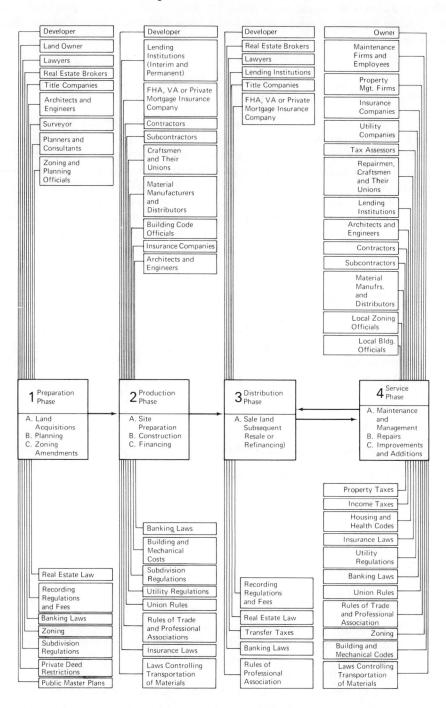

Preparation Phase	Production Phase	Distribution Phase	Service Phase
Developer	Developer	Developer	Owner
Land Owner	Lending Institutions (Interim and Permanent)	Real Estate Brokers	Maintenance Firms and Employees
Lawyers		Lawyers	Property Mgt. Firms
Real Estate Brokers	FHA, VA or Private Mortgage Insurance Company	Lending Institutions	Insurance Companies
Title Companies		Title Companies	Utility Companies
Architects and Engineers	Contractors	FHA, VA or Private Mortgage Insurance Company	Tax Assessors
Surveyor	Subcontractors		Repairmen, Craftsmen and Their Unions
Planners and Consultants	Craftsmen and Their Unions		Lending Institutions
Zoning and Planning Officials	Material Manufacturers and Distributors		Architects and Engineers
	Building Code Officials		Contractors
	Insurance Companies		Subcontractors
	Architects and Engineers		Material Manufrs. and Distributors
			Local Zoning Officials
			Local Bldg. Officials

1 Preparation Phase	**2** Production Phase	**3** Distribution Phase	**4** Service Phase
A. Land Acquisitions B. Planning C. Zoning Amendments	A. Site Preparation B. Construction C. Financing	A. Sale (and Subsequent Resale or Refinancing)	A. Maintenance and Management B. Repairs C. Improvements and Additions
Real Estate Law	Banking Laws		Property Taxes
Recording Regulations and Fees	Building and Mechanical Costs		Income Taxes
Banking Laws	Subdivision Regulations		Housing and Health Codes
Zoning	Utility Regulations	Recording Regulations and Fees	Insurance Laws
Subdivision Regulations	Union Rules	Real Estate Law	Utility Regulations
Private Deed Restrictions	Rules of Trade and Professional Associations	Transfer Taxes	Banking Laws
Public Master Plans	Insurance Laws	Banking Laws	Union Rules
	Laws Controlling Transportation of Materials	Rules of Professional Association	Rules of Trade and Professional Association
			Zoning
			Building and Mechanical Codes
			Laws Controlling Transportation of Materials

Source: The President's Committee on Urban Housing, *A Decent Home* (Washington, D.C.: U.S. Government Printing Office, 1969), p. 115.

adequate amounts of capital to facilitate his project. Additionally, material and labor in key areas may be a premium that would allow a firm to complete a project that another firm without access to such national markets would be unable to complete at a feasible cost.

Unorganized Industry Nationally

In the economic sense, the unorganized nature of the production process in real estate is most dramatic in the building codes and zoning regulations that exist in nearly every locality. Such regulations are municipal in their nature and vary to nearly infinite extremes between localities. As a result of such parameters, it is a physical impossibility to build units that will satisfy all the regulations of all the cities and counties in all the 50 states. Such requirements enforce the prevailing tendency for construction firms to be local in their origin and small scale in their operations. The result is lower operating economies subject to greater frequencies of fluctuations, and a higher cost to the builders, owners and consumers of real property services.

OPERATION BREAKTHROUGH

Indeed, the characteristics in the production process of real estate services were so contrary to what most persons felt was the efficient way to produce improvements that the federal government entered the picture through the U.S. Department of Housing and Urban Development (HUD) after its formation in 1965. At that time, HUD found the constraints in the production of adequate housing for the citizens to be:

1—A fragmented housing market

2—Restrictive building and zoning codes

3—Shortages and inefficiency of skilled labor

4—Processing red tape

5—Poor use of land

6—Restrictive labor practices

7—Inadequate management methods

8—Absence of adequate short-term and long-term financing.

In an attempt to overcome some of those industry shortcomings several research and experimental programs were started. Primarily they were aimed at the more technical nature of the industry problems. Such concepts as manufactured housing and modular units constructed off site to be later assembled on site, and various other technical aspects of the production problems, were addressed in the federal program. In 1970 there were 73 contracts awarded in the HUD experiment for a total of $27 million dollars. In the following year, 1971, 65 contracts were awarded for a total of nearly $26 million.

As a result of these and many other research projects relating to the real estate and construction area, significant advancement has been made in the areas of design and material improvements in the construction of housing units. Although in some cases the acceptance of a new method or process has been slow, the industry and the ultimate consumers of technologic advancement have benefited from some of the real progress made during the past ten years.

Technology has actually not been the major obstacle to the solution of some of the major social problems. We have the industrial capacity to construct, and the technical skills to design, entire cities in single buildings or structures compatible with our environment and enriching to the lives of those who inhabit them. The major problem is in being human beings and being blessed or cursed with that capacity of will and individual direction that may enrich the life of the individual and coincidentally hamper progress on the group or species level. Individualism in the production processes of real estate correlates very highly with the fractionalism of property ownership in the land-use planning and patterns that develop. We have come to the conclusion that zoning regulations are necessary to overcome some of the disadvantages of fractionalization of ownership. When one looks at the major problem areas identified with the production process in real estate, there are many similarities with the justifications for zoning in land use.

CURRENT PROBLEM AREA IN THE PRODUCTION PROCESS

Many of the constraints found by HUD mentioned earlier are currently found on the construction scene. The housing market is by its very nature severely fragmented. This fragmentation persists into the contemporary market. Although a few large planned communities are beginning to appear, the majority of housing starts are still spread out among the major cities in the nation. Additionally, even within one major city or area the housing starts are not concentrated in one area, but rather are spread out in various areas throughout the major metropolitan areas and their fringe areas. As a result, there is very little promise in the future of alleviating the fragmentary nature of the housing production industry. Some centralization and concentration will increase as the new planned communities increase in number and size, but the current population trends dictate that this will be short lived as our population begins to stabilize. Some additional concentration may occur in the rebuilding efforts being introduced in the larger major cities. The migration of major population segments back into the central cities may lessen fragmentation. It is also a short-lived promise, however, and would not permanently alleviate the fragmented character of the production sector of the real estate industry.

The presence of extensive red tape in processing production commitments and the actual exchange in the market place is an area of increasing and growing magnitude. With the growth of environmental considerations and the "social advantages and disadvantages" associated with given proposed projects being a required part of the pre-construction process, the future does not hold bright promise for any substantial reduction in the processing time required in the production process. In part, the extensive planning and processing steps prior to actual construction are reflective of the very nature of the real estate commodity itself.

Referring to the classes of estates in real property, and the technicalities involved in the ownership of real property, much of the "red tape" is more reflective of the product itself than of the various social and government requirements relating to it. Through some consolidation on the part of government agencies regulating the various aspects of real property use and transfer, there is the prospect of some reduction in the processing times associated with improving real property. The impetus for such improvement, however, appears to be directed at the governmental sector rather than the private sector involved in real estate production and improvement.

With respect to the poor use of land, the rising costs of real estate services and real property will direct nearly all national attention to the efficient use of real property wherever it is under significant growth pressure from the major population centers. To the extent that such poor land use is the function of outdated and shortsighted planning and zoning regulations, the economic pressures placed upon the major population segments of our nation, and to some extent the world, will force such changes in those regulations because of economic pressures. Improved planning on the part of municipal planning agencies, with the coordination implied in the regional planning concept, should overcome some of the shortcomings resulting from the fractionalization of ownership and competing municipal interests. The result should be more improved land use within regions for the benefit of all the population segments within the regions concerned.

The one major flaw in such analysis is the planning function itself. As the Figure 15–4 illustrates, the planning departments of most municipalities have an advisory function only. In most municipal organizations the planning department is staffed by well-trained and experienced urban planners. That department is within the city administration. In proposed projects the planning department researches the possible impact of the projects and makes a professional recommendation to the planning commission on whether the project should be approved or disapproved in light of the land use plans of the city. The planning commission is generally composed of a wide variety of public citizens without extensive economic or planning knowledge. The commission then makes its decision based upon the planning department's analysis and recommendation and upon the personal beliefs of the commission members.

If the project is refused a permit, the principals may appeal to the city council, which is composed of elected representatives of the public rather than the appointed members that sit on the planning commission. If the appeal is denied there is still one more avenue for the principals to take. Through a procedure known as a special use permit, or a variance permit, the developers may circumvent the entire procedure. Since the mayor and the city council are most often politicians, they are subject to political pressure if it originates from the proper sources and is intense enough to provoke action. The special use permits are most often associated with very large projects by very important people on the local political scene. Through the issuance of a special use permit, the entire land use plan of an area may be contradicted. It is in these ways that the best plans for a region or municipality may be totally ignored in the actual patterns of land use that develop. Until the persons with the expertise in economics and urban

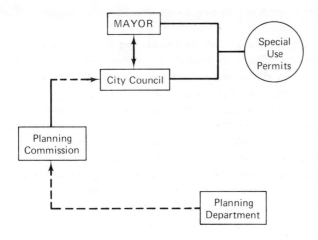

Figure 15–4

planning inherit some power or authority to enforce their planning decisions, the instances of poor land use relative to the total good of the community and its citizens will continue to reappear.

PROBLEM AREAS LIKELY TO BE SOLVED

The four problem areas likely to hold promise of solution in the future of real estate are: (1) restrictive building and zoning codes, (2) the shortages and inefficient use of skilled labor that characterize the industry, (3) the restrictive labor practices, and (4) the general absence of short-term and long-term financing. The reasons for promise in these areas as opposed to the other areas is that they are more specific in the nature of the problem concerned. Where the previous problems were indicative of the very nature of the real estate product and the basic nature of the market process of supply and demand, the four topics listed above are more reflective of specific practices of those operating within the market for real estate services and their production capabilities.

Restrictive building codes are fairly common in the municipal jurisdictions that have formal building codes that date much before the 1960s. Rather than specifying what materials a building and its parts must be built from, a rewording of the codes in terms of what objectives are to be reached or maintained would open the area to innovation in technical materials and handling beyond what now exists. Additionally, such rewriting of building codes could be stimulated from the governmental level with very little procedural problems. The cooperation of the various elements of the industry that possess an inappropriate advantage stemming from the requirements of such codes would be the largest single obstacle for effort on the part of local or regional governmental bodies. Specific state or federal governmental influence or pressure could substantially reduce resistance to such a rewriting to the benefit of the majority of the citizenry of those areas.

The restrictive zoning codes present another more complex issue. Both areas are totally within the jurisdiction of local municipalities, and could not be unilaterally removed or modified by the federal or state governments. The major impetus for changes will probably be in the area of certain economic incentives originating from the state or federal level to promote changes for the benefit of regional planning and improvement. As long as certain groups are the recipients of distinct economic advantages that would not, or that they believe would not, persist if changes were made, then the changes will not be made. However, if the economic returns to the region of the major elements of a region or the real estate production industry within a region are such that they outweigh the economic strength of the specific groups, then changes in building and zoning codes will succeed. Because of the move toward regional planning agencies at the impetus of the federal government, there is a very real hope that the zoning codes that are restrictive will be modified in the best interests of the citizens of the entire regions concerned.

The problems of shortages and inefficient use of skilled labor is a major problem in the industry as a whole. Many of the problems are a result of the small economies of scale of the majority of firms operating within the industry. It is possible that as the size and scope of firms operating within the industry grows, much of this problem will be addressed. However, it remains for the industry to restructure itself and provide the necessary opportunity for firms of a national scope to enter the market. With a firm of national scale, certain economies of scale would become available and labor could be employed on a more permanent scale. As the size of projects grows materially and financially, there is the hope that incentives will begin to appear in the industry sufficient to attract internal structural changes.

The problem of restrictive labor practices became most apparent when Operation Breakthrough attempted to introduce the manufacturing techniques of major industry to the construction industry. By manufacturing units in a centralized location and facility of substantial size, large cost savings could be realized. Material could be purchased on a bulk scale and the division of labor could be achieved.

It was the division of labor that led to many if not most of the problems in adapting these techniques to the industry at large. It was not necessary to employ journeyman carpenters and plumbers and electricians when producing housing units on the assembly line basis where each station in the line only performed one task of a relatively simple and/or routine nature. A journeyman carpenter, for instance, is required to be proficient at building forms for cement, floors and wall studs and framing, hanging doors and windows and doing finish cabinet work, but the tasks performed on the assembly line would involve many more people each doing only one part. The resultant lower skills required would not necessarily justify the wages earned by the person capable of performing all those tasks. Through the strong organization of the skilled trades labor force, displacement of their members with less-skilled and lower-paid personnel was and is a major issue. The trend toward subcontracting for framing off-site and buying cabinets premade at an off-site location gives promise that such innovations are in fact creeping into the production process in real estate. The economic benefits to be derived by the producers and consumers of real estate buildings are such that continued division of labor seems assured. The stability of the labor force in the specialized areas also is an attraction to those composing the skilled trades in the construction industry. Improved cooperation between organized labor and governmental interests would significantly advance such trends to the benefit of the majority if not all in the industry.

The last major problem area, that of an absence of adequate short- and long-term financing in the production process, is a continual problem throughout the entire real estate sector of our economy. It is a problem not only in the production process but also in the marketing area of real estate.

Figure 15–5 reflects the fundamental problem involved in the financing of real estate. Banks and major financial institutions raise capital through various short-term accounts. These short-term accounts are the borrowed funds for such institutions. Being short-term in nature they fluctuate according to the current economic conditions prevailing in the money and financial markets. However, the funds generated through such accounts are the funds used to finance the long-lived real estate interests. Generally these real estate interests are long-term loans of one form or another. Since the loans are relatively fixed in the amounts they will return to the financial institutions, and the short-term accounts are forever fluctuating, the result is an alternate profit and loss depending upon the spread between the two.

Disintermediation

When the returns capable of being earned in the short-term interest accounts are substantially below the returns promised in other forms of investments, there is a shift

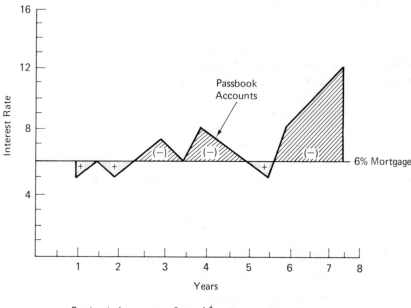

Passbook Accounts — Cost of $ to Banks = Short Term
Mortgages   — Price of Product = Profit = Long Term

Figure 15–5

from the lower to the higher returns. This involves the withdrawal of funds from the savings institutions and the reinvestment of such funds in other areas. Generally these other areas are not real estate oriented. The result is a decrease in the amount of funds available for real estate financing. Such flow of funds out of the savings institutions into other higher yielding investments on a short-term basis is called *disintermediation*.

Because of the nature of the real estate industry and the financial industry that interacts with it, the consequences of such fluctuations are severe in terms of productivity level and the economies of scale to be realized through more stability. The lack of funds in the real estate sector has a rather immediate impact upon the production of real estate improvements and also upon the marketing of units already completed or offered for resale. There is the capacity on the part of the nation to substantially alleviate some of the more severe of the consequences of such fluctuations in the money markets.

One solution has been to advocate the variable rate mortgage. The effect would be to make the rate of return earned on the part of financial institutions on their mortgages follow the pattern of the short-term passbook accounts, which represent the cost of borrowed capital to the same such institutions. The fundamental problem of borrowing short-term and lending long-term would be addressed by making the loans subject to the short-term fluctuations. The result would be costs based upon the short-term and profits keyed to the same short-term conditions.

The other fundamental solution would be to finance real estate loans with capital raised in the long-term market. By issuing long-term bonds bearing a fixed interest rate, the proceeds from the bonds could be used to finance long-term real estate mortgages at a fixed spread above the costs of the bonds. The ultimate impact of such an approach would be to loan money in the long-term from the funds borrowed in the same long-term time frame.

It is obvious that something must be done, hopefully in the near future, to equate the time parameters of the debt market largely supportive of the real estate industry. The continued fluctuation between feast and famine, mostly famine in the inflationary market, that has plagued the whole of the real estate production process and the financing complexities that evolved in the financing involved in the marketing segments of the whole real estate industry cannot continue to be tolerated indefinitely. It would also appear that the role of the federal and state governments could be significantly expanded in this particular area. The capacity for such an innovation on the part of the private sector would seem to be far below that necessary to substantially solve the short-term versus long-term problem and its manifestations on the national real estate level.

REFERENCES

1—U.S., Department of Commerce, Bureau of the Census, *Statistical Abstract of the United States, 1973*. Washington, D.C.: U.S. Printing Office, 1974.

2—U.S., Department of Housing and Urban Development, A Decent Home. Report of the President's Commission on Housing. Washington, D.C.: U.S. Printing Office, 1968.

GOVERNMENT PARTICIPATION IN REAL ESTATE

REAL ESTATE AS A "BUNDLE OF RIGHTS"

In the ultimate sense, real estate ownership is essentially the purchase or sale of rights to use specific real property within certain parameters. The physical asset is not capable of being in anyone's possession in the way that tradeable items such as bread, clothing or other smaller items can be. Real estate is not portable, and therefore cannot accompany the owner when he or she moves about. The entire asset itself is rather more abstract than normal goods exchanged in the market place.

The rights to use, which are the essence of real property ownership, are legally defined. The rights are also enforced through the legal system of the governing authorities under which they are subject. The property object itself must be capable of being owned, and must also have a police power to defend and enforce the claims to ownership. Therefore, the government of any area is fundamentally involved in the ownership of real property. The governing authority defines the abstract property rights that are the subject of the market exchange. That same governing authority must stand to enforce the rights of the principals in the exchange of any ownership concept to have any meaning or validity. In this way the governments—federal, state and local—are basic to the very nature of real property. Such a role in real property is so basic that there always has been and probably always will be a strong and direct involvement on the parts of governing bodies and the real property located within their jurisdiction.

EARLY HISTORY

The history of government involvement in the real estate sector was essentially one of physical involvement of land acquisition and disposal prior to the early 1900s. The federal government acquired many major parcels of land in several major events in our early history, as shown in Figure 16–1. As is true with most nations of the world, the United States acquired most of its lands through military efforts and various treaties as the direct result of military campaigns. In some of the acquisitions, there was an actual agreement to buy the subject lands for monetary compensation. The Louisiana Purchase, the Gladstone Purchase and the Territory of Alaska are examples of major lands that were purchased by the federal government during the early history of the United States. In most other cases, however, the acquisition of lands was through military conquests of various sorts.

The second major activity on the part of the federal government involving real estate was to give these newly acquired lands to those who agreed to settle permanently in the new areas. The various homestead areas under the homestead acts of Congress included most of the midwest and central areas after the Louisiana Purchase. There was also extensive homestead activity in the far west, particularly the northwestern states. Giving federally acquired lands to settlers who agreed to establish themselves in the new territories was an active part of the federal government's policies involving real estate throughout the 1800s, and in fact is active in the present day in the more primitive areas of the Alaskan frontier.

The federal government's activities in the real estate sector were never explicitly defined or declared until the 1930s. Until that time the role of the federal government was

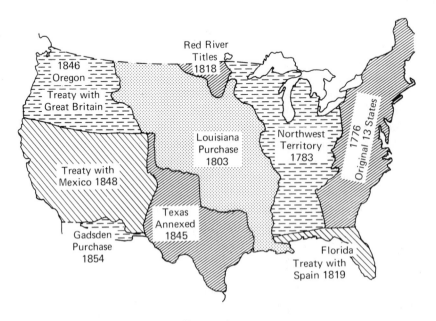

Figure 16–1

primarily one of acquiring various land areas and then disposing of those land areas in such a way as to encourage permanent settling of the areas involved. Formal policy relating to the objectives of government involvement in real estate was not forthcoming until the country was in the depths of the depression in the early 1930s. Then it was mandatory that the federal government take a position in relation to the inequities and impact nationally of the sudden collapse of the real estate sector almost totally.

Birth of Federal Policy

Although some attention was given to the need for housing on the part of the nation as a whole as early as the turn of the century, and some federal public housing was actually produced after World War I, the manifestation of an active role on the part of the federal government was not evident until the depression era of the 1930s. In the early 1930s the nation was faced with the nearly complete collapse of the real estate mortgage markets and the concurrent high levels of unemployment and low economic activity. It was at this time that the federal government declared its intention of returning the economy to its feet in the economic sense. This was the first time that a definitive objective had been issued from the federal level relating to its objectives in reference to the real estate sector and the involvement of the federal government in that sector.

As a result of this objective, the federal government set about the task of reorganizing the activities in the real estate sector and instituting various specific programs to overcome some of the major problem areas that had come to light during the economic depression and its manifestations. Atlhough much of the detail of the governmental involvement during this period was discussed earlier in the chapter relating to the history of real estate finance, it may be appropriate to mention some of those activities on the part of the federal government that originated at this time. The first major problem was the collapse of the savings and loan industry, which had to be dealt with before anything else could be done. In 1931, the Federal Home Loan Bank System was created and actually became a reality in 1932. In 1933, the Home Owners Loan Corporation was formed to buy mortgages that were threatened with foreclosure. The National Housing Act of 1934 instituted the program of mortgage insurance programs to be administered by the Federal Housing Authority. Finally at this time the secondary mortgage market was established through the creation of the Federal National Mortgage Association in 1938. There also was the first direct involvement in the housing of the poor through public and subsidized housing that began through the Housing Act of 1937.

Contemporary Federal Policies

During and following the Second World War the scope as well as the objectives of involvement in real estate by the federal government changed from the focus born out of the depression years. Under the G.I. Bill of Rights passed in 1944, the veteran's mortgage guarantee program was born and placed under the direction of the Veterans Administration. Through such a program, veterans returning from World War II could borrow 100 percent of the cost of a new home. The need for programs suitable to fill the needs of the nation with thousands of returning veterans and the starting of new family units was the major impetus behind such programs. At this time the FNMA was also modified so that it could make commitments in advance to support the low interest rates of the VA loans. Because of the sudden jump in activity there was increased pressure on interest rates that hurt some of the VA projects.

Shortly after the war there was increased interest in providing adequate housing for those below the average income levels. The Housing Act of 1949 authorized certain public housing programs in addition to slum clearance and urban renewal projects. The Housing Act of 1949 was most noted for its statement of national housing policy. For the second time in the history of the federal government there was an explicit declaration of the intent and objectives of its involvement in the real estate sector. In the 1949 Act the federal government declared that there be the goal of "a decent home and a suitable living environment for every American Family."

In the decade of the 1950s there was little new legislation from the federal level that changed the directions already established since the end of the Second World War. The Housing Act of 1954 did bring one new area into focus from both the national and the local perspective. Under the provisions of that act local government was required to develop plans for community improvement before eligibility for various assistance was established.

In the Housing Acts of 1959, 1961, 1965 and 1968 the major part of the federal programs specifically aimed at the lower economic groups in an attempt to provide adequate housing to segments of the national populace that could not normally afford such housing. Some other aspects of the legislation during the period of the 1960s was the creation of the Department of Housing and Urban Development (HUD) in 1965, which was a cabinet-level department focusing upon real estate and housing and the authorization of large appropriations with which to finance these federal subsidy programs in the 1968 Act.

CONSTITUTIONAL IMPLICATIONS

Through the Constitution of the United States governing bodies have an inherent obligation to protect and enhance the health and welfare of the citizens of the country. It is through this obligation that the state and local governments of the individual states and the federal government have a direct interest in the use and distribution of real estate resources among the citizenry. As was cited earlier, control over land use and improvements within certain well defined parameters is a function and obligation on the part of local as well as state governments. As a result, each municipality has some form of legislation to regulate the building and improving of real property within their jurisdiction. Building codes are potent forms of government involvement in the real estate sector. They directly touch the land and improvements in the areas and have a very telling impact many times on the costs and resultant land-use patterns that develop in the area.

We have discussed zoning codes in the earlier chapters relating to land use patterns and control. It should be noted that although municipal zoning codes did not come into their own until the early 1930s, political and social pressure they reflect have been and are a strong form of informal government influence. The issuance of building permits, which are required in nearly all municipal jurisdictions, is often a political as well as economic consideration. In such cases, the social and political pressures that exist relative to a land use decision weigh quite heavily on the eventual outcome. Governing bodies are forever political in nature, and therefore they will continue to reflect local attitudes of social as well as political nature.

INDIRECT GOVERNMENTAL INFLUENCES

As we have seen in the preceding chapter, the sector of our national economy involving real estate constitutes a very large segment of our whole economic profile. When one reflects upon the multitude of supporting sectors of industry and commerce that largely service and depend upon the real estate sector, it is no surprise that nearly every economic decision at the federal level as well as the state level has a real impact upon real estate activity and economic well-being. Such policies that may emanate from the federal level that have substantial impact upon monetary policy, fiscal policy, imports and exports, balance of trade, balance of payments, inflationary trends and employment are all areas that have or tend to have a real and measurable impact upon the level of real estate activity in the nation as a whole, and particular areas even more so.

Monetary Policy

The regulation of the total money supply of the nation is the basic subject of monetary policy. As the quantity of money available largely determines the prevailing interest rates, which in turn affect the general level of economic activity within the nation, monetary policy has a very real impact upon the real estate sector of the nation. Prior to World War II, monetary policy was rather undefined through regulation in the direct sense. The major problem confronting federal authorities at that time in our history was how to deal with sudden and dramatic deflation of the economy. After the depression, the Federal Reserve System was more active in its support of the monetary activities on the part of the Treasury.

Since the war, inflation has been the major focus of monetary policy. Because real estate services normally constitute nearly one-fourth of the total personal expenditures on the part of the population, and as it is one single industry or product expenditure, the impact of inflation and monetary policy in reaction to it are quickly discernible by the majority of the people. When the prices of real estate services escalate during periods of rapid inflation, the impact upon the nation is dramatic and severe. Likewise, when the supply of money is curtailed relative to the demand for money, the rise in the interest rates particularly in the real estate sector affects a substantial portion of the economy. The most direct area of impact is in the financing of real estate as discussed in the previous chapter in reference to new units. The problem of disintermediation in the savings and loan sector during times of escalating demand for funds and a stagnant or trailing supply of money is often directly related to the actions on the part of federal monetary authorities.

Fiscal Policy

The general area of federal government expenditure policy is the basic focus of fiscal affairs. When the federal government spends more money than it takes in from taxes and other revenue sources, the net impact is an increase in the money supply in the form of federal debt. In the case of a budget surplus, where the federal government spends less than it takes in, the net impact on the economy is the reduction in the money supply and economic activity. It is through such policies that the federal government raised the level of economic activity during the early 1930s to stimulate the economic recovery. The case of inflation and overheated economic pressure calls for the reverse procedure of a federal government surplus to slow down the inflation and growth rate. Such a policy as federal budget surpluses and higher taxes is politically not the most popular item in most campaigns. As a result, the general nature of inflation is much more pervasive and more difficult to deal with in a political democracy.

Another element of federal fiscal policy that should be mentioned is the specific nature of such activity. Rather than affecting the entire economy rather generally, fiscal policy will identify and affect select elements in the economy directly. An increase in Defense Department contracts will affect only those areas that are directly related to defense contractors and subcontractors. Other areas without such industries will not reap the benefits of such expenditures until the spent funds have percolated through the entire system. Therefore, it is very important to identify those areas within one's operating area that are subject to the fiscal policies on the part of the federal and state governments. Such areas as retirement communities, educational plants, scientific research, veterans and agriculture are areas not normally followed in the published business indicators. Yet, such areas may in fact live or die in the economic sense on the basis of federal fiscal expenditure patterns.

The case of Boeing, Inc., in Seattle is an illustration of the impact of fiscal policies that may affect specific areas dramatically, while at the same time having very little impact upon areas having little such industry within their areas. In that city, Boeing was one of the major employers and constituted one of the largest basic industries in that economic region. In the late 1960s the federal government severely cut back on its development contracts for the supersonic transport (SST), for which Boeing was a major contractor and developer. As a result the unemployment rate in that area increased dramatically. Nearly one-third of the work force was laid off or terminated as the direct result of cutoff of funds from the federal authorities for the SST.

Communities that contain large proportions of retired people would be much more sensitive to fiscal policies relating to social security and military and government retirement benefits. Wherever there is one segment of the local regional economy dependent upon some fiscal program on the national or state level, normal business indicators will fall short of accurately predicting future economic trends when those indicators are not expanded to include certain fiscal and federal program legislation in the current time frame.

International Trade

At the national level, international trade is a vital economic factor affecting the balance of payments with foreign countries. When a nation exports more than it imports, the result is a payment in money for the difference by the foreign nation. The payment or transfer of funds from one nation to another results in a net increase in the country receiving the funds. Through the banking system of the nation this increase is multiplied as it percolates through the economy. The multiplier discussed earlier in the section relating to real estate finance comes into the picture in relation to a positive balance of payments situation where the nation has a "favorable" balance of trade. It will be recalled that with a reserve requirement of 20 percent the result of the multiplier effect is a multiplier of five. That means for every unit of net gain in the money base, as through payments by foreign countries, one unit will become five units after passing from one segment of the economy to another. Such an increase in the monetary profile of a nation as the result of foreign trade is a vitally important consideration on the part of the federal authorities.

It should also be noted that such increases in the total funds within a nation also decrease the interest rates prevailing in the nation. The market for funds is not unlike the market for most other commodities in that the price of those funds in terms of interest rates reflects the interaction of the supply for funds and the demand for funds. If the supply of funds increases, and there is not a corresponding increase in the demand for funds at the same time, the price of that commodity, money, will drop. Figure 16–2 illustrates this process of a sudden increase in supply without a change in the demand function. With an increase in the total available funds from S_1 to S_2, the price as reflected in interest rates buyers are willing to pay drops from i_1 to i_2. This is an over-

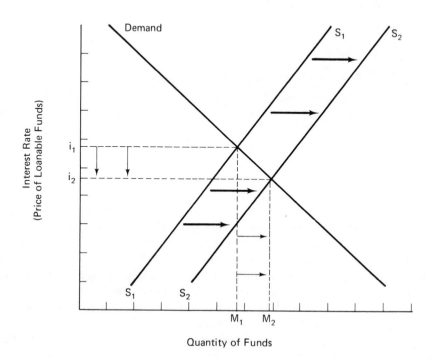

Figure 16–2

simplified example to be sure; however, the market generally behaves this way over time. The major area of oversimplification is the demand for funds, which in the real world fluctuates greatly and changes dramatically in the short term. During periods of over-heated expansion, demand may, in fact, exceed all available supply and will drive interest rates far above any level prevailing prior to that period. Because the central banking system has some powerful tools at its disposal through the reserve requirement, discount window and the Open Market Committee operating in the major money market, there is rarely any sudden decline of major proportions in the available supply of total money in the system.

Specific Agencies

Among the agencies of the federal government that operate directly in the real estate sector are the following:

1—Department of Housing and Urban Development

2—Federal Housing Authority

3—Veterans Administration

4—Federal Home Loan Banks

5—GNMA

6—FNMA

7—General Services Administration

8—All branches of the military services

9—National Park Service

10—Department of Agriculture

11—Department of Transportation

This is only a partial list, but gives some indication of the number and extent of in-volvement in real estate on the part of the federal government and its various agencies.

An inventory of land ownership in a given region will aid the researcher in gauging the possible impact of various agencies and their policy decisions upon the real estate activity of the given area under study. Some of the departments will affect real es-tate activity in nearly all areas of the nation. Others will have greater impact upon certain areas that are more subject to their influence. Areas with large sections of land ownership in the hands of federal agencies will be more sensitive to policy changes emanating from those sectors of the federal government having jurisdiction over such land areas. Notably, the military and park services control large portions of land areas in the western regions of the country. Significant changes in the use to which such lands are to be or are being put can have a dramatic impact upon the regional economies and the level of real estate activity in the private sector that lies within the same regions.

Trends of Government Involvement

During the first 200 years of this nation, the federal government was involved in the acquisition and granting of real property to the nearly complete exclusion of any other action relating to real estate. It was not until the depression of the early 1930s that conditions compelled the federal government to formally declare its objectives in real estate involvement. At that time, the first objective was to aid the nation in its economic recovery from the depression. As a result, the programs that developed out of this era were broad general programs designed to aid all of the nation and the economic recovery.

After World War II, there were more specific conditions that brought the focus of the federal government on the real estate sector. At this time the second formal objective of federal participation in the real estate sector was formulated. That objective was the promotion of a "decent home and living environment for every American citizen." Although the focus was on the real estate sector for what it was in its own right, the programs that resulted were also generally national in scope and influenced all of real estate in general. Programs such as the VA insured loan program, the restructuring of the secondary mortgage market and the creation of HUD on the cabinet level were indicative of the type of programs that developed out of this period.

Since the late 1960s, policies relating to the real estate sector on the part of the federal governmental bodies have been more specific and detailed in content than those of previous years. Several programs have aimed specifically at the lower income portions of the national population, more than at any time previously. Additionally, in numerous instances land use decisions have been aided by the actions on the part of the federal government. The programs such as Operation Breakthrough and the Model Cities program have been aimed at specific problems within the real estate sector and the problems of trying to insure a "decent home for every American."

Generally, then, we have seen the role of the federal government begin with an absence of formal policy, definition of national economic goals to include real estate, the development of specific general programs to aid the real estate industry in aggregate and, during the past decade, the formation of goals and policy aimed at specific elements of the national real estate sector.

IMPLICATIONS FOR THE FUTURE

As with the private industrialist producing a product for sale in the market place, the major tasks in terms of real estate are: (1) producing the proper blend of real estate services to fill the needs of the buyers in the market now and in the future, and (2) producing that blend at a cost that will allow the product to sell in the market at a price the greatest number of potential consumers can afford and are willing to pay, and at the same time give the producing sector an adequate profit to make the entire venture worthwhile in terms of risks and returns. These will always present the greatest tests of ingenuity and creativeness that characterize the free-enterprise system under which the United States operates. They are the same major problem areas confronting most industrialists manufacturing products for the consuming public. The real estate product is by far more complex and very few instances exist, if any, where one major group has the power to make all the decisions from the market location, the product manufacture, through the sale and maintenance and resale of the product. Indeed, many of the problems associated with real estate originate from the number of groups and individuals included in the decision-making process.

COSTS OF THE REAL ESTATE PRODUCT

In spite of all the political debate and various legislative voices of concern for environmental and social concern over national, state and local benefits to the major segments of society, the one area of most concern and dramatic impact is the cost of real estate services. Every individual in the country is made aware of the cost impact of real estate services on their personal incomes. Although altruistic motivations are admirable and indeed may yield valuable social benefits, the dollar impact of real estate choices usually prevails as the number one issue.

Current trends in the real estate sector indicate that the costs of adequate housing are escalating faster than the incomes of the majority of persons in the United States, if not the entire world. For this reason, it is the opinion of the author that costs will be the major focus of the future involvement on the part of the federal and state governments in the real estate sector. More particularly, the financing of real property will receive the majority of that interest. The problem of disintermediation in the major financial institutions supporting real estate financing is but one of the major symptoms of needed restructuring of the whole of real estate finance. The impact of fluctuating availability and terms of the financing of construction and sales of real estate services on other major elements of the economy are serious ills built into the current structure of the real estate industry. The powerful influence of the federal government in the areas of monetary and fiscal policy, and the even stronger influence of the various federal agencies directly involved in the real estate sector, seem to point to the role of the federal government in the changes within the financing of real estate services in production and marketing.

In addition to the financing of real estate services, the overcoming of some of the localization and low economies of scale that characterize the real estate sector may also be a major area for federal government influence. It would seem that through providing adequate economic incentives, the federal government may gain the cooperation of the local governments and the various segments of organized labor sufficient to allow national production of the real estate resources able to overcome some of the ill effects of fluctuating local economies and the predominance of local small-scale producers.

PROPER BLEND OF REAL
ESTATE RESOURCES

The possibilities for drastic innovation and change from the typical form of real estate product found in the market today appear to be much less optimistic. The reeducation of the majority of real estate consumers away from the individual structure and individuality expressed in most of the real estate resources would be a substantial task. The major impetus for such a change in consumer preferences would have to emanate from the significant cost advantages inherent in such a change. Recent successes occurring in the areas of condominiums would seem to point to the possibilities for such a change in life styles and product preferences in the real estate product market. The major advantages continue to be the apparent lower cost of luxury and/or adequate housing when compared to that to be found in the more traditional single-family residence mode.

The recent trends in environmental concern and evaluation would seem to add further importance to more well planned and larger scale projects the condominium procepts typify. With the rising costs of the real estate product itself, and the even more increasing planning and processing costs associated with it, development will raise the cost of the end product in real estate services. When the costs of real estate services rise faster relative to incomes of the population, there will be significant modification of the product to bring it into the market at a price adequate to be marketed. Such modifications as the planned unit development, townhouses and condominiums are some of the more recent trends in product modification that the future of real estate will be looking at in the solution of the inefficient uses and high costs of the more traditional real estate project.

REFERENCES

1—Chamberlain, Neil W. *The Limits of Corporate Responsibility.* New York: Basic Books, Inc., 1973.

2—Commoner, Barry. "The Closing Circle," *The New Yorker*, 2 October 1971, p. 46.

3—Heller, Walter. "Economic Growth and Ecology." *Monthly Labor Review* 44: November 1971, pp. 19–20.

4—Kratovil, Robert. *Real Estate Law.* Englewood Cliffs, N.J.: Prentice-Hall, Inc., 1974.

5—Mylroie, Gerald R. et. al. *California Environmental Law: A Guide.* Claremont, Ca.: Center for California Public Affairs, 1972.

6—Solow, Robert M. "The Economist's Approach to Pollution and its Control." *Science* 173. August, 1971, pp. 498–503.

Appendix
Interest and Present Value Tables

Period	Compound Interest Amount	Compound One Per Period	Present Value Of $1 In Future	Present Value Of $1 Per Period	Period
1	1.0008333000	1.0000000000	.9991673938	.9991673947	1
2	1.0016672944	2.0008332893	.9983354809	1.9975028681	2
3	1.0025019837	3.0025005880	.9975042606	2.9950071403	3
4	1.0033373686	4.0050025681	.9966737323	3.9916808592	4
5	1.0041734497	5.0083399376	.9958438956	4.9875247570	5
6	1.0050102274	6.0125133925	.9950147498	5.9825395176	6
7	1.0058477024	7.0175236169	.9941862944	6.9767258010	7
8	1.0066858753	8.0233713189	.9933585287	7.9700843394	8
9	1.0075247467	9.0300571943	.9925314523	8.9626157926	9
10	1.0083643170	10.0375819393	.9917050644	9.9543208448	10
11	1.0092045870	11.0459462619	.9908793647	10.9452002160	11
12	1.0100455572	12.0551508460	.9900543524	11.9352545662	12
13	1.0108872282	13.0651963999	.9892300270	12.9244845914	13
14	1.0117296005	14.0760836313	.9884063879	13.9128909876	14
15	1.0125726748	15.0878132365	.9875834347	14.9004744270	15
16	1.0134164516	16.1003859114	.9867611666	15.8872355934	16
17	1.0142609315	17.1138023641	.9859395831	16.8731751710	17
18	1.0151061151	18.1280632905	.9851186837	17.8582938558	18
19	1.0159520031	19.1431694108	.9842984678	18.8425923317	19
20	1.0167985959	20.1591214089	.9834789348	19.8260712589	20
21	1.0176458941	21.1759200048	.9826600842	20.8087313453	21
22	1.0184938985	22.1935658946	.9818419153	21.7905732509	22
23	1.0193426094	23.2120597984	.9810244277	22.7715976839	23
24	1.0201920276	24.2314024121	.9802076206	23.7518053042	24
25	1.0210421536	25.2515944318	.9793914937	24.7311967959	25
26	1.0218929881	26.2726365895	.9785760463	25.7097728429	26
27	1.0227445315	27.2945295812	.9777612778	26.6875341294	27
28	1.0235967845	28.3172741030	.9769471877	27.6644813033	28
29	1.0244497477	29.3408708868	.9761337755	28.6406150846	29
30	1.0253034217	30.3653206408	.9753210404	29.6159361214	30
31	1.0261578070	31.3906240610	.9745089821	30.5904451098	31
32	1.0270129043	32.4167818673	.9736975999	31.5641427097	32
33	1.0278687142	33.4437947678	.9728868932	32.5370295932	33
34	1.0287252372	34.4716634825	.9720768616	33.5091064563	34
35	1.0295824739	35.5003887195	.9712675044	34.4803739590	35
36	1.0304404250	36.5299711988	.9704588210	35.4508327853	36
37	1.0312990910	37.5604116285	.9696508110	36.4204836073	37
38	1.0321584725	38.5917107164	.9688434738	37.3893270731	38
39	1.0330185702	39.6238691828	.9680368087	38.3573638786	39
40	1.0338793846	40.6568877595	.9672308152	39.3245946958	40
41	1.0347409163	41.6907671427	.9664254929	40.2910201848	41
42	1.0356031659	42.7255080523	.9656208410	41.2566410296	42
43	1.0364661340	43.7611112204	.9648168591	42.2214578903	43
44	1.0373298212	44.7975773551	.9640135467	43.1854714389	44
45	1.0381942282	45.8349071763	.9632109030	44.1486823353	45
46	1.0390593554	46.8731014041	.9624089277	45.1110912637	46
47	1.0399252036	47.9121607584	.9616076200	46.0726988840	47
48	1.0407917732	48.9520859714	.9608069796	47.0335058682	48
49	1.0416590650	49.9928777391	.9600070057	47.9935128765	49
50	1.0425270795	51.0345368055	.9592076980	48.9527205688	50
51	1.0433958173	52.0770638786	.9584090557	49.9111296172	51
52	1.0442652791	53.1204597024	.9576110784	50.8687407056	52
53	1.0451354653	54.1647249850	.9568137655	51.8255544702	53
54	1.0460063767	55.2098604464	.9560171164	52.7815715829	54
55	1.0468780138	56.2558668187	.9552211306	53.7367927157	55
56	1.0477503773	57.3027448338	.9544258076	54.6912185167	56
57	1.0486234677	58.3504952118	.9536311468	55.6448496700	57
58	1.0494972856	59.3991186847	.9528371476	56.5976868235	58
59	1.0503718317	60.4486159606	.9520438095	57.5497306252	59
60	1.0512471065	61.4989877955	.9512511319	58.5009817593	60
61	1.0521231108	62.5502349094	.9504591143	59.4514408736	61
62	1.0529998449	63.6023580103	.9496677562	60.4011086283	62
63	1.0538773097	64.6553578543	.9488770569	61.3499856834	63
64	1.0547555057	65.7092351734	.9480870160	62.2980727109	64
65	1.0556344334	66.7639906756	.9472976329	63.2453703348	65

Period	Compound Interest Amount	Compound One Per Period	Present Value Of $1 In Future	Present Value Of $1 Per Period	Period	RATE
1	1.0010000000	1.0000000000	.9990009990	.9990010000	1	
2	1.0020010000	2.0010000000	.9980029960	1.9970040000	2	
3	1.0030030010	3.0030010000	.9970059900	2.9940099900	3	
4	1.0040060040	4.0060040000	.9960099800	3.9900199700	4	
5	1.0050100100	5.0100100000	.9950149651	4.9850349300	5	
6	1.0060150200	6.0150200100	.9940209441	5.9790558700	6	
7	1.0070210350	7.0210350300	.9930279162	6.9720837900	7	
8	1.0080280561	8.0280560700	.9920358803	7.9641196800	8	
9	1.0090360841	9.0360841200	.9910448355	8.9551645100	9	
10	1.0100451202	10.0451202100	.9900547807	9.9452192900	10	
11	1.0110551653	11.0551653300	.9890657150	10.9342850100	11	
12	1.0120662205	12.0662204900	.9880776374	11.9223626400	12	
13	1.0130782867	13.0782867100	.9870905468	12.9094531900	13	
14	1.0140913650	14.0913650000	.9861044424	13.8955576300	14	
15	1.0151054564	15.1054563600	.9851193231	14.8806769500	15	
16	1.0161205618	16.1205618200	.9841351879	15.8648121400	16	
17	1.0171366824	17.1366823800	.9831520358	16.8479641700	17	
18	1.0181538191	18.1538190600	.9821698660	17.8301340400	18	
19	1.0191719729	19.1719728800	.9811886773	18.8113227200	19	
20	1.0201911449	20.1911448600	.9802084688	19.7915311900	20	
21	1.0212113360	21.2113360000	.9792292396	20.7707604300	21	
22	1.0222325473	22.2325473400	.9782509886	21.7490114200	22	
23	1.0232547799	23.2547798800	.9772737149	22.7262851300	23	
24	1.0242780347	24.2780346600	.9762974175	23.7025825400	24	
25	1.0253023127	25.3023127000	.9753220954	24.6779046500	25	
26	1.0263276150	26.3276150100	.9743477476	25.6522523900	26	
27	1.0273539426	27.3539426300	.9733743732	26.6256267700	27	
28	1.0283812966	28.3812965700	.9724019713	27.5980287400	28	
29	1.0294096779	29.4096778700	.9714305407	28.5694592800	29	
30	1.0304390875	30.4390875400	.9704600807	29.5399193500	30	
31	1.0314695266	31.4695266300	.9694905901	30.5094099500	31	
32	1.0325009962	32.5009961600	.9685220680	31.4779320200	32	
33	1.0335334972	33.5334971500	.9675545135	32.4454865300	33	
34	1.0345670307	34.5670306500	.9665879256	33.4120744500	34	
35	1.0356015977	35.6015976800	.9656223032	34.3776967600	35	
36	1.0366371993	36.6371992800	.9646576456	35.3423544000	36	
37	1.0376738365	37.6738364800	.9636939516	36.3060483600	37	
38	1.0387115103	38.7115103100	.9627312204	37.2687795700	38	
39	1.0397502218	39.7502218300	.9617694510	38.2305490300	39	
40	1.0407899721	40.7899720500	.9608086423	39.1913576700	40	
41	1.0418307620	41.8307620200	.9598487935	40.1512064600	41	
42	1.0428725927	42.8725927800	.9588899036	41.1100963600	42	
43	1.0439154654	43.9154653700	.9579319717	42.0680283300	43	
44	1.0449593808	44.9593808400	.9569749967	43.0250033300	44	
45	1.0460043402	46.0043402200	.9560189777	43.9810223100	45	
46	1.0470503446	47.0503445600	.9550639138	44.9360862300	46	
47	1.0480973949	48.0973949000	.9541098040	45.8901960200	47	
48	1.0491454923	49.1454923000	.9531566473	46.8433526800	48	
49	1.0501946378	50.1946377900	.9522044429	47.7955571200	49	
50	1.0512448324	51.2448324300	.9512531897	48.7468103100	50	
51	1.0522960773	52.2960772600	.9503028868	49.6971131900	51	
52	1.0533483733	53.3483733400	.9493535333	50.6464667300	52	
53	1.0544017217	54.4017217100	.9484051282	51.5948718500	53	
54	1.0554561234	55.4561234300	.9474576705	52.5423295200	54	
55	1.0565115796	56.5115795600	.9465111593	53.4888406900	55	
56	1.0575680911	57.5680911400	.9455655937	54.4344062800	56	
57	1.0586256592	58.6256592300	.9446209728	55.3790272500	57	
58	1.0596842849	59.6842848900	.9436772955	56.3227045500	58	
59	1.0607439692	60.7439691700	.9427345609	57.2654391100	59	
60	1.0618047131	61.8047131400	.9417927681	58.2072318800	60	
61	1.0628665179	62.8665178600	.9408519162	59.1480838000	61	
62	1.0639293844	63.9293843700	.9399120042	60.0879958000	62	
63	1.0649933138	64.9933137600	.9389730312	61.0269688300	63	
64	1.0660583071	66.0583070700	.9380349962	61.9650038300	64	
65	1.0671243654	67.1243653800	.9370978983	62.9021017300	65	

RATE

¹⁄₁₀ %

Period	Compound Interest Amount	Compound One Per Period	Present Value Of $1 In Future	Present Value Of $1 Per Period	Period
1	1.0012500000	1.0000000000	.9987515605	.9987515680	1
2	1.0025015625	2.0012500000	.9975046797	1.9962562480	2
3	1.0037546895	3.0037515600	.9962593555	2.9925156000	3
4	1.0050093828	4.0075062480	.9950155860	3.9875311840	4
5	1.0062656445	5.0125156320	.9937733693	4.9813045520	5
6	1.0075234766	6.0187812720	.9925327034	5.9738372480	6
7	1.0087828809	7.0263047520	.9912935865	6.9651308400	7
8	1.0100438595	8.0350876320	.9900560164	7.9551868560	8
9	1.0113064144	9.0451314960	.9888199914	8.9440068560	9
10	1.0125705474	10.0564379040	.9875855096	9.9315923520	10
11	1.0138362606	11.0690084560	.9863525688	10.9179449280	11
12	1.0151035559	12.0828447120	.9851211674	11.9030660960	12
13	1.0163724353	13.0979482720	.9838913033	12.8869574000	13
14	1.0176429009	14.1143207040	.9826629745	13.8696203680	14
15	1.0189149545	15.1319636080	.9814361793	14.8510565520	15
16	1.0201885982	16.1508785600	.9802109157	15.8312674640	16
17	1.0214638340	17.1710671600	.9789871817	16.8102546480	17
18	1.0227406637	18.1925309920	.9777649755	17.7880196240	18
19	1.0240190896	19.2152716560	.9765442951	18.7645639200	19
20	1.0252991134	20.2392907440	.9753251387	19.7398890560	20
21	1.0265807373	21.2645898640	.9741075043	20.7139965680	21
22	1.0278639633	22.2911706000	.9728913901	21.6868879520	22
23	1.0291487932	23.3190345600	.9716767941	22.6585647440	23
24	1.0304352292	24.3481833520	.9704637144	23.6290284560	24
25	1.0317232732	25.3786185840	.9692521492	24.5982806080	25
26	1.0330129273	26.4103418560	.9680420966	25.5663227040	26
27	1.0343041935	27.4433547840	.9668335547	26.5331562640	27
28	1.0355970737	28.4776589760	.9656265215	27.4987827840	28
29	1.0368915701	29.5132560480	.9644209953	28.4632037760	29
30	1.0381876845	30.5501476240	.9632169741	29.4264207520	30
31	1.0394854191	31.5883353040	.9620144560	30.3884352080	31
32	1.0407847759	32.6278207280	.9608134392	31.3492486480	32
33	1.0420857569	33.6686055040	.9596139218	32.3088625760	33
34	1.0433883641	34.7106912560	.9584159019	33.2672784720	34
35	1.0446925995	35.7540796240	.9572193777	34.2244978480	35
36	1.0459984653	36.7987722240	.9560243473	35.1805222000	36
37	1.0473059634	37.8447706880	.9548308087	36.1353530080	37
38	1.0486150958	38.8920766480	.9536387603	37.0889917680	38
39	1.0499258647	39.9406917440	.9524482000	38.0414399680	39
40	1.0512382720	40.9906176080	.9512591261	38.9926990880	40
41	1.0525523199	42.0418558800	.9500715367	39.9427706240	41
42	1.0538680103	43.0944082000	.9488854299	40.8916560560	42
43	1.0551853453	44.1482762160	.9477008039	41.8393568640	43
44	1.0565043270	45.2034615600	.9465176569	42.7858745200	44
45	1.0578249574	46.2599658880	.9453359869	43.7312105120	45
46	1.0591472386	47.3177908400	.9441557921	44.6753662960	46
47	1.0604711726	48.3769380800	.9429770708	45.6183433680	47
48	1.0617967616	49.4374092560	.9417998210	46.5601431920	48
49	1.0631240075	50.4992060160	.9406240410	47.5007672320	49
50	1.0644529125	51.5623300240	.9394497288	48.4402169600	50
51	1.0657834787	52.6267829360	.9382768827	49.3784938400	51
52	1.0671157080	53.6925664160	.9371055008	50.3155993440	52
53	1.0684496027	54.7596821200	.9359355814	51.2515349200	53
54	1.0697851647	55.8281317280	.9347671224	52.1863020480	54
55	1.0711223961	56.8979168880	.9336001223	53.1199021680	55
56	1.0724612991	57.9690392880	.9324345791	54.0523367520	56
57	1.0738018757	59.0415005840	.9312704910	54.9836072400	57
58	1.0751441281	60.1153024560	.9301078561	55.9137150960	58
59	1.0764880582	61.1904465840	.9289466728	56.8426617680	59
60	1.0778336683	62.2669346480	.9277869391	57.7704487120	60
61	1.0791809604	63.3447683120	.9266286533	58.6970773600	61
62	1.0805299366	64.4239492720	.9254718135	59.6225491760	62
63	1.0818805990	65.5044792080	.9243164180	60.5468655920	63
64	1.0832329498	66.5863598080	.9231624649	61.4700280560	64
65	1.0845869910	67.6695927600	.9220099525	62.3920380080	65

Period	Compound Interest Amount	Compound One Per Period	Present Value Of $1 In Future	Present Value Of $1 Per Period	Period	RATE
						⅙ %
1	1.0016667000	1.0000000000	.9983360733	.9983360773	1	
2	1.0033361779	2.0016666947	.9966749152	1.9950109858	2	
3	1.0050084383	3.0050028739	.9950165212	2.9900275094	3	
4	1.0066834859	4.0100113158	.9933608866	3.9833883962	4	
5	1.0083613252	5.0166947981	.9917080068	4.9750964001	5	
6	1.0100419610	6.0250561229	.9900578774	5.9651542809	6	
7	1.0117253980	7.0350980860	.9884104936	6.9535647747	7	
8	1.0134116407	8.0468234835	.9867658510	7.9403306234	8	
9	1.0151006939	9.0602351233	.9851239449	8.9254545689	9	
10	1.0167925622	10.0753358193	.9834847708	9.9089393412	10	
11	1.0184872504	11.0921283794	.9818483242	10.8907876642	11	
12	1.0201847631	12.1106156297	.9802146005	11.8710022620	12	
13	1.0218851050	13.1308003960	.9785803952	12.8495858643	13	
14	1.0235882809	14.1526854983	.9769553038	13.8265411652	14	
15	1.0252942955	15.1762737805	.9753297218	14.8018708886	15	
16	1.0270031535	16.2015680746	.9737068446	15.7755777284	16	
17	1.0287148597	17.2285712306	.9720866677	16.7476644027	17	
18	1.0304294187	18.2572860863	.9704691868	17.7181335813	18	
19	1.0321468354	19.2877155097	.9688543971	18.6869879822	19	
20	1.0338671146	20.3198623448	.9672422944	19.6542302814	20	
21	1.0355902609	21.3537294594	.9656328741	20.6198631547	21	
22	1.0373162792	22.3893197156	.9640261317	21.5838892782	22	
23	1.0390451742	23.4266359993	.9624220629	22.5463113458	23	
24	1.0407769508	24.4656811724	.9608206631	23.5071320094	24	
25	1.0425116138	25.5064581208	.9592219279	24.4663539329	25	
26	1.0442491679	26.5489697366	.9576258529	25.4239797924	26	
27	1.0459896180	27.5932189056	.9560324336	26.3800122278	27	
28	1.0477329688	28.6392085198	.9544416657	27.3344538849	28	
29	1.0494792254	29.6869414892	.9528535447	28.2873074339	29	
30	1.0512283924	30.7364207176	.9512680662	29.2385755025	30	
31	1.0529804748	31.7876491090	.9496852259	30.1882607248	31	
32	1.0547354773	32.8406295854	.9481050192	31.1363657467	32	
33	1.0564934050	33.8953650627	.9465274419	32.0828931901	33	
34	1.0582542625	34.9518584628	.9449524896	33.0278456771	34	
35	1.0600180549	36.0101127257	.9433801579	33.9712258355	35	
36	1.0617847870	37.0701307854	.9418104424	34.9130362813	36	
37	1.0635544637	38.1319155697	.9402433389	35.8532796184	37	
38	1.0653270899	39.1954700306	.9386788428	36.7919584568	38	
39	1.0671026706	40.2607971261	.9371169500	37.7290754125	39	
40	1.0688812106	41.3278997960	.9355576561	38.6646330653	40	
41	1.0706627149	42.3967810044	.9340009567	39.5986340193	41	
42	1.0724471885	43.4674437211	.9324468475	40.5310808724	42	
43	1.0742346362	44.5398909102	.9308953243	41.4619761925	43	
44	1.0750250630	45.6141255415	.9293463827	42.3913225715	44	
45	1.0778184740	46.6901506090	.9278000184	43.3191225955	45	
46	1.0796148741	47.7679690826	.9262562271	44.2453788204	46	
47	1.0814142682	48.8475839563	.9247150046	45.1700938261	47	
48	1.0832166613	49.9289982240	.9231763646	46.0932701746	48	
49	1.0850220586	51.0122148857	.9216402488	47.0149104218	49	
50	1.0868304648	52.0972369413	.9201067070	47.9350171297	50	
51	1.0886418852	53.1840674087	.9185757168	48.8535928481	51	
52	1.0904563246	54.2727092938	.9170472741	49.7706401212	52	
53	1.0922737881	55.3631656207	.9155213746	50.6861614988	53	
54	1.0940942809	56.4554394072	.9139980142	51.6001595068	54	
55	1.0959178078	57.5495336893	.9124771884	52.5126367013	55	
56	1.0977443740	58.6454514970	.9109588932	53.4235955901	56	
57	1.0995739846	59.7431958661	.9094431244	54.3330387112	57	
58	1.1014066445	60.8427698506	.9079298777	55.2409685906	58	
59	1.1032423590	61.9441764985	.9064191489	56.1473877422	59	
60	1.1050811330	63.0474188576	.9049109338	57.0522986740	60	
61	1.1069229717	64.1524999880	.9034052283	57.9557038999	61	
62	1.1087678803	65.2594229615	.9019020282	58.8576059339	62	
63	1.1106158637	66.3681908442	.9004013293	59.7580072599	63	
64	1.1124669271	67.4788067079	.8989031275	60.6569103918	64	
65	1.1143210758	68.5912736305	.8974074185	61.5543178076	65	

Period	Compound Interest Amount	Compound One Per Period	Present Value Of $1 In Future	Present Value Of $1 Per Period	Period
1	1.0025000000	1.0000000000	.9975062344	.9975062360	1
2	1.0050062500	2.0025000000	.9950186877	1.9925249240	2
3	1.0075187656	3.0075062480	.9925373443	2.9850622680	3
4	1.0100375625	4.0150250120	.9900621889	3.9751244520	4
5	1.0125626564	5.0250625760	.9875932059	4.9627176600	5
6	1.0150940631	6.0376252320	.9851303799	5.9478480400	6
7	1.0176317982	7.0527192960	.9826736957	6.9305217360	7
8	1.0201758777	8.0703510920	.9802231378	7.9107448720	8
9	1.0227263174	9.0905269760	.9777786911	8.8885235680	9
10	1.0252831332	10.1132532880	.9753403402	9.8638639040	10
11	1.0278463411	11.1385364240	.9729080701	10.8367719760	11
12	1.0304159569	12.1663827640	.9704818654	11.8072538400	12
13	1.0329919968	13.1967987200	.9680617111	12.7753155520	13
14	1.0355744768	14.2297907160	.9656475921	13.7409631440	14
15	1.0381634130	15.2653651920	.9632394934	14.7042026360	15
16	1.0407588215	16.3035286080	.9608373999	15.6650400400	16
17	1.0433607186	17.3442874280	.9584412967	16.6234813360	17
18	1.0459691204	18.3876481480	.9560511687	17.5795325040	18
19	1.0485840432	19.4336172680	.9536670012	18.5331995040	19
20	1.0512055033	20.4822013120	.9512887793	19.4844882840	20
21	1.0538335170	21.5334068120	.9489164881	20.4334047720	21
22	1.0564681008	22.5872403320	.9465501128	21.3799548840	22
23	1.0591092711	23.6437084320	.9441896387	22.3241445240	23
24	1.0617570443	24.7028177040	.9418350511	23.2659795760	24
25	1.0644114369	25.7645747480	.9394863352	24.2054659120	25
26	1.0670724655	26.8289861840	.9371434765	25.1426093880	26
27	1.0697401466	27.8960586480	.9348064604	26.0774158440	27
28	1.0724144970	28.9657987960	.9324752722	27.0098911200	28
29	1.0750955332	30.0382132920	.9301498975	27.9400410160	29
30	1.0777832721	31.1133088280	.9278303217	28.8678713400	30
31	1.0804777303	32.1910921000	.9255165303	29.7933878680	31
32	1.0831789246	33.2715698280	.9232085091	30.7165963760	32
33	1.0858868719	34.3547487520	.9209062435	31.6375026200	33
34	1.0886015891	35.4406356240	.9186097192	32.5561123400	34
35	1.0913230930	36.5292372160	.9163189218	33.4724312640	35
36	1.0940514008	37.6205603080	.9140338373	34.3864651000	36
37	1.0967865293	38.7146117080	.9117544511	35.2982195520	37
38	1.0995284956	39.8113982360	.9094807493	36.2077003000	38
39	1.1022773168	40.9109267320	.9072127175	37.1149130160	39
40	1.1050330101	42.0132040480	.9049503416	38.0198633560	40
41	1.1077955927	43.1182370600	.9026936076	38.9225569680	41
42	1.1105650816	44.2260326520	.9004425013	39.8229994680	42
43	1.1133414943	45.3365977360	.8981970088	40.7211964800	43
44	1.1161248481	46.4499392280	.8959571160	41.6171535920	44
45	1.1189151602	47.5660640760	.8937228090	42.5108764000	45
46	1.1217124481	48.6849792360	.8914940738	43.4023704760	46
47	1.1245167292	49.8066916840	.8892708966	44.2916413720	47
48	1.1273280210	50.9312084120	.8870532634	45.1786946320	48
49	1.1301463411	52.0585364360	.8848411605	46.0635357960	49
50	1.1329717069	53.1886827760	.8826345741	46.9461703680	50
51	1.1358041362	54.3216544840	.8804334904	47.8266038600	51
52	1.1386436466	55.4574586200	.8782378956	48.7048417560	52
53	1.1414902557	56.5961022640	.8760477762	49.5808895320	53
54	1.1443439813	57.7375925200	.8738631184	50.4547526480	54
55	1.1472048413	58.8819365040	.8716839086	51.3264365600	55
56	1.1500728534	60.0291413440	.8695101333	52.1959466920	56
57	1.1529480355	61.1792141960	.8673417788	53.0632884720	57
58	1.1558304056	62.3321622320	.8651788317	53.9284673040	58
59	1.1587199816	63.4879926400	.8630212785	54.7914885840	59
60	1.1616167816	64.6467126200	.8608691058	55.6523576880	60
61	1.1645208235	65.8083294000	.8587223000	56.5110799880	61
62	1.1674321256	66.9728502240	.8565808479	57.3676608360	62
63	1.1703507059	68.1402823520	.8544447361	58.2221055720	63
64	1.1732765826	69.3106330560	.8523139512	59.0744195240	64
65	1.1762097741	70.4839096400	.8501884800	59.9246080040	65

Period	Compound Interest Amount	Compound One Per Period	Present Value Of $1 In Future	Present Value Of $1 Per Period	Period
1	1.0033333000	1.0000000000	.9966777740	.9966777758	1
2	1.0066777109	2.0033332973	.9933665851	1.9900443584	2
3	1.0100332697	3.0100110101	.9900663968	2.9801107581	3
4	1.0134000136	4.0200442804	.9867771725	3.9668879309	4
5	1.0167779799	5.0334442924	.9834988757	4.9503868029	5
6	1.0201672059	6.0502222722	.9802314701	5.9306182732	6
7	1.0235677293	7.0703894789	.9769749196	6.9075931929	7
8	1.0269795876	8.0939572076	.9737291881	7.8813223832	8
9	1.0304028186	9.1209367954	.9704942397	8.8518166232	9
10	1.0338374603	10.1513396154	.9672700384	9.8190866619	10
11	1.0372835507	11.1851770738	.9640565487	10.7831432094	11
12	1.0407411280	12.2224606246	.9608537350	11.7439969430	12
13	1.0442102304	13.2632017520	.9576615617	12.7016585036	13
14	1.0476908964	14.3074119821	.9544799935	13.6561384994	14
15	1.0511831644	15.3551028800	.9513089953	14.6074474935	15
16	1.0546870733	16.4062860439	.9481485318	15.5555960250	16
17	1.0582026617	17.4609731167	.9449985680	16.5005945939	17
18	1.0617299686	18.5191757778	.9418590692	17.4424536615	18
19	1.0652690331	19.5809057481	.9387300005	18.3811836648	19
20	1.0688198944	20.6461747817	.9356113273	19.3167949929	20
21	1.0723825918	21.7149946749	.9325030150	20.2492980050	21
22	1.0759571646	22.7873772658	.9294050292	21.1787030330	22
23	1.0795436527	23.8633344313	.9263173356	22.1050203702	23
24	1.0831420955	24.9428780848	.9232399000	23.0282602706	24
25	1.0867525331	26.0260201812	.9201726884	23.9484329613	25
26	1.0903750053	27.1127727117	.9171156668	24.8655486245	26
27	1.0940095523	28.2031477185	.9140688012	25.7796174272	27
28	1.0976562143	29.2971572706	.9110320581	26.6906494855	28
29	1.1013150318	30.3948134851	.9080054037	27.5986548885	29
30	1.1049860452	31.4961285153	.9049888045	28.5036436924	30
31	1.1086692952	32.6011145621	.9019822271	29.4056259203	31
32	1.1123648225	33.7097838568	.8989856383	30.3046115591	32
33	1.1160726682	34.8221486785	.8959990048	31.2006105631	33
34	1.1197928732	35.9382213482	.8930222936	32.0936328563	34
35	1.1235254788	37.0580142201	.8900554717	32.9836883299	35
36	1.1272705263	38.1815396994	.8870985062	33.8707868359	36
37	1.1310280571	39.3088102271	.8841513645	34.7549381994	37
38	1.1347981130	40.4398382834	.8812140138	35.6361522125	38
39	1.1385807355	41.5746363964	.8782864217	36.5144386344	39
40	1.1423759667	42.7132171332	.8753685557	37.3898071911	40
41	1.1461838485	43.8555930969	.8724603835	38.2622675727	41
42	1.1500044231	45.0017769478	.8695618729	39.1318294483	42
43	1.1538377328	46.1517813698	.8666729918	39.9985024390	43
44	1.1576838202	47.3056191042	.8637937083	40.8622961480	44
45	1.1615427276	48.4633029220	.8609239903	41.7232201362	45
46	1.1654144980	49.6248456515	.8580638062	42.5812839438	46
47	1.1692991742	50.7902601476	.8552131243	43.4364970690	47
48	1.1731967991	51.9595593226	.8523719130	44.2888689827	48
49	1.1771074160	53.1327561216	.8495401409	45.1384091231	49
50	1.1810310681	54.3098635376	.8467177765	45.9851268983	50
51	1.1849677990	55.4908946059	.8439047887	46.8290316863	51
52	1.1889176522	56.6758624036	.8411011462	47.6701328323	52
53	1.1928806714	57.8647800558	.8383068181	48.5084396514	53
54	1.1968569005	59.0576607296	.8355217734	49.3439614256	54
55	1.2008463836	60.2545176282	.8327459812	50.1767074071	55
56	1.2048491649	61.4553640116	.8299794108	51.0066868179	56
57	1.2088652886	62.6602131761	.8272220316	51.8339088471	57
58	1.2128947993	63.8690784658	.8244738131	52.6583826628	58
59	1.2169377415	65.0819732667	.8217347247	53.4801173882	59
60	1.2209941601	66.2989110071	.8190047362	54.2991221222	60
61	1.2250640999	67.5199051661	.8162838174	55.1154059401	61
62	1.2291476061	68.7449692677	.8135719380	55.9289778778	62
63	1.2332447238	69.9741168722	.8108690682	56.7398469475	63
64	1.2373554984	71.2073615966	.8081751779	57.5480221252	64
65	1.2414799755	72.4447170942	.8054902373	58.3535123601	65

RATE

$1/3 \%$

Period	Compound Interest Amount	Compound One Per Period	Present Value Of $1 In Future	Present Value Of $1 Per Period	Period
1	1.0050000000	1.0000000000	.9950248756	.9950248760	1
2	1.0100250000	2.0050000000	.9900745031	1.9850993800	2
3	1.0150751250	3.0150250000	.9851487593	2.9702481400	3
4	1.0201505006	4.0301001240	.9802475217	3.9504956600	4
5	1.0252512531	5.0502506240	.9753706684	4.9258663280	5
6	1.0303775094	6.0755018780	.9705180780	5.8963844060	6
7	1.0355293969	7.1058793880	.9656896298	6.8620740360	7
8	1.0407070439	8.1414087840	.9608852038	7.8229592400	8
9	1.0459105791	9.1821158280	.9561046804	8.7790639200	9
10	1.0511401320	10.2280264080	.9513479407	9.7304118620	10
11	1.0563958327	11.2791665400	.9466148664	10.6770267280	11
12	1.0616778119	12.3355623720	.9419053397	11.6189320680	12
13	1.0669862009	13.3972401840	.9372192435	12.5561513100	13
14	1.0723211319	14.4642263840	.9325564612	13.4887077700	14
15	1.0776827376	15.5365475160	.9279168768	14.4166246480	15
16	1.0830711513	16.6142302540	.9233003749	15.3399250240	16
17	1.0884865070	17.6973014060	.9187068407	16.2586318640	17
18	1.0939289396	18.7857879120	.9141361599	17.1727680240	18
19	1.0993985843	19.8797168520	.9095882188	18.0823562420	19
20	1.1048955772	20.9791154360	.9050629043	18.9874191460	20
21	1.1104200551	22.0840110140	.9005601038	19.8879792500	21
22	1.1159721553	23.1944310680	.8960797052	20.7840589560	22
23	1.1215520161	24.3104032240	.8916215972	21.6756805540	23
24	1.1271597762	25.4319552400	.8871856689	22.5628662220	24
25	1.1327955751	26.5591150160	.8827718098	23.4456380320	25
26	1.1384595530	27.6919105920	.8783799103	24.3240179420	26
27	1.1441518507	28.8303701440	.8740098610	25.1980278020	27
28	1.1498726100	29.9745219960	.8696615532	26.0676893580	28
29	1.1556219730	31.1243946060	.8653348788	26.9330242360	29
30	1.1614000829	32.2800165780	.8610297302	27.7940539660	30
31	1.1672070833	33.4414166600	.8567460002	28.6507999640	31
32	1.1730431187	34.6086237440	.8524835823	29.5032835480	32
33	1.1789083343	35.7816668640	.8482423704	30.3515259180	33
34	1.1848028760	36.9605751980	.8440222591	31.1955481780	34
35	1.1907268904	38.1453780740	.8398231434	32.0353713220	35
36	1.1966805248	39.3361049640	.8356449188	32.8710162400	36
37	1.2026639274	40.5327854880	.8314874814	33.7025037200	37
38	1.2086772471	41.7354494160	.8273507278	34.5298544480	38
39	1.2147206333	42.9441266640	.8232345550	35.3530890040	39
40	1.2207942365	44.1588472960	.8191388607	36.1722278640	40
41	1.2268982077	45.3796415320	.8150635430	36.9872914060	41
42	1.2330326987	46.6065397400	.8110085005	37.7982999080	42
43	1.2391978622	47.8395724400	.8069736323	38.6052735400	43
44	1.2453938515	49.0787703020	.8029588381	39.4082323780	44
45	1.2516208208	50.3241641520	.7989640180	40.2071963960	45
46	1.2578789249	51.5757849740	.7949890727	41.0021854700	46
47	1.2641683195	52.8336638980	.7910339031	41.7932193720	47
48	1.2704891611	54.0978322180	.7870984111	42.5803177840	48
49	1.2768416069	55.3683213800	.7831824986	43.3635002820	49
50	1.2832258149	56.6451629860	.7792860683	44.1427863500	50
51	1.2896419440	57.9283888020	.7754090231	44.9181953740	51
52	1.2960901537	59.2180307460	.7715512668	45.6897466400	52
53	1.3025706045	60.5141208980	.7677127033	46.4574593420	53
54	1.3090834575	61.8166915040	.7638932371	47.2213525800	54
55	1.3156288748	63.1257749600	.7600927732	47.9814453540	55
56	1.3222070192	64.4414038360	.7563112171	48.7377565720	56
57	1.3288180543	65.7636108540	.7525484748	49.4903050460	57
58	1.3354621446	67.0924289100	.7488044525	50.2391094980	58
59	1.3421394553	68.4278910540	.7450790572	50.9841885560	59
60	1.3488501525	69.7700305080	.7413721962	51.7255607520	60
61	1.3555944033	71.1188806620	.7376837774	52.4632445300	61
62	1.3623723753	72.4744750640	.7340137088	53.1972582380	62
63	1.3691842372	73.8368474400	.7303618993	53.9276201380	63
64	1.3760301584	75.2060316780	.7267282580	54.6543483960	64
65	1.3829103092	76.5820618360	.7231126946	55.3774610900	65

Period	Compound Interest Amount	Compound One Per Period	Present Value Of $1 In Future	Present Value Of $1 Per Period	Period	
1	1.0066667000	1.0000000000	.9933774506	.9933774506	1	
2	1.0133778449	2.0066666987	.9867987593	1.9801762086	2	
3	1.0201337310	3.0200445438	.9802636357	2.9604398458	3	
4	1.0269346565	4.0401782756	.9737717913	3.9342116369	4	
5	1.0337809218	5.0671129314	.9673229394	4.9015345763	5	
6	1.0406728291	6.1008938530	.9609167954	5.8624513717	6	
7	1.0476106826	7.1415666822	.9545530765	6.8170044475	7	
8	1.0545947887	8.1891773651	.9482315015	7.7652359503	8	
9	1.0616254558	9.2437721541	.9419517915	8.7071877421	9	
10	1.0687029942	10.3053976090	.9357136692	9.6429014100	10	
11	1.0758277165	11.3741006045	.9295168591	10.5724182699	11	
12	1.0829999371	12.4499283199	.9233610878	11.4957793571	12	
13	1.0902199728	13.5329282569	.9172460833	12.4130254399	13	
14	1.0974881423	14.6231482308	.9111715758	13.3241970165	14	
15	1.1048047665	15.7206363733	.9051372969	14.2293343138	15	
16	1.1121701684	16.8254411388	.8991429804	15.1284772931	16	
17	1.1195846733	17.9376113069	.8931883616	16.0216656547	17	
18	1.1270486085	19.0571959815	.8872731775	16.9089388333	18	
19	1.1345623034	20.1842445888	.8813971670	17.7903359998	19	
20	1.1421260899	21.3188068925	.8755600707	18.6658960700	20	
21	1.1497403019	22.4609329833	.8697616308	19.5356577017	21	
22	1.1574052756	23.6106732851	.8640015914	20.3996592932	22	
23	1.1651213493	24.7680785606	.8582796981	21.2579389908	23	
24	1.1728888638	25.9331999100	.8525956984	22.1105346888	24	
25	1.1807081620	27.1060887741	.8469493412	22.9574840311	25	
26	1.1885795891	28.2867969355	.8413403773	23.7988244079	26	
27	1.1965034927	29.4753765251	.8357685591	24.6345929665	27	
28	1.2044802225	30.6718800171	.8302336405	25.4648266069	28	
29	1.2125101308	31.8763602397	.8247353771	26.2895619842	29	
30	1.2205935721	33.0888703706	.8192735263	27.1088355108	30	
31	1.2287309033	34.3094639432	.8138478469	27.9226833576	31	
32	1.2369224836	35.5381948460	.8084580993	28.7311414568	32	
33	1.2451686747	36.7751173294	.8031040455	29.5342455023	33	
34	1.2534698407	38.0202860036	.7977854493	30.3320309508	34	
35	1.2618263481	39.2737558447	.7925020757	31.1245330268	35	
36	1.2702385658	40.5355821936	.7872536915	31.9117867191	36	
37	1.2787068653	41.8058207584	.7820400650	32.6938267839	37	
38	1.2872316203	43.0845276239	.7768609660	33.4706877496	38	
39	1.2958132074	44.3717592437	.7717161658	34.2424039150	39	
40	1.3044520053	45.6675724511	.7666054374	35.0090093525	40	
41	1.3131483955	46.9720244574	.7615285549	35.7705379078	41	
42	1.3219027619	48.2851728531	.7564852944	36.5270232034	42	
43	1.3307154910	49.6070756146	.7514754332	37.2784986350	43	
44	1.3395869720	50.9377911050	.7464987499	38.0249973855	44	
45	1.3485175964	52.2773780776	.7415550250	38.7665524112	45	
46	1.3575077587	53.6258956740	.7366440402	39.5031964510	46	
47	1.3665578557	54.9834034320	.7317655786	40.2349620292	47	
48	1.3756682869	56.3499612882	.7269194249	40.9618814541	48	
49	1.3848394547	57.7256295754	.7221053651	41.6839868196	49	
50	1.3940717639	59.1104690297	.7173231866	42.4013100064	50	
51	1.4033656221	60.5045407938	.7125726783	43.1138826841	51	
52	1.4127214397	61.9079064155	.7078536305	43.8217363148	52	
53	1.4221396297	63.3206278549	.7031658348	44.5249021495	53	
54	1.4316206080	64.7427674847	.6985090843	45.2234112334	54	
55	1.4411647931	66.1743880931	.6938831734	45.9172944065	55	
56	1.4507726064	67.6155528867	.6892878978	46.6065823046	56	
57	1.4604444722	69.0663254924	.6847230546	47.2913053595	57	
58	1.4701808173	70.5267699657	.6801884423	47.9714938020	58	
59	1.4799820718	71.9969507822	.6756838607	48.6471776621	59	
60	1.4898486683	73.4769328543	.6712091109	49.3183867731	60	
61	1.4997810424	74.9667815216	.6667639954	49.9851507687	61	
62	1.5097796327	76.4665625647	.6623483178	50.6474990865	62	
63	1.5198448805	77.9763421978	.6579618834	51.3054609702	63	
64	1.5299772304	79.4961870776	.6536044982	51.9590654687	64	
65	1.5401771296	81.0261643077	.6492759701	52.6083414388	65	

	Period	Compound Interest Amount	Compound One Per Period	Present Value Of $1 In Future	Present Value Of $1 Per Period	Period
	1	1.0075000000	1.0000000000	.9925558313	.9925558320	1
	2	1.0150562500	2.0075000000	.9851670782	1.9777229107	2
	3	1.0226691719	3.0225562493	.9778333282	2.9555562373	3
	4	1.0303391907	4.0452254213	.9705541719	3.9261104093	4
	5	1.0380667346	5.0755646120	.9633292029	4.8894396120	5
	6	1.0458522351	6.1136313467	.9561580178	5.8455976307	6
	7	1.0536961269	7.1594835813	.9490402162	6.7946378467	7
	8	1.0615988478	8.2131797080	.9419754007	7.7366132467	8
	9	1.0695608392	9.2747785560	.9349631768	8.6715764240	9
	10	1.0775825455	10.3443393960	.9280031532	9.5995795773	10
	11	1.0856644146	11.4219219413	.9210949411	10.5206745187	11
	12	1.0938068977	12.5075863560	.9142381550	11.4349126733	12
	13	1.1020104494	13.6013932533	.9074324119	12.3423450853	13
	14	1.1102755278	14.7034037027	.9006773319	13.2430224173	14
	15	1.1186025942	15.8136792307	.8939725378	14.1369949547	15
	16	1.1269921137	16.9322818240	.8873176554	15.0243126093	16
	17	1.1354445545	18.0592739387	.8807123131	15.9050249240	17
	18	1.1439603887	19.1947184933	.8741561420	16.7791810653	18
	19	1.1525400916	20.3386788813	.8676487762	17.6468298413	19
	20	1.1611841423	21.4912189733	.8611898523	18.5080196947	20
	21	1.1698930234	22.6524031160	.8547790097	19.3627987040	21
	22	1.1786672210	23.8222961387	.8484158905	20.2112145947	22
	23	1.1875072252	25.0009633600	.8421001395	21.0533147333	23
	24	1.1964135294	26.1884705853	.8358314040	21.8891461373	24
	25	1.2053866309	27.3848841147	.8296093340	22.7187554720	25
	26	1.2144270306	28.5902707453	.8234335821	23.5421890533	26
	27	1.2235352333	29.8046977760	.8173038036	24.3594928573	27
	28	1.2327117476	31.0282330093	.8112196562	25.1707125133	28
	29	1.2419570857	32.2609447573	.8051808002	25.9758933133	29
	30	1.2512717638	33.5029018427	.7991868984	26.7750802120	30
	31	1.2606563021	34.7541736067	.7932376163	27.5683178280	31
	32	1.2701112243	36.0148299080	.7873326216	28.3556504493	32
	33	1.2796370585	37.2849411320	.7814715847	29.1371220347	33
	34	1.2892343364	38.5645781907	.7756541784	29.9127762133	34
	35	1.2989035940	39.8538125280	.7698800778	30.6826562907	35
	36	1.3086453709	41.1527161213	.7641489606	31.4468052520	36
	37	1.3184602112	42.4613614920	.7584605068	32.2052657587	37
	38	1.3283486628	43.7798217040	.7528143988	32.9580801573	38
	39	1.3383112778	45.1081703667	.7472103214	33.7052904787	39
	40	1.3483486123	46.4464816440	.7416479617	34.4469384400	40
	41	1.3584612269	47.7948302560	.7361270091	35.1830654493	41
	42	1.3686496861	49.1532914840	.7306470155	35.9137126053	42
	43	1.3789145588	50.5219411693	.7252080948	36.6389207000	43
	44	1.3892564180	51.9008557280	.7198095233	37.3587302227	44
	45	1.3996758411	53.2901121467	.7144511398	38.0731813627	45
	46	1.4101734099	54.6897879880	.7091326449	38.7823140080	46
	47	1.4207497105	56.0999613973	.7038537419	39.4861677493	47
	48	1.4314053333	57.5207111080	.6986141359	40.1847818853	48
	49	1.4421408733	58.9521164413	.6934135344	40.8781954200	49
	50	1.4529569299	60.3942573147	.6882516470	41.5664470667	50
	51	1.4638541068	61.8472142440	.6831281856	42.2495752520	51
	52	1.4748330126	63.3110683507	.6780428641	42.9276181160	52
	53	1.4858942602	64.7859013640	.6729953986	43.6006135160	53
	54	1.4970384672	66.2717956240	.6679855073	44.2685990227	54
	55	1.5082662557	67.7688340907	.6630129105	44.9316119333	55
	56	1.5195782526	69.2771003467	.6580773305	45.5896892640	56
	57	1.5309750895	70.7966786000	.6531784918	46.2428677560	57
	58	1.5424574027	72.3276536893	.6483161209	46.8911838760	58
	59	1.5540258332	73.8701110920	.6434899463	47.5346738227	59
	60	1.5656810269	75.4241369253	.6386996986	48.1733735213	60
	61	1.5774236346	76.9898179520	.6339451103	48.8073186320	61
	62	1.5892543119	78.5672415867	.6292259159	49.4365445480	62
	63	1.6011737192	80.1564958987	.6245418520	50.0610864000	63
	64	1.6131825221	81.7576696173	.6198926571	50.6809790560	64
	65	1.6252813911	83.3708521400	.6152780715	51.2962571280	65

Period	Compound Interest Amount	Compound One Per Period	Present Value Of $1 In Future	Present Value Of $1 Per Period	Period	
1	1.0100000000	1.0000000000	.9900990099	.9900990100	1	
2	1.0201000000	2.0100000000	.9802960494	1.9703950600	2	
3	1.0303010000	3.0301000000	.9705901479	2.9409852080	3	
4	1.0406040100	4.0604010000	.9609803445	3.9019655520	4	
5	1.0510100501	5.1010050100	.9514656876	4.8534312400	5	
6	1.0615201506	6.1520150600	.9420452353	5.7954764750	6	
7	1.0721353521	7.2135352100	.9327180547	6.7281945290	7	
8	1.0828567056	8.2856705620	.9234832225	7.6516777520	8	
9	1.0936852727	9.3685272680	.9143398242	8.5660175760	9	
10	1.1046221254	10.4622125410	.9052869547	9.4713045310	10	
11	1.1156683467	11.5668346660	.8963237175	10.3676282480	11	
12	1.1268250301	12.6825030130	.8874492253	11.2550774740	12	
13	1.1380932804	13.8093280430	.8786625993	12.1337400730	13	
14	1.1494742132	14.9474213230	.8699629696	13.0037030420	14	
15	1.1609689554	16.0968955360	.8613494748	13.8650525170	15	
16	1.1725786449	17.2578644920	.8528212622	14.7178737800	16	
17	1.1843044314	18.4304431370	.8443774873	15.5622512670	17	
18	1.1961474757	19.6147475680	.8360173142	16.3982685810	18	
19	1.2081089504	20.8108950440	.8277399150	17.2260084960	19	
20	1.2201900399	22.0190039940	.8195444703	18.0455529660	20	
21	1.2323919403	23.2391940340	.8114301687	18.8569831350	21	
22	1.2447158598	24.4715859750	.8033962066	19.6603793420	22	
23	1.2571630183	25.7163018340	.7954417887	20.4558211300	23	
24	1.2697346485	26.9734648530	.7875661274	21.2433872580	24	
25	1.2824319950	28.2431995010	.7797684430	22.0231557010	25	
26	1.2952563150	29.5256314960	.7720479634	22.7952036640	26	
27	1.3082088781	30.8208878110	.7644039241	23.5596075880	27	
28	1.3212909669	32.1290966890	.7568355684	24.3164431570	28	
29	1.3345038766	33.4503876560	.7493421470	25.0657853040	29	
30	1.3478489153	34.7848915330	.7419229178	25.8077082220	30	
31	1.3613274045	36.1327404480	.7345771463	26.5422853680	31	
32	1.3749406785	37.4940678530	.7273041053	27.2695894730	32	
33	1.3886900853	38.8690085310	.7201030745	27.9896925480	33	
34	1.4025769862	40.2576986160	.7129733411	28.7026658890	34	
35	1.4166027560	41.6602756030	.7059141991	29.4085800880	35	
36	1.4307687836	43.0768783590	.6989249496	30.1075050380	36	
37	1.4450764714	44.5076471420	.6920049006	30.7995099380	37	
38	1.4595272361	45.9527236140	.6851533670	31.4846633050	38	
39	1.4741225085	47.4122508500	.6783696703	32.1630329750	39	
40	1.4888637336	48.8863733580	.6716531389	32.8346861140	40	
41	1.5037523709	50.3752370920	.6650031078	33.4996892220	41	
42	1.5187898946	51.8789894630	.6584189186	34.1581081410	42	
43	1.5339777936	53.3977793570	.6518999194	34.8100080600	43	
44	1.5493175715	54.9317571510	.6454454648	35.4554535250	44	
45	1.5648107472	56.4810747230	.6390549156	36.0945084410	45	
46	1.5804588547	58.0458854700	.6327276392	36.7272360800	46	
47	1.5962634432	59.6263443240	.6264630091	37.3536990890	47	
48	1.6122260777	61.2226077680	.6202604051	37.9739594940	48	
49	1.6283483385	62.8348338450	.6141192129	38.5880787070	49	
50	1.6446318218	64.4631821840	.6080388247	39.1961175310	50	
51	1.6610781401	66.1078140060	.6020186383	39.7981361700	51	
52	1.6776889215	67.7688921460	.5960580577	40.3941942280	52	
53	1.6944658107	69.4465810670	.5901564928	40.9843507200	53	
54	1.7114104688	71.1410468780	.5843133592	41.5686640800	54	
55	1.7285245735	72.8524573470	.5785280784	42.1471921580	55	
56	1.7458098192	74.5809819200	.5728000777	42.7199922350	56	
57	1.7632679174	76.3267917390	.5671287898	43.2871210250	57	
58	1.7809005966	78.0900596570	.5615136532	43.8486346790	58	
59	1.7987096025	79.8709602530	.5559541121	44.4045887910	59	
60	1.8166966986	81.6696698560	.5504496159	44.9550384070	60	
61	1.8348636655	83.4863665540	.5449996197	45.5000380260	61	
62	1.8532123022	85.3212302200	.5396035839	46.0396416100	62	
63	1.8717444252	87.1744425220	.5342609742	46.5739025840	63	
64	1.8904618695	89.0461869470	.5289712615	47.1028738460	64	
65	1.9093664882	90.9366488170	.5237339223	47.6266077680	65	

RATE

1%

Period	Compound Interest Amount	Compound One Per Period	Present Value Of $1 In Future	Present Value Of $1 Per Period	Period
1	1.0200000000	1.0000000000	.9803921569	.9803921570	1
2	1.0404000000	2.0200000000	.9611687812	1.9415609385	2
3	1.0612080000	3.0604000000	.9423223345	2.8838832730	3
4	1.0824321600	4.1216080000	.9238454260	3.8077286990	4
5	1.1040808032	5.2040401600	.9057308098	4.7134595090	5
6	1.1261624193	6.3081209630	.8879713822	5.6014308910	6
7	1.1486856676	7.4342833820	.8705601786	6.4719910690	7
8	1.1716593810	8.5829690500	.8534903712	7.3254814405	8
9	1.1950925686	9.7546284310	.8367552659	8.1622367065	9
10	1.2189944200	10.9497209995	.8203482999	8.9825850065	10
11	1.2433743084	12.1687154195	.8042630391	9.7868480455	11
12	1.2682417946	13.4120897280	.7884931756	10.5753412210	12
13	1.2936066305	14.6803315225	.7730325251	11.3483737460	13
14	1.3194787631	15.9739381530	.7578750246	12.1062487710	14
15	1.3458683383	17.2934169160	.7430147300	12.8492635005	15
16	1.3727857051	18.6392852545	.7284458137	13.5777093145	16
17	1.4002414192	20.0120709595	.7141625625	14.2918718770	17
18	1.4282462476	21.4123123785	.7001593750	14.9920312520	18
19	1.4568111725	22.8405586260	.6864307598	15.6784620115	19
20	1.4859473960	24.2973697985	.6729713331	16.3514333445	20
21	1.5156663439	25.7833171945	.6597758168	17.0112091615	21
22	1.5459796708	27.2989835385	.6468390361	17.6580481975	22
23	1.5768992642	28.8449632095	.6341559177	18.2922041155	23
24	1.6084372495	30.4218624735	.6217214879	18.9139256030	24
25	1.6406059945	32.0302997230	.6095308705	19.5234564735	25
26	1.6734181144	33.6709057175	.5975792848	20.1210357585	26
27	1.7068864766	35.3443238320	.5858620440	20.7068978025	27
28	1.7410242062	37.0512103085	.5743745529	21.2812723555	28
29	1.7758446903	38.7922345145	.5621123068	21.8443846620	29
30	1.8113615841	40.5680792050	.5520708890	22.3964555510	30
31	1.8475888158	42.3794407890	.5412459696	22.9377015210	31
32	1.8845405921	44.2270296050	.5306333035	23.4683348245	32
33	1.9222314039	46.1115701970	.5202287289	23.9885635535	33
34	1.9606760320	48.0338016010	.5100281656	24.4985917190	34
35	1.9998895527	49.9944776330	.5000276134	24.9986193325	35
36	2.0398873437	51.9943671855	.4902231504	25.4888424825	36
37	2.0806850906	54.0342545295	.4806109317	25.9694534145	37
38	2.1222987924	56.1149396200	.4711871880	26.4406406025	38
39	2.1647447682	58.2372384120	.4619482235	26.9025888255	39
40	2.2080396636	60.4019831805	.4528904152	27.3554792410	40
41	2.2522004569	62.6100228440	.4440102110	27.7994894520	41
42	2.2972444660	64.8622233010	.4353041284	28.2347935805	42
43	2.3431893553	67.1594677670	.4267687533	28.6615623335	43
44	2.3900531425	69.5026571225	.4184007386	29.0799630720	44
45	2.4378542053	71.8927102650	.4101968025	29.4901598745	45
46	2.4866112894	74.3305644700	.4021537280	29.8923136025	46
47	2.5363435152	76.8171757595	.3942683607	30.2865819635	47
48	2.5870703855	79.3535192745	.3865376086	30.6731195720	48
49	2.6388117932	81.9405896600	.3789584398	31.0520780115	49
50	2.6915880291	84.5794014535	.3715278821	31.4236058940	50
51	2.7454197897	87.2709894825	.3642430217	31.7878489155	51
52	2.8003281854	90.0164092720	.3571010017	32.1449499170	52
53	2.8563347492	92.8167374575	.3500990212	32.4950489385	53
54	2.9134614441	95.6730722070	.3432343345	32.8382832730	54
55	2.9717306730	98.5865336510	.3365042496	33.1747875225	55
56	3.0311652865	101.5582643240	.3299061270	33.5046936495	56
57	3.0917885922	104.5894296105	.3234373794	33.8281310290	57
58	3.1536243641	107.6812182025	.3170954700	34.1452264990	58
59	3.2166968513	110.8348425665	.3108779118	34.4561044110	59
60	3.2810307884	114.0515394180	.3047822665	34.7608866775	60
61	3.3466514041	117.3325702065	.2988061436	35.0596928210	61
62	3.4135844322	120.6792216105	.2929471996	35.3526400205	62
63	3.4818561209	124.0928060425	.2872031369	35.6398431575	63
64	3.5514932433	127.5746621635	.2815717028	35.9214148600	64
65	3.6225231081	131.1261554070	.2760506890	36.1974655490	65

Period	Compound Interest Amount	Compound One Per Period	Present Value Of $1 In Future	Present Value Of $1 Per Period	Period
1	1.0300000000	1.0000000000	.9708737864	.9708737867	1
2	1.0609000000	2.0300000000	.9425959091	1.9134696957	2
3	1.0927270000	3.0909000000	.9151416594	2.8286113550	3
4	1.1255088100	4.1836270000	.8884870479	3.7170984030	4
5	1.1592740743	5.3091358100	.8626087844	4.5797071873	5
6	1.1940522965	6.4684098840	.8374842567	5.4171914440	6
7	1.2298738654	7.6624621807	.8130915113	6.2302829553	7
8	1.2667700814	8.8923360460	.7894092343	7.0196921897	8
9	1.3047731838	10.1591061273	.7664167323	7.7861089220	9
10	1.3439163793	11.4638793113	.7440939149	8.5302028370	10
11	1.3842338707	12.8077956907	.7224212766	9.2526241133	11
12	1.4257608868	14.1920295613	.7013798802	9.9540039937	12
13	1.4685337135	15.6177904483	.6809513400	10.6349553337	13
14	1.5125897249	17.0863241617	.6611178058	11.2960731393	14
15	1.5579674166	18.5989138867	.6418619474	11.9379350870	15
16	1.6047064391	20.1568813030	.6231669392	12.5611020260	16
17	1.6528476323	21.7615877423	.6050164458	13.1661184720	17
18	1.7024330612	23.4144353743	.5873946076	13.7535130797	18
19	1.7535060531	25.1168684357	.5702860268	14.3237991063	19
20	1.8061112347	26.8703744887	.5536757542	14.8774748607	20
21	1.8602945717	28.6764857233	.5375492759	15.4150241363	21
22	1.9161034089	30.5367802953	.5218925009	15.9369166373	22
23	1.9735865111	32.4528837040	.5066917484	16.4436083857	23
24	2.0327941065	34.4264702153	.4919337363	16.9355421223	24
25	2.0937779297	36.4592643217	.4776055693	17.4131476913	25
26	2.1565912675	38.5530422513	.4636947274	17.8768424190	26
27	2.2212890056	40.7096335190	.4501890558	18.3270314747	27
28	2.2879276757	42.9309225243	.4370767532	18.7641082277	28
29	2.3565655060	45.2188502000	.4243463623	19.1884545900	29
30	2.4272624712	47.5754157060	.4119867595	19.6004413497	30
31	2.5000803453	50.0026781773	.3999871452	20.0004284947	31
32	2.5750827557	52.5027585227	.3883370341	20.3887655290	32
33	2.6523352384	55.0778412783	.3770262467	20.7657917757	33
34	2.7319052955	57.7301765167	.3660448997	21.1318366753	34
35	2.8138624544	60.4620818123	.3553833978	21.4872200733	35
36	2.8982783280	63.2759442667	.3450324251	21.8322524983	36
37	2.9852266778	66.1742225947	.3349829369	22.1672354353	37
38	3.0747834782	69.1594492723	.3252261524	22.4924615877	38
39	3.1670269825	72.2342327507	.3157535460	22.8082151337	39
40	3.2620377920	75.4012597330	.3065568408	23.1147719743	40
41	3.3598989258	78.6632975250	.2976280008	23.4123999750	41
42	3.4606958935	82.0231964510	.2889592240	23.7013591990	42
43	3.5645167703	85.4838923443	.2805429360	23.9819021350	43
44	3.6714522734	89.0484091147	.2723717825	24.2542739177	44
45	3.7815958417	92.7198613883	.2644386238	24.5187125413	45
46	3.8950437169	96.5014572300	.2567365279	24.7754490693	46
47	4.0118950284	100.3965009467	.2492587650	25.0247078343	47
48	4.1322518793	104.4083959753	.2419988009	25.2667066353	48
49	4.2562194356	108.5406478543	.2349502922	25.5016569273	49
50	4.3839060187	112.7968672900	.2281070798	25.7297640070	50
51	4.5154231993	117.1807733087	.2214631843	25.9512271913	51
52	4.6508858952	121.6961965080	.2150128003	26.1662399917	52
53	4.7904124721	126.3470824033	.2087502915	26.3749902833	53
54	4.9341248463	131.1374948753	.2026701859	26.5776604690	54
55	5.0821485917	136.0716197217	.1967671708	26.7744276400	55
56	5.2346130494	141.1537683133	.1910360882	26.9654637280	56
57	5.3916514409	146.3883813627	.1854719303	27.1509356583	57
58	5.5534009841	151.7800328037	.1800698352	27.3310054937	58
59	5.7200030136	157.3334337877	.1748250827	27.5058305763	59
60	5.8916031040	163.0534368013	.1697330900	27.6755636663	60
61	6.0683511972	168.9450399053	.1647894078	27.8403530740	61
62	6.2504017331	175.0133911027	.1599897163	28.0003427903	62
63	6.4379137851	181.2637928357	.1553298216	28.1556726120	63
64	6.6310511986	187.7017066207	.1508056521	28.3064782640	64
65	6.8299827346	194.3327578193	.1464132544	28.4528915187	65

RATE

3%

Period	Compound Interest Amount	Compound One Per Period	Present Value Of $1 In Future	Present Value Of $1 Per Period	Period
1	1.0400000000	1.0000000000	.9615384615	.9615384618	1
2	1.0816000000	2.0400000000	.9245562130	1.8860946748	2
3	1.1248640000	3.1216000000	.8889963587	2.7750910333	3
4	1.1698585600	4.2464640000	.8548041910	3.6298952245	4
5	1.2166529024	5.4163225600	.8219271068	4.4518223313	5
6	1.2653190185	6.6329754623	.7903145257	5.2421368568	6
7	1.3159317792	7.8982944808	.7599178132	6.0020546700	7
8	1.3685690504	9.2142262600	.7306902050	6.7327448750	8
9	1.4233118124	10.5827953105	.7025867356	7.4353316108	9
10	1.4802442849	12.0061071228	.6755641688	8.1108957795	10
11	1.5394540563	13.4863514078	.6495809316	8.7604767110	11
12	1.6010322186	15.0258054640	.6245970496	9.3850737605	12
13	1.6650735073	16.6268376828	.6005740861	9.9856478468	13
14	1.7316764476	18.2919111900	.5774750828	10.5631229295	14
15	1.8009435055	20.0235876375	.5552645027	11.1183874323	15
16	1.8729812457	21.8245311430	.5339081757	11.6522956080	16
17	1.9479004956	23.6975123888	.5133732459	12.1656688538	17
18	2.0258165154	25.6454128843	.4936281210	12.6592969748	18
19	2.1068491760	27.6712293998	.4746424241	13.1339393988	19
20	2.1911231430	29.7780785758	.4563869462	13.5903263450	20
21	2.2787680688	31.9692017188	.4388336021	14.0291599473	21
22	2.3699187915	34.2479697875	.4219553867	14.4511153338	22
23	2.4647155432	36.6178885790	.4057263333	14.8568416673	23
24	2.5633041649	39.0826041223	.3901214743	15.2469631415	24
25	2.6658363315	41.6459082870	.2751168023	15.6220799438	25
26	2.7724697847	44.3117446185	.3606892329	15.9827691768	26
27	2.8833685761	47.0842144033	.3468165701	16.3295857468	27
28	2.9987033192	49.9675829795	.3334774713	16.6630632180	28
29	3.1186514519	52.9662862985	.3206514147	16.9837146328	29
30	3.2433975100	56.0849377505	.3083186680	17.2920333008	30
31	3.3731334104	59.3283352605	.2964602577	17.5884935585	31
32	3.5080587468	62.7014686710	.2850579401	17.8735514985	32
33	3.6483810967	66.2095274178	.2740941731	18.1476456718	33
34	3.7943163406	69.8579085145	.2635520896	18.4111977613	34
35	3.9460889942	73.6522248553	.2534154707	18.6646132320	35
36	4.1039325540	77.5983138495	.2436687219	18.9082819538	36
37	4.2680898561	81.7022464033	.2342968479	19.1425788018	37
38	4.4388134504	85.9703362595	.2252854307	19.3678642325	38
39	4.6163659884	90.4091497100	.2166206064	19.5844848390	39
40	4.8010206279	95.0255156983	.2082890447	19.7927738835	40
41	4.9930614531	99.8265363263	.2002779276	19.9930518110	41
42	5.1927839112	104.8195977793	.1925749303	20.1856267415	42
43	5.4004952676	110.0123816905	.1851682023	20.3707949438	43
44	5.6165150783	115.4128769580	.1780463483	20.5488412920	44
45	5.8411756815	121.0293920365	.1711984118	20.7200397040	45
46	6.0748227087	126.8705677178	.1646138575	20.8846535615	46
47	6.3178156171	132.9453904265	.1582825553	21.0429361168	47
48	6.5705282418	139.2632060438	.1521947647	21.1951308815	48
49	6.8333493714	145.8337342855	.1463411199	21.3414720015	49
50	7.1066833463	152.6670836568	.1407126153	21.4821846168	50
51	7.3909506801	159.7737670030	.1353005917	21.6174852085	51
52	7.6865887073	167.1647176833	.1300967228	21.7475819313	52
53	7.9940522556	174.8513063905	.1250930027	21.8726749338	53
54	8.3138143459	182.8453586463	.1202817333	21.9929566673	54
55	8.6463669197	191.1591729920	.1156555128	22.1086121800	55
56	8.9922215965	199.8055399118	.1112072239	22.2198194038	56
57	9.3519104603	208.7977615083	.1069300229	22.3267494268	57
58	9.7259868787	218.1496719685	.1028173297	22.4295667565	58
59	10.1150263539	227.8756588473	.0988628171	22.5284295735	59
60	10.5196274081	237.9906852013	.0950604010	22.6234899745	60
61	10.9404125044	248.5103126093	.0914042318	22.7148942063	61
62	11.3780290045	259.4507251135	.0878886844	22.8027828908	62
63	11.8331501647	270.8287541183	.0845083504	22.8872912410	63
64	12.3064761713	282.6619042830	.0812580292	22.9685492703	64
65	12.7987352182	294.9683804543	.0781327204	23.0466819908	65

Period	Compound Interest Amount	Compound One Per Period	Present Value Of $1 In Future	Present Value Of $1 Per Period	Period	RATE
1	1.0500000000	1.0000000000	.9523809524	.9523809524	1	**5%**
2	1.1025000000	2.0500000000	.9070294785	1.8594104310	2	
3	1.1576250000	3.1525000000	.8638375985	2.7232480294	3	
4	1.2155062500	4.3101250000	.8227024748	3.5459505042	4	
5	1.2762815625	5.5256312500	.7835261665	4.3294766708	5	
6	1.3400956406	6.8019128124	.7462153966	5.0756920674	6	
7	1.4071004227	8.1420084530	.7106813301	5.7863733974	7	
8	1.4774554438	9.5491088756	.6768393620	6.4632127594	8	
9	1.5513282160	11.0265643194	.6446089162	7.1078216756	9	
10	1.6288946268	12.5778925354	.6139132535	7.7217349292	10	
11	1.7103393581	14.2067871622	.5846792891	8.3064142184	11	
12	1.7958563260	15.9171265204	.5568374182	8.8632516366	12	
13	1.8856491423	17.7129828464	.5303213506	9.3935729872	13	
14	1.9799315994	19.5986319886	.5050679530	9.8986409402	14	
15	2.0789281794	21.5785635882	.4810170981	10.3796580382	15	
16	2.1828745884	23.6574917676	.4581115220	10.8377695602	16	
17	2.2920183178	25.8403663560	.4362966876	11.2740662478	17	
18	2.4066192337	28.1323846738	.4155206549	11.6895869028	18	
19	2.5269501954	30.5390039074	.3957339570	12.0853208598	19	
20	2.6532977051	33.0659541028	.3768894829	12.4622103426	20	
21	2.7859625904	35.7192518080	.3589423646	12.8211527072	21	
22	2.9252607199	38.5052143984	.3418498711	13.1630025784	22	
23	3.0715237559	41.4304751182	.3255713058	13.4885738842	23	
24	3.2250999437	44.5019988742	.3100679103	13.7986417944	24	
25	3.3863549409	47.7270988178	.2953027717	14.0939445662	25	
26	3.5556726879	51.1134537588	.2812407350	14.3751853010	26	
27	3.7334563223	54.6691264468	.2678483190	14.6430336200	27	
28	3.9201291385	58.4025827690	.2550936371	14.8981272572	28	
29	4.1161355954	62.3227119076	.2429463211	15.1410735784	29	
30	4.3219423752	66.4388475030	.2313774487	15.3724510270	30	
31	4.5380394939	70.7607898780	.2203594749	15.5928105018	31	
32	4.7649414686	75.2988293720	.2098661666	15.8026766684	32	
33	5.0031885420	80.0637708406	.1998725396	16.0025492080	33	
34	5.2533479691	85.0669593826	.1903547996	16.1929040076	34	
35	5.5160153676	90.3203073518	.1812902854	16.3741942930	35	
36	5.7918161360	95.8363227194	.1726574146	16.5468517076	36	
37	6.0814069428	101.6281388554	.1644356330	16.7112873406	37	
38	6.3854772899	107.7095457980	.1566053647	16.8678927054	38	
39	6.7047511544	114.0950230880	.1491479664	17.0170406718	39	
40	7.0399887121	120.7997742424	.1420456823	17.1590863540	40	
41	7.3919881477	127.8397629546	.1352816022	17.2943679562	41	
42	7.7615875551	135.2317511022	.1288396211	17.4232075774	42	
43	8.1496669329	142.9933386574	.1227044011	17.5459119784	43	
44	8.5571502795	151.1430055902	.1168613344	17.6627733128	44	
45	8.9850077935	159.7001558698	.1112965089	17.7740698218	45	
46	9.4342581832	168.6851636632	.1059966752	17.8800664970	46	
47	9.9059710923	178.1194218464	.1009492144	17.9810157114	47	
48	10.4012696469	188.0253929388	.0961421090	18.0771578204	48	
49	10.9213331293	198.4266625856	.0915639133	18.1687217336	49	
50	11.4673997858	209.3479957150	.0872037270	18.2559254606	50	
51	12.0407697750	220.8153955008	.0830511685	18.3389766292	51	
52	12.6428082638	232.8561652758	.0790963510	18.4180729802	52	
53	13.2749486770	245.4989735396	.0753298581	18.4934028382	53	
54	13.9386961108	258.7739222166	.0717427220	18.5651455602	54	
55	14.6356309164	272.7126183274	.0683264019	18.6334719622	55	
56	15.3674124622	287.3482492438	.0650727637	18.6985447258	56	
57	16.1357830853	302.7156617060	.0619740607	18.7605187866	57	
58	16.9425722396	318.8514447912	.0590229149	18.8195417014	58	
59	17.7897008515	335.7940170308	.0562122999	18.8757540014	59	
60	18.6791858941	353.5837178824	.0535355237	18.9292895252	60	
61	19.6131451888	372.2629037764	.0509862131	18.9802757382	61	
62	20.5938024483	391.8760489654	.0485582982	19.0288340364	62	
63	21.6234925707	412.4698514136	.0462459983	19.0750800348	63	
64	22.7046671992	434.0933439842	.0440438079	19.1191238426	64	
65	23.8399005592	456.7980111834	.0419464837	19.1610703262	65	

Period	Compound Interest Amount	Compound One Per Period	Present Value Of $1 In Future	Present Value Of $1 Per Period	Period
1	1.0600000000	1.0000000000	.9433962264	.9433962265	1
2	1.1236000000	2.0600000000	.8899964400	1.8333926665	2
3	1.1910160000	3.1836000000	.8396192830	2.6730119495	3
4	1.2624769600	4.3746160000	.7920936632	3.4651056128	4
5	1.3382255776	5.6370929600	.7472581729	4.2123637857	5
6	1.4185191123	6.9753185375	.7049605404	4.9173243260	6
7	1.5036302590	8.3938376498	.6650571136	5.5823814397	7
8	1.5938480745	9.8974679088	.6274123713	6.2097938110	8
9	1.6894789590	11.4913159833	.5918984635	6.8016922745	9
10	1.7908476965	13.1807949423	.5583947769	7.3600870515	10
11	1.8982985583	14.9716426388	.5267875254	7.8868745768	11
12	2.0121964718	16.8699411972	.4969693636	8.3838439405	12
13	2.1329282601	18.8821376690	.4688390222	8.8526829627	13
14	2.2609039558	21.0150659292	.4423009644	9.2949839270	14
15	2.3965581931	23.2759698848	.4172650607	9.7122489878	15
16	2.5403516847	25.6725280780	.3936462837	10.1058952715	16
17	2.6927727858	28.2128797627	.3713644186	10.4772596902	17
18	2.8543391529	30.9056525485	.3503437911	10.8276034813	18
19	3.0255995021	33.7599917013	.3305130105	11.1581164917	19
20	3.2071354722	36.7855912035	.3118047269	11.4699212187	20
21	3.3995636005	39.9927266757	.2941554027	11.7640766213	21
22	3.6035374166	43.3922902762	.2775050969	12.0415817183	22
23	3.8197496616	46.9958276928	.2617972612	12.3033789795	23
24	4.0489346413	50.8155773543	.2469785483	12.5503575278	24
25	4.2918707197	54.8645119957	.2329986305	12.7833561583	25
26	4.5493829629	59.1563827153	.2198100288	13.0031661872	26
27	4.8223459407	63.7057656783	.2073679517	13.2105341388	27
28	5.1116866971	68.5281116190	.1956301431	13.4061642818	28
29	5.4183878990	73.6397983162	.1845567388	13.5907210207	29
30	5.7434911729	79.0581862152	.1741101309	13.7648311515	30
31	6.0881006433	84.8016773880	.1642548405	13.9290859920	31
32	6.4533866819	90.8897780313	.1549573967	14.0840433887	32
33	6.8405898828	97.3431647132	.1461862233	14.2302296120	33
34	7.2510252758	104.1837545960	.1379115314	14.3681411435	34
35	7.6860867923	111.4347798718	.1301052183	14.4982463617	35
36	8.1472519999	119.1208666642	.1227407720	14.6209871337	36
37	8.6360871198	127.2681186640	.1157931811	14.7367803148	37
38	9.1542523470	135.9042057838	.1092388501	14.8460191650	38
39	9.7035074879	145.0584581308	.1030555190	14.9490746838	39
40	10.2857179371	154.7619656187	.0972221877	15.0462968717	40
41	10.9028610134	165.0476835558	.0917190450	15.1380159167	41
42	11.5570326742	175.9505445692	.0865274010	15.2245433175	42
43	12.2504546346	187.5075772433	.0816296235	15.3061729412	43
44	12.9854819127	199.7580318780	.0770090788	15.3831820198	44
45	13.7646108274	212.7435137907	.0726500743	15.4558320943	45
46	14.5904874771	226.5081246180	.0685378060	15.5243699003	46
47	15.4659167257	241.0986120952	.0646583075	15.5890282078	47
48	16.3938717293	256.5645288208	.0609984033	15.6500266112	48
49	17.3775040330	272.9584005502	.0575456635	15.7075722747	49
50	18.4201542750	290.3359045832	.0542883618	15.7618606365	50
51	19.5253635315	308.7560588582	.0512154357	15.8130760722	51
52	20.6968853434	328.2814223897	.0483164488	15.8613925208	52
53	21.9386984640	348.9783077330	.0455815554	15.9069740763	53
54	23.2550203718	370.9170061970	.0430014674	15.9499755437	54
55	24.6503215941	394.1720265688	.0405674221	15.9905429658	55
56	26.1293408898	418.8223481628	.0382711529	16.0288141187	56
57	27.6971013432	444.9516890527	.0361048612	16.0649189798	57
58	29.3589274238	472.6487903958	.0340611898	16.0989801697	58
59	31.1204630692	502.0077178197	.0321331979	16.1311133677	59
60	32.9876908533	533.1281808888	.0303143377	16.1614277053	60
61	34.9669523045	566.1158717422	.0285984318	16.1900261372	61
62	37.0649694428	601.0828240467	.0269796526	16.2170057897	62
63	39.2888676094	638.1477934895	.0254525025	16.2424582922	63
64	41.6461996659	677.4366610988	.0240117948	16.2664700870	64
65	44.1449716459	719.0828607648	.0226526366	16.2891227235	65

Period	Compound Interest Amount	Compound One Per Period	Present Value Of $1 In Future	Present Value Of $1 Per Period	Period
1	1.0700000000	1.0000000000	.9345794393	.9345794393	1
2	1.1449000000	2.0700000000	.8734387283	1.8080181676	2
3	1.2250430000	3.2149000000	.8162978769	2.6243160444	3
4	1.3107960100	4.4399430000	.7628952120	3.3872112566	4
5	1.4025517307	5.7507390100	.7129861795	4.1001974360	5
6	1.5007303518	7.1532907406	.6663422238	4.7665396597	6
7	1.6057814765	8.6540210924	.6227497419	5.3892894017	7
8	1.7181861798	10.2598025690	.5820091046	5.9712985063	8
9	1.8384592124	11.9779887489	.5439337426	6.5152322489	9
10	1.9671513573	13.8164479611	.5083492921	7.0235815410	10
11	2.1048519523	15.7835993184	.4750927964	7.4986743374	11
12	2.2521915890	17.8884512709	.4440119592	7.9426862966	12
13	2.4098450002	20.1406428597	.4149644479	8.3576507446	13
14	2.5785341502	22.5504878600	.3878172410	8.7454679856	14
15	2.7590315407	25.1290220101	.3624460196	9.1079140051	15
16	2.9521637486	27.8880535509	.3387345978	9.4466486030	16
17	3.1588152110	30.8402172994	.3165743905	9.7632229934	17
18	3.3799322757	33.9990325104	.2958639163	10.0590869097	18
19	3.6165275350	37.3789647861	.2765083330	10.3355952427	19
20	3.8696844625	40.9954923211	.2584190028	10.5940142456	20
21	4.1405623749	44.8651767837	.2415130867	10.8355273323	21
22	4.4304017411	49.0057391586	.2257131652	11.0612404976	22
23	4.7405298630	53.4361408996	.2109468833	11.2721873809	23
24	5.0723669534	58.1766707626	.1971466199	11.4693340009	24
25	5.4274326401	63.2490377160	.1842491775	11.6535831783	25
26	5.8073529249	68.6764703561	.1721954930	11.8257786713	26
27	6.2138676297	74.4838232810	.1609303673	11.9867090386	27
28	6.6488383638	80.6976909107	.1504022124	12.1371112510	28
29	7.1142570492	87.3465292744	.1405628154	12.2776740664	29
30	7.6122550427	94.4607863237	.1313671172	12.4090411836	30
31	8.1451128956	102.0730413663	.1227730067	12.5318141903	31
32	8.7152707983	110.2181542620	.1147411277	12.6465553180	32
33	9.3253397542	118.9334250603	.1072346988	12.7537900169	33
34	9.9781135370	128.2587648146	.1002193447	12.8540093616	34
35	10.6765814846	138.2368783516	.0936629390	12.9476723006	35
36	11.4239421885	148.9134598361	.0875354570	13.0352077574	36
37	12.2236181417	160.3374020247	.0818088383	13.1170165957	37
38	13.0792714117	172.5610201664	.0764568582	13.1934734540	38
39	13.9948204105	185.6402915781	.0714550077	13.2649284617	39
40	14.9744578392	199.6351119886	.0667803810	13.3317088427	40
41	16.0226698880	214.6095698279	.0624115710	13.3941204137	41
42	17.1442567801	230.6322397157	.0583285711	13.4524489849	42
43	18.3443547547	247.7764964959	.0545126832	13.5069616680	43
44	19.6284595875	266.1208512506	.0509464329	13.5579081010	44
45	21.0024517587	285.7493108381	.0476134887	13.6055215897	45
46	22.4726233818	306.7517625969	.0444985876	13.6500201773	46
47	24.0457070185	329.2243859786	.0415874650	13.6916076423	47
48	25.7289065098	353.2700929971	.0388667898	13.7304744321	48
49	27.5299299655	378.9989995069	.0363241026	13.7667985347	49
50	29.4570250631	406.5289294724	.0339477594	13.8007462941	50
51	31.5190168175	435.9859545354	.0317268780	13.8324731720	51
52	33.7253479947	467.5049713530	.0296512878	13.8621244599	52
53	36.0861223543	501.2303193477	.0277114839	13.8898359439	53
54	38.6121509191	537.3164417020	.0258985831	13.9157345270	54
55	41.3150014835	575.9285926211	.0242042833	13.9399388103	55
56	44.2070515873	617.2435941046	.0226208255	13.9625596357	56
57	47.3015451984	661.4506456920	.0211409584	13.9837005941	57
58	50.6126533623	708.7521908904	.0197579051	14.0034584991	58
59	54.1555390977	759.3648442527	.0184653318	14.0219238310	59
60	57.9464268345	813.5203833504	.0172573195	14.0391811506	60
61	62.0026767130	871.4668101850	.0161283360	14.0553094864	61
62	66.3428640829	933.4694868979	.0150732112	14.0703826976	62
63	70.9868645687	999.8123509807	.0140871132	14.0844698109	63
64	75.9559450885	1070.7992155494	.0131655264	14.0976353373	64
65	81.2728612447	1146.7551606379	.0123042303	14.1099395676	65

RATE

7%

Period	Compound Interest Amount	Compound One Per Period	Present Value Of $1 In Future	Present Value Of $1 Per Period	Period
1	1.0725000000	1.0000000000	.9324009324	.9324009324	1
2	1.1502562500	2.0725000000	.8693714987	1.8017724312	2
3	1.2336498281	3.2227562499	.8106027960	2.6123752272	3
4	1.3230894407	4.4564060781	.7558068028	3.3681820301	4
5	1.4190134251	5.7794955188	.7047149677	4.0728969977	5
6	1.5218918984	7.1985089439	.6570768929	4.7299738906	6
7	1.6322290611	8.7204008422	.6126591076	5.3426329982	7
8	1.7505656680	10.3526299033	.5712439232	5.9138769215	8
9	1.8774816789	12.1031955713	.5326283666	6.4465052881	9
10	2.0135991006	13.9806772502	.4966231857	6.9431284738	10
11	2.1595850354	15.9942763509	.4630519214	7.4061803952	11
12	2.3161549505	18.1538613863	.4317500432	7.8379304383	12
13	2.4840761844	20.4700163368	.4025641429	8.2404945812	13
14	2.6641717078	22.9540925212	.3753511822	8.6158457633	14
15	2.8573241566	25.6182642291	.3499777922	8.9658235556	15
16	3.0644801580	28.4755883857	.3263196198	9.2921431753	16
17	3.2866549694	31.5400685437	.3042607178	9.5964038931	17
18	3.5249374547	34.8267235131	.2836929769	9.8800968701	18
19	3.7804954202	38.3516609679	.2645155962	10.1446124662	19
20	4.0545813381	42.1321563880	.2466345885	10.3912470548	20
21	4.3485384851	46.1867377261	.2299623203	10.6212093752	21
22	4.6638075253	50.5352762113	.2144170819	10.8356264570	22
23	5.0019335709	55.1990837366	.1999226871	11.0355491440	23
24	5.3645737548	60.2010173074	.1864080998	11.2219572439	24
25	5.7535053520	65.5655910623	.1738070861	11.3957643299	25
26	6.1706344900	71.3190964143	.1620578891	11.5578222190	26
27	6.6180054906	77.4897309043	.1511029269	11.7089251459	27
28	7.0978108886	84.1077363949	.1408885099	11.8498136566	28
29	7.6124021781	91.2055472836	.1313645780	11.9811782339	29
30	8.1643013360	98.8179494617	.1224844550	12.1036626891	30
31	8.7562131828	106.9822507975	.1142046201	12.2178673091	31
32	9.3910386386	115.7384639804	.1064844943	12.3243518034	32
33	10.0718889399	125.1295026190	.0992862417	12.4236380451	33
34	10.8021008880	135.2013915589	.0925745844	12.5162126295	34
35	11.5852532024	146.0034924469	.0863166288	12.6025292582	35
36	12.4251840596	157.5887456492	.0804817052	12.6830109634	36
37	13.3260099039	170.0139297088	.0750412169	12.7580521804	37
38	14.2921456219	183.3399396128	.0699685006	12.8280206810	38
39	15.3283261795	197.6320852348	.0652386952	12.8932593763	39
40	16.4396298275	212.9604114142	.0608286203	12.9540879964	40
41	17.6315029900	229.4000412418	.0567166622	13.0108046588	41
42	18.9097869568	247.0315442319	.0528826688	13.0636873274	42
43	20.2807465112	265.9413311887	.0493078497	13.1129951771	43
44	21.7511006332	286.2220776999	.0459746850	13.1589698622	44
45	23.3280554292	307.9731783331	.0428668392	13.2018367012	45
46	25.0193394478	331.3012337622	.0399690808	13.2418057821	46
47	26.8332415577	356.3205732099	.0372672082	13.2790729903	47
48	28.7786515707	383.1538147677	.0347479797	13.3138209699	48
49	30.8651038095	411.9324663383	.0323990487	13.3462200186	49
50	33.1028238357	442.7975701479	.0302089032	13.3764289218	50
51	35.5027785638	475.9003939836	.0281668095	13.4045957313	51
52	38.0767300097	511.4031725474	.0262627594	13.4308584908	52
53	40.8372929354	549.4799025571	.0244874214	13.4553459121	53
54	43.7979966732	590.3171954926	.0228320945	13.4781780066	54
55	46.9733514320	634.1151921658	.0212886662	13.4994666728	55
56	50.3789194108	681.0885435978	.0198495722	13.5193162451	56
57	54.0313910681	731.4674630086	.0185077597	13.5378240047	57
58	57.9486669206	785.4988540767	.0172566524	13.5550806571	58
59	62.1499452723	843.4475209972	.0160901188	13.5711707759	59
60	66.6558163046	905.5974662697	.0150024417	13.5861732177	60
61	71.4883629866	972.2532825742	.0139882907	13.6001615083	61
62	76.6712693032	1043.7416455608	.0130426953	13.6132042034	62
63	82.2299363276	1120.4129148640	.0121610212	13.6253652247	63
64	88.1916067114	1202.6428511916	.0113389475	13.6367041723	64
65	94.5854981980	1290.8344579030	.0105724452	13.6472766175	65

Period	Compound Interest Amount	Compound One Per Period	Present Value Of $1 In Future	Present Value Of $1 Per Period	Period
1	1.0750000000	1.0000000000	.9302325581	.9302325583	1
2	1.1556250000	2.0750000000	.8653326122	1.7955651704	2
3	1.2422968750	3.2306250000	.8049605695	2.6005257400	3
4	1.3354691406	4.4729218749	.7488005298	3.3493262697	4
5	1.4356293262	5.8083910156	.6965586324	4.0458849020	5
6	1.5433015256	7.2440203417	.6479615185	4.6938464205	6
7	1.6590491401	8.7873218673	.6027549009	5.2966013213	7
8	1.7834778256	10.4463710075	.5607022334	5.8573035548	8
9	1.9172386625	12.2298488329	.5215834729	6.3788870277	9
10	2.0610315622	14.1470874955	.4851939283	6.8640809560	10
11	2.2156089293	16.2081190576	.4513431891	7.3154241452	11
12	2.3817795990	18.4237279869	.4198541294	7.7352782745	12
13	2.5604130690	20.8055075860	.3905619808	8.1258402555	13
14	2.7524440491	23.3659206549	.3633134706	8.4891537260	14
15	2.9588773528	26.1183647040	.3379660191	8.8271197451	15
16	3.1807931543	29.0772420569	.3143869945	9.1415067396	16
17	3.4193526408	32.2580352112	.2924530182	9.4339597579	17
18	3.6758040889	35.6773878520	.2720493192	9.7060090771	18
19	3.9514893956	39.3531919409	.2530691342	9.9590782112	19
20	4.2478511002	43.3046813364	.2354131481	10.1944913592	20
21	4.5664399328	47.5525324367	.2189889749	10.4134803341	21
22	4.9089229277	52.1189723695	.2037106744	10.6171910085	22
23	5.2770921473	57.0278952972	.1894983017	10.8066893103	23
24	5.6728740583	62.3049874444	.1762774900	10.9829668003	24
25	6.0983396127	67.9778615028	.1639790605	11.1469458607	25
26	6.5557150837	74.0762011155	.1525386609	11.2994845216	26
27	7.0473937149	80.6319161992	.1418964287	11.4413809504	27
28	7.5759482436	87.6793099141	.1319966779	11.5733776283	28
29	8.1441443618	95.2552581577	.1227876073	11.6961652356	29
30	8.7549551890	103.3994025195	.1142210301	11.8103862656	30
31	9.4115768281	112.1543577085	.1062521210	11.9166383867	31
32	10.1174450903	121.5659345367	.0988391823	12.0154775689	32
33	10.8762534720	131.6833796269	.0919434254	12.1074209944	33
34	11.6919724824	142.5596330989	.0855287678	12.1929497623	34
35	12.5688704186	154.2516055813	.0795616445	12.2725114068	35
36	13.5115357000	166.8204759999	.0740108321	12.3465222388	36
37	14.5249008775	180.3320116999	.0688472857	12.4153695245	37
38	15.6142684433	194.8569125775	.0640439867	12.4794135112	38
39	16.7853385766	210.4711810208	.0595758016	12.5389893127	39
40	18.0442389698	227.2565195973	.0554193503	12.5944086631	40
41	19.3975568925	245.3007585671	.0515528840	12.6459615469	41
42	20.8523736595	264.6983154596	.0479561711	12.6939177181	42
43	22.4163016839	285.5506891191	.0446103918	12.7385281099	43
44	24.0975243102	307.9669908031	.0414980388	12.7800261488	44
45	25.9048386335	332.0645151133	.0386028268	12.8186289756	45
46	27.8477015310	357.9693537468	.0359096064	12.8545385820	46
47	29.9362791458	385.8170552779	.0334042850	12.8879428669	47
48	32.1815000818	415.7533344236	.0310737535	12.9190166204	48
49	34.5951125879	447.9348345055	.0289058172	12.9479224376	49
50	37.1897460320	482.5299470933	.0268891323	12.9748115699	50
51	39.9789769844	519.7196931253	.0250131463	12.9998247161	51
52	42.9774002582	559.6986701097	.0232680431	13.0230927592	52
53	46.2007052776	602.6760703680	.0216446912	13.0447374504	53
54	49.6657581734	648.8767756456	.0201345965	13.0648720469	54
55	53.3906900364	698.5425338191	.0187298572	13.0836019041	55
56	57.3949917892	751.9332238555	.0174231230	13.1010250271	56
57	61.6996161734	809.3282156447	.0162075563	13.1172325833	57
58	66.3270873864	871.0278318180	.0150767965	13.1323093799	58
59	71.3016189403	937.3549192043	.0140249270	13.1463343068	59
60	76.6492403609	1008.6565381447	.0130464437	13.1593807505	60
61	82.3979333879	1085.3057785055	.0121362267	13.1715169773	61
62	88.5777783920	1167.7037118935	.0112895132	13.1828064905	62
63	95.2211117714	1256.2814902855	.0105018728	13.1933083632	63
64	102.3626951543	1351.5026020568	.0097691840	13.2030775472	64
65	110.0398972908	1453.8652972111	.0090876130	13.2121651603	65

RATE

7½%

Period	Compound Interest Amount	Compound One Per Period	Present Value Of $1 In Future	Present Value Of $1 Per Period	Period
1	1.0775000000	1.0000000000	.9280742459	.9280742461	1
2	1.1610062500	2.0775000000	.8613218060	1.7893960520	2
3	1.2509842344	3.2385062499	.7993705856	2.5887666375	3
4	1.3479355125	4.4894904843	.7418752535	3.3306418910	4
5	1.4524005148	5.8374259969	.6885153164	4.0191572075	5
6	1.5649615547	7.2898265116	.6389933331	4.6581505405	6
7	1.6862460751	8.8547880663	.5930332558	5.2511837964	7
8	1.8169301460	10.5410341414	.5503788917	5.8015626880	8
9	1.9577422323	12.3579642874	.5107924749	6.3123551628	9
10	2.1094672553	14.3157065196	.4740533410	6.7864085039	10
11	2.2729509676	16.4251737750	.4399566969	7.2263652008	11
12	2.4491046675	18.6981247425	.4083124798	7.6346776805	12
13	2.6389102793	21.1472294101	.3789442968	8.0136219773	13
14	2.8434258259	23.7861396893	.3516884425	8.3653104197	14
15	3.0637913274	26.6295655152	.3263929861	8.6917034058	15
16	3.3012351553	29.6933568427	.3029169244	8.9946203303	16
17	3.5570808798	32.9945919979	.2811293962	9.2757497265	17
18	3.8327546480	36.5516728778	.2609089524	9.5366586788	18
19	4.1297931333	40.3844275259	.2421428793	9.7788015581	19
20	4.4498521011	44.5142206591	.2247265701	10.0035281281	20
21	4.7947156389	48.9640727603	.2085629421	10.2120910702	21
22	5.1663061009	53.7587883991	.1935618952	10.4056529654	22
23	5.5666948238	58.9250945001	.1796398099	10.5852927754	23
24	5.9981136726	64.4917893239	.1667190811	10.7520118565	24
25	6.4629674822	70.4899029965	.1547276855	10.9067395419	25
26	6.9638474621	76.9528704787	.1435987800	11.0503383221	26
27	7.5035456404	83.9167179408	.1332703295	11.1836086515	27
28	8.0850704275	91.4202635812	.1236847606	11.3072934121	28
29	8.7116633857	99.5053340088	.1147886409	11.4220820530	29
30	9.3868172981	108.2169973945	.1065323813	11.5286144343	30
31	10.1142956387	117.6038146925	.0988699595	11.6274843938	31
32	10.8981535507	127.7181103312	.0917586631	11.7192430569	32
33	11.7427604508	138.6162638818	.0851588521	11.8044019090	33
34	12.6528243858	150.3590243326	.0790337374	11.8834356465	34
35	13.6334182757	163.0118487185	.0733491763	11.9567848226	35
36	14.6900081921	176.6452669942	.0680734814	12.0248583041	36
37	15.8284838269	191.3352751862	.0631772450	12.0880355490	37
38	17.0551913235	207.1637590132	.0586331740	12.1466687230	38
39	18.3769686511	224.2189503366	.0544159387	12.2010846617	39
40	19.8011837216	242.5959189877	.0505020313	12.2515866930	40
41	21.3357754600	262.3971027094	.0468696346	12.2984563276	41
42	22.9892980581	283.7328781693	.0434985008	12.3419548284	42
43	24.7709686576	306.7221762275	.0403698383	12.3823246667	43
44	26.6907187286	331.4931448850	.0374662073	12.4197908741	44
45	28.7592494301	358.1838636137	.0347714221	12.4545622961	45
46	30.9880912609	386.9431130437	.0322704613	12.4868327574	46
47	33.3896683336	417.9312043046	.0299493840	12.5167821414	47
48	35.9773676295	451.3208726383	.0277952520	12.5445773934	48
49	38.7656136208	487.2982402677	.0257960576	12.5703734510	49
50	41.7699486764	526.0638538885	.0239406567	12.5943141076	50
51	45.0071196988	567.8338025649	.0222187069	12.6165328146	51
52	48.4951714754	612.8409222636	.0206206096	12.6371534241	52
53	52.2535472648	661.3360937391	.0191374567	12.6562908809	53
54	56.3031971778	713.5896410039	.0177609807	12.6740518617	54
55	60.6666949591	769.8928381817	.0164835088	12.6905353705	55
56	65.3683638184	830.5595331408	.0152979200	12.7058332905	56
57	70.4344120143	895.9278969592	.0141976056	12.7200308960	57
58	75.8930789455	966.3623089735	.0131764321	12.7332073281	58
59	81.7747925637	1042.2553879190	.0122287073	12.7454360354	59
60	88.1123389874	1124.0301804827	.0113491483	12.7567851836	60
61	94.9410452589	1212.1425194701	.0105328522	12.7673180359	61
62	102.2989762665	1307.0835647290	.0097752489	12.7770933048	62
63	110.2271469272	1409.3825409956	.0090721753	12.7861654800	63
64	118.7697508140	1519.6096879227	.0084196523	12.7945851323	64
65	127.9744065021	1638.3794387368	.0078140624	12.8023991947	65

Period	Compound Interest Amount	Compound One Per Period	Present Value Of $1 In Future	Present Value Of $1 Per Period	Period
1	1.0800000000	1.0000000000	.9259259259	.9259259260	1
2	1.1664000000	2.0800000000	.8573388203	1.7832647463	2
3	1.2597120000	3.2464000000	.7938322410	2.5770969873	3
4	1.3604889600	4.5061120000	.7350298528	3.3121268401	4
5	1.4693280768	5.8666009600	.6805831970	3.9927100371	5
6	1.5868743229	7.3359290368	.6301696269	4.6228796640	6
7	1.7138242688	8.9228033596	.5834903953	5.2063700593	7
8	1.8509302103	10.6366276285	.5402688845	5.7466389438	8
9	1.9990046271	12.4875578388	.5002489671	6.2468879109	9
10	2.1589249973	14.4865624659	.4631934881	6.7100813990	10
11	2.3316389971	16.6454874631	.4288828593	7.1389642584	11
12	2.5181701168	18.9771246601	.3971137586	7.5360780170	12
13	2.7196237262	21.4952965770	.3676979247	7.9037759416	13
14	2.9371936243	24.2149203031	.3404610414	8.2442369830	14
15	3.1721691142	27.1521139274	.3152417050	8.5594786880	15
16	3.4259426433	30.3242830416	.2918904676	8.8513691555	16
17	3.7000180548	33.7502256880	.2702689514	9.1216381070	17
18	3.9960194992	37.4502437398	.2502490291	9.3718871361	18
19	4.3157010591	41.4462632389	.2317120640	9.6035992001	19
20	4.6609571438	45.7619642980	.2145482074	9.8181474075	20
21	5.0338337154	50.4229214419	.1986557476	10.0168031551	21
22	5.4365404126	55.4567551573	.1839405070	10.2007436621	22
23	5.8714636456	60.8932955699	.1703152843	10.3710589464	23
24	6.3411807372	66.7647592155	.1576993373	10.5287582838	24
25	6.8484751962	73.1059399526	.1460179049	10.6747761886	25
26	7.3963532119	79.9544151489	.1352017638	10.8099779525	26
27	7.9880614689	87.3507683609	.1251868183	10.9351647708	27
28	8.6271063864	95.3388298296	.1159137207	11.0510784915	28
29	9.3172748973	103.9659362161	.1073275192	11.1584060106	29
30	10.0626568891	113.2832111134	.0993773325	11.2577833433	30
31	10.8676694402	123.3458680024	.0920160483	11.3497993919	31
32	11.7370829954	134.2135374426	.0852000451	11.4349994369	32
33	12.6760496350	145.9506204380	.0788889306	11.5138883675	33
34	13.6901336059	158.6266700731	.0730453061	11.5869336736	34
35	14.7853442943	172.3168036790	.0676345427	11.6545682164	35
36	15.9681718379	187.1021479733	.0626245766	11.7171927929	36
37	17.2456255849	203.0703198111	.0579857190	11.7751785120	37
38	18.6252756317	220.3159453960	.0536904806	11.8288689925	38
39	20.1152976822	238.9412210278	.0497134080	11.8785824005	39
40	21.7245214968	259.0565187099	.0460309333	11.9246133338	40
41	23.4624832165	280.7810402068	.0426212345	11.9672345684	41
42	25.3394818739	304.2435234233	.0394641061	12.0066986744	42
43	27.3666404238	329.5830052971	.0365408389	12.0432395134	43
44	29.5559716577	356.9496457209	.0338341101	12.0770736235	44
45	31.9204493903	386.5056173786	.0313278797	12.1084015033	45
46	34.4740853415	418.4260667689	.0290072961	12.1374087993	46
47	37.2320121688	452.9001521104	.0268586075	12.1642674068	47
48	40.2105731423	490.1321642793	.0248690810	12.1891364878	48
49	43.4274189937	530.3427374216	.0230269268	12.2121634146	49
50	46.9016125132	573.7701564154	.0213212286	12.2334846431	50
51	50.6537415143	620.6717689285	.0197418783	12.2532265214	51
52	54.7060408354	671.3255104429	.0182795169	12.2715060384	52
53	59.0825241023	726.0315512783	.0169254786	12.2884315170	53
54	63.8091260304	785.1140753805	.0156717395	12.3041032565	54
55	68.9138561129	848.9232014110	.0145108699	12.3186141264	55
56	74.4269646019	917.8370575239	.0134359906	12.3320501170	56
57	80.3811217701	992.2640221258	.0124407321	12.3444908491	57
58	86.8116115117	1072.6451438959	.0115191964	12.3560100455	58
59	93.7565404326	1159.4567554075	.0106659680	12.3666759680	59
60	101.2570636672	1253.2132958401	.0098758542	12.3765518223	60
61	109.3576287606	1354.4703595074	.0091443095	12.3856961318	61
62	118.1062390614	1463.8279882680	.0084669532	12.3941630849	62
63	127.5547381864	1581.9342273294	.0078397715	12.4020028564	63
64	137.7591172413	1709.4889655158	.0072590477	12.4092619041	64
65	148.7798466206	1847.2480827570	.0067213404	12.4159832445	65

Period	Compound Interest Amount	Compound One Per Period	Present Value Of $1 In Future	Present Value Of $1 Per Period	Period
1	1.0825000000	1.0000000000	.9237875289	.9237875290	1
2	1.1718062500	2.0825000000	.8533833985	1.7771709274	2
3	1.2684802656	3.2543062499	.7883449409	2.5655158682	3
4	1.3731298875	4.5227865155	.7282632248	3.2937790931	4
5	1.4864131033	5.8959164032	.6727604848	3.9665395779	5
6	1.6090421843	7.3823295064	.6214877458	4.5880273238	6
7	1.7417881645	8.9913716907	.5741226289	5.1621499526	7
8	1.8854856881	10.7331598552	.5303673246	5.6925172772	8
9	2.0410382573	12.6186455432	.4899467202	6.1824639975	9
10	2.2094239135	14.6596838005	.4526066699	6.6350706674	10
11	2.3917013864	16.8691077141	.4181123972	7.0531830646	11
12	2.5890167508	19.2608091005	.3862470182	7.4394300828	12
13	2.8026106327	21.8498258513	.3568101785	7.7962402612	13
14	3.0338260099	24.6524364840	.3296167930	8.1258570543	14
15	3.2841166558	27.6862624939	.3044958827	8.4303529370	15
16	3.5550562799	30.9703791497	.2812894990	8.7116424360	16
17	3.8483484229	34.5254354296	.2598517312	8.9714941673	17
18	4.1658371678	38.3737838525	.2400477886	9.2115419559	18
19	4.5095187342	42.5396210202	.2217531535	9.4332951093	19
20	4.8815540297	47.0491397544	.2048527977	9.6381479070	20
21	5.2842822372	51.9306937842	.1892404597	9.8273883668	21
22	5.7202355218	57.2149760215	.1748179767	10.0022063434	22
23	6.1921549523	62.9352115432	.1614946667	10.1637010101	23
24	6.7030077359	69.1273664955	.1491867590	10.3128877692	24
25	7.2560058741	75.8303742314	.1378168675	10.4507046366	25
26	7.8546263587	83.0863801055	.1273135034	10.5780181401	26
27	8.5026330333	90.9410064642	.1176106267	10.6956287668	27
28	9.2041002586	99.4436394976	.1086472302	10.8042759971	28
29	9.9634385299	108.6477397561	.1003669563	10.9046429535	29
30	10.7854222086	118.6111782859	.0927177426	10.9973606960	30
31	11.6752195408	129.3966004945	.0856514943	11.0830121903	31
32	12.6384251529	141.0718200354	.0791237823	11.1621359726	32
33	13.6810952280	153.7102451882	.0730935633	11.2352295359	33
34	14.8097855844	167.3913404164	.0675229222	11.3027524581	34
35	16.0315928951	182.2011260006	.0623768335	11.3651292915	35
36	17.3541993089	198.2327188958	.0576229408	11.4227522324	36
37	18.7859207519	215.5869182046	.0532313541	11.4759835865	37
38	20.3357592139	234.3728389565	.0491744611	11.5251580475	38
39	22.0134593491	254.7085981704	.0454267539	11.5705848015	39
40	23.8295697454	276.7220575195	.0419646687	11.6125494702	40
41	25.7955092494	300.5516272648	.0387664376	11.6513159078	41
42	27.9236387624	326.3471365142	.0358119516	11.6871278594	42
43	30.2273389603	354.2707752766	.0330826343	11.7202104937	43
44	32.7210944246	384.4981142370	.0305613250	11.7507718187	44
45	35.4205847146	417.2192086615	.0282321709	11.7790039895	45
46	38.3427829535	452.6397933761	.0260805274	11.8050845168	46
47	41.5060625472	490.9825763296	.0240928659	11.8291773828	47
48	44.9303127073	532.4886388768	.0222566891	11.8514340719	48
49	48.6370635057	577.4189515841	.0205604518	11.8719945236	49
50	52.6496212449	626.0560150898	.0189934890	11.8909880126	50
51	56.9932149976	678.7056363348	.0175459482	11.9085339608	51
52	61.6951552349	735.6988513324	.0162087282	11.9247426890	52
53	66.7850055418	797.3940065673	.0149734209	11.9397161099	53
54	72.2947684990	864.1790121091	.0138322595	11.9535483695	54
55	78.2590869002	936.4737806081	.0127780688	11.9663264383	55
56	84.7154615694	1014.7328675084	.0118042206	11.9781306589	56
57	91.7044871489	1099.4483290778	.0109045918	11.9890352508	57
58	99.2701073387	1191.1528162267	.0100735259	11.9991087767	58
59	107.4598911941	1290.4229235653	.0093057976	12.0084145743	59
60	116.3253322177	1397.8828147595	.0085965798	12.0170111542	60
61	125.9221721256	1514.2081469772	.0079414132	12.0249525673	61
62	136.3107513260	1640.1303191028	.0073361785	12.0322887458	62
63	147.5563883104	1776.4410704288	.0067770702	12.0390658160	63
64	159.7297903460	1923.9974587392	.0062605729	12.0453263888	64
65	172.9074980495	2083.7272490852	.0057834392	12.0511098281	65

Period	Compound Interest Amount	Compound One Per Period	Present Value Of $1 In Future	Present Value Of $1 Per Period	Period	
1	1.0850000000	1.0000000000	.9216589862	.9216589862	1	
2	1.1772250000	2.0850000000	.8494552868	1.7711142731	2	
3	1.2772891250	3.2622250000	.7829080984	2.5540223714	3	
4	1.3858587006	4.5395141249	.7215742843	3.2755966556	4	
5	1.5036566902	5.9253728255	.6650454233	3.9406420789	5	
6	1.6314675088	7.4290295158	.6129450906	4.5535871696	6	
7	1.7701422471	9.0604970246	.5649263508	5.1185135204	7	
8	1.9206043381	10.8306392716	.5206694477	5.6391829681	8	
9	2.0838557068	12.7512436098	.4798796753	6.1190626434	9	
10	2.2609834419	14.8350993166	.4422854150	6.5613480585	10	
11	2.4531670345	17.0960827586	.4076363272	6.9689843856	11	
12	2.6616862324	19.5492497931	.3757016841	7.3446860698	12	
13	2.8879295622	22.2109360254	.3462688333	7.6909549029	13	
14	3.1334035750	25.0988655876	.3191417818	8.0100966848	14	
15	3.3997428788	28.2322691626	.2941398911	8.3042365759	15	
16	3.6887210235	31.6320120414	.2710966738	8.5753332496	16	
17	4.0022623105	35.3207330649	.2498586855	8.8251919352	17	
18	4.3424546069	39.3229953754	.2302845028	9.0554764379	18	
19	4.7115632485	43.6654499824	.2122437814	9.2677202193	19	
20	5.1120461246	48.3770132308	.1956163884	9.4633366076	20	
21	5.5465700452	53.4890593554	.1802916022	9.6436282098	21	
22	6.0180284991	59.0356294007	.1661673753	9.8097955851	22	
23	6.5295609215	65.0536578998	.1531496546	9.9629452398	23	
24	7.0845735998	71.5832188212	.1411517554	10.1040969952	24	
25	7.6867623558	78.6677924211	.1300937838	10.2341907789	25	
26	8.3401371560	86.3545547768	.1199021049	10.3540928838	26	
27	9.0490488143	94.6946919328	.1105088524	10.4646017362	27	
28	9.8182179635	103.7437407472	.1018514769	10.5664532132	28	
29	10.6527664904	113.5619587107	.0938723289	10.6603255421	29	
30	11.5582516421	124.2147252011	.0865182755	10.7468438175	30	
31	12.5407030317	135.7729768432	.0797403461	10.8265841636	31	
32	13.6066627894	148.3136798748	.0734934065	10.9000775702	32	
33	14.7632291265	161.9203426642	.0677358586	10.9678134287	33	
34	16.0181036022	176.6835717907	.0624293627	11.0302427915	34	
35	17.3796424084	192.7016753928	.0575385832	11.0877813747	35	
36	18.8569120231	210.0813178013	.0530309522	11.1408123268	36	
37	20.4597495342	228.9382298144	.0488764637	11.1896887806	37	
38	22.1988282446	249.3979793486	.0450474227	11.2347362033	38	
39	24.0857286454	271.5968075932	.0415183620	11.2762545652	39	
40	26.1330155803	295.6825362387	.0382657714	11.3145203366	40	
41	28.3543219046	321.8155518189	.0352679921	11.3497883287	41	
42	30.7644392665	350.1698737235	.0325050618	11.3822933905	42	
43	33.3794166042	380.9343129901	.0299585823	11.4122519728	43	
44	36.2166670155	414.3137295942	.0276115966	11.4398635694	44	
45	39.2950837118	450.5303966098	.0254484761	11.4653120455	45	
46	42.6351658273	489.8254803216	.0234548167	11.4887668622	46	
47	46.2591549227	532.4606461489	.0216173426	11.5103842048	47	
48	50.1911830911	578.7198010716	.0199238181	11.5303080229	48	
49	54.4574336538	628.9109841627	.0183629660	11.5486709888	49	
50	59.0863155144	683.3684178165	.0169243926	11.5655953814	50	
51	64.1086523331	742.4547333309	.0155985185	11.5811939000	51	
52	69.5578877815	806.5633856641	.0143765148	11.5955704147	52	
53	75.4703082429	876.1212734455	.0132502440	11.6088206587	53	
54	81.8852844435	951.5915816884	.0122122065	11.6210328652	54	
55	88.8455336212	1033.4768661319	.0112554898	11.6322883551	55	
56	96.3974039790	1122.3223997532	.0103737233	11.6426620784	56	
57	104.5911833172	1218.7198037321	.0095610353	11.6522231136	57	
58	113.4814338992	1323.3109870494	.0088120141	11.6610351279	58	
59	123.1273557806	1436.7924209486	.0081216720	11.6691567999	59	
60	133.5931810220	1559.9197767292	.0074854120	11.6766422119	60	
61	144.9486014089	1693.5129757512	.0068989972	11.6835412091	61	
62	157.2692325286	1838.4615591601	.0063585228	11.6898997319	62	
63	170.6371172935	1995.7307916887	.0058603897	11.6957601215	63	
64	185.1412722635	2166.3679089822	.0054012808	11.7011614024	64	
65	200.8782804059	2351.5091812458	.0049781390	11.7061395413	65	

RATE

8½%

223

Period	Compound Interest Amount	Compound One Per Period	Present Value Of $1 In Future	Present Value Of $1 Per Period	Period
1	1.0875000000	1.0000000000	.9195402299	.9195402299	1
2	1.1826562500	2.0875000000	.8455542344	1.7650944643	2
3	1.2861386719	3.2701562499	.7775211351	2.5426155993	3
4	1.3986758057	4.5562949218	.7149619633	3.2575775626	4
5	1.5210599387	5.9549707274	.6574362881	3.9150138506	5
6	1.6541526833	7.4760306662	.6045391155	4.5195529662	6
7	1.7988910431	9.1301833495	.5558980372	5.0754510034	7
8	1.9562940094	10.9290743926	.5111706089	5.5866216123	8
9	2.1274697352	12.8853684018	.4700419392	6.0566635515	9
10	2.3136233370	15.0128381370	.4322224729	6.4888860245	10
11	2.5160653790	17.3264614741	.3974459521	6.8863319765	11
12	2.7362210996	19.8425268530	.3654675421	7.2517995186	12
13	2.9756404459	22.5787479527	.3360621077	7.5878616263	13
14	3.2360089849	25.5543883985	.3090226278	7.8968842541	14
15	3.5191597711	28.7903973834	.2841587382	8.1810429922	15
16	3.8270862510	32.3095571544	.2612953914	8.4423383837	16
17	4.1619562980	36.1366434055	.2402716243	8.6826100080	17
18	4.5261274741	40.2985997034	.2209394246	8.9035494327	18
19	4.9221636280	44.8247271775	.2031626893	9.1067121219	19
20	5.3528529455	49.7468908055	.1868162661	9.2935283880	20
21	5.8212275782	55.0997437510	.1717850722	9.4653134602	21
22	6.3305849913	60.9209713293	.1579632848	9.6232767450	22
23	6.8845111781	67.2515563206	.1452535952	9.7685303403	23
24	7.4869059061	74.1360674986	.1335665243	9.9020968647	24
25	8.1420101729	81.6229734048	.1228197925	10.0249166571	25
26	8.8544360631	89.7649835777	.1129377402	10.1378543974	26
27	9.6291992186	98.6194196407	.1038507956	10.2417051930	27
28	10.4717541502	108.2486188593	.0954949845	10.3372001705	28
29	11.3880326383	118.7203730095	.0878114800	10.4250116575	29
30	12.3844854942	130.1084056478	.0807461885	10.5057578459	30
31	13.4681279749	142.4928911421	.0742493687	10.5800072146	31
32	14.6465891727	155.9610191169	.0682752816	10.6482824962	32
33	15.9281657254	170.6076082897	.0627818681	10.7110643643	33
34	17.3218802262	186.5357740150	.0577304534	10.7687948178	34
35	18.8375447461	203.8576542414	.0530854744	10.8218802922	35
36	20.4858299114	222.6951989874	.0488142294	10.8706945216	36
37	22.2783400287	243.1810288989	.0448866477	10.9155811693	37
38	24.2276947812	265.4593689275	.0412750783	10.9568562477	38
39	26.3476180745	289.6870637087	.0379540950	10.9948103426	39
40	28.6530346560	316.0346817832	.0349003173	11.0297106599	40
41	31.1601751884	344.6877164392	.0320922458	11.0618029057	41
42	33.8866905174	375.8478916277	.0295101110	11.0913130167	42
43	36.8517759377	409.7345821451	.0271357343	11.1184487510	43
44	40.0763063323	446.5863580829	.0249523993	11.1434011504	44
45	43.5829831363	486.6626644151	.0229447350	11.1663458854	45
46	47.3964941608	530.2456475514	.0210986069	11.1874444923	46
47	51.5436873998	577.6421417121	.0294010179	11.2068455102	47
48	56.0537600473	629.1858291120	.0178400164	11.2246855266	48
49	60.9584640514	685.2395891592	.0164046128	11.2410901394	49
50	66.2923296559	746.1980532107	.0150847014	11.2561748408	50
51	72.0929085008	812.4903828666	.0138709898	11.2700458306	51
52	78.4010379947	884.5832913674	.0127549332	11.2828007639	52
53	85.2611288192	962.9843293622	.0117286742	11.2945294381	53
54	92.7214775909	1048.2454581814	.0107849878	11.3053144257	54
55	100.8346068801	1140.9669357722	.0099172301	11.3152316559	55
56	109.6576349821	1241.8015426522	.0091192921	11.3243509480	56
57	119.2526780430	1351.4591776344	.0083855559	11.3327365039	57
58	129.6872873718	1470.7118556774	.0077108560	11.3404473599	58
59	141.0349250168	1600.3991430491	.0070904423	11.3475378022	59
60	153.3754809558	1741.4340680659	.0065199470	11.3540577491	60
61	166.7958355394	1894.8095490217	.0059953535	11.3600531026	61
62	181.3904711491	2061.6053845611	.0055129688	11.3655660714	62
63	197.2621373746	2242.9958557102	.0050693966	11.3706354680	63
64	214.5225743949	2440.2579930849	.0046615141	11.3752969821	64
65	233.2932996545	2654.7805674798	.0042864497	11.3795834318	65

Period	Compound Interest Amount	Compound One Per Period	Present Value Of $1 In Future	Present Value Of $1 Per Period	Period
1	1.0900000000	1.0000000000	.9174311927	.9174311927	1
2	1.1881000000	2.0900000000	.8416799933	1.7591111860	2
3	1.2950290000	3.2781000000	.7721834801	2.5312946660	3
4	1.4115816100	4.5731290000	.7084252111	3.2397198771	4
5	1.5386239549	5.9847106100	.6499313863	3.8896512634	5
6	1.6771001108	7.5233345649	.5962673269	4.4859185903	6
7	1.8280391208	9.2004346757	.5470342448	5.0329528351	7
8	1.9925626417	11.0284737966	.5018662797	5.5348191148	8
9	2.1718932794	13.0210364382	.4604277795	5.9952468943	9
10	2.3673636746	15.1929297177	.4224108069	6.4176577012	10
11	2.5804264053	17.5602933922	.3875328504	6.8051905516	11
12	2.8126647818	20.1407197976	.3555347251	7.1607252767	12
13	3.0658046121	22.9533845793	.3261786469	7.4869039236	13
14	3.3417270272	26.0191891914	.2992464650	7.7861503886	14
15	3.6424824597	29.3609162187	.2745380413	8.0606884299	15
16	3.9703058811	33.0033986783	.2518697627	8.3125581926	16
17	4.3276334104	36.9737045594	.2310731768	8.5436313693	17
18	4.7171204173	41.3013379698	.2119937402	8.7556251094	18
19	5.1416612548	46.0184583871	.1944896699	8.9501147793	19
20	5.6044107678	51.1601196419	.1784308898	9.1285456691	20
21	6.1088077369	56.7645304097	.1636980640	9.2922437331	21
22	6.6586004332	62.8733381466	.1501817101	9.4424254432	22
23	7.2578744722	69.5319385798	.1377813854	9.5802068287	23
24	7.9110831747	76.7898130520	.1264049408	9.7066117694	24
25	8.6230806604	84.7008962267	.1159678356	9.8225796050	25
26	9.3991579198	93.3239768870	.1063925097	9.9289721147	26
27	10.2450821326	102.7231348069	.0976078070	10.0265799218	27
28	11.1671395246	112.9682169396	.0895484468	10.1161283686	28
29	12.1721820818	124.1353564641	.0821545384	10.1982829070	29
30	13.2676784691	136.3075385459	.0753711361	10.2736540431	30
31	14.4617695314	149.5752170150	.0691478313	10.3428018743	31
32	15.7633287892	164.0369865463	.0634383773	10.4062402518	32
33	17.1820283802	179.8003153356	.0582003462	10.4644405979	33
34	18.7284109344	196.9823437157	.0533948130	10.5178354110	34
35	20.4139679185	215.7107546501	.0489860670	10.5668214779	35
36	22.2512250312	236.1247225687	.0449413459	10.6117628238	36
37	24.2538352840	258.3759475998	.0412305925	10.6529934163	37
38	26.4366804595	282.6297828838	.0378262317	10.6908196480	38
39	28.8159817009	309.0664633433	.0347029648	10.7255226129	39
40	31.4094200540	337.8824450442	.0318375824	10.7573601953	40
41	34.2362678588	369.2918650982	.0292087912	10.7865689866	41
42	37.3175319661	403.5281329571	.0267970562	10.8133660427	42
43	40.6761098431	440.8456649232	.0245844552	10.8379504979	43
44	44.3369597290	481.5217747663	.0225545461	10.8605050439	44
45	48.3272861046	525.8587344953	.0206922441	10.8811972880	45
46	52.6767418540	574.1860205999	.0189837102	10.9001809982	46
47	57.4176486209	626.8627624539	.0174162479	10.9175972460	47
48	62.5852369967	684.2804110748	.0159782090	10.9335754551	48
49	68.2179083264	746.8656480714	.0146589074	10.9482343624	49
50	74.3575200758	815.0835563979	.0134485389	10.9616829013	50
51	81.0496968826	889.4410764738	.0123381091	10.9740210104	51
52	88.3441696021	970.4907733664	.0113193661	10.9853403766	52
53	96.2951448663	1058.8349429584	.0103847396	10.9957251161	53
54	104.9617079042	1155.1300878248	.0095272840	11.0052524001	54
55	114.4082616156	1260.0917957290	.0087406275	11.0139930276	55
56	124.7050051610	1374.5000573446	.0080189243	11.0220119519	56
57	135.9284556255	1499.2050625057	.0073568113	11.0293687632	57
58	148.1620166318	1635.1335181311	.0067493682	11.0361181314	58
59	161.4965981287	1783.2955347629	.0061920809	11.0423102123	59
60	176.0312919602	1944.7921328916	.0056808082	11.0479910204	60
61	191.8741082367	2120.8234248519	.0052117506	11.0532027711	61
62	209.1427779780	2312.6975330886	.0047814226	11.0579841937	62
63	227.9656279960	2521.8403110664	.0043866262	11.0623708199	63
64	248.4825345156	2749.8059390624	.0040244277	11.0663952476	64
65	270.8459626220	2998.2884735781	.0036921355	11.0700873831	65

RATE

9%

Period	Compound Interest Amount	Compound One Per Period	Present Value Of $1 In Future	Present Value Of $1 Per Period	Period
1	1.0925000000	1.0000000000	.9153318078	.9153318078	1
2	1.1935562500	2.0925000000	.8378323183	1.7531641262	2
3	1.3039602031	3.2860562499	.7668945706	2.5200586966	3
4	1.4245765219	4.5900164531	.7019629936	3.2220216904	4
5	1.5563498502	6.0145929750	.6425290560	3.8645507464	5
6	1.7003122113	7.5709428252	.5881272824	4.4526780286	6
7	1.8575910909	9.2712550365	.5383316086	4.9910096373	7
8	2.0294182668	11.1288461274	.4927520444	5.4837616817	8
9	2.2171394565	13.1582643942	.4510316196	5.9347933013	9
10	2.4222248562	15.3754038506	.4128435878	6.3476368891	10
11	2.6462806554	17.7976287068	.3778888675	6.7255257566	11
12	2.8910616160	20.4439093623	.3458937002	7.0714194569	12
13	3.1584848155	23.3349709783	.3166075059	7.3880269628	13
14	3.4506446609	26.4934557937	.2898009208	7.6778278836	14
15	3.7698292921	29.9441004547	.2652640007	7.9430918843	15
16	4.1185385016	33.7139297467	.2428045773	8.1858964616	16
17	4.4995033130	37.8324682483	.2222467527	8.4081432143	17
18	4.9157073694	42.3319715613	.2034295219	8.6115727362	18
19	5.3704103011	47.2476789307	.1862055120	8.7977782482	19
20	5.8671732539	52.6180892318	.1704398280	8.9682180762	20
21	6.4098867799	58.4852624857	.1560089958	9.1242270720	21
22	7.0028013071	64.8951492656	.1427999962	9.2670270682	22
23	7.6505604280	71.8979505728	.1307093787	9.3977364469	23
24	8.3582372676	79.5485110008	.1196424519	9.5173788988	24
25	9.1313742148	87.9067482683	.1095125418	9.6268914405	25
26	9.9760263297	97.0381224831	.1002403128	9.7271317533	26
27	10.8998087652	107.0141488128	.0917531467	9.8188849001	27
28	11.9069485760	117.9129575779	.0839845737	9.9028694737	28
29	13.0083413192	129.8199061539	.0768737517	9.9797432254	29
30	14.2116128913	142.8282474732	.0703649901	10.0501082155	30
31	15.5261870837	157.0398603644	.0644073136	10.1145155291	31
32	16.9623593890	172.5660474482	.0589540628	10.1734695918	32
33	18.5313776324	189.5284068372	.0539625288	10.2274321206	33
34	20.2455300634	208.0597844696	.0493936191	10.2768257398	34
35	22.1182415943	228.3053145331	.0452115506	10.3220372904	35
36	24.1641789418	250.4235561274	.0413835704	10.3634208608	36
37	26.3993654939	274.5877350692	.0378796983	10.4013005590	37
38	28.8413068021	300.9871005630	.0346724927	10.4359730518	38
39	31.5091276813	329.8284073651	.0317368354	10.4677098872	39
40	34.4237219918	361.3375350464	.0290497350	10.4967596222	40
41	37.6079162760	395.7612570382	.0265901464	10.5233497685	41
42	41.0866485316	433.3691733143	.0243388068	10.5476885754	42
43	44.8871635207	474.4558218458	.0222780840	10.5699666594	43
44	49.0392261464	519.3429853666	.0203918389	10.5903584983	44
45	53.5753545650	568.3822115130	.0186652988	10.6090237971	45
46	58.5310748622	621.9575660779	.0170849417	10.6261087387	46
47	63.9451992870	680.4886409401	.0156383905	10.6417471293	47
48	69.8601302210	744.4338402271	.0143143163	10.6560614456	48
49	76.3221922665	814.2939704481	.0131023490	10.6691637946	49
50	83.3819950511	890.6161627146	.0119929968	10.6811567914	50
51	91.0948295933	973.9981577657	.0109775714	10.6921343628	51
52	99.5211013307	1065.0929873590	.0100481203	10.7021824831	52
53	108.7268032038	1164.6140886897	.0091973641	10.7113798472	53
54	118.7840325002	1273.3408918935	.0084186399	10.7197984872	54
55	129.7715555064	1392.1249243937	.0077058489	10.7275043361	55
56	141.7754243908	1521.8964799001	.0070534086	10.7345577448	56
57	154.8896511469	1663.6719042909	.0064562093	10.7410139541	57
58	169.2169438780	1818.5615554378	.0059095737	10.7469235277	58
59	184.8695111867	1987.7784993158	.0054092208	10.7523327484	59
60	201.9699409715	2172.6480105025	.0049512318	10.7572839803	60
61	220.6521605114	2374.6179514741	.0045320200	10.7618160003	61
62	241.0624853586	2595.2701119853	.0041483020	10.7659643023	62
63	263.3607652543	2836.3325973440	.0037970728	10.7697613751	63
64	287.7216360404	3099.6933625984	.0034755815	10.7732369566	64
65	314.3358873741	3387.4149986387	.0031813103	10.7764182669	65

Period	Compound Interest Amount	Compound One Per Period	Present Value Of $1 In Future	Present Value Of $1 Per Period	Period
1	1.0950000000	1.0000000000	.9132420091	.9132420092	1
2	1.1990250000	2.0950000000	.8340109672	1.7472529764	2
3	1.3129323750	3.2940250000	.7616538514	2.5089068278	3
4	1.4376609506	4.6069573749	.6955742935	3.2044811213	4
5	1.5742387409	6.0446183256	.6352276653	3.8397087865	5
6	1.7237914213	7.6188570665	.5801165893	4.4198253759	6
7	1.8875516063	9.3426484878	.5297868395	4.9496122154	7
8	2.0668690090	11.2302000942	.4838235978	5.4334358132	8
9	2.2632215648	13.2970691032	.4418480345	5.8752838476	9
10	2.4782276135	15.5602906679	.4035141867	6.2787980343	10
11	2.7136592367	18.0385182814	.3685061066	6.6473041409	11
12	2.9714568642	20.7521775181	.3365352572	6.9838393981	12
13	3.2537452663	23.7236343823	.3073381344	7.2911775325	13
14	3.5628510666	26.9773796487	.2806740954	7.5718516279	14
15	3.9013219180	30.5402307153	.2563233748	7.8281750026	15
16	4.2719475002	34.4415526333	.2340852737	8.0622602764	16
17	4.6777825127	38.7135001335	.2137765057	8.2760367821	17
18	5.1221718514	43.3912826461	.1952296856	8.4712664677	18
19	5.6087781773	48.5134544975	.1782919503	8.6495584180	19
20	6.1416121041	54.1222326747	.1628236989	8.8123821168	20
21	6.7250652540	60.2638447788	.1486974419	8.9610795588	21
22	7.3639464531	66.9889100328	.1357967506	9.0968763094	22
23	8.0635213662	74.3528564860	.1240152974	9.2208916067	23
24	8.8295558960	82.4163778522	.1132559793	9.3341475861	24
25	9.6683637061	91.2459337481	.1034301181	9.4375777042	25
26	10.5868582582	100.9142974542	.0944567289	9.5320344331	26
27	11.5926097927	111.5011557124	.0862618528	9.6182962859	27
28	12.6939077230	123.0937655051	.0787779478	9.6970742337	28
29	13.8998289567	135.7876732281	.0719433313	9.7690175651	29
30	15.2203127076	149.6875021847	.0657016724	9.8347192375	30
31	16.6662424148	164.9078148923	.0600015273	9.8047207648	31
32	18.2495354442	181.5740573071	.0547959154	9.9495166802	32
33	19.9832413114	199.8235927513	.0500419319	9.9995586121	33
34	21.8816492360	219.8068340626	.0457003944	10.0452590064	34
35	23.9604059134	241.6884832985	.0417355200	10.0869945264	35
36	26.2366444751	265.6488892119	.0381146301	10.1251091566	36
37	28.7291257003	291.8855336871	.0348078814	10.1599170380	37
38	31.4583926418	320.6146593874	.0317880195	10.1917050575	38
39	34.4469399428	352.0730520292	.0290301548	10.2207352123	39
40	37.7193992373	386.5199919719	.0265115569	10.2472467693	40
41	41.3027421649	424.2393912093	.0242114675	10.2714582367	41
42	45.2265026705	465.5421333741	.0221109292	10.2935691660	42
43	49.5230204243	510.7686360447	.0201926294	10.3137617955	43
44	54.2277073646	560.2916564689	.0184407575	10.3322025529	44
45	59.3793395642	614.5193638335	.0168408744	10.3490434274	45
46	65.0203768228	673.8987033977	.0153797940	10.3644232214	46
47	71.1973126209	738.9190802204	.0140454740	10.3784686953	47
48	77.9610573199	810.1163928414	.0128269169	10.3912956121	48
49	85.3673577653	888.0774501614	.0117140793	10.4030096915	49
50	93.4772567530	973.4448079267	.0106977893	10.4137074807	50
51	102.3575961446	1066.9220646797	.0097696706	10.4234771514	51
52	112.0815677783	1169.2796608243	.0089220736	10.4323992251	52
53	122.7293167173	1281.3612286026	.0081480124	10.4405472375	53
54	134.3886018054	1404.0905453199	.0074411073	10.4479883447	54
55	147.1555189769	1538.4791471253	.0067955317	10.4547838764	55
56	161.1352932797	1685.6346661022	.0062059651	10.4609898416	56
57	176.4431461413	1846.7699593819	.0056675480	10.4666573896	57
58	193.2052450247	2023.2131055232	.0051758429	10.4718332324	58
59	211.5597433021	2216.4183505479	.0047267972	10.4765600297	59
60	231.6579189157	2427.9780938499	.0043167098	10.4808767394	60
61	253.6654212127	2659.6360127657	.0039422007	10.4848189401	61
62	277.7636362280	2913.3014339784	.0036001833	10.4884191234	62
63	304.1511816696	3191.0650702064	.0032878386	10.4917069620	63
64	333.0455439282	3495.2162518760	.0030025923	10.4947095543	64
65	364.6848706014	3828.2617958042	.0027420935	10.4974516478	65

RATE
9½%

227

Period	Compound Interest Amount	Compound One Per Period	Present Value Of $1 In Future	Present Value Of $1 Per Period	Period
1	1.0975000000	1.0000000000	.9111617312	.9111617313	1
2	1.2045062500	2.0975000000	.8302157004	1.7413774317	2
3	1.3219456094	3.3020062499	.7564607749	2.4978382066	3
4	1.4508353063	4.6239518593	.6892581092	3.1870963157	4
5	1.5922917487	6.0747871656	.6280256120	3.8151219278	5
6	1.7475401941	7.6670789143	.5722329039	4.3873548317	6
7	1.9179253631	9.4146191084	.5213967234	4.9087515551	7
8	2.1049230860	11.3325444715	.4750767411	5.3838282962	8
9	2.3101530869	13.4374675574	.4328717459	5.8167000422	9
10	2.5353930128	15.7476206443	.3944161694	6.2111162115	10
11	2.7825938316	18.2830136571	.3593769197	6.5704931312	11
12	3.0538967302	21.0656074887	.3274504963	6.8979436275	12
13	3.3516516613	24.1195042189	.2983603611	7.1963039886	13
14	3.6784376983	27.4711558802	.2718545432	7.4681585318	14
15	4.0370853739	31.1495935786	.2477034562	7.7158619880	15
16	4.4307011979	35.1866789525	.2256979100	7.9415598979	16
17	4.8626945647	39.6173801504	.2056472984	8.1472071963	17
18	5.3368072847	44.4800747150	.1873779484	8.3345851447	18
19	5.8571459950	49.8168819997	.1707316159	8.5053167605	19
20	6.4282177295	55.6740279947	.1555641147	8.6608808752	20
21	7.0549689581	62.1022457242	.1417440680	8.8026249433	21
22	7.7428284315	69.1572146823	.1291517704	8.9317787136	22
23	8.4977542036	76.9000431138	.1176781507	9.0494548644	23
24	9.3262852385	85.3977973174	.1072238275	9.1566786919	24
25	10.2355980492	94.7240825559	.0976982483	9.2543769403	25
26	11.2335688590	104.9596806050	.0890189051	9.3433958453	26
27	12.3288418228	116.1932494641	.0811106197	9.4245064650	27
28	13.5309039005	128.5220912869	.0739048926	9.4984113576	28
29	14.8501670308	142.0529951873	.0673393099	9.5657506676	29
30	16.2980583163	156.9031622181	.0613570022	9.6271076697	30
31	17.8871190021	173.2012205344	.0559061523	9.6830138222	31
32	19.6311131048	191.0883395364	.0509395466	9.7339533687	32
33	21.5451466325	210.7194526412	.0464141654	9.7803675342	33
34	23.6457984292	232.2645992737	.0422908113	9.8226583454	34
35	25.9512637760	255.9103977030	.0385337689	9.8611921143	35
36	28.4815119942	281.8616614790	.0351104955	9.8963026098	36
37	31.2584594136	310.3431734732	.0319913399	9.9282939497	37
38	34.3061592065	341.6016328869	.0291492847	9.9574432344	38
39	37.6510097291	375.9077920933	.0265597127	9.9840029471	39
40	41.3219831777	413.5588018225	.0242001938	10.0082031408	40
41	45.3508765375	454.8807850001	.0220502905	10.0302534313	41
42	49.7725869999	500.2316615376	.0200913808	10.0503448121	42
43	54.6254142324	550.0042485375	.0183064973	10.0686513094	43
44	59.9513921201	604.6296627699	.0166801798	10.0853314892	44
45	65.7966528518	664.5810548901	.0151983415	10.1005298308	45
46	72.2118265048	730.3777077418	.0138481472	10.1143779779	46
47	79.2524795891	802.5895342567	.0126179017	10.1269958797	47
48	86.9795963490	881.8420138357	.0114969492	10.1384928288	48
49	95.4601069930	968.8216101847	.0104755801	10.1489684090	49
50	104.7674674248	1064.2817171777	.0095449477	10.1585133567	50
51	114.9822954988	1169.0491846026	.0086969911	10.1672103478	51
52	126.1930693099	1284.0314801013	.0079243655	10.1751347132	52
53	138.4968935676	1410.2245494112	.0072203786	10.1823550918	53
54	152.0003406904	1548.7214429788	.0065789326	10.1889340244	54
55	166.8203739078	1700.7217836692	.0059944716	10.1949284961	55
56	183.0853603638	1867.5421575770	.0054619332	10.2003904292	56
57	200.9361829992	2050.6275179407	.0049767045	10.2053671337	57
58	220.5274608417	2251.5637009400	.0045345827	10.2099017163	58
59	242.0288882737	2472.0911617816	.0041317382	10.2140334546	59
60	265.6267048804	2714.1200500554	.0037646817	10.2177981363	60
61	291.5253086062	2979.7467549358	.0034302339	10.2212283702	61
62	319.9490261953	3271.2720635419	.0031254979	10.2243538680	62
63	351.1440562494	3591.2210897373	.0028478341	10.2272017021	63
64	385.3806017337	3942.3651459868	.0025948374	10.2297965395	64
65	422.9552104027	4327.7457477204	.0023643165	10.2321608560	65

Period	Compound Interest Amount	Compound One Per Period	Present Value Of $1 In Future	Present Value Of $1 Per Period	Period
1	1.10000000000	1.0000000000	.9090909091	.9090909091	1
2	1.21000000000	2.1000000000	.8264462810	1.7355371901	2
3	1.33100000000	3.3100000000	.7513148009	2.4868519910	3
4	1.46410000000	4.6410000000	.6830134554	3.1698654464	4
5	1.61051000000	6.1051000000	.6209213231	3.7907867695	5
6	1.77156100000	7.7156100000	.5644739301	4.3552606995	6
7	1.94871710000	9.4871710000	.5131581182	4.8684188177	7
8	2.14358881000	11.4358881000	.4665073802	5.3349261980	8
9	2.35794769100	13.5794769100	.4240976184	5.7590238163	9
10	2.59374246010	15.9374246010	.3855432894	6.1445671058	10
11	2.85311670611	18.5311670611	.3504938995	6.4950610052	11
12	3.13842837672	21.3842837672	.3186308177	6.8136918229	12
13	3.45227121439	24.5227121439	.2896643797	7.1033562027	13
14	3.79749833583	27.9749833583	.2633312543	7.3666874570	14
15	4.17724816941	31.7724816941	.2393920494	7.6060795064	15
16	4.59497298635	35.9497298635	.2176291358	7.8237086421	16
17	5.05447028499	40.5447028499	.1978446689	8.0215533110	17
18	5.55991731349	45.5991731349	.1798587899	8.2014121010	18
19	6.11590904484	51.1590904484	.1635079908	8.3649200918	19
20	6.72749994932	57.2749994932	.1486436280	8.5135637198	20
21	7.40024994425	64.0024994425	.1351305709	8.6486942907	21
22	8.14027493868	71.4027493868	.1228459736	8.7715402643	22
23	8.95430243255	79.5430243255	.1116781578	8.8832184221	23
24	9.84973267580	88.4973267580	.1015255980	8.9847440201	24
25	10.8347059434	98.3470594338	.0922959982	9.0770400183	25
26	11.9181765377	109.1817653772	.0839054529	9.1609454712	26
27	13.1099941915	121.0999419149	.0762776844	9.2372231556	27
28	14.4209936106	134.2099361064	.0693433495	9.3065665051	28
29	15.8630929717	148.6309297171	.0630394086	9.3696059137	29
30	17.4494022689	164.4940226888	.0573085533	9.4269144670	30
31	19.1943424958	181.9434249577	.0520986848	9.4790131519	31
32	21.1137767454	201.1377674535	.0473624407	9.5263755926	32
33	23.2251544199	222.2515441988	.0430567643	9.5694323569	33
34	25.5476698619	245.4766986187	.0391425130	9.6085748699	34
35	28.1024368481	271.0243684806	.0355841027	9.6441589727	35
36	30.9126805329	299.1268053287	.0323491843	9.6765081570	36
37	34.0039485862	330.0394858615	.0294083494	9.7059165063	37
38	37.4043434448	364.0434344477	.0267348631	9.7326513694	38
39	41.1447777893	401.4477778925	.0243044210	9.7569557904	39
40	45.2592555682	442.5925556817	.0220949282	9.7790507185	40
41	49.7851811250	487.8518112499	.0200862983	9.7991370168	41
42	54.7636992375	537.6369923749	.0182602712	9.8173972880	42
43	60.2400691612	592.4006916124	.0166002465	9.8339975346	43
44	66.2640760774	652.6407607736	.0150911332	9.8490886678	44
45	72.8904836851	718.9048368510	.0137192120	9.8628078798	45
46	80.1795320536	791.7953205361	.0124720109	9.8752798908	46
47	88.1974852590	871.9748525897	.0113381918	9.8866180825	47
48	97.0172337849	960.1723378487	.0103074470	9.8969255296	48
49	106.7189571634	1057.1895716335	.0093704064	9.9062959360	49
50	117.3908528797	1163.9085287969	.0085185513	9.9148144873	50
51	129.1299381677	1281.2993816766	.0077441375	9.9225586248	51
52	142.0429319844	1410.4293198443	.0070401250	9.9295987498	52
53	156.2472251829	1552.4722518287	.0064001137	9.9359988635	53
54	171.8719477012	1708.7194770116	.0058182851	9.9418171486	54
55	189.0591424713	1880.5914247127	.0052893501	9.9471064987	55
56	207.9650567184	2069.6505671840	.0048085001	9.9519149989	56
57	228.7615623902	2277.6156239024	.0043713637	9.9562863626	57
58	251.6377186293	2506.3771862927	.0039739670	9.9602603296	58
59	276.8014904922	2758.0149049219	.0036126973	9.9638730270	59
60	304.4816395414	3034.8163954141	.0032842703	9.9671572972	60
61	334.9298034956	3339.2980349555	.0029857003	9.9701429975	61
62	368.4227838451	3674.2278384511	.0027142730	9.9728572705	62
63	405.2650622296	4042.6506222962	.0024675209	9.9753247913	63
64	445.7915684526	4447.9156845259	.0022432008	9.9775679921	64
65	490.3707252978	4893.7072529784	.0020392734	9.9796072656	65

RATE

10%

229

RATE	Period	Compound Interest Amount	Compound One Per Period	Present Value Of $1 In Future	Present Value Of $1 Per Period	Period
10¼%	1	1.1025000000	1.0000000000	.9070294785	.9070294785	1
	2	1.2155062500	2.1025000000	.8227024748	1.7297319533	2
	3	1.3400956406	3.3180062500	.7462153966	2.4759473500	3
	4	1.4774554438	4.6581018905	.6768393620	3.1527867119	4
	5	1.6288946268	6.1355573343	.6139132535	3.7666999655	5
	6	1.7958563260	7.7644519612	.5568374182	4.3235373837	6
	7	1.9799315994	9.5603082871	.5050679530	4.8286053367	7
	8	2.1828745884	11.5402398866	.4581115220	5.2867168586	8
	9	2.4066192337	13.7231144750	.4155206549	5.7022375136	9
	10	2.6532977051	16.1297337087	.3768894829	6.0791269964	10
	11	2.9252607199	18.7830314139	.3418498711	6.4209768675	11
	12	3.2250999437	21.7082921338	.3100679103	6.7310447778	12
	13	3.5556726879	24.9333920775	.2812407350	7.0122855127	13
	14	3.9201291385	28.4890647654	.2550936371	7.2673791499	14
	15	4.3219423752	32.4091939039	.2313774487	7.4987565985	15
	16	4.7649414686	36.7311362790	.2098661666	7.7086227651	16
	17	5.2533479691	41.4960777476	.1903547996	7.8989775647	17
	18	5.7918161360	46.7494257168	.1726574146	8.0716349793	18
	19	6.3854772899	52.5412418527	.1566053647	8.2282403441	19
	20	7.0399887121	58.9267191426	.1420456823	8.3702860263	20
	21	7.7615875551	65.9667078547	.1288396211	8.4991256475	21
	22	8.5571502795	73.7282954099	.1168613344	8.6159869819	22
	23	9.4342581832	82.2854456894	.1059966752	8.7219836571	23
	24	10.4012696469	91.7197038726	.0961421090	8.8181257660	24
	25	11.4673997858	102.1209735195	.0872037270	8.9053294930	25
	26	12.6428082638	113.5883733053	.0790963510	8.9844258440	26
	27	13.9386961108	126.2311815691	.0717427220	9.0561685660	27
	28	15.3674124622	140.1698776799	.0650727637	9.1212413297	28
	29	16.9425722396	155.5372901420	.0590229149	9.1802642446	29
	30	18.6791858941	172.4798623817	.0535355237	9.2337997684	30
	31	20.5938024483	191.1590482758	.0485582982	9.2823580665	31
	32	22.7046671992	211.7528507240	.0440438079	9.3264018744	32
	33	25.0318955871	234.4575179232	.0399490321	9.3663509065	33
	34	27.5976648848	259.4894135103	.0362349497	9.4025858563	34
	35	30.4264255355	287.0870783952	.0328661676	9.4354520238	35
	36	33.5451341529	317.5135039307	.0298105828	9.4652626066	36
	37	36.9835104036	351.0586380836	.0270390774	9.4923016840	37
	38	40.7743202199	388.0421484872	.0245252403	9.5168269243	38
	39	44.9536880425	428.8164687071	.0222451159	9.5390720402	39
	40	49.5614410668	473.7701567497	.0201769759	9.5592490160	40
	41	54.6414887762	523.3315978165	.0183011119	9.5775501279	41
	42	60.2422413758	577.9730865597	.0165996480	9.5941497759	42
	43	66.4170711168	638.2153279684	.0150563700	9.6092061460	43
	44	73.2248209062	704.6323990852	.0136565715	9.6228627175	44
	45	80.7303650491	777.8572199914	.0123869129	9.6352496303	45
	46	89.0052274667	858.5875850406	.0112352951	9.6464849255	46
	47	98.1282632820	947.5928125072	.0101907439	9.6566756694	47
	48	108.1864102684	1045.7210757892	.0092433051	9.6659189744	48
	49	119.2755173209	1153.9074860577	.0083839502	9.6743029247	49
	50	131.5012578463	1273.1830033785	.0076044900	9.6819074147	50
	51	144.9801367755	1404.6842612248	.0068974966	9.6888049113	51
	52	159.8406007950	1549.6643980004	.0062562327	9.6950611440	52
	53	176.2242623765	1709.5049987954	.0056745875	9.7007357316	53
	54	194.2872492701	1885.7292611720	.0051470182	9.7058827498	54
	55	214.2016923203	2080.0165104420	.0046684972	9.7105512469	55
	56	236.1573657832	2294.2182027624	.0042344646	9.7147857115	56
	57	260.3634957759	2530.3755685456	.0038407842	9.7186264957	57
	58	287.0507540930	2790.7390643215	.0034837045	9.7221102002	58
	59	316.4734563875	3077.7898184144	.0031598227	9.7252700228	59
	60	348.9119856672	3394.2632748020	.0028660523	9.7281360751	60
	61	384.6754641981	3743.1752604691	.0025995939	9.7307356691	61
	62	424.1046992784	4127.8507246672	.0023579083	9.7330935774	62
	63	467.5754309544	4551.9554239456	.0021386924	9.7352322698	63
	64	515.5019126273	5019.5308549000	.0019398570	9.7371721267	64
	65	568.3408586716	5535.0327675273	.0017595075	9.7389316342	65

Period	Compound Interest Amount	Compound One Per Period	Present Value Of $1 In Future	Present Value Of $1 Per Period	Period
1	1.1050000000	1.0000000000	.9049773756	.9049773756	1
2	1.2210250000	2.1050000000	.8189840503	1.7239614259	2
3	1.3492326250	3.3260250000	.7411620365	2.4651234624	3
4	1.4909020506	4.6752576250	.6707348746	3.1358583370	4
5	1.6474467659	6.1661596756	.6069998865	3.7428582235	5
6	1.8204286764	7.8136064415	.5493211643	4.2921793878	6
7	2.0115736874	9.6340351179	.4971232256	4.7893026134	7
8	2.2227889246	11.6456088052	.4498852720	5.2391878854	8
9	2.4561817616	13.8683977298	.4071359928	5.6463238782	9
10	2.7140808466	16.3245794914	.3684488623	6.0147727405	10
11	2.9990593355	19.0386603381	.3334378844	6.3482106249	11
12	3.3139605657	22.0377196735	.3017537415	6.6499643664	12
13	3.6619264251	25.3516802393	.2730803091	6.9230446755	13
14	4.0464286998	29.0136066645	.2471315014	7.1701761770	14
15	4.4713037132	33.0600353642	.2236484176	7.3938245945	15
16	4.9407906031	37.5313390774	.2023967580	7.5962213525	16
17	5.4595736165	42.4721296806	.1831644869	7.7793858393	17
18	6.0328288462	47.9317032970	.1657597166	7.9451455560	18
19	6.6662758750	53.9645321432	.1500087933	8.0951543493	19
20	7.3662348419	60.6308080183	.1357545641	8.2309089134	20
21	8.1396895003	67.9970428602	.1228548091	8.3537637226	21
22	8.9943568979	76.1367323606	.1111808227	8.4649445453	22
23	9.9387643721	85.1310892584	.1006161292	8.5655606745	23
24	10.9823346312	95.0698536306	.0910553205	8.6566159950	24
25	12.1354797675	106.0521882617	.0824030050	8.7390190000	25
26	13.4097051431	118.1876680292	.0745728552	8.8135918552	26
27	14.8177241831	131.5973731723	.0674867468	8.8810786020	27
28	16.3735852223	146.4150973554	.0610739790	8.9421525810	28
29	18.0928116707	162.7886825777	.0552705692	8.9974231503	29
30	19.9925568961	180.8814942484	.0500186147	9.0474417650	30
31	22.0917753702	200.8740511445	.0452657146	9.0927074796	31
32	24.4114117840	222.9658265147	.0409644476	9.1336719272	32
33	26.9746100214	247.3772382988	.0370718983	9.1707438255	33
34	29.8069440736	274.3518483201	.0335492293	9.2042930548	34
35	32.9366732013	304.1587923937	.0303612934	9.2346543483	35
36	36.3950238875	337.0954655950	.0274762837	9.2621306319	36
37	40.2165013957	373.4904894826	.0248654151	9.2869960470	37
38	44.4392340422	413.7069908782	.0225026381	9.3094986850	38
39	49.1053536167	458.1462249205	.0203643783	9.3298630634	39
40	54.2614157464	507.2515785370	.0184293017	9.3482923650	40
41	59.9588643998	561.5129942835	.0166781011	9.3649704661	41
42	66.2545451617	621.4718586832	.0150933041	9.3800637703	42
43	73.2112724037	687.7264038450	.0136590988	9.3937228690	43
44	80.8984560061	760.9376762488	.0123611753	9.4060840444	44
45	89.3927938868	841.8361322549	.0111865840	9.4172706284	45
46	98.7790372449	931.2289261416	.0101236055	9.4273942338	46
47	109.1508361556	1030.0079633865	.0091616339	9.4365558677	47
48	120.6116739519	1139.1587995421	.0082910714	9.4448469391	48
49	133.2758997169	1259.7704734940	.0075032320	9.4523501711	49
50	147.2698691871	1393.0463732109	.0067902552	9.4591404264	50
51	162.7332054518	1540.3162423980	.0061450274	9.4652854537	51
52	179.8201920242	1703.0494478498	.0055611107	9.4708465645	52
53	198.7013121868	1882.8696398741	.0050326794	9.4758792439	53
54	219.5649499664	2081.5709520609	.0045544610	9.4804337049	54
55	242.6192697129	2301.1359020272	.0041216842	9.4845553890	55
56	268.0942930327	2543.7551717401	.0037300309	9.4882854199	56
57	296.2441938012	2811.8494647729	.0033755936	9.4916610135	57
58	327.3498341503	3108.0936585740	.0030548358	9.4947158493	58
59	361.7215667360	3435.4434927242	.0027645573	9.4974804067	59
60	399.7023312433	3797.1650594603	.0025018618	9.4999822685	60
61	441.6710760239	4196.8673907036	.0022641283	9.5022463969	61
62	488.0465390064	4638.5384667275	.0020489849	9.5042953817	62
63	539.2914256021	5126.5850057339	.0018542850	9.5061496668	63
63	595.9170252903	5665.8764313360	.0016780860	9.5078277527	64
65	658.4883129458	6261.7934566263	.0015186298	9.5093463826	65

RATE

10½%

231

RATE	Period	Compound Interest Amount	Compound One Per Period	Present Value Of $1 In Future	Present Value Of $1 Per Period	Period
10¾%	1	1.1075000000	1.0000000000	.9029345372	.9029345373	1
	2	1.2265562500	2.1075000000	.8152907786	1.7182253158	2
	3	1.3584110469	3.3340562500	.7361542019	2.4543795177	3
	4	1.5044402344	4.6924672968	.6646990536	3.1190785713	4
	5	1.6661675596	6.1969075313	.6001797324	3.7192583036	5
	6	1.8452805723	7.8630750909	.5419230089	4.2611813126	6
	7	2.0436482338	9.7083556632	.4893210013	4.7505023139	7
	8	2.2633404189	11.7520038969	.4418248318	5.1923271457	8
	9	2.5066495140	14.0153443158	.3989389001	5.5912660458	9
	10	2.7761143367	16.5219938298	.3602157111	5.9514817569	10
	11	3.0745466279	19.2981081665	.3252512064	6.2767329633	11
	12	3.4050603904	22.3726547944	.2936805476	6.5704135109	12
	13	3.7711043824	25.7777151848	.2651743093	6.8355878203	13
	14	4.1764981035	29.5488195672	.2394350423	7.0750228625	14
	15	4.6254716496	33.7253176707	.2161941691	7.2912170316	15
	16	5.1227098519	38.3507893203	.1952091820	7.4864262137	16
	17	5.6734011610	43.4734991722	.1762611124	7.6626873261	17
	18	6.2832917858	49.1469003332	.1591522460	7.8218395721	18
	19	6.9587456528	55.4301921191	.1437040596	7.9655436317	19
	20	7.7068108105	62.3889377718	.1297553586	8.0952989902	20
	21	8.5352929726	70.0957485823	.1171605946	8.2124595849	21
	22	9.4528369672	78.6310415550	.1057883473	8.3182479322	22
	23	10.4690169411	88.0838785221	.0955199524	8.4137678846	23
	24	11.5944362623	98.5528954633	.0862482640	8.5000161487	24
	25	12.8408381605	110.1473317255	.0778765364	8.5778926850	25
	26	14.2212282628	122.9881698860	.0703174143	8.6482100993	26
	27	15.7500103010	137.2093981487	.0634920220	8.7117021213	27
	28	17.4431364084	152.9594084498	.0573291395	8.7690312607	28
	29	19.3182735723	170.4025448581	.0517644600	8.8207957207	29
	30	21.3949879813	189.7208184304	.0467399188	8.8675356395	30
	31	23.6949491893	211.1158064116	.0422030869	8.9097387264	31
	32	26.2421562271	234.8107556009	.0381066248	8.9478453512	32
	33	29.0631880215	261.0529118280	.0344077876	8.9822531388	33
	34	32.1874807338	290.1160998496	.0310679798	9.0133211185	34
	35	35.6476349127	322.3035805833	.0280523519	9.0413734705	35
	36	39.4797556658	357.9512154961	.0253294374	9.0667029079	36
	37	43.7238293999	397.4309711620	.0228708238	9.0895737317	37
	38	48.4241410604	441.1548005619	.0206508567	9.1102245885	38
	39	53.6297362244	489.5789416222	.0186463718	9.1288709603	39
	40	59.3949328685	543.2086778467	.0168364531	9.1457074133	40
	41	65.7798881519	602.6036107152	.0152022150	9.1609096283	41
	42	72.8512261282	668.3834988671	.0137266049	9.1746362332	42
	43	80.6827329370	741.2347249953	.0123942257	9.1870304589	43
	44	89.3561267277	821.9174579323	.0111911744	9.1982216333	44
	45	98.9619103510	911.2735846600	.0101048979	9.2083265313	45
	46	109.6003157137	1010.2354950110	.0091240613	9.2174505926	46
	47	121.3823496529	1119.8358107247	.0082384301	9.2256890226	47
	48	134.4309522406	1241.2181603776	.0074387630	9.2331277857	48
	49	148.8822796065	1375.6491126181	.0067167161	9.2398445017	49
	50	164.8871246641	1524.5313922246	.0060647549	9.2459092567	50
	51	182.6124905655	1689.4185168887	.0054760767	9.2513853333	51
	52	202.2433333013	1872.0310074543	.0049445388	9.2563298721	52
	53	223.9844916312	2074.2743407556	.0044645948	9.2607944669	53
	54	248.0628244816	2298.2588323869	.0040312369	9.2648257037	54
	55	274.7295781134	2546.3216568685	.0036399430	9.2684656467	55
	56	304.2630077606	2821.0512349819	.0032866302	9.2717522769	56
	57	336.9712810948	3125.3142427424	.0029676119	9.2747198889	57
	58	373.1956938125	3462.2855238372	.0026795593	9.2773994482	58
	59	413.3142308973	3835.4812176497	.0024194667	9.2798189149	59
	60	457.7455107188	4248.7954485471	.0021846200	9.2820035349	60
	61	506.9531531211	4706.5409592659	.0019725689	9.2839761037	61
	62	561.4506170816	5213.4941123870	.0017811005	9.2857572043	62
	63	621.8065584179	5774.9447294686	.0016082172	9.2873654215	63
	64	688.6507634478	6396.7512878864	.0014521148	9.2888175364	64
	65	762.6807205184	7085.4020513342	.0013111647	9.2901287009	65

Period	Compound Interest Amount	Compound One Per Period	Present Value Of $1 In Future	Present Value Of $1 Per Period	Period	
1	1.1100000000	1.0000000000	.9009009009	.9009009009	1	
2	1.2321000000	2.1100000000	.8116224332	1.7125233342	2	
3	1.3676310000	3.3421000000	.7311913813	2.4437147155	3	
4	1.5180704100	4.7097310000	.6587309741	3.1024456896	4	
5	1.6850581551	6.2278014100	.5934513281	3.6958970177	5	
6	1.8704145522	7.9128595651	.5346408361	4.2305378538	6	
7	2.0761601529	9.7832741172	.4816584109	4.7121962646	7	
8	2.3045377697	11.8594342701	.4339264963	5.1461227610	8	
9	2.5580369244	14.1639720398	.3909247714	5.5370475324	9	
10	2.8394209861	16.7220089642	.3521844788	5.8892320112	10	
11	3.1517572945	19.5614299503	.3172833142	6.2065153254	11	
12	3.4984505969	22.7131872448	.2858408236	6.4923561490	12	
13	3.8832801626	26.2116378417	.2575142555	6.7498704045	13	
14	4.3104409805	30.0949180044	.2319948248	6.9818652293	14	
15	4.7845894883	34.4053589848	.2090043467	7.1908695759	15	
16	5.3108943321	39.1899484732	.1882922042	7.3791617802	16	
17	5.8950927086	44.5008428053	.1696326164	7.5487943965	17	
18	6.5435529065	50.3959355138	.1528221769	7.7016165735	18	
19	7.2633437262	56.9394884204	.1376776369	7.8392942104	19	
20	8.0623115361	64.2028321465	.1240339071	7.9633281175	20	
21	8.9491658051	72.2651436827	.1117422586	8.0750703761	21	
22	9.9335740437	81.2143094878	.1006687015	8.1757390775	22	
23	11.0262671885	91.1478835315	.0906925239	8.2664316014	23	
24	12.2391565792	102.1741507199	.0817049764	8.3481365778	24	
25	13.5854638029	114.4133072992	.0736080869	8.4217446647	25	
26	15.0798648212	127.9987711021	.0663135918	8.4880582565	26	
27	16.7386499516	143.0786359233	.0597419746	8.5478002311	27	
28	18.5799014462	159.8172858748	.0538215987	8.6016218298	28	
29	20.6236906053	178.3971873211	.0484879268	8.6501097566	29	
30	22.8922965719	199.0208779265	.0436828169	8.6937925735	30	
31	25.4104491948	221.9131744984	.0393538891	8.7331464626	31	
32	28.2055986063	247.3236236932	.0354539542	8.7686004168	32	
33	31.3082144529	275.5292222994	.0319404992	8.8005409160	33	
34	34.7521180428	306.8374367524	.0287752245	8.8293161405	34	
35	38.5748510275	341.5895547951	.0259236257	8.8552397663	35	
36	42.8180846405	380.1644058225	.0233546178	8.8785943840	36	
37	47.5280739509	422.9824904631	.0210401962	8.8996345802	37	
38	52.7561620855	470.5105644140	.0189551317	8.9185897119	38	
39	58.5593399150	523.2667264995	.0170766952	8.9356664072	39	
40	65.0008673056	581.8260664145	.0153844101	8.9510508173	40	
41	72.1509627092	646.8269337201	.0138598289	8.9649106462	41	
42	80.0875686072	718.9778964294	.0124863324	8.9773969785	42	
43	88.8972011540	799.0654650365	.0112489481	8.9886459266	43	
44	98.6758932810	887.9626661905	.0101341875	8.9987801141	44	
45	109.5302415419	986.6385594715	.0091298986	9.0079100127	45	
46	121.5785681115	1096.1688010135	.0082251339	9.0161351465	46	
47	134.9522106037	1217.7473691249	.0074100305	9.0235451771	47	
48	149.7969537702	1352.6995797286	.0066757032	9.0302208803	48	
49	166.2746186849	1502.4965334988	.0060141470	9.0362350273	49	
50	184.5648267402	1668.7711521837	.0054181505	9.0416531777	50	
51	204.8669576816	1853.3359789239	.0048812166	9.0465343944	51	
52	227.4023230266	2058.2029366055	.0043974925	9.0509318868	52	
53	252.4165785595	2285.6052596322	.0039617049	9.0548935917	53	
54	280.1824022011	2538.0218381917	.0035691035	9.0584626953	54	
55	311.0024664432	2818.2042403928	.0032154086	9.0616781038	55	
56	345.2127377520	3129.2067068360	.0028967645	9.0645748684	56	
57	383.1861389047	3474.4194445880	.0026096977	9.0671845661	57	
58	425.3366141842	3857.6055834926	.0023510790	9.0695356451	58	
59	472.1236417445	4282.9421976768	.0021180892	9.0716537344	59	
60	524.0572423363	4755.0658394213	.0019081885	9.0735619228	60	
61	581.7035389933	5279.1230817576	.0017190887	9.0752810115	61	
62	645.6909282826	5860.8266207510	.0015487286	9.0768297402	62	
63	716.7169303937	6506.5175490336	.0013952510	9.0782249911	63	
64	795.5557927370	7223.2344794273	.0012569829	9.0794819740	64	
65	883.0669299381	8018.7902721643	.0011324170	9.0806143910	65	

RATE
11%

233

Period	Compound Interest Amount	Compound One Per Period	Present Value Of $1 In Future	Present Value Of $1 Per Period	Period
1	1.1125000000	1.0000000000	.8988764045	.8988764045	1
2	1.2376562500	2.1125000000	.8079787906	1.7068551951	2
3	1.3768925781	3.3501562500	.7262730702	2.4331282652	3
4	1.5317929932	4.7270488281	.6528297260	3.0859579912	4
5	1.7041197049	6.2588418212	.5868132368	3.6727712281	5
6	1.8958331717	7.9629615261	.5274725724	4.2002438005	6
7	2.1091144035	9.8587946979	.4741326494	4.6743764500	7
8	2.3463897739	11.9679091013	.4261866511	5.1005631011	8
9	2.6103586235	14.3142988753	.3830891246	5.4836522257	9
10	2.9040239686	16.9246574988	.3443497749	5.8280020006	10
11	3.2307266651	19.8286814674	.3095278876	6.1375298882	11
12	3.5941834149	23.0594081324	.2782273147	6.4157572028	12
13	3.9985290491	26.6535915473	.2500919683	6.6658491711	13
14	4.4483635671	30.6521205964	.2248017692	6.8906509404	14
15	4.9488044684	35.1004841635	.2020690060	7.0927199464	15
16	5.5055449711	40.0492886319	.1816350616	7.2743550080	16
17	6.1249187803	45.5548336030	.1632674711	7.4376224791	17
18	6.8139721431	51.6797523833	.1467572774	7.5843797565	18
19	7.5805440092	58.4937245265	.1319166538	7.7162964103	19
20	8.4333552103	66.0742685357	.1185767675	7.8348731779	20
21	9.3821076714	74.5076237460	.1065858584	7.9414590363	21
22	10.4375947845	83.8897314174	.0958075132	8.0372665494	22
23	11.6118241977	94.3273262019	.0861191130	8.1233856624	23
24	12.9181544200	105.9391503996	.0774104386	8.2007961011	24
25	14.3714467922	118.8573048196	.0695824168	8.2703785178	25
26	15.9882345563	133.2287516117	.0625459926	8.3329245104	26
27	17.7869109439	149.2169861680	.0562211169	8.3891456274	27
28	19.7879384251	167.0038971119	.0505358354	8.4396814628	28
29	22.0140814979	186.7918355371	.0454254701	8.4851069328	29
30	24.4906656664	208.8059170349	.0408318832	8.5259388160	30
31	27.2458655539	233.2965827014	.0367028164	8.5626416324	31
32	30.3110254287	260.5424482553	.0329912956	8.5956329280	32
33	33.7210157895	290.8534736841	.0296550972	8.6252880252	33
34	37.5146300658	324.5744894735	.0266562671	8.6519442923	34
35	41.7350259482	362.0891195393	.0239606895	8.6759049819	35
36	46.4302163673	403.8241454875	.0215376985	8.6974426804	36
37	51.6536157087	450.2543618548	.0193597290	8.7168024092	37
38	57.4646474759	501.9079775635	.0174020036	8.7342044128	38
39	63.9294203169	559.3726250394	.0156422504	8.7498466632	39
40	71.1214801026	623.3020453563	.0140604498	8.7639071130	40
41	79.1226466141	694.4235254588	.0126386066	8.7765457196	41
42	88.0239443582	773.5461720730	.0113605452	8.7879062648	42
43	97.9266380985	861.5701164312	.0102117260	8.7981179908	43
44	108.9433848846	959.4967545298	.0091790796	8.8072970704	44
45	121.1995156841	1068.4401394144	.0082508581	8.8155479284	45
46	134.8344611986	1189.6396550985	.0074165016	8.8229644300	46
47	150.0033380834	1324.4741162971	.0066665183	8.8296309484	47
48	166.8787136178	1474.4774543804	.0059923760	8.8356233244	48
49	185.6525688998	1641.3561679983	.0053864054	8.8410097298	49
50	206.5384829010	1827.0087368981	.0048417127	8.8458514425	50
51	229.7740622274	2033.5472197991	.0043521013	8.8502035438	51
52	255.6236442280	2263.3212820266	.0039120012	8.8541155451	52
53	284.3813042036	2518.9449262546	.0035164056	8.8576319506	53
54	316.3742009266	2803.3262304582	.0031608140	8.8607927646	54
55	351.9662985308	3119.7004313847	.0028411811	8.8636339457	55
56	391.5625071155	3471.6667299156	.0025538707	8.8661878164	56
57	435.6132891660	3863.2292370310	.0022956141	8.8684834305	57
58	484.6197841972	4298.8425261971	.0020634733	8.8705469037	58
59	539.1395099194	4783.4623103942	.0018548075	8.8724017113	59
60	599.7927047853	5322.6018203136	.0016672427	8.8740689540	60
61	667.2693840736	5922.3945250988	.0014986451	8.8755675990	61
62	742.3371897819	6589.6639091724	.0013470967	8.8769146958	62
63	825.8501236324	7332.0010989544	.0012108735	8.8781255692	63
64	918.7582625410	8157.8512225868	.0010884256	8.8792139948	64
65	1022.1185670769	9076.6094851277	.0009783601	8.8801923549	65

Period	Compound Interest Amount	Compound One Per Period	Present Value Of $1 In Future	Present Value Of $1 Per Period	Period
1	1.1150000000	1.0000000000	.8968609865	.8968609866	1
2	1.2432250000	2.1150000000	.8043596292	1.7012206157	2
3	1.3861958750	3.3582250000	.7213987706	2.4226193863	3
4	1.5456084006	4.7444208750	.6469944131	3.0696137994	4
5	1.7233533667	6.2900292756	.5802640476	3.6498778470	5
6	1.9215390039	8.0133826423	.5204161862	4.1702940332	6
7	2.1425159893	9.9349216462	.4667409742	4.6370350074	7
8	2.3889053281	12.0774376355	.4186017705	5.0556367779	8
9	2.6636294408	14.4663429636	.3754275969	5.4310643748	9
10	2.9699468265	17.1299724043	.3367063649	5.7677707397	10
11	3.3114907116	20.0999192309	.3019788026	6.0697495423	11
12	3.6923121434	23.4114099424	.2708330068	6.3405825492	12
13	4.1169280399	27.1037220858	.2428995577	6.5834821070	13
14	4.5903747645	31.2206501257	.2178471370	6.8013292439	14
15	5.1182678624	35.8110248901	.1953785982	6.9967078421	15
16	5.7068686665	40.9292927525	.1752274423	7.1719352843	16
17	6.3631585632	46.6361614190	.1571546568	7.3290899411	17
18	7.0949217980	52.9993199823	.1409458805	7.4700358217	18
19	7.9108378047	60.0942417802	.1264088614	7.5964446831	19
20	8.8205841523	68.0050795849	.1133711762	7.7098158593	20
21	9.8349513298	76.8256637372	.1016781849	7.8114940442	21
22	10.9659707327	86.6606150670	.0911911972	7.9026852415	22
23	12.2270573670	97.6265857997	.0817858271	7.9844710686	23
24	13.6331689642	109.8536431666	.0733505176	8.0578215862	24
25	15.2009833950	123.4868121308	.0657852176	8.1236068037	25
26	16.9490964855	138.6877955258	.0590001951	8.1826069989	26
27	18.8982425813	155.6368920113	.0529149732	8.2355219721	27
28	21.0715404782	174.5351345926	.0474573751	8.2829793471	28
29	23.4947676331	195.6066750708	.0425626682	8.3255420154	29
30	26.1966659110	219.1014427039	.0381727966	8.3637148120	30
31	29.2092824907	245.2981086149	.0342356920	8.3979505041	31
32	32.5683499772	274.5073911057	.0307046565	8.4286551606	32
33	36.3137102245	307.0757410828	.0275378086	8.4561929691	33
34	40.4897869003	343.3894513073	.0246975861	8.4808905553	34
35	45.1461123939	383.8792382077	.0221503015	8.5030408568	35
36	50.3379153192	429.0253506015	.0198657412	8.5229065980	36
37	56.1267755809	479.3632659207	.0178168083	8.5407234063	37
38	62.5813547727	535.4900415016	.0159792003	8.5567026065	38
39	69.7782105715	598.0713962743	.0143311213	8.5710337278	39
40	77.8027047873	667.8496068458	.0128530236	8.5838867514	40
41	86.7500158378	745.6523116330	.0115273754	8.5954141269	41
42	96.7262676592	832.4023274709	.0103384533	8.6057525802	42
43	107.8497884400	929.1285951301	.0092721554	8.6150247356	43
44	120.2525141106	1036.9783835700	.0083158345	8.6233405700	44
45	134.0815532333	1157.2308976806	.0074581475	8.6307987175	45
46	149.5009318551	1291.3124509138	.0066889215	8.6374876390	46
47	166.6935390184	1440.8133827690	.0059990328	8.6434866717	47
48	185.8632960056	1607.5069217874	.0053802984	8.6488669702	48
49	207.2375750462	1793.3702177930	.0048253798	8.6536923500	49
50	231.0698961765	2000.6077928391	.0043276949	8.6580200448	50
51	257.6429342368	2231.6776890157	.0038813407	8.6619013855	51
52	287.2718716740	2489.3206232524	.0034810230	8.6653824085	52
53	320.3081369165	2776.5924949264	.0031219937	8.6685044023	53
54	357.1435726620	3096.9006318430	.0027999944	8.6713043966	54
55	398.2150835181	3454.0442045050	.0025112057	8.6738156023	55
56	444.0098181227	3852.2592880230	.0022522024	8.6760678049	56
57	495.0709472068	4296.2691061457	.0020199125	8.6780877173	57
58	552.0041061355	4791.3400533524	.0018115807	8.6798992981	58
59	615.4845783411	5343.3441594880	.0016247361	8.6815240342	59
60	686.2653048504	5958.8287378291	.0014571624	8.6829811965	60
61	765.1858149081	6645.0940426795	.0013068721	8.6842880687	61
62	853.1821836226	7410.2798575876	.0011720826	8.6854601513	62
63	951.2981347392	8263.4620412102	.0010511952	8.6865113464	63
64	1060.6974202342	9214.7601759493	.0009427759	8.6874541223	64
65	1182.6776235611	10275.4575961835	.0008455390	8.6882996613	65

Period	Compound Interest Amount	Compound One Per Period	Present Value Of $1 In Future	Present Value Of $1 Per Period	Period
1	1.1175000000	1.0000000000	.8948545861	.8948545862	1
2	1.2488062500	2.1175000000	.8007647303	1.6956193165	2
3	1.3955409844	3.3663062500	.7165679913	2.4121873078	3
4	1.5595170500	4.7618472343	.6412241533	3.0534114611	4
5	1.7427603034	6.3213642843	.5738023743	3.6272138355	5
6	1.9475346391	8.0641245878	.5134696862	4.1406835217	6
7	2.1763699592	10.0116592269	.4594807035	4.6001642252	7
8	2.4320934294	12.1880291860	.4111684148	5.0113326400	8
9	2.7178644073	14.6201226154	.3679359417	5.3792685817	9
10	3.0372134752	17.3379870227	.3292491648	5.7085177465	10
11	3.3940860585	20.3752004979	.2946301251	6.0031478716	11
12	3.7928911704	23.7692865563	.2636511187	6.2667989902	12
13	4.2385558829	27.5621777267	.2359294127	6.5027284029	13
14	4.7365861991	31.8007336096	.2111225169	6.7138509198	14
15	5.2931350775	36.5373198088	.1889239525	6.9027748723	15
16	5.9150784491	41.8304548863	.1690594653	7.0718343376	16
17	6.6101001669	47.7455333355	.1512836379	7.2231179756	17
18	7.3867869365	54.3556335024	.1353768572	7.3584948327	18
19	8.2547344016	61.7424204389	.1211426015	7.4796374342	19
20	9.2246656938	69.9971548405	.1084050125	7.5880424467	20
21	10.3085639128	79.2218205343	.0970067226	7.6850491693	21
22	11.5198201725	89.5303844471	.0868069106	7.7718560799	22
23	12.8733990428	101.0502046196	.0776795621	7.8495356420	23
24	14.3860234303	113.9236036624	.0695119124	7.9190475544	24
25	16.0763811834	128.3096270928	.0622030536	7.9812506079	25
26	17.9653559725	144.3860082762	.0556626878	8.0369132957	26
27	20.0762852992	162.3513642486	.0498100114	8.0867233071	27
28	22.4352488219	182.4276495478	.0445727172	8.1312960243	28
29	25.0713905584	204.8628983697	.0398861004	8.1711821246	29
30	28.0172789491	229.9342889282	.0356922598	8.2068743844	30
31	31.3093092256	257.9515678772	.0319393824	8.2388137669	31
32	34.9881530596	289.2608771028	.0285811028	8.2673948697	32
33	39.0992610441	324.2490301624	.0255759309	8.2929708006	33
34	43.6934242168	363.3482912065	.0228867391	8.3158575397	34
35	48.8274015622	407.0417154231	.0204803034	8.3363378431	35
36	54.5646212458	455.8691169854	.0183268935	8.3546647366	36
37	60.9759642422	510.4337382312	.0163999047	8.3710646413	37
38	68.1406400406	571.4097024734	.0146755299	8.3857401711	38
39	76.1471652454	639.5503425140	.0131324652	8.3988726363	39
40	85.0944571617	715.6975077594	.0117516467	8.4106242831	40
41	95.0930558782	800.7919649212	.0105160150	8.4211402981	41
42	106.2664899439	895.8850207994	.0094103042	8.4305506023	42
43	118.7528025123	1002.1515107433	.0084208539	8.4389714563	43
44	132.7062568075	1120.9043132557	.0075354397	8.4465068959	44
45	148.2992419824	1253.6105700632	.0067431228	8.4532500187	45
46	165.7244029154	1401.9098120456	.0060341144	8.4592841331	46
47	185.1970202579	1567.6342149610	.0053996549	8.4646837860	47
48	206.9576701382	1752.8312352190	.0048319060	8.4695156940	48
49	231.2751963795	1959.7889053572	.0043238532	8.4738395472	49
50	258.4500319541	2191.0641017367	.0038692199	8.4777087671	50
51	288.8179107087	2449.5141336907	.0034623891	8.4811711563	51
52	322.7540152169	2738.3320443994	.0030983348	8.4842694911	52
53	360.6776120049	3061.0860596163	.0027725591	8.4870420501	53
54	403.0572314155	3421.7636716212	.0024810372	8.4895230874	54
55	450.4164561068	3824.8209030367	.0022201676	8.4917432549	55
56	503.3403896994	4275.2373591436	.0019867271	8.4937299820	56
57	562.4828854890	4778.5777488429	.0017778319	8.4955078140	57
58	628.5746245340	5341.0606343319	.0015909010	8.4970987149	58
59	702.4321429168	5969.6352588660	.0014236251	8.4985223400	59
60	784.9679197095	6672.0674017827	.0012739374	8.4997962774	60
61	877.2016502753	7457.0353214922	.0011399887	8.5009362661	61
62	980.2728441827	8334.2369717675	.0010201241	8.5019563903	62
63	1095.4549033742	9314.5098159502	.0009128628	8.5028692530	63
64	1224.1708545206	10409.9647193243	.0008168794	8.5036861325	64
65	1368.0109299268	11634.1355738450	.0007309883	8.5044171208	65

Period	Compound Interest Amount	Compound One Per Period	Present Value Of $1 In Future	Present Value Of $1 Per Period	Period
1	1.1200000000	1.0000000000	.8928571429	.8928571429	1
2	1.2544000000	2.1200000000	.7971938776	1.6900510204	2
3	1.4049280000	3.3744000000	.7117802478	2.4018312683	3
4	1.5735193600	4.7793280000	.6355180784	3.0373493467	4
5	1.7623416832	6.3528473600	.5674268557	3.6047762024	5
6	1.9738226852	8.1151890432	.5066311212	4.1114073236	6
7	2.2106814074	10.0890117283	.4523492153	4.5637565389	7
8	2.4759631763	12.2996931358	.4038832280	4.9676397668	8
9	2.7730787575	14.7756563121	.3606100250	5.3282497918	9
10	3.1058482083	17.5487350695	.3219732366	5.6502230284	10
11	3.4785499933	20.6545832778	.2874761041	5.9376991326	11
12	3.8959759925	24.1331332712	.2566750929	6.1943742255	12
13	4.3634931117	28.0291092638	.2291741901	6.4235484157	13
14	4.8871122851	32.3926023754	.2046198126	6.6281682283	14
15	5.4735657593	37.2797146604	.1826962613	6.8108644895	15
16	6.1303936504	42.7532804197	.1631216618	6.9739861513	16
17	6.8660408884	48.8836740701	.1456443409	7.1196304923	17
18	7.6899657950	55.7497149585	.1300395901	7.2496700824	18
19	8.6127616904	63.4396807535	.1161067769	7.3657768593	19
20	9.6462930933	72.0524424439	.1036667651	7.4694436243	20
21	10.8038482645	81.6987355372	.0925596117	7.5620032361	21
22	12.1003100562	92.5025838017	.0826425104	7.6446457465	22
23	13.5523472629	104.6028938578	.0737879557	7.7184337023	23
24	15.1786289345	118.1552411208	.0658821033	7.7843158056	24
25	17.0000644066	133.3338700553	.0588233066	7.8431391121	25
26	19.0400721354	150.3339344619	.0525208094	7.8956599215	26
27	21.3248807917	169.3740065974	.0468935798	7.9425535013	27
28	23.8838664867	190.6988873891	.0418692677	7.9844227691	28
29	26.7499304651	214.5827538758	.0373832747	8.0218060438	29
30	29.9599221209	241.3326843409	.0333779239	8.0551839678	30
31	33.5551127754	271.2926064618	.0298017177	8.0849856855	31
32	37.5817263085	304.8477192373	.0266086766	8.1115943620	32
33	42.0915334655	342.4294455457	.0237577469	8.1353521089	33
34	47.1425174813	384.5209790112	.0212122740	8.1565643830	34
35	52.7996195791	431.6634964925	.0189395304	8.1755039134	35
36	59.1355739286	484.4631160717	.0169102950	8.1924142084	36
37	66.2318428000	543.5986900003	.0150984777	8.2075126861	37
38	74.1796639360	609.8305328003	.0134807836	8.2209934698	38
39	83.0812236084	684.0101967363	.0120364140	8.2330298837	39
40	93.0509704414	767.0914203447	.0107467982	8.2437766818	40
41	104.2170868943	860.1423907860	.0095953555	8.2533720374	41
42	116.7231373216	964.3594776803	.0085672817	8.2619393191	42
43	130.7299138002	1081.0826150020	.0076493587	8.2695886778	43
44	146.4175034563	1211.8125288023	.0068297845	8.2764184623	44
45	163.9876038710	1358.2300322585	.0060980219	8.2825164842	45
46	183.6661163355	1522.2176361295	.0054446624	8.2879611466	46
47	205.7060502958	1705.8837524651	.0048613057	8.2928224523	47
48	230.3907763313	1911.5898027609	.0043404515	8.2971629038	48
49	258.0376694911	2141.9805790923	.0038754032	8.3010383070	49
50	289.0021898300	2400.0182485833	.0034601814	8.3044984884	50
51	323.6824526096	2689.0204384133	.0030894477	8.3075879361	51
52	362.5243469228	3012.7028910229	.0027584354	8.3103463715	52
53	406.0272685535	3375.2272379457	.0024628888	8.3128092603	53
54	454.7505407799	3781.2545064991	.0021990078	8.3150082681	54
55	509.3206056735	4236.0050472790	.0019633998	8.3169716680	55
56	570.4390783543	4745.3256529525	.0017530356	8.3187247036	56
57	638.8917677568	5315.7647313068	.0015652103	8.3202899139	57
58	715.5587798876	5954.6564990637	.0013975092	8.3216874231	58
59	801.4258334742	6670.2152789513	.0012477761	8.3229351993	58
60	897.5969334911	7471.6411124254	.0011140858	8.3240492850	60
61	1005.3085655100	8369.2380459165	.0009947195	8.3250440045	61
62	1125.9455933712	9374.5466114265	.0008881424	8.3259321468	62
63	1261.0590645757	10500.4922047977	.0007929843	8.3267251312	63
64	1412.3861523248	11761.5512693734	.0007080217	8.3274331528	64
65	1581.8724906038	13173.9374216982	.0006321622	8.3280653150	65

RATE

12%

Period	Compound Interest Amount	Compound One Per Period	Present Value Of $1 In Future	Present Value Of $1 Per Period	Period
1	1.1225000000	1.0000000000	.8908685969	.8908685969	1
2	1.2600062500	2.1225000000	.7936468569	1.6845154538	2
3	1.4143570156	3.3825062500	.7070350618	2.3915505157	3
4	1.5876157500	4.7968632656	.6298753335	3.0214258491	4
5	1.7820986794	6.3844790156	.5611361546	3.5825620037	5
6	2.0004057676	8.1665776950	.4998985787	4.0824605824	6
7	2.2454554742	10.1669834627	.4453439454	4.5278045278	7
8	2.5205237698	12.4124389369	.3967429357	4.9245474634	8
9	2.8292879316	14.9329627066	.3534458225	5.2779932860	9
10	3.1758757032	17.7622506382	.3148737839	5.5928670699	10
11	3.5649204768	20.9381263414	.2805111661	5.8733782360	11
12	4.0016232352	24.5030468182	.2498985890	6.1232768249	12
13	4.4918220816	28.5046700535	.2226268053	6.3459036302	13
14	5.0420702865	32.9964921350	.1983312297	6.5442348599	14
15	5.6597238966	38.0385624216	.1766870643	6.7209219242	15
16	6.3530400740	43.6982863182	.1574049571	6.8783268812	16
17	7.1312874830	50.0513263922	.1402271332	7.0185540144	17
18	8.0048701997	57.1826138753	.1249239494	7.1434779639	18
19	8.9854667992	65.1874840749	.1112908235	7.2547687874	19
20	10.0861864821	74.1729508741	.0991454998	7.3539142873	20
21	11.3217443261	84.2591373562	.0883256123	7.4422398996	21
22	12.7086580061	95.5808816824	.0786865143	7.5209264139	22
23	14.2654686118	108.2895396885	.0700993446	7.5910257584	23
24	16.0129885168	122.5550083003	.0624493048	7.6534750633	24
25	17.9745796101	138.5679968171	.0556341245	7.7091091878	25
26	20.1764656123	156.5425764273	.0495626944	7.7586718822	26
27	22.6480826499	176.7190420396	.0441538481	7.8028257302	27
28	25.4224727745	199.3671246895	.0393352767	7.8421610069	28
29	28.5367256893	224.7895974639	.0350425627	7.8772035696	28
30	32.0324745863	253.3263231532	.0312183187	7.9084218883	29
31	35.9564527231	285.3587977395	.0278114198	7.9362333081	31
32	40.3611181817	321.3152504626	.0247763205	7.9610096286	32
33	45.3053551589	361.6763686442	.0220724459	7.9830820744	33
34	50.8552611659	406.9817238032	.0196636489	8.0027457233	34
35	57.0850306587	457.8369849691	.0175177273	8.0202634506	35
36	64.0779469144	514.9220156278	.0156059931	8.0358694438	36
37	71.9274954114	578.9999625422	.0139028892	8.0497723330	37
38	80.7386135993	650.9274579536	.0123856474	8.0621579804	38
39	90.6290937652	731.6660715530	.0110339843	8.0731919647	39
40	101.7311577515	822.2951653182	.0098298301	8.0830217949	40
41	114.1932245760	924.0263230697	.0087570870	8.0917788819	41
42	128.1818945866	1038.2195476458	.0078014138	8.0995802957	42
43	143.8841766735	1166.4014422324	.0069500346	8.1065303302	43
44	161.5099883160	1310.2856189059	.0061915675	8.1127218977	44
45	181.2949618847	1471.7956072218	.0055158731	8.1182377708	45
46	203.5035947156	1653.0905691065	.0049139181	8.1231516889	46
47	228.4327850682	1856.5941638220	.0043776553	8.1275293442	47
48	256.4158012391	2085.0269488903	.0038999157	8.1314292599	48
49	287.8267368908	2341.4427501293	.0034743124	8.1349035723	49
50	323.0855121600	2629.2694870202	.0030951558	8.1379987282	50
51	362.6634873996	2952.3549991802	.0027573771	8.1407561052	51
52	407.0897646060	3315.0184865798	.0024564607	8.1432125659	52
53	456.9582607703	3722.1082511858	.0021883837	8.1454009496	53
54	512.9356477146	4179.0665119560	.0019495623	8.1473505119	54
55	575.7702645597	4692.0021596706	.0017368038	8.1490873158	55
56	646.3021219682	5267.7724242303	.0015472640	8.1506345797	56
57	725.4741319093	5914.0745461985	.0013784089	8.1520129887	57
58	814.3447130682	6639.5486781078	.0012279812	8.1532409698	58
59	914.1019404191	7453.8933911761	.0010939699	8.1543349397	59
60	1026.0794281204	8367.9953315951	.0009745834	8.1553095231	60
61	1151.7741580652	9394.0747597155	.0008682258	8.1561777489	61
62	1292.8664924281	10545.8489177807	.0007734751	8.1569512240	62
63	1451.2426377506	11838.7154102088	.0006890646	8.1576402887	63
64	1629.0198608750	13289.9580479594	.0006138661	8.1582541547	64
65	1828.5747938322	14918.9779088344	.0005468740	8.1588010287	65

Period	Compound Interest Amount	Compound One Per Period	Present Value Of $1 In Future	Present Value Of $1 Per Period	Period	RATE
						12½%
1	1.1250000000	1.0000000000	.8888888889	.8888888890	1	
2	1.2656250000	2.1250000000	.7901234568	1.6790123457	2	
3	1.4238281250	3.3906250000	.7023319616	2.3813443073	3	
4	1.6018066406	4.8144531250	.6242950770	3.0056393842	4	
5	1.8020324707	6.4162597656	.5549289573	3.5605683416	5	
6	2.0272865295	8.2182922363	.4932701843	4.0538385258	6	
7	2.2806973457	10.2455787658	.4384623860	4.4923009118	7	
8	2.5657845140	12.5262761116	.3897443431	4.8820452550	8	
9	2.8865075782	15.0920606255	.3464394161	5.2284846711	9	
10	3.2473210255	17.9785682037	.3079461477	5.5364308188	10	
11	3.6532361537	21.2258892292	.2737299090	5.8101607278	11	
12	4.1098906729	24.8791253828	.2433154747	6.0534762025	12	
13	4.6236270070	28.9890160557	.2162804219	6.2697566245	13	
14	5.2015803828	33.6126430626	.1922492640	6.4620058884	14	
15	5.8517779307	38.8142234455	.1708882346	6.6328941230	15	
16	6.5832501720	44.6660013762	.1519006530	6.7847947760	16	
17	7.4061564435	51.2492515482	.1350228027	6.9198175787	17	
18	8.3319259990	58.6554079918	.1200202690	7.0398378478	18	
19	9.3734167488	66.9873339907	.1066846836	7.1465225314	19	
20	10.5450938424	76.3607507395	.0948308299	7.2413533612	20	
21	11.8632305728	86.9058445820	.0842940710	7.3256474322	21	
22	13.3461343943	98.7690751547	.0749280631	7.4005754953	22	
23	15.0144011936	112.1152095491	.0666027228	7.4671782180	23	
24	16.8912013428	127.1296107427	.0592024202	7.5263806382	24	
25	19.0026015107	144.0208120856	.0526243735	7.5790050118	25	
26	21.3779266995	163.0234135963	.0467772209	7.6257822327	26	
27	24.0501675370	184.4013402958	.0415797519	7.6673619846	27	
28	27.0564384791	208.4515078328	.0369597795	7.7043217641	28	
29	30.4384932890	235.5079463119	.0328531373	7.7371749014	29	
30	34.2433049501	265.9464396010	.0292027887	7.7663776902	30	
31	38.5237180689	300.1897445510	.0259580344	7.7923357246	31	
32	43.3391828275	338.7134626199	.0230738084	7.8154095330	32	
33	48.7565806809	382.0526454474	.0205100519	7.8359195849	33	
34	54.8511532661	430.8092261284	.0182311572	7.8541507421	34	
35	61.7075474243	485.6603793945	.0162054731	7.8703562152	35	
36	69.4209908523	547.3679268187	.0144048650	7.8847610802	36	
37	78.0986147089	616.7889176711	.0128043244	7.8975654046	37	
38	87.8609415475	694.8875323800	.0113816217	7.9089470263	38	
39	98.8435592409	782.7484739275	.0101169971	7.9190640234	39	
40	111.1990041461	881.5920331685	.0089928863	7.9280569097	40	
41	125.0988796643	992.7910373145	.0079936767	7.9360505864	41	
42	140.7362396224	1117.8899169788	.0071054904	7.9431560768	42	
43	158.3282695752	1258.6261566012	.0063159915	7.9494720683	43	
44	178.1193032720	1416.9544261763	.0056142146	7.9550862830	44	
45	200.3842161811	1595.0737294484	.0049904130	7.9600766959	45	
46	225.4322432037	1795.4579456294	.0044359227	7.9645126186	46	
47	253.6112736041	2020.8901888331	.0039430424	7.9684556610	47	
48	285.3126828047	2274.5014624373	.0035049266	7.9719605875	48	
49	320.9767681552	2559.8141452419	.0031154903	7.9750760778	49	
50	361.0988641746	2880.7909133971	.0027693247	7.9778454026	50	
51	406.2362221965	3241.8897775718	.0024616219	7.9803070245	51	
52	457.0157499710	3648.1259997683	.0021881084	7.9824951329	52	
53	514.1427187174	4105.1417497394	.0019449852	7.9844401181	53	
54	578.4105585517	4619.2844684567	.0017288758	7.9861689938	54	
55	650.7118783767	5197.6950270138	.0015367785	7.9877057723	55	
56	732.0508631738	5848.4069053906	.0013660253	7.9890717976	56	
57	823.5572210706	6580.4577685644	.0012142447	7.9902860423	57	
58	926.5018737044	7404.0149896350	.0010793286	7.9913653710	58	
59	1042.3146079174	8330.5168633394	.0009594032	7.9923247742	59	
60	1172.6039339071	9372.8314712568	.0008528029	7.9931775771	60	
61	1319.1794256455	10545.4354051638	.0007580470	7.9939356241	61	
62	1484.0768538512	11864.6148308094	.0006738196	7.9946094436	62	
63	1669.5864605826	13348.6916846606	.0005989507	7.9952083943	63	
64	1878.2847681554	15018.2781452431	.0005324006	7.9957407950	64	
65	2113.0703641748	16896.5629133985	.0004732450	7.9962140400	65	

12¾%

Period	Compound Interest Amount	Compound One Per Period	Present Value Of $1 In Future	Present Value Of $1 Per Period	Period
1	1.1275000000	1.0000000000	.8869179601	.8869179602	1
2	1.2712562500	2.1275000000	.7866234679	1.6735414281	2
3	1.4333414219	3.3987562500	.6976704815	2.3712119096	3
4	1.6160924532	4.8320976718	.6187764803	2.9899883899	4
5	1.8221442409	6.4481901250	.5488039737	3.5387923635	5
6	2.0544676317	8.2703343660	.4867441008	4.0255364643	6
7	2.3164122547	10.3248019976	.4317020850	4.4572385493	7
8	2.6117548172	12.6412142523	.3828843326	4.8401228819	8
9	2.9447535564	15.2529690695	.3395869912	5.1797098731	9
10	3.3202096348	18.1977226258	.3011858015	5.4808956746	10
11	3.7435363632	21.5179322606	.2671270967	5.7480227712	11
12	4.2208372495	25.2614686238	.2369198197	5.9849425909	12
13	4.7589939989	29.4823058734	.2101284432	6.1950710340	13
14	5.3657657337	34.2412998723	.1863666902	6.3814377242	14
15	6.0499008648	39.6070656060	.1652919647	6.5467296889	15
16	6.8212632250	45.6569664708	.1466004121	6.6933301010	16
17	7.6909742862	52.4782296958	.1300225385	6.8233526395	17
18	8.6715735077	60.1692039820	.1153193246	6.9386719641	18
19	9.7771991299	68.8407774897	.1022787801	7.0409507442	19
20	11.0237920190	78.6179766197	.0907128870	7.1316636312	20
21	12.4293255014	89.6417686387	.0804548887	7.2121185199	21
22	14.0140645029	102.0710941402	.0713568858	7.2834754057	22
23	15.8008577270	116.0851586431	.0632877036	7.3467631093	23
24	17.8154670872	131.8860163700	.0561310010	7.4028941102	24
25	20.0869391408	149.7014834573	.0497835929	7.4526777031	25
26	22.6480238813	169.7884225980	.0441539626	7.4968316657	26
27	25.5356469261	192.4364464793	.0391609425	7.5359926082	27
28	28.7914419092	217.9720934054	.0347325432	7.5707251514	28
29	32.4623507526	246.7635353146	.0308049164	7.6015300678	29
30	36.6013004736	279.2258860672	.0273214336	7.6288515013	30
31	41.2679662840	315.8271865408	.0242318701	7.6530833715	31
32	46.5296319852	357.0951528247	.0214916808	7.6745750523	32
33	52.4621600633	403.6247848099	.0190613577	7.6936364100	33
34	59.1510854713	456.0869448732	.0169058605	7.7105422705	34
35	66.6928488689	515.2380303445	.0149941113	7.7255363819	35
36	75.1961870997	581.9308792134	.0132985466	7.7388349285	36
37	84.7837009549	657.1270663131	.0117947198	7.7506296483	37
38	95.5936228267	741.9107672680	.0104609489	7.7610905972	38
39	107.7818097371	837.5043900947	.0092780034	7.7703686006	39
40	121.5239904786	945.2861998318	.0082288279	7.7785974285	40
41	137.0182992646	1066.8101903104	.0072982952	7.7858957237	41
42	154.4881324208	1203.8284895749	.0064729891	7.7923687129	42
43	174.1853693045	1358.3166219958	.0057410103	7.7981097231	43
44	196.3940038908	1532.5019913002	.0050918051	7.8032015283	44
45	221.4342393869	1728.8959951910	.0045160134	7.8077175417	45
46	249.6671049087	1950.3302345778	.0040053334	7.8117228751	46
47	281.4996607845	2199.9973394865	.0035524021	7.8152752773	47
48	317.3908675346	2481.4970002711	.0031506893	7.8184259666	48
49	357.8582031452	2798.8878678056	.0027944029	7.8212203695	49
50	403.4851240462	3156.7460709508	.0024784061	7.8236987756	50
51	454.9294773621	3560.2311949971	.0021981429	7.8258969185	51
52	512.9329857258	4015.1606723592	.0019495724	7.8278464909	52
53	578.3319414058	4528.0936580850	.0017291108	7.8295756017	53
54	652.0692639351	5106.4255994909	.0015335794	7.8311091811	54
55	735.2080950868	5758.4948634260	.0013601591	7.8324693402	55
56	828.9471272104	6493.7029585128	.0012063496	7.8336756898	56
57	934.6378859297	7322.6500857231	.0010699331	7.8347456229	57
58	1053.8042163857	8257.2879716529	.0009489429	7.8356945657	58
59	1188.1642539749	9311.0921880386	.0008416345	7.8365362002	59
60	1339.6551963567	10499.2564420135	.0007464607	7.8372826609	60
61	1510.4612338922	11838.9116383703	.0006620494	7.8379447104	61
62	1703.0450412135	13349.3728722624	.0005871835	7.8385318939	62
63	1920.1832839682	15052.4179134759	.0005207836	7.8390526776	63
64	2165.0066526741	16972.6011974442	.0004618923	7.8395145699	64
65	2441.0450008901	19137.6078501183	.0004096606	7.8399242305	65

Period	Compound Interest Amount	Compound One Per Period	Present Value Of $1 In Future	Present Value Of $1 Per Period	Period
1	1.1300000000	1.0000000000	.8849557522	.8849557522	1
2	1.2769000000	2.1300000000	.7831466834	1.6681024356	2
3	1.4428970000	3.4069000000	.6930501623	2.3611525979	3
4	1.6304726900	4.8497970000	.6133187277	2.9744713256	4
5	1.8424351793	6.4802706100	.5427599360	3.5172312616	5
6	2.0819517526	8.3227057892	.4803185274	3.9975497890	6
7	2.3526054804	10.4046575418	.4250606437	4.4226104328	7
8	2.6584441929	12.7572630223	.3761598617	4.7987702945	8
9	3.0040419380	15.4157072152	.3328848334	5.1316551278	9
10	3.3945673899	18.4197491532	.2945883481	5.4262434760	10
11	3.8358611506	21.8143165432	.2606976532	5.6869411292	11
12	4.3345231002	25.6501776938	.2307058878	5.9176470170	12
13	4.8980111032	29.9847007939	.2041645025	6.1218115195	13
14	5.5347525466	34.8827118972	.1806765509	6.3024880703	14
15	6.2542703777	40.4174644438	.1598907530	6.4623788233	15
16	7.0673255268	46.6717348215	.1414962416	6.6038750648	16
17	7.9860778453	53.7390603483	.1252179129	6.7290929778	17
18	9.0242679652	61.7251381935	.1108123123	6.8399052901	18
19	10.1974228006	70.7494061588	.0980639932	6.9379692832	19
20	11.5230877647	80.9468289594	.0867822949	7.0247515781	20
21	13.0210891741	92.4699167241	.0767984910	7.1015500692	21
22	14.7138307668	105.4910058982	.0679632664	7.1695133355	22
23	16.6266287665	120.2048366650	.0601444835	7.2296578191	23
24	18.7880905061	136.8314654315	.0532252067	7.2828830257	24
25	21.2305422719	155.6195559375	.0471019528	7.3299849785	25
26	23.9905127672	176.8500982095	.0416831441	7.3716681225	26
27	27.1092794270	200.8406109767	.0368877381	7.4085558607	27
28	30.6334857525	227.9498904037	.0326440160	7.4411998767	28
29	34.6158389003	258.5833761562	.0288885098	7.4700883865	29
30	39.1158979573	293.1992150565	.0255650529	7.4956534394	30
31	44.2009646918	332.3151130138	.0226239406	7.5182773800	31
32	49.9470901017	376.5160777055	.0200211864	7.5382985664	32
33	56.4402118150	426.4631678073	.0177178641	7.5560164304	33
34	63.7774393509	482.9033796222	.0156795257	7.5716959562	34
35	72.0685064665	546.6808189732	.0138756865	7.5855716426	35
36	81.4374123072	618.7493254397	.0122793686	7.5978510112	36
37	92.0242759071	700.1867377468	.0108666978	7.6087177090	37
38	103.9874317750	792.2110136539	.0096165468	7.6183342558	38
39	117.5057979058	896.1984454289	.0085102184	7.6268444741	39
40	132.7815516335	1013.7042433347	.0075311667	7.6343756408	40
41	150.0431533459	1146.4857949682	.0066647493	7.6410403901	41
42	169.5487632808	1296.5289483141	.0058980082	7.6469383983	42
43	191.5901025073	1466.0777115949	.0052194763	7.6521578746	43
44	216.4968158333	1657.6678141023	.0046190056	7.6567768802	44
45	244.6414018916	1874.1646299356	.0040876156	7.6608644958	45
46	276.4447841375	2118.8060318272	.0036173589	7.6644818547	46
47	312.3826060754	2395.2508159648	.0032012026	7.6676830572	47
48	352.9923448652	2707.6334220402	.0028329226	7.6705159798	48
49	398.8813496977	3060.6257669055	.0025070112	7.6730229910	49
50	450.7359251584	3459.5071166032	.0022185940	7.6752415850	50
51	509.3315954290	3910.2430417615	.0019633575	7.6772049425	51
52	575.5447028348	4419.5746371905	.0017374845	7.6789424270	52
53	650.3655142033	4995.1193400253	.0015375969	7.6804800238	53
54	734.9130310497	5645.4848542286	.0013607052	7.6818407291	54
55	830.4517250862	6380.3978852784	.0012041639	7.6830448930	55
56	938.4104493474	7210.8496103645	.0010656318	7.6841105248	56
57	1060.4038077626	8149.2600597119	.0009430370	7.6850535618	57
58	1198.2563027717	9209.6638674745	.0008345460	7.6858881078	58
59	1354.0296221320	10407.9201702462	.0007385363	7.6866266441	59
60	1530.0534730092	11761.9497923782	.0006535719	7.6872802160	60
61	1728.9604245004	13292.0032653874	.0005783822	7.6878585982	61
62	1953.7252796854	15020.9636898878	.0005118427	7.6883704409	62
63	2207.7095660445	16974.6889695732	.0004529581	7.6888233990	63
64	2494.7118096303	19182.3985356177	.0004008479	7.6892242469	64
65	2819.0243448822	21677.1103452479	.0003547327	7.6895789796	65

RATE

13%

Period	Compound Interest Amount	Compound One Per Period	Present Value Of $1 In Future	Present Value Of $1 Per Period	Period
1	1.1400000000	1.0000000000	.8771929825	.8771929825	1
2	1.2996000000	2.1400000000	.7694675285	1.6466605109	2
3	1.4815440000	3.4396000000	.6749715162	2.3216320271	3
4	1.6889601600	4.9211440000	.5920802774	2.9137123045	4
5	1.9254145824	6.6101041600	.5193686644	3.4330809689	5
6	2.1949726239	8.5355187424	.4555865477	3.8886675166	6
7	2.5022687913	10.7304913663	.3996373225	4.2883048391	7
8	2.8525864221	13.2327601576	.3505590549	4.6388638939	8
9	3.2519485212	16.0853465796	.3075079924	4.9463718368	9
10	3.7072213141	19.3372951008	.2697438095	5.2161156464	10
11	4.2262322981	23.0445164149	.2366173768	5.4527330231	11
12	4.8179048198	27.2707487130	.2075591024	5.6602921255	12
13	5.4924114946	32.0886535329	.1820693881	5.8423615136	13
14	6.2613491038	37.5810650274	.1597099896	6.0020715032	14
15	7.1379379784	43.8424141313	.1400964821	6.1421679853	15
16	8.1372492954	50.9803521097	.1228916509	6.2650596362	16
17	9.2764641967	59.1176014051	.1077996938	6.3728593300	17
18	10.5751691843	68.3940656018	.0945611349	6.4674204649	18
19	12.0556928700	78.9692347860	.0829483640	6.5503688289	19
20	13.7434898719	91.0249276561	.0727617228	6.6231305516	20
21	15.6675784539	104.7684175279	.0638260726	6.6869566243	21
22	17.8610394375	120.4359959819	.0559877830	6.7429444073	22
23	20.3615849587	138.2970354193	.0491120903	6.7920564976	23
24	23.2122068529	158.6586203780	.0430807810	6.8351372786	24
25	26.4619158123	181.8708272309	.0377901588	6.8729274374	25
26	30.1665840261	208.3327430433	.0331492621	6.9060766994	26
27	34.3899057897	238.4993270694	.0290783001	6.9351549995	27
28	39.2044926003	272.8892328591	.0255072808	6.9606622803	28
29	44.6931215643	312.0937254594	.0223748077	6.9830370880	29
30	50.9501585833	356.7868470236	.0196270243	7.0026641123	30
31	58.0831807850	407.7370056069	.0172166880	7.0198808002	31
32	66.2148260949	465.8201863919	.0151023579	7.0349831581	32
33	75.4849017482	532.0350124868	.0132476823	7.0482308404	33
34	86.0527879929	607.5199142349	.0116207740	7.0598516144	34
35	98.1001783119	693.5727022279	.0101936614	7.0700452759	35
36	111.8342032756	791.6728805398	.0089418082	7.0789870841	36
37	127.4909917342	903.5070838154	.0078436914	7.0868307755	37
38	145.3397305769	1030.9980755495	.0068804311	7.0937112066	38
39	165.6872928577	1176.3378061264	.0060354659	7.0997466724	39
40	188.8835138578	1342.0250989841	.0052942683	7.1050409407	40
41	215.3272057979	1530.9086128419	.0046440950	7.1096850357	41
42	245.4730146096	1746.2358186398	.0040737675	7.1137588033	42
43	279.8392366549	1991.7088332494	.0035734803	7.1173322836	43
44	319.0167297866	2271.5480699042	.0031346318	7.1204669154	44
45	363.6790719567	2590.5647996909	.0027496771	7.1232165925	45
46	414.5941420307	2954.2438716476	.0024119974	7.1256285899	46
47	472.6373219150	3368.8380136782	.0021157872	7.1277443771	47
48	538.8065469831	3841.4753355932	.0018559537	7.1296003308	48
49	614.2394635607	4380.2818825762	.0016280296	7.1312283604	49
50	700.2329884592	4994.5213461369	.0014280961	7.1326564564	50
51	798.2656068435	5694.7543345961	.0012527159	7.1339091724	51
52	910.0227918015	6493.0199414396	.0010988736	7.1350080459	52
53	1037.4259826538	7403.0427332411	.0009639242	7.1359719701	53
54	1182.6656202253	8440.4687158949	.0008455475	7.1368175176	54
55	1348.2388070568	9623.1343361201	.0007417084	7.1375592260	55
56	1536.9922400448	10971.3731431770	.0006506214	7.1382098474	56
57	1752.1711536510	12508.3653832217	.0005707205	7.1387805679	57
58	1997.4751151622	14260.5365368728	.0005006320	7.1392811999	58
59	2277.1216312849	16258.0116520350	.0004391509	7.1397203508	59
60	2595.9186596648	18535.1332833199	.0003852201	7.1401055709	60
61	2959.3472720179	21131.0519429847	.0003379124	7.1404434832	61
62	3373.6558901004	24090.3992150026	.0002964143	7.1407398976	62
63	3845.9677147144	27464.0551051029	.0002600126	7.1409999101	63
64	4384.4031947744	31310.0228198174	.0002280812	7.1412279914	64
65	4998.2196420429	35694.4260145918	.0002000712	7.1414280626	65

Period	Compound Interest Amount	Compound One Per Period	Present Value Of $1 In Future	Present Value Of $1 Per Period	Period
1	1.1500000000	1.0000000000	.8695652174	.8695652174	1
2	1.3225000000	2.1500000000	.7561436673	1.6257088847	2
3	1.5208750000	3.4725000000	.6575162324	2.2832251171	3
4	1.7490062500	4.9933750000	.5717532456	2.8549783627	4
5	2.0113571875	6.7423812500	.4971767353	3.3521550981	5
6	2.3130607656	8.7537384375	.4323275959	3.7844826939	6
7	2.6600198805	11.0667992031	.3759370399	4.1604197339	7
8	3.0590228625	13.7268190835	.3269017738	4.4873215077	8
9	3.5178762919	16.7858419461	.2842624120	4.7715839197	9
10	4.0455577357	20.3037182380	.2471847061	5.0187686259	10
11	4.6523913961	24.3492759737	.2149432227	5.2337118486	11
12	5.3502501055	29.0016673698	.1869071502	5.4206189988	12
13	6.1527876213	34.3519174753	.1625279567	5.5831469555	13
14	7.0757057645	40.5047050965	.1413286580	5.7244756135	14
15	8.1370616292	47.5804108611	.1228944852	5.8473700987	15
16	9.3576208735	55.7174724902	.1068647697	5.9542348684	16
17	10.7612640046	65.0750933637	.0929258867	6.0471607551	17
18	12.3754536053	75.8363573683	.0808051189	6.1279658741	18
19	14.2317716460	88.2118109736	.0702653208	6.1982311948	19
20	16.3665373929	102.4435826196	.0611002789	6.2593314737	20
21	18.8215180019	118.8101200125	.0531306773	6.3124621511	21
22	21.6447457022	137.6316380145	.0462005890	6.3586527401	22
23	24.8914575575	159.2763837166	.0401744252	6.3988371653	23
24	28.6251761911	184.1678412741	.0349342828	6.4337714481	24
25	32.9189526198	212.7930174652	.0303776372	6.4641490853	25
26	37.8567955128	245.7119700850	.0264153367	6.4905644220	26
27	43.5353148397	283.5687655978	.0229698580	6.5135342800	27
28	50.0656120656	327.1040804375	.0199737896	6.5335080696	28
29	57.5754538755	377.1696925031	.0173685127	6.5508765823	29
30	66.2117719568	434.7451463785	.0151030545	6.5659796367	30
31	76.1435377503	500.9569183353	.0131330909	6.5791127276	31
32	87.5650684128	577.1004560856	.0114200790	6.5905328066	32
33	100.6998286748	664.6655244985	.0099305035	6.6004633101	33
34	115.8048029760	765.3653531733	.0086352204	6.6090985305	34
35	133.1755234224	881.1701561493	.0075088873	6.6166074179	35
36	153.1518519358	1014.3456795717	.0065294672	6.6231368851	36
37	176.1246297261	1167.4975315074	.0056777976	6.6288146827	37
38	202.5433241850	1343.6221612335	.0049372153	6.6337518980	38
39	232.9248228128	1546.1654854185	.0042932307	6.6380451287	39
40	267.8635462347	1779.0903082313	.0037332441	6.6417783728	40
41	308.0430781699	2046.9538544660	.0032462992	6.6450246720	41
42	354.2495398954	2354.9969326359	.0028228689	6.6478475409	42
43	407.3869708797	2709.2464725313	.0024546686	6.6503022095	43
44	468.4950165117	3116.6334434111	.0021344944	6.6524367039	44
45	538.7692689884	3585.1284599227	.0018560821	6.6542927860	45
46	619.5846593367	4123.8977289111	.0016139844	6.6559067704	46
47	712.5223582372	4743.4823882478	.0014034647	6.6573102351	47
48	819.4007119727	5456.0047464849	.0012204041	6.6585306393	48
49	942.3108187687	6275.4054584577	.0010612210	6.6595918603	49
50	1083.6574415840	7217.7162772263	.0009228008	6.6605146611	50
51	1246.2060578216	8301.3737188103	.0008024355	6.6613170966	51
52	1433.1369664948	9547.5797766319	.0006977700	6.6620148666	52
53	1648.1075114690	10980.7167431267	.0006067565	6.6626216231	53
54	1895.3236381894	12628.8242545957	.0005276144	6.6631492375	54
55	2179.6221839178	14524.1478927850	.0004587951	6.6636080326	55
56	2506.5655115054	16703.7700767027	.0003989523	6.6640069849	56
57	2882.5503382312	19210.3355882082	.0003469150	6.6643538999	57
58	3314.9328889659	22092.8859264394	.0003016652	6.6646555651	58
59	3812.1728223108	25407.8188154053	.0002623176	6.6649178827	59
60	4383.9987456574	29219.9916377161	.0002281023	6.6651459850	60
61	5041.5985575060	33603.9903833735	.0001983498	6.6653443348	61
62	5797.8383411319	38645.5889408796	.0001724781	6.6644168129	62
63	6667.5140923017	44443.4272820115	.0001499809	6.6656667938	63
64	7667.6412061470	51110.9413743133	.0001304182	6.6657972120	64
65	8817.7873870690	58778.5825804603	.0001134071	6.6659106191	65

RATE

15%

243

Period	Compound Interest Amount	Compound One Per Period	Present Value Of $1 In Future	Present Value Of $1 Per Period	Period
1	1.1600000000	1.0000000000	.8620689655	.8620689656	1
2	1.3456000000	2.1600000000	.7431629013	1.6052318669	2
3	1.5608960000	3.5056000000	.6406476735	2.2458895404	3
4	1.8106393600	5.0664960000	.5522910979	2.7981806383	4
5	2.1003416576	6.8771353600	.4761130154	3.2742936537	5
6	2.4363963228	8.9774770176	.4104422547	3.6847359084	6
7	2.8262197345	11.4138733404	.3538295299	4.0385654383	7
8	3.2784148920	14.2400930749	.3050254568	4.3435908951	8
9	3.8029612747	17.5185079668	.2629529800	4.6065438751	9
10	4.4114350786	21.3214692415	.2266836034	4.8332274785	10
11	5.1172646912	25.7329043202	.1954168995	5.0286443780	11
12	5.9360270418	30.8501690114	.1684628444	5.1971072224	12
13	6.8857913685	36.7861960533	.1452265900	5.3423338124	13
14	7.9875179875	43.6719874218	.1251953362	5.4675291487	14
15	9.2655208655	51.6595054093	.1079270140	5.5754561626	15
16	10.7480042040	60.9250262748	.0930405293	5.6684966919	16
17	12.4676848766	71.6730304787	.0802073528	5.7487040448	17
18	14.4625144569	84.1407153553	.0691442697	5.8178483144	18
19	16.7765167700	98.6032298122	.0596071290	5.8774554435	19
20	19.4607594531	115.3797465821	.0513854561	5.9288408996	20
21	22.5744809656	134.8405060353	.0442978070	5.9731387066	21
22	26.1863979201	157.4149870009	.0381877646	6.0113264712	22
23	30.3762215874	183.6013849211	.0329204867	6.0442469579	23
24	35.2364170414	213.9776065084	.0283797299	6.0726266879	24
25	40.8742437680	249.2140235498	.0244652844	6.0970919723	25
26	47.4141227708	290.0882673178	.0210907624	6.1181827348	26
27	55.0003824142	337.5023900886	.0181816918	6.1363644265	27
28	63.8004436004	392.5027725028	.0156738722	6.1520382987	28
29	74.0085145765	456.3032161032	.0135119588	6.1655502575	29
30	85.8498769088	530.3117306798	.0116482403	6.1771984979	30
31	99.5858572142	616.1616075885	.0100415865	6.1872400844	31
32	115.5195943684	715.7474648027	.0086565401	6.1958966244	32
33	134.0027294674	831.2670591711	.0074625346	6.2033591590	33
34	155.4431661822	965.2697886385	.0064332194	6.2097923785	34
35	180.3140727713	1120.7129548206	.0055458788	6.2153382573	35
36	209.1643244147	1301.0270275919	.0047809300	6.2201191873	36
37	242.6306163211	1510.1913520067	.0041214914	6.2242406788	37
38	281.4515149324	1752.8219683278	.0035530098	6.2277936886	38
39	326.4837573216	2034.2734832602	.0030629395	6.2308566281	39
40	378.7211584931	2360.7572405818	.0026404651	6.2334970932	40
41	439.3165438520	2739.4783990749	.0022762630	6.2357733562	41
42	509.6071908683	3178.7949429269	.0019622957	6.2377356519	42
43	591.1443414072	3688.4021337952	.0016916342	6.2394272861	43
44	685.7274360324	4279.5464752024	.0014583054	6.2408855915	44
45	795.4438257976	4965.2739112348	.0012571598	6.2421427513	45
46	922.7148379252	5760.7177370324	.0010837584	6.2432265098	46
47	1070.3492119932	6683.4325749576	.0009342745	6.2441607843	47
48	1241.6050859121	7753.7817869508	.0008054091	6.2449661933	48
49	1440.2618996581	8995.3868728629	.0006943182	6.2456605115	49
50	1670.7038036034	10435.6487725210	.0005985501	6.2462590616	50
51	1938.0164121799	12106.3525761244	.0005159915	6.2467750531	51
52	2248.0990381287	14044.3689883043	.0004448203	6.2472198734	52
53	2607.7948842293	16292.4680264330	.0003834657	6.2476033391	53
54	3025.0420657060	18900.2629106623	.0003305739	6.2479339131	54
55	3509.0487962189	21925.3049763683	.0002849775	6.2482188906	55
56	4070.4966036140	25434.3537725872	.0002456703	6.2484645608	56
57	4721.7760601922	29504.8503762011	.0002117847	6.2486763456	57
58	5477.2602298229	34226.6264363933	.0001825730	6.2488589186	58
59	6353.6218665946	39703.8866662163	.0001573905	6.2490163091	59
60	7370.2013652497	46057.5085328109	.0001356815	6.2491519906	60
61	8549.4335836897	53427.7098980606	.0001169668	6.2492689574	61
62	9917.3429570801	61977.1434817503	.0001008335	6.2493697909	62
63	11504.1178302129	71894.4864388304	.0000869254	6.2494567163	63
64	13344.7766830469	83398.6042690433	.0000749357	6.2495316520	64
65	15479.9409523344	96743.3809520902	.0000645997	6.2495962518	65

Period	Compound Interest Amount	Compound One Per Period	Present Value Of $1 In Future	Present Value Of $1 Per Period	Period
1	1.1700000000	1.0000000000	.8547008547	.8547008547	1
2	1.3689000000	2.1700000000	.7305135510	1.5852144058	2
3	1.6016130000	3.5389000000	.6243705564	2.2095849622	3
4	1.8738872100	5.1405130000	.5336500482	2.7432350104	4
5	2.1924480357	7.0144002100	.4561111523	3.1993461628	5
6	2.5651642018	9.2068482456	.3898385917	3.5891847545	6
7	3.0012421161	11.7720124474	.3331953776	3.9223801321	7
8	3.5114532758	14.7732545635	.2847823740	4.2071625061	8
9	4.1084003327	18.2847078393	.2434037384	4.4505662445	9
10	4.8068283892	22.3931081720	.2080373833	4.6586036278	10
11	5.6239892154	27.1999365612	.1778097293	4.8364133571	11
12	6.5800673820	32.8239257766	.1519741276	4.9883874846	12
13	7.6986788370	39.4039931587	.1298924168	5.1182799014	13
14	9.0074542393	47.1026719957	.1110191596	5.2292990611	14
15	10.5387214599	56.1101262349	.0948881706	5.3241872317	15
16	12.3303041081	66.6488476949	.0811010005	5.4052882322	16
17	14.4264558065	78.9791518031	.0693170945	5.4746053267	17
18	16.8789532936	93.4056076095	.0592453799	5.5338507066	18
19	19.7483753535	110.2845609032	.0506370768	5.5844877834	19
20	23.1055991636	130.0329362567	.0432795528	5.6277673362	20
21	27.0355510215	153.1385354204	.0369910708	5.6647584071	21
22	31.6292546951	180.1720864419	.0316162998	5.6963747069	22
23	37.0062279933	211.8013411370	.0270224785	5.7233971854	23
24	43.2972867521	248.8075691302	.0230961355	5.7464933208	24
25	50.6578255000	292.1048558824	.0197402867	5.7662336075	25
26	59.2696558350	342.7626813824	.0168720399	5.7831046475	26
27	69.3454973270	402.0323372175	.0144205470	5.7975261944	27
28	81.1342318726	471.3778345444	.0123252538	5.8098514482	28
29	94.9270512909	552.5120664170	.0105344050	5.8203858532	29
30	111.0646500103	647.4391177079	.0090037649	5.8293896181	30
31	129.9456405121	758.5037677182	.0076955256	5.8370851437	31
32	152.0363993992	888.4494082303	.0065773723	5.8436625160	32
33	177.8825872970	1040.4858076295	.0056216857	5.8492842017	33
34	208.1226271375	1218.3683949265	.0048048596	5.8540890613	34
35	243.5034737509	1426.4910220640	.0041067176	5.8581957789	35
36	284.8990642885	1669.9944958149	.0035100150	5.8617057939	36
37	333.3319052176	1954.8935601034	.0030000129	5.8647058068	37
38	389.9983291046	2288.2254653210	.0025641135	5.8672699204	38
39	456.2980450523	2678.2237944255	.0021915500	5.8694614704	39
40	533.8687127112	3134.5218394779	.0018731197	5.8713345901	40
41	624.6263938722	3668.3905521891	.0016009570	5.8729355471	41
42	730.8128808304	4293.0169460613	.0013683393	5.8743038864	42
43	855.0510705716	5023.8298268917	.0011695208	5.8754734072	43
44	1000.4097525688	5878.8808974634	.0009995904	5.8764729976	44
45	1170.4794105055	6879.2906400321	.0008543508	5.8773273484	45
46	1369.4609102914	8049.7700605376	.0007302143	5.8780575627	46
47	1602.2692650409	9419.2309708289	.0006241148	5.8786816775	47
48	1874.6550400979	11021.5002358699	.0005334315	5.8792151090	48
49	2193.3463969145	12896.1552759678	.0004559243	5.8796710334	49
50	2566.2152843900	15089.5016728823	.0003896789	5.8800607123	50
51	3002.4718827363	17655.7169572723	.0003330589	5.8803937712	51
52	3512.8921028015	20658.1888400086	.0002846657	5.8806784369	52
53	4110.0837602777	24171.0809428101	.0002433040	5.8809217409	53
54	4808.7979995249	28281.1647030878	.0002079522	5.8811296931	54
55	5626.2936594442	33089.9627026126	.0001777369	5.8813074300	55
56	6582.7635815497	38716.2563620568	.0001519119	5.8814593419	56
57	7701.8333904131	45299.0199436065	.0001298392	5.8815891811	57
58	9011.1450667833	53000.8533340196	.0001109737	5.8817001548	58
59	10543.0397281365	62011.9984008029	.0000948493	5.8817950041	59
60	12335.3564819197	72555.0381289394	.0000810678	5.8818760719	60
61	14432.3670838461	84890.3946108592	.0000692887	5.8819453606	61
62	16885.8694880999	99322.7616947052	.0000592211	5.8820045817	62
63	19756.4673010769	116208.6311828051	.0000506163	5.8820551981	63
64	23115.0667422599	135965.0984838820	.0000432618	5.8820984599	64
65	27044.6280884441	159080.1652261419	.0000369759	5.8821354358	65

RATE

17%

245

Period	Compound Interest Amount	Compound One Per Period	Present Value Of $1 In Future	Present Value Of $1 Per Period	Period
1	1.1800000000	1.0000000000	.8474576271	.8474576272	1
2	1.3924000000	2.1800000000	.7181844298	1.5656420569	2
3	1.6430320000	3.5724000000	.6086308727	2.1742729296	3
4	1.9387777600	5.2154320000	.5157888752	2.6900618047	4
5	2.2877577568	7.1542097600	.4371092162	3.1271710209	5
6	2.6995541530	9.4419675168	.3704315392	3.4976025602	6
7	3.1854739006	12.1415216698	.3139250332	3.8115275933	7
8	3.7588592027	15.3269955704	.2660381637	4.0775657571	8
9	4.4354538592	19.0858547731	.2254560710	4.3030218281	9
10	5.2338355538	23.5213086322	.1910644669	4.4940862949	10
11	6.1759259535	28.7551441860	.1619190398	4.6560053347	11
12	7.2875926251	34.9310701394	.1372195252	4.7932248599	12
13	8.5993592976	42.2186627646	.1162877332	4.9095125932	13
14	10.1472439712	50.8180220622	.0985489265	5.0080615196	14
15	11.9737478860	60.9652660334	.0835160394	5.0915775590	15
16	14.1290225055	72.9390139194	.0707763046	5.1623538636	16
17	16.6722465565	87.0680364249	.0599799191	5.2223337827	17
18	19.6732509367	103.7402829814	.0508304399	5.2731642226	18
19	23.2144361053	123.4135339181	.0430766440	5.3162408666	19
20	27.3930346042	146.6279700233	.0365056305	5.3527464972	20
21	32.3237808330	174.0210046276	.0309369750	5.3836834722	21
22	38.1420613829	206.3447854605	.0262177754	5.4099012476	22
23	45.0076324318	244.4868468434	.0222184538	5.4321197014	23
24	53.1090062695	289.4944792752	.0188291981	5.4509488994	24
25	62.6686273981	342.6034855448	.0159569475	5.4669058470	25
26	73.9489803297	405.2721129428	.0135228369	5.4804286839	26
27	87.2597967891	479.2210932726	.0114600313	5.4918887152	27
28	102.9665602111	566.4808900616	.0097118909	5.5016006061	28
29	121.5005410491	669.4474502727	.0082304160	5.5098310221	29
30	143.3706384379	790.9479913218	.0069749288	5.5168059509	30
31	169.1773533568	934.3186297597	.0059109566	5.5227169076	31
32	199.6292769610	1103.4959831165	.0050092853	5.5277261929	32
33	235.5625468139	1303.1252600774	.0042451570	5.5319713499	33
34	277.9638052405	1538.6878068914	.0035975907	5.5355689406	34
35	327.9972901837	1816.6516121318	.0030488057	5.5386177463	35
36	387.0368024168	2144.6489023156	.0025837336	5.5412014799	36
37	456.7034268518	2531.6857047324	.0021896048	5.5433910847	37
38	538.9100436852	2988.3891315842	.0018555973	5.5452466819	38
39	635.9138515485	3527.2991752694	.0015725401	5.5468192219	39
40	750.3783448272	4163.2130268179	.0013326611	5.5481518831	40
41	885.4464468961	4913.5913716451	.0011293738	5.5492812568	41
42	1044.8268073374	5799.0378185412	.0009570964	5.5502383532	42
43	1232.8956326582	6843.8646258787	.0008110987	5.5510494519	43
44	1454.8168465366	8076.7602585368	.0006873717	5.5517368237	44
45	1716.6838789132	9531.5771050734	.0005825184	5.5523193421	45
46	2025.6869771176	11248.2609839867	.0004936597	5.5528130018	46
47	2390.3106329988	13273.9479611043	.0004183557	5.5532313574	47
48	2820.5665469386	15664.2585941031	.0003545387	5.5535858961	48
49	3328.2685253875	18484.8251410417	.0003004565	5.5538863527	49
50	3927.3568599573	21813.0936664292	.0002546242	5.5541409768	50
51	4634.2810947496	25740.4505263864	.0002157832	5.5543567601	51
52	5468.4516918045	30374.7316211359	.0001828671	5.5545396272	52
53	6452.7729963293	35843.1833129404	.0001549721	5.5546945993	53
54	7614.2721356686	42295.9563092697	.0001313323	5.5548259316	54
55	8984.8411200889	49910.2284449383	.0001112986	5.5549372302	55
56	10602.1125217049	58895.0695650272	.0000943208	5.5550315510	56
57	12510.4927756118	69497.1820867321	.0000799329	5.5551114839	57
58	14762.3814752219	82007.6748623439	.0000677397	5.5551792237	58
59	17419.6101407618	96770.0563375658	.0000574066	5.5552366302	59
60	20555.1399660990	114189.6664783276	.0000486496	5.5552852798	60
61	24255.0651599968	134744.8064444266	.0000412285	5.5553265083	61
62	28620.9768887962	158999.8716044234	.0000349394	5.5553614478	62
63	33772.7527287795	187620.8484932196	.0000296097	5.5553910574	63
64	39851.8482199599	221393.6012219992	.0000250929	5.5554161504	64
65	47025.1808995526	261245.4494419590	.0000212652	5.5554374156	65

Period	Compound Interest Amount	Compound One Per Period	Present Value Of $1 In Future	Present Value Of $1 Per Period	Period
1	1.1900000000	1.0000000000	.8403361345	.8403361345	1
2	1.4161000000	2.1900000000	.7061648189	1.5465009534	2
3	1.6851590000	3.6061000000	.5934158142	2.1399167675	3
4	2.0053392100	5.2912590000	.4986687514	2.6385855189	4
5	2.3863536599	7.2965982100	.4190493709	3.0576348898	5
6	2.8397608553	9.6829518699	.3521423285	3.4097772184	6
7	3.3793154178	12.5227127252	.2959179231	3.7056951415	7
8	4.0213853472	15.9020281429	.2486705236	3.9543656651	8
9	4.7854485631	19.9234134901	.2089668266	4.1633324917	9
10	5.6946837901	24.7088620532	.1756023753	4.3389348670	10
11	6.7766737102	30.4035458434	.1475650212	4.4864998882	11
12	8.0642417152	37.1802195536	.1240042195	4.6105041077	12
13	9.5964476411	45.2444612688	.1042052265	4.7147093343	13
14	11.4197726929	54.8409089098	.0875674172	4.8022767515	14
15	13.5895295045	66.2606816027	.0735860649	4.8758628164	15
16	16.1715401104	79.8502111073	.0618370293	4.9376998457	16
17	19.2441327314	96.0217512176	.0519638902	4.9896637359	17
18	22.9005179503	115.2658839490	.0436671346	5.0333308705	18
19	27.2516163609	138.1664018993	.0366950711	5.0700259416	19
20	32.4294234694	165.4180182602	.0308361942	5.1008621358	20
21	38.5910139286	197.8474417296	.0259127682	5.1267749041	21
22	45.9233065751	236.4384556582	.0217754355	5.1485503395	22
23	54.6487348243	282.3617622333	.0182986853	5.1668490248	23
24	65.0319944410	337.0104970576	.0153770465	5.1822260713	24
25	77.3880733847	402.0424914986	.0129218878	5.1951479591	25
26	92.0918073278	479.4305648833	.0108587292	5.2060066883	26
27	109.5892507201	571.5223722111	.0091249825	5.2151316708	27
28	130.4112083569	681.1116229313	.0076680526	5.2227997234	28
29	155.1893379448	811.5228312882	.0064437416	5.2292434651	29
30	184.6753121543	966.7121692329	.0054149089	5.2346583740	30
31	219.7636214636	1151.3874813872	.0045503437	5.2392087176	31
32	261.5187095417	1371.1511028508	.0038238182	5.2430325358	32
33	311.2072643546	1632.6698123924	.0032132926	5.2462458284	33
34	370.3366445819	1943.8770767470	.0027002459	5.2489460743	34
35	440.7006070525	2314.2137213289	.0022691142	5.2512151885	35
36	524.4337223925	2754.9143283814	.0019068186	5.2531220072	36
37	624.0761296470	3279.3480507739	.0016023686	5.2547243758	37
38	742.6505942800	3903.4241804209	.0013465282	5.2560709040	38
39	883.7542071932	4646.0747747009	.0011315363	5.2572024404	39
40	1051.6675065599	5529.8289818941	.0009508709	5.2581533112	40
41	1251.4843328063	6581.4964884540	.0007990512	5.2589523624	41
42	1489.2663560395	7832.9808212603	.0006714716	5.2596238339	42
43	1772.2269636869	9322.2471772997	.0005642618	5.2601880957	43
44	2108.9500867875	11094.4741409867	.0004741696	5.2606622653	44
45	2509.6506032771	13203.4242277741	.0003984618	5.2610607272	45
46	2986.4842178997	15713.0748310512	.0003348419	5.2613955691	46
47	3553.9162193007	18699.5590489509	.0002813797	5.2616769488	47
48	4229.1603009678	22253.4752682516	.0002364536	5.2619134024	48
49	5032.7007581517	26482.6355692195	.0001987005	5.2621121028	49
50	5988.9139022005	31515.3363273712	.0001669752	5.2622790780	50
51	7126.8075436186	37504.2502295717	.0001403153	5.2624193933	51
52	8480.9009769062	44631.0577731982	.0001179120	5.2625373053	52
53	10092.2721625183	53111.9587500965	.0000990857	5.2626363910	53
54	12009.8038733968	63204.2309126148	.0000832653	5.2627196563	54
55	14291.6666093422	75214.0347860116	.0000699708	5.2627896272	55
56	17007.0832651172	89505.7013953538	.0000587990	5.2628484262	56
57	20238.4290854895	106512.7846604711	.0000494109	5.2628978372	57
58	24083.7306117325	126751.2137459606	.0000415218	5.2629393589	58
59	28659.6394279617	150834.9443576931	.0000348923	5.2629742512	59
60	34104.9709192744	179494.5837856548	.0000293212	5.2630035725	60
61	40584.9153939366	213599.5547049292	.0000246397	5.2630282122	61
62	48296.0493187845	254184.4700988658	.0000207056	5.2630489178	62
63	57472.2986893536	302480.5194176503	.0000173997	5.2630663175	63
64	68392.0354403307	359952.8181070038	.0000146216	5.2630809391	64
65	81386.5221739936	428344.8535473346	.0000122870	5.2630932261	65

RATE

19%

Period	Compound Interest Amount	Compound One Per Period	Present Value Of $1 In Future	Present Value Of $1 Per Period	Period
1	1.2000000000	1.0000000000	.8333333333	.8333333334	1
2	1.4400000000	2.2000000000	.6944444444	1.5277777778	2
3	1.7280000000	3.6400000000	.5787037037	2.1064814815	3
4	2.0736000000	5.3680000000	.4822530864	2.5887345680	4
5	2.4883200000	7.4416000000	.4018775720	2.9906121400	5
6	2.9859840000	9.9299200000	.3348979767	3.3255101166	6
7	3.5831808000	12.9159040000	.2790816472	3.6045917639	7
8	4.2998169600	16.4990848000	.2325680394	3.8371598032	8
9	5.1597803520	20.7989017600	.1938066995	4.0309665027	9
10	6.1917364224	25.9586821120	.1615055829	4.1924720856	10
11	7.4300837069	32.1504185344	.1345879857	4.3270600713	11
12	8.9161004483	39.5805022413	.1121566548	4.4392167261	12
13	10.6993205379	48.4966026895	.0934638790	4.5326806051	13
14	12.8391846455	59.1959232274	.0778865658	4.6105671709	14
15	15.4070215746	72.0351078729	.0649054715	4.6754726425	15
16	18.4884258895	87.4421294475	.0540878929	4.7295605354	16
17	22.1861110674	105.9305553370	.0450732441	4.7746337795	17
18	26.6233332809	128.1166664044	.0375610368	4.8121948163	18
19	31.9479999371	154.7399996853	.0313008640	4.8434956802	19
20	38.3375999245	186.6879996224	.0260840533	4.8695797335	20
21	46.0051199094	225.0255995468	.0217367111	4.8913164446	21
22	55.2061438912	271.0307194562	.0181139259	4.9094303705	22
23	66.2473726695	326.2368633475	.0150949383	4.9245253088	23
24	79.4968472034	392.4842360170	.0125791152	4.9371044240	24
25	95.3962166441	471.9810832203	.0104825960	4.9475870200	25
26	114.4754599729	567.3772998644	.0087354967	4.9563225167	26
27	137.3705519675	681.8527598373	.0072795806	4.9636020972	27
28	164.8446623610	819.2233118048	.0060663171	4.9696684144	28
29	197.8135948331	984.0679741657	.0050552643	4.9747236787	29
30	237.3763137998	1181.8815689988	.0042127202	4.9789363989	30
31	284.8515765597	1419.2578827986	.0035106002	4.9824469991	31
32	341.8218918717	1704.1094593583	.0029255002	4.9853724992	32
33	410.1862702460	2045.9313512300	.0024379168	4.9878104160	33
34	492.2235242952	2456.1176214760	.0020315973	4.9898420134	34
35	590.6682291542	2948.3411457712	.0016929978	4.9915350112	35
36	708.8018749851	3539.0093749255	.0014108315	4.9929458426	36
37	850.5622499821	4247.8112499106	.0011756929	4.9941215355	37
38	1020.6746999785	5098.3734998927	.0009797441	4.9951012796	38
39	1224.8096399742	6119.0481998712	.0008164534	4.9959177330	39
40	1469.7715679691	7343.8578398454	.0006803778	4.9965981109	40
41	1763.7258815629	8813.6294078145	.0005669815	4.9971650924	41
42	2116.4710578755	10577.3552893774	.0004724846	4.9976375770	42
43	2539.7652694506	12693.8263472529	.0003937372	4.9980313142	43
44	3047.7183233407	15233.5916167035	.0003281143	4.9983594285	44
45	3657.2619880088	18281.3099400442	.0002734286	4.9986328571	45
46	4388.7143856106	21938.5719280530	.0002278572	4.9988607142	46
47	5266.4572627327	26327.2863136636	.0001898810	4.9990505952	47
48	6319.7487152793	31593.7435763964	.0001582341	4.9992088294	48
49	7583.6984583351	37913.4922916756	.0001318618	4.9993406911	49
50	9100.4381500021	45497.1907500107	.0001098848	4.9994505760	50
51	10920.5257800026	54597.6289000129	.0000915707	4.9995421466	51
52	13104.6309360031	65518.1546800155	.0000763089	4.9996184555	52
53	15725.5571232037	78622.7856160186	.0000635908	4.9996820463	53
54	18870.6685478445	94348.3427392223	.0000529923	4.9997350386	54
55	22644.8022574133	113219.0112870667	.0000441602	4.9997791988	55
56	27173.7627088960	135863.8135444801	.0000368002	4.9998159990	56
57	32608.5152506752	163037.5762533761	.0000306668	4.9998466659	57
58	39130.2183008103	195646.0915040513	.0000255557	4.9998722216	58
59	46956.2619609723	234776.3098048616	.0000212964	4.9998935180	59
60	56347.5143531668	281732.5717658339	.0000177470	4.9999112650	60
61	67617.0172238001	338080.0861190007	.0000147892	4.9999260542	61
62	81140.4206685602	405697.1033428009	.0000123243	4.9999383785	62
63	97368.5048022722	486837.5240113610	.0000102703	4.9999486487	63
64	116842.2057627266	584206.0288136332	.0000085586	4.9999572073	64
65	140210.6469152720	701048.2345763599	.0000071321	4.9999643394	65

Period	Compound Interest Amount	Compound One Per Period	Present Value Of $1 In Future	Present Value Of $1 Per Period	Period
1	1.2100000000	1.0000000000	.8264462810	.8264462810	1
2	1.4641000000	2.2100000000	.6830134554	1.5094597364	2
3	1.7715610000	3.6741000000	.5644739301	2.0739336664	3
4	2.1435888100	5.4456610000	.4665073802	2.5404410467	4
5	2.5937424601	7.5892498100	.3855432894	2.9259843361	5
6	3.1384283767	10.1829922701	.3186308177	3.2446151538	6
7	3.7974983358	13.3214206468	.2633312543	3.5079464081	7
8	4.5949729864	17.1189189826	.2176291358	3.7255755439	8
9	5.5599173135	21.7138919690	.1798587899	3.9054343338	9
10	6.7274999493	27.2738092825	.1486436280	4.0540779618	10
11	8.1402749387	34.0013092318	.1228459736	4.1769239354	11
12	9.8497326758	42.1415841705	.1015255980	4.2784495334	12
13	11.9181765377	51.9913168463	.0839054529	4.362354963	13
14	14.4209936106	63.9094933840	.0693433495	4.4316983358	14
15	17.4494022689	78.3304869947	.0573085533	4.4890068890	15
16	21.1137767454	95.7798892636	.0473624407	4.5363693298	16
17	25.5476698619	116.8936660089	.0391425130	4.5755118428	17
18	30.9126805329	142.4413358708	.0323491843	4.6078610271	18
19	37.4043434448	173.3540164037	.0267348631	4.6345958902	19
20	45.2592555682	210.7583598484	.0220949282	4.6566908183	20
21	54.7636992375	256.0176154166	.0182602712	4.6749510895	21
22	66.2640760774	310.7813146541	.0150911332	4.6900422228	22
23	80.1795320536	377.0453907315	.0124720109	4.7025142337	23
24	97.0172337849	457.2249227851	.0103074470	4.7128216808	24
25	117.3908528797	554.2421565700	.0085185513	4.7213402320	25
26	142.0429319844	671.6330094497	.0070401250	4.7283803570	26
27	171.8719477012	813.6759414341	.0058182851	4.7341986422	27
28	207.9650567184	985.5478891352	.0048085001	4.7390071423	28
29	251.6377186293	1193.5129458537	.0039739670	4.7429811093	29
30	304.4816395414	1445.1506644829	.0032842703	4.7462653796	30
31	368.4227838451	1749.6323040243	.0027142730	4.7489796526	31
32	445.7915684526	2118.0550878695	.0022432008	4.7512228534	32
33	539.4077978276	2563.8466563220	.0018538850	4.7530767383	33
34	652.6834353714	3103.2544541497	.0015321363	4.7546088747	34
35	789.7469567994	3755.9378895211	.0012662284	4.7558751030	35
36	955.5938177273	4545.6848463206	.0010464697	4.7569215728	36
37	1156.2685194501	5501.2786640479	.0008648510	4.7577864238	37
38	1399.0849085346	6657.5471834980	.0007147529	4.7585011767	38
39	1692.8927393268	8056.6320920325	.0005907049	4.7590918816	39
40	2048.4002145855	9749.5248313593	.0004881859	4.7595800674	40
41	2478.5642596484	11797.9250459448	.0004034594	4.7599835268	41
42	2999.0627541746	14276.4893055932	.0003334375	4.7603169643	42
43	3628.8659325512	17275.5520597678	.0002755682	4.7605925325	43
44	4390.9277783870	20904.4179923190	.0002277423	4.7608202748	44
45	5313.0226118483	25295.3457707060	.0001882168	4.7610084916	45
46	6428.7573603364	30608.3683825543	.0001555511	4.7611640426	46
47	7778.7964060071	37037.1257428907	.0001285546	4.7612925972	47
48	9412.3436512685	44815.9221488978	.0001062435	4.7613988407	48
49	11388.9358180349	54228.2658001663	.0000878045	4.7614866452	49
50	13780.6123398223	65617.2016182013	.0000725657	4.7615592109	50
51	16674.5409311849	79397.8139580235	.0000599717	4.7616191826	51
52	20176.1945267338	96072.3548892085	.0000495634	4.7616687459	52
53	24413.1953773479	116248.5494159423	.0000409615	4.7617097074	53
54	29539.9664065909	140661.7447932001	.0000338524	4.7617435598	54
55	35743.3593519750	170201.7111998811	.0000279772	4.7617715370	55
56	43249.4648158898	205945.0705518561	.0000231217	4.7617946587	56
57	52331.8524272266	249194.5353677459	.0000191088	4.7618137675	57
58	63321.5414369442	301526.3877949726	.0000157924	4.7618295600	58
59	76619.0651387025	364847.9292319168	.0000130516	4.7618426115	59
60	92709.0688178301	441466.9943706193	.0000107864	4.7618533980	60
61	112177.9732695744	534176.0631884494	.0000089144	4.7618623124	61
62	135735.3476561850	646354.0364580238	.0000073673	4.7618696797	62
63	164239.7706639838	782089.3841142088	.0000060887	4.7618757683	63
64	198730.1225034204	946329.1547781926	.0000050319	4.7618808003	64
65	240463.4482291387	1145059.2772816130	.0000041586	4.7618849589	65

RATE

21%

249

Period	Compound Interest Amount	Compound One Per Period	Present Value Of $1 In Future	Present Value Of $1 Per Period	Period
1	1.2200000000	1.0000000000	.8196721311	.8196721312	1
2	1.4884000000	2.2200000000	.6718624026	1.4915345338	2
3	1.8158480000	3.7084000000	.5507068874	2.0422414211	3
4	2.2153345600	5.5242480000	.4513990880	2.4936405091	4
5	2.7027081632	7.7395825600	.3699992525	2.8636397616	5
6	3.2973039591	10.4422907232	.3032780758	3.1669178374	6
7	4.0227108301	13.7395946823	.2485885867	3.4155064240	7
8	4.9077072127	17.7623055124	.2037611366	3.6192675607	8
9	5.9874027995	22.6700127251	.1670173251	3.7862848858	9
10	7.3046314154	28.6574155246	.1368994468	3.9231843326	10
11	8.9116503268	35.9620469401	.1122126613	4.0353969940	11
12	10.8722133987	44.8736972669	.0919775913	4.1273745852	12
13	13.2641003464	55.7459106656	.0753914682	4.2027660535	13
14	16.1822024227	69.0100110120	.0617962854	4.2645623389	14
15	19.7422869556	85.1922134347	.0506526930	4.3152150319	15
16	24.0855900859	104.9345003904	.0415186008	4.3567336327	16
17	29.3844199048	129.0200904763	.0340316400	4.3907652727	17
18	35.8489922838	158.4045103810	.0278947869	4.4186600596	18
19	43.7357705863	194.2535026649	.0228645794	4.4415246390	19
20	53.3576401153	237.9892732511	.0187414585	4.4602660976	20
21	65.0963209406	291.3469133664	.0153618513	4.4756279488	21
22	79.4175115475	356.4432343070	.0125916814	4.4882196302	22
23	96.8893640880	435.8607458545	.0103210503	4.4985406805	23
24	118.2050241874	532.7501099426	.0084598773	4.5070005578	24
25	144.2101295086	650.9551341300	.0069343256	4.5139348835	25
26	175.9363580005	795.1652636385	.0056838735	4.5196187569	26
27	214.6423567606	971.1016216390	.0046589127	4.5242776696	27
28	261.8636752479	1185.7439783996	.0038187809	4.5280964505	28
29	319.4736838025	1447.6076536475	.0031301483	4.5312265988	29
30	389.7578942390	1767.0813374500	.0025656953	4.5337922941	30
31	475.5046309716	2156.8392316890	.0021030289	4.5358953230	31
32	580.1156497853	2632.3438626605	.0017237942	4.5376191172	32
33	707.7410927381	3212.4595124459	.0014129461	4.5390320633	33
34	863.4441331405	3920.2006051840	.0011581525	4.5401902158	34
35	1053.4018424314	4783.6447383245	.0009493053	4.5411395212	35
36	1285.1502477663	5837.0465807559	.0007781191	4.5419176403	36
37	1567.8833022749	7122.1968285221	.0006378026	4.5425554429	37
38	1912.8176287753	8690.0801307970	.0005227890	4.5430782319	38
39	2333.6375071059	10602.8977595724	.0004285156	4.5435067475	39
40	2847.0377586692	12936.5352666783	.0003512423	4.5438579897	40
41	3473.3860655765	15783.5730253475	.0002879035	4.5441458932	41
42	4237.5310000033	19256.9590909240	.0002359865	4.5443818797	42
43	5169.7878200040	23494.4900909272	.0001934315	4.5445753112	43
44	6307.1411404049	28664.2779109312	.0001585504	4.5447338617	44
45	7694.7121912939	34971.4190513361	.0001299594	4.5448638210	45
46	9387.5488733786	42666.1312426300	.0001065241	4.5449703451	46
47	11452.8096255219	52053.6801160087	.0000873148	4.5450576600	47
48	13972.4277431367	63506.4897415306	.0000715695	4.5451292295	48
49	17046.3618466268	77478.9174846673	.0000586635	4.5451878930	49
50	20796.5614528847	94525.2793312941	.0000480849	4.5452359779	50
51	25371.8049725194	115321.8407841789	.0000394138	4.5452753917	51
52	30953.6020664736	140693.6457566982	.0000323064	4.5453076981	52
53	37763.3945210978	171647.2478231718	.0000264807	4.5453341788	53
54	46071.3413157393	209410.6423442696	.0000217055	4.5453558843	54
55	56207.0364052020	255481.9836600090	.0000177914	4.5453736756	55
56	68572.5844143464	311689.0200652109	.0000145831	4.5453882587	56
57	83658.5529855026	380261.6044795573	.0000119534	4.5454002120	57
58	102063.4346423132	463920.1574650600	.0000097978	4.5454100099	58
59	124517.3902636221	565983.5921073731	.0000080310	4.5454180409	59
60	151911.2161216190	690500.9823709952	.0000065828	4.5454246237	60
61	185331.6836683751	842412.1984926142	.0000053957	4.5454300194	61
62	226104.6540754177	1027743.8821609893	.0000044227	4.5454344421	62
63	275847.6779720095	1253848.5362364070	.0000036252	4.5454380674	63
64	336534.1671258516	1529696.2142084165	.0000029715	4.5454410388	64
65	410571.6838935390	1866230.3813342681	.0000024356	4.5454434745	65

Period	Compound Interest Amount	Compound One Per Period	Present Value Of $1 In Future	Present Value Of $1 Per Period	Period
1	1.2300000000	1.0000000000	.8130081301	.8130081301	1
2	1.5129000000	2.2300000000	.6609822196	1.4739903497	2
3	1.8608670000	3.7429000000	.5373839184	2.0113742680	3
4	2.2888664100	5.6037670000	.4368974946	2.4482717627	4
5	2.8153056843	7.8926334100	.3552012151	2.8034729777	5
6	3.4628259917	10.7079390943	.2887814757	3.0922544535	6
7	4.2592759698	14.1707650860	.2347816876	3.3270361410	7
8	5.2389094428	18.4300410557	.1908794208	3.5179155618	8
9	6.4438586147	23.6689504986	.1551865210	3.6731020828	9
10	7.9259460961	30.1128091133	.1261679032	3.7992699860	10
11	9.7489136981	38.0387552093	.1025755311	3.9018455171	11
12	11.9911638487	47.7876689074	.0833947407	3.9852402578	12
13	14.7491315339	59.7788327562	.0678006022	4.0530408600	13
14	18.1414317867	74.5279642901	.0551224408	4.1081633008	14
15	22.3139610977	92.6693960768	.0448149925	4.1529782933	15
16	27.4461721501	114.9833571745	.0364349533	4.1894132467	16
17	33.7587917447	142.4295293246	.0296219132	4.2190351599	17
18	41.5233138459	176.1883210693	.0240828563	4.2431180162	18
19	51.0736760305	217.7116349152	.0195795580	4.2626975741	19
20	62.8206215175	268.7853109457	.0159183398	4.2786159139	20
21	77.2693644665	331.6059324632	.0129417397	4.2915576536	21
22	95.0413182939	408.8752969298	.0105217396	4.3020793932	22
23	116.9008215014	503.9166152237	.0085542598	4.3106336530	23
24	143.7880104468	620.8174367251	.0069546828	4.3175883358	24
25	176.8592528495	764.6054471719	.0056542136	4.3232425494	25
26	217.5368810049	941.4647000214	.0045969217	4.3278394711	26
27	267.5703636361	1159.0015810263	.0037373347	4.3315768057	27
28	329.1115472724	1426.5719446624	.0030384835	4.3346152892	28
29	404.8072031450	1755.6834919347	.0024703118	4.3370856010	29
30	497.9128598683	2160.4906950797	.0020083836	4.3390939846	30
31	612.4328176381	2658.4035549481	.0016328322	4.3407268167	31
32	753.2923656948	3270.8363725861	.0013275058	4.3420543225	32
33	926.5496098046	4024.1287382810	.0010792730	4.3431335956	33
34	1139.6560200597	4950.6783480856	.0008774577	4.3440110533	34
35	1401.7769046734	6090.3343681453	.0007133803	4.3447244336	35
36	1724.1855927483	7492.1112728187	.0005799840	4.3453044176	36
37	2120.7482790804	9216.2968655670	.0004715317	4.3457759492	37
38	2608.5203832689	11337.0451446474	.0003833591	4.3461593083	38
39	3208.4800714208	13945.5655279163	.0003116741	4.3464709824	39
40	3946.4304878475	17154.0455993370	.0002533935	4.3467243759	40
41	4854.1095000525	21100.4760871846	.0002060110	4.3469303870	41
42	5970.5546850645	25954.5855872370	.0001674886	4.3470978756	42
43	7343.7822626294	31925.1402723015	.0001361696	4.3472340452	43
44	9032.8521830341	39268.9225349309	.0001107070	4.3473447522	44
45	11110.4081851320	48301.7747179650	.0000900057	4.3474347579	45
46	13665.8020677123	59412.1829030970	.0000731754	4.3475079332	46
47	16808.9365432861	73077.9849708093	.0000594922	4.3475674254	47
48	20674.9919482419	89886.9215140954	.0000483676	4.3476157930	48
49	25430.2400963376	110561.9134623373	.0000393233	4.3476551163	49
50	31279.1953184952	135992.1535586750	.0000319701	4.3476870864	50
51	38473.4102417491	167271.3488771702	.0000259920	4.3477130784	51
52	47322.2945973515	205744.7591189193	.0000211317	4.3477342101	52
53	58206.4223547423	253067.0537162708	.0000171802	4.3477513903	53
54	71593.8994963330	311273.4760710131	.0000139677	4.3477653580	54
55	88060.4963804896	382867.3755673461	.0000113558	4.3477767138	55
56	108314.4105480022	470927.8719478357	.0000092324	4.3477859462	56
57	133226.7249740427	579242.2824958379	.0000075060	4.3477934522	57
58	163868.8717180726	712469.0074698807	.0000061024	4.3477995546	58
59	201558.7122132292	876337.8791879532	.0000049613	4.3478045160	59
60	247917.2160222720	1077896.5914011824	.0000040336	4.3478085496	60
61	304938.1757073945	1325813.8074234544	.0000032794	4.3478118289	61
62	375073.9561200953	1630751.9831308489	.0000026661	4.3478144950	62
63	461340.9660277172	2005825.9392509442	.0000021676	4.3478166627	63
64	567449.3882140921	2467166.9052786613	.0000017623	4.3478184249	64
65	697962.7475033333	3034616.2934927535	.0000014327	4.3478198577	65

RATE

23%

Period	Compound Interest Amount	Compound One Per Period	Present Value Of $1 In Future	Present Value Of $1 Per Period	Period
1	1.2400000000	1.0000000000	.8064516129	.8064516129	1
2	1.5376000000	2.2400000000	.6503642040	1.4568158169	2
3	1.9066240000	3.7776000000	.5244872613	1.9813030781	3
4	2.3642137600	5.6842240000	.4229735978	2.4042766759	4
5	2.9316250624	8.0484377600	.3411077401	2.7453844161	5
6	3.6352150774	10.9800628224	.2760868872	3.0204713033	6
7	4.5076666959	14.6152778998	.2218442639	3.2423155672	7
8	5.5895067030	19.1229445957	.1789066644	3.4212222316	8
9	6.9309883117	24.7124512987	.1442795681	3.5655017997	9
10	8.5944255065	31.6434396104	.1163544904	3.6818562901	10
11	10.6570876280	40.2378651168	.0938342664	3.7756905565	11
12	13.2147886588	50.8949527449	.0756727955	3.8513633520	12
13	16.3863379369	64.1097414037	.0610264480	3.9123898000	13
14	20.3190590417	80.4960793406	.0492148774	3.9616046775	14
15	25.1956332118	100.8151383823	.0396894173	4.0012940947	15
16	31.2425851826	126.0107715941	.0320075946	4.0333016893	16
17	38.7408056264	157.2533567767	.0258125763	4.0591142655	17
18	48.0385989767	195.9941624031	.0208165938	4.0799308593	18
19	59.5678627312	244.0327613798	.0167875756	4.0967184350	19
20	73.8641497866	303.6006241110	.0135383674	4.1102568024	20
21	91.5915457354	377.4647738976	.0109180383	4.1211748406	21
22	113.5735167119	469.0563196330	.0088048696	4.1299797102	22
23	140.8311607228	582.6298363450	.0071007013	4.1370804115	23
24	174.6306392963	723.4609970678	.0057263720	4.1428067834	24
25	216.5419927274	898.0916363640	.0046180419	4.1474248253	25
26	268.5120709819	1114.6336290914	.0037242274	4.1511490527	26
27	332.9549680176	1383.1457000733	.0030034092	4.1541524619	27
28	412.8641603418	1716.1006680910	.0024221042	4.1565745660	28
29	511.9515588239	2128.9648284328	.0019533098	4.1585278758	29
30	634.8199329416	2640.9163872567	.0015752498	4.1601031257	30
31	787.1767168476	3275.7363201983	.0012703628	4.1613734885	31
32	976.0991288910	4062.9130370458	.0010244861	4.1623979745	32
33	1210.3629198249	5039.0121659369	.0008261985	4.1632241730	33
34	1500.8500205828	6249.3750857617	.0006662891	4.1638904621	34
35	1861.0540255227	7750.2251063445	.0005373299	4.1644277920	35
36	2307.7069916481	9611.2791318672	.0004333306	4.1648611226	36
37	2861.5566696437	11918.9861235154	.0003494601	4.1652105828	37
38	3548.3302703582	14780.5427931590	.0002818227	4.1654924055	38
39	4399.9295352441	18328.8730635172	.0002272764	4.1657196818	39
40	5455.9126237027	22728.8025987614	.0001832874	4.1659029692	40
41	6765.3316533914	28184.7152224641	.0001478124	4.1660507816	41
42	8389.0112502053	34950.0468758555	.0001192036	4.1661699852	42
43	10402.3739502546	43339.0581260608	.0000961319	4.1662661171	43
44	12898.9436983157	53741.4320763154	.0000775257	4.1663436428	44
45	15994.6901859115	66640.3757746311	.0000625207	4.1664061636	45
46	19833.4158305302	82635.0659605426	.0000504200	4.1664565835	46
47	24593.4356298575	102468.4817910728	.0000406613	4.1664972448	47
48	30495.8601810233	127061.9174209303	.0000327913	4.1665300361	48
49	37814.8666244689	157557.7776019535	.0000264446	4.1665564808	49
50	46890.4346143414	195372.6442264224	.0000213263	4.1665778070	50
51	58144.1389217833	242263.0788407638	.0000171986	4.1665950057	51
52	72098.7322630113	300407.2177625471	.0000138699	4.1666088756	52
53	89402.4280061340	372505.9500255584	.0000111854	4.1666200610	53
54	110859.0107276062	461908.3780316924	.0000090205	4.1666290814	54
55	137465.1733022317	572767.3887592986	.0000072746	4.1666363560	55
56	170456.8148947673	710232.5620615303	.0000058666	4.1666422226	56
57	211366.4504695114	880689.3769562975	.0000047311	4.1666469537	57
58	262094.3985821941	1092055.8274258089	.0000038154	4.1666507691	58
59	324997.0542419207	1354150.2260080031	.0000030770	4.1666538460	59
60	402996.3472599817	1679147.2802499238	.0000024814	4.1666563286	60
61	499715.4706023773	2082143.6275099055	.0000020011	4.1666583286	61
62	619647.1835469479	2581859.0981122829	.0000016138	4.1666599424	62
63	768362.5075982154	3201506.2816592308	.0000013015	4.1666612439	63
64	952769.5094217871	3969868.7892574461	.0000010496	4.1666622935	64
65	1181434.1916830160	4922638.2986792332	.0000008464	4.1666631399	65

Period	Compound Interest Amount	Compound One Per Period	Present Value Of $1 In Future	Present Value Of $1 Per Period	Period
1	1.2500000000	1.0000000000	.8000000000	.8000000000	1
2	1.5625000000	2.2500000000	.6400000000	1.4400000000	2
3	1.9531250000	3.8125000000	.5120000000	1.9520000000	3
4	2.4414062500	5.7656250000	.4096000000	2.3616000000	4
5	3.0517578125	8.2070312500	.3276800000	2.6892800000	5
6	3.8146972656	11.2587890625	.2621440000	2.9514240000	6
7	4.7683715820	15.0734863281	.2097152000	3.1611392000	7
8	5.9604644775	19.8418579101	.1677721600	3.3289113600	8
9	7.4505805969	25.8023223877	.1342177280	3.4631290880	9
10	9.3132257462	33.2529029846	.1073741824	3.5705032704	10
11	11.6415321827	42.5661287308	.0858993459	3.6564026163	11
12	14.5519152284	54.2076609134	.0687194767	3.7251220931	12
13	18.1898940355	68.7595761418	.0549755814	3.7800976745	13
14	22.7373675443	86.9494701773	.0439804651	3.8240781396	14
15	28.4217094304	109.6868377216	.0351843721	3.8592625117	15
16	35.5271367880	138.1085471520	.0281474977	3.8874100093	16
17	44.4089209850	173.6356839400	.0225179981	3.9099280075	17
18	55.5111512313	218.0446049250	.0180143965	3.9279424060	18
19	69.3889390391	273.5557561563	.0144115188	3.9423539248	19
20	86.7361737988	342.9446951954	.011529215 0	3.9538831398	20
21	108.4202172486	429.6808689942	.0092233720	3.9631065119	21
22	135.5252715607	538.1010862427	.0073786976	3.9704852095	22
23	169.4065894509	673.6263578034	.0059029581	3.9763881676	23
24	211.7582368136	843.0329472543	.0047223665	3.9811105341	24
25	264.6977960170	1054.7911840678	.0037778932	3.9848884273	25
26	330.8722450212	1319.4889800848	.0030223145	3.9879107418	26
27	413.5903062765	1650.3612251060	.0024178516	3.9903285935	27
28	516.9878828456	2063.9515313826	.0019342813	3.9922628748	28
29	646.2348535571	2580.9394142282	.0015474250	3.9938102998	29
30	807.7935669463	3227.1742677852	.0012379400	3.9950482399	30
31	1009.7419586829	4034.9678347316	.0009903520	3.9960385919	31
32	1262.1774483536	5044.7097934144	.0007922816	3.9968308735	32
33	1577.7218104420	6306.8872417681	.0006338253	3.9974646988	33
34	1972.1522630525	7884.6090522101	.0005070602	3.9979717590	34
35	2465.1903288157	9856.7613152626	.0004056482	3.9983774072	35
36	3081.4879110196	12321.9516440783	.0003245186	3.9987019258	36
37	3851.8598887745	15403.4395550979	.0002596148	3.9989615406	37
38	4814.8248609681	19255.2994438723	.0002076919	3.9991692325	38
39	6018.5310762101	24070.1243048404	.0001661535	3.9993353860	39
40	7523.1638452626	30088.6553810506	.0001329228	3.9994683088	40
41	9403.9548065783	37611.8192263132	.0001063382	3.9995746471	41
42	11754.9435082229	47015.7740328915	.0000850706	3.9996597176	42
43	14693.6793852786	58770.7175411144	.0000680565	3.9997277741	43
44	18367.0992315982	73464.3969263930	.0000544452	3.9997822193	44
45	22958.8740394978	91831.4961579912	.0000435561	3.9998257754	45
46	28698.5925493723	114790.3701974890	.0000348449	3.9998606204	46
47	35873.2406867153	143488.9627468612	.0000278759	3.9998884963	47
48	44841.5508583941	179362.2034335766	.0000223007	3.9999107970	48
49	56051.9385729927	224203.7542919707	.0000178406	3.9999286376	49
50	70064.9232162409	280255.6928649634	.0000142725	3.9999429101	50
51	87581.1540203011	350320.6160812042	.0000114180	3.9999543281	51
52	109476.4425253763	437901.7701015053	.0000091344	3.9999634625	52
53	136845.5531567204	547378.2126268816	.0000073075	3.9999707700	53
54	171056.9414459005	684223.7657836021	.0000058460	3.9999766160	54
55	213821.1768073757	855280.7072295026	.0000046768	3.9999812928	55
56	267276.4710092196	1069101.8840368782	.0000037414	3.9999850342	56
57	334095.5887615245	1336378.3550460978	.0000029932	3.9999880274	57
58	417619.4859519056	1670473.9438076222	.0000023945	3.9999904219	58
59	522024.3674398820	2088093.4297595278	.0000019156	3.9999923376	59
60	652530.4467998525	2610117.7871994098	.0000015325	3.9999938700	60
61	815663.0584998156	3262648.2339992622	.0000012260	3.9999950960	61
62	1019578.8231247695	4078311.2924990778	.0000009808	3.9999960768	62
63	1274473.5289059618	5097890.1156238473	.0000007846	3.9999968615	63
64	1593091.9111324523	6372363.6445298091	.0000006277	3.9999974892	64
65	1991364.8889155653	7965455.5556622614	.0000005022	3.9999979914	65

RATE

25%

INDEX